TROUT UNLIMITED HAS COMMISSIONED
DOUGLAS C. MAULDIN
AT THE DERRYDALE PRESS TO PUBLISH THEIR
EXCLUSIVE LIMITED EDITION
FLY FISHERMAN'S GOLD LIBRARY
TWO THOUSAND AND FIVE HUNDRED COPIES OF
TROUT FISHING AND SPORT IN MAORILAND
BY G. D. HAMILTON
HAVE BEEN PRINTED

THIS IS COPY ⎯⎯⎯⎯⎯ OF 2500
IN A LIMITED EDITION

FOREWORD

This new edition of *Trout Fishing & Sport in Maoriland* by Captain G. D. Hamilton is a welcome and timely addition to The Derrydale Press collection of *Fly Fisherman's Gold* classic international angling books. It is also the first New Zealand book in the series, although it was not in fact the very first New Zealand written and published book on fishing. That honour fell to W. H. Spackman's *Trout in New Zealand, where to go and how to catch them*, published in Wellington in 1892.

Spackman's book is fascinating and unique, but it is what is says, a slim where-to-go and how-to-do-it guide. Hamilton's book, published twelve years later in 1904, is a rollicking rumbustious account of New Zealand trout fishing when just about every little stream and creek throughout the entire country began to teem with trout of sheer size and weight, numbers, and condition beyond most fishermen's wildest dreams. By 1904, introduced acclimatized species, browns and rainbows, dominated every freshwater river system throughout the country. The Angler's Eldorado was established. That it lasted as long as it did was due only to the country's remoteness and sparse population.

But first, more about this book and its writer. Captain Hamilton, as he seemed universally known and seemingly expected to be so addressed, was so large and flamboyant a character, as well as being something of a mystery, that he deserves a book all to himself. Even then would remain many question marks, many doubts, and perhaps no more than the shadow of the real man flitting through the pages.

George Douglas Hamilton was born in France on 15th July 1835. He was descended from the brother of Lord Hamilton, Regent of Scotland. Educated in France and on the Continent for ten years, he received his further education at Edinburgh University, followed by "private instruction in permanent fortification and military drawing." Although receiving a commission in the 11th Hussars in 1851 nothing is known of this episode in his life.

He arrived in Wellington on 11th May 1857 and by his own account at once bought himself a horse and rode to Dr. Featherston's station at Akitio without a guide and at once took charge of the stock there. With the exception of a rough road of sorts between Wellington and Lower Hutt around the harbour bay there was no vestige of road or bridge at that time between Wellington and Napier. In 1858 he became manager and part-stock-owner of St Hill's station at Tukituki, Hawke's Bay.

As to his knowledge and past experience of sheep, Hamilton claimed to know more about them than any man then in the Colony. It is round about this period that Hamilton's account of his own life once more seems to leave many questions unanswered.

Between 1862 and 1870 Hamilton served as Captain in command of Scouts, Armed Constabulary, Militia and the Maori Contingents in charge of the country between Napier, Taupo, the Upper Waikato, and North and West Urewera; and was present at several engagements and skirmishes; being wounded slightly four times, and awarded the NZ War Medal.

He took up land in the Mangatoro country, near

Dannevirke, about 1857, then dense bush and reputedly near impenetrable. Later described as an island of farm husbandry in a sea of wild native bush, Hamilton leased more than 30,000 acres of land from the Maori tribes. He was the first white settler in the district and appears at first to have quickly won the respect and esteem of all the local Maoris. Hamilton's dream was to create a grand estate, and build a mansion at Mangatoro that would be an antipodean version of the Hamilton ancestral home in Scotland.

Hamilton was an extremely fit and physical man—he talks of challenging all the local Maoris to wrestling matches, and quite obviously relished such activities.

In this respect it soon becomes apparent that Hamilton was both a complex character and not all that he seemed. Most biographies are compiled from an assortment of facts and the opinions of people who knew them well, without too much regard—if any—for what the subject of the biography had to say about himself.

In the case of Captain Hamilton the strange fact emerges that we know nothing about him other than what he said about himself. What often appears to be source material turns out to have been copied without comment from some provincial newspaper interview he gave later on in his lifetime. In the end it must be accepted that we have little but Hamilton's own image of himself.

That image was undoubtedly both grand and heroic. The few facts that are available seem to be about a different man altogether. Maybe, in disappointed and disillusioned old age, he simply chose to forget some of the more mundane happenings and lived on in his unfulfilled dream to have established a grand country estate and founding dynasty in the still wild heartland of New Zealand.

The Mangatoro Estate consisted of 30,750 acres. One gets the impression that to Hamilton himself this was only the beginning, so grand was his view of what he was to hack out of the Seventy Mile Bush. First living in a tent, then a shack, followed by a humble cottage, Hamilton then set about building the grand mansion of his dreams. Only the ground floor was ever built, as shown in the frontispiece photograph of this book.

The Mangatoro Stream ran in front of the house. It was stocked with brown trout from Hamilton's private hatchery. Most of the streams of the Wairarapa and southern Hawke's Bay were stocked with Mangatoro Hatchery fish.

These were the first brown trout to be introduced into the North Island. The ova were obtained from Otago, in the South Island, in 1870.

In the early days Hamilton suffered many reverses of fortune as both the local and more distant Maori tribes objected to the Mangatoro wool clip being transported across their land or down their rivers. He was engaged in constant argument with them over ever-increasing tolls imposed on his wool. Before long the tolls exceeded its value. At the same time he was involved in litigation and lawsuits that went on for years, ending sadly in 1910 when the Bank of New Zealand foreclosed on the property, dividing it into twenty farms and grazing runs.

Hamilton emerged a ruined man. He and his wife

went to live in a mill whare at Tiratu, where he died in poverty in 1911. I knew someone who told me her mother remembered Captain Hamilton in his latter days, shuffling into Dannevirke, unkept, wearing an old and voluminously enveloping coat, in which capacious pockets he would carry back his few meagre subsistence purchases from the local shops.

During his time he devised a better holding fly hook, and had them manufactured for him in England. It speaks well of their design for the firm of Partridge of Redditch make them to this day.

Hamilton, as you will read, deemed five flies only as being essential for any circumstances of fly fishing. For him all the rest were useless and unnecessary impedimenta. In his view (and one, incidentally, coming back into the present mainstream of much informed fly fishing speculation, after a hundred years of contempt) all that really mattered was to be careful in suiting the size and colour of the fly to the existing conditions of water and weather. For him these five flies in three colours in all would do more execution than all the endless list of other existing flies. He did add one rider: if "used by a skillful fly fisher."

I have said little, in fact, about Captain Hamilton's book as such. But, as you will see, it speaks for itself eloquently enough. Here, then, is his book; like him a little larger than life; but, also like him, touched by something akin to grandeur, especially a grandeur of spirit.

Bryn Hammond
Hampshire, England
April 1994

RESIDENCE OF THE AUTHOR.

RIVER IN FRONT OF THE HOUSE.

TROUT-FISHING

AND

SPORT

IN

MAORILAND.

BY

G. D. HAMILTON,

Late Captain of Scouts and Maori Contingent, &c. ; President of the Hawke's Bay Angling and Shooting Club; late President of the Woodville District and Dannevirke Jockey Clubs; late President of the Bush District Farmers' Club.

DERRYDALE PRESS

TO

MY NEPHEW

Lord Garioch,

In memory of our Rambles
By the River-sides of Britain;

AND TO THE

ANGLERS AND SPORTSMEN

OF

Maoriland and Britain,

This volume is Inscribed with the best wishes of

THE AUTHOR.

His Excellency the Governor of New Zealand, Earl of Ranfurly, who has been all over the country, writes :—

" The book on trout-fishing and sport should prove invaluable to visitors to the country, and the hints to beginners should be of much assistance to those who have not yet found out the pleasure and healthy exercise which is obtainable so easily and is within the reach of all."

CONTENTS.

CHAPTER V.

How to Proceed on Arriving at the River.

CHAPTER VI.

Playing and Landing.

CHAPTER VII.

Facts for Trout-fishers.

CHAPTER VIII.

Artificial-fly Fishing.

CHAPTER IX.
ARTIFICIAL MINNOW FISHING.

CHAPTER X.
NATURAL MINNOW AND FISH-TAIL FISHING.

CHAPTER XI.
WORM, GRUB, CREEPER, CICADA, GRASSHOPPER FISHING.

CHAPTER XII.
LAKE FISHING.

CHAPTER XIII.

DIRECTIONS AND EXPLANATIONS FOR USING THE GUIDE TO THE RIVERS AND LAKES.

It is advised to read this Chapter — Number of Rivers, Streams, Burns, Lakes mentioned, One Thousand — Length of Course of Rivers, Streams, Burns—Length, Breadth, and Height above Sea-level of Lakes — Called " River," " Stream," " Burn " according to Length, &c. — Map issued with Book, Ordinary Map—Where Description of Main Rivers and Tributaries begun — Rivers Discharging into Lakes — How Distances to reach Rivers calculated — Distances given closely approximate — " Ice-" or " Snow-fed," Meaning of—" Bottom," Meaning of— " Bed," Meaning of — Banks, Description of — " Wadeable," Meaning of—" Landing," Meaning of—Kinds of Trout in Rivers and Lakes – Rivers and Lakes stocked with Trout from the Sea —Brown and Bull Trout—Bull Trout—Habits of Bull Trout— Thames Trout, Original Habits of—Where caught in this Country—Large Trout in most Rivers and Lakes, and Weight of— Sea-trout (*Salmo trutta*)—Rainbow trout (*Salmo irideus*) — Trout, how caught for some Distance above Sea-outlet of Rivers —Trout vary in Appearance in each River or Lake— Lures and Baits for Fishing near the Mouths of Rivers for Sea-run Trout —Tackle for—Effect of Weather and Tide on Fishing near Sea-outlet of Rivers—Feeding-time of Trout in Tidal Water — Heaviest Takes often at Night — Average Weight of Trout in and near Tidal Water—Average Weight of Trout throughout the Country—Glacier- and Perpetual-snow-fed Rivers under Different Influence from Others — Large Shingle-bed Rivers divide into several Channels—Widths of Beds and Lengths of Bridges—Good Fishing in Branch Channels—Increase of Trout—First Introduction of Trout—Photographs of " Takes " of Trout in all of the Provincial Districts, including " Takes " in Brackish Water—Own " Takes "—Secretaries of Acclimatisation Societies should be visited for Information about Size and Nature of Streams, &c.—The Government Tourist Department

CHAPTER XIV.

Hints for Approaching Game in Field and Forest.

CHAPTER XV.

Deer-stalking; Winged Game; Cattle Shooting; and Pig Hunting.

CHAPTER XVI.

North Island—East Coast, from Doubtless Bay to Port Nicholson.

CHAPTER XVII.

North Island—West Coast, from Ahipara Bay to Porirua Harbour.

ALPHABETICAL LIST

ILLUSTRATIONS.

Detached Maps of the North Island and Middle and Stewart Islands, showing stocked water; railways open and under construction; roads; tracks; coastal steamer routes; and towns: drawn in connection with the book.

ILLUSTRATIONS DESCRIBED IN DETAIL.

INTRODUCTION.

AT the request of many friends, the following pages on trout-fishing have been produced. There did not seem to be any book in the country which dealt in such a way with the subject as to be of much use to beginners. A few pages on the other sports available are also added.

A defect of most books on sport, as far as the beginner is concerned, is the absence of explanation of details. I have endeavoured to remedy this by going into detail as much as possible.

Trout-fishing, unlike most other sport, is suited to all degrees of men—to the working man, or to the hardworked lawyer, medical man, merchant, or literary man, all of whom may find in this a means of taking moderate exercise, and of occupying the mind and preventing *ennui* while taking a much-needed holiday in the country. The invalid may take it easily; the active athlete, with limbs of iron, nerves of steel, cool of head, quick of eye and hand, will have all the advantage in this sport which these qualities give elsewhere.

It is a sport which to excel in requires more cool nerve than any other I am acquainted with in temperate climates. Many men who can rush a horse over a big fence, or shoot well with either rifle or gun, are often entirely disconcerted by the rush of a trout at the minnow with which they are fishing, the trout being missed in consequence. The fact is, there are far more trout than birds missed from want of nerve. The difference is that the miss of the trout is not so noticeable, being in the water, while the bird flies away in sight.

Trout-fishing is a sport that gives scope for close observation, and rewards it better than any other, and it is also a sport where intelligence gives all the advantage. A knowledge of the habits of the trout, the effect on them of different conditions of weather and water, and where to look for them at different times, are essential to any great success.

We have magnificent trout in this country; finer, on the whole, than those to be found anywhere else. Their introduction has been a great success.

My claim to help the beginner and the visitor is based on some sixty years' experience of trout-fishing and sport in Britain and Maoriland. I know this country well, and have been practically all over it, and have visited, with few exceptions, all the rivers and lakes mentioned—some thousand in number, the combined length of which is about eighteen thousand miles.

My efforts at settlement have converted some 40,000 acres of the country to English grasses. Of this area 10,000 acres were virgin forest.

In Britain, before coming to this country, some forty-five years ago, I had in about five years fished about a hundred rivers and lakes, having fished and shot from the north of Scotland to the south of

England, besides a good deal abroad; killing game from deer to partridges, and landing nearly ten thousand trout, and a good proportion of sea-trout and salmon. Much the greater number of the fish were taken with artificial fly. The largest number taken by me in a day with artificial fly was over 132. (We counted trout in Scotland by the dozen.) The weight would probably be about 30 lb. to 40 lb. This is not given as a proof of skill, for the trout were there in great numbers, and rose freely. They were taken in the Whitadder River, among the Scotch Lammermuir Hills. My thirteenth year was not reached then. With much greater skill since, the bag has not been over ninety in a day, either in river or lake.

My opportunities of observing the habits of trout and salmon have been exceptionally good. In Britain I lived nearly always, summer and winter, on the bank of a salmon and trout river, chiefly by the Tweed. There, seven miles from the nearest hamlet, I had only to go ten yards from the house to a high bank to see salmon and trout life in fresh water all through the year. I have lived in this country for over forty years on the bank of a river; for many years seventy miles from the nearest habitation. This river was some thirty years ago stocked with trout by myself, and by going fifty yards from the house to a high cliff overhanging the river trout-life could be seen at all times.

The early days of my life were entirely given to sport—the rod, the gun, and the horse. It was

ii—Sport.

difficult to decide which was favourite. Luckily, the three came mostly at different times of the year, and so were not entirely rivals.

The style of fishing Scotch rivers requires little, if any, alteration to be adapted to those here, excepting that the trout, which average quite 2 lb., and half this weight in the small streams— about six times the average weight of British trout —*require tackle stout in proportion ;* and it should be noted that all the following directions for tackle and fishing are intended to apply to comparatively large trout. The rods in use in Britain, for the different kinds of trout lures and fishing, are sufficiently heavy for this country. Even the natural baits are very similar in both countries.

The rods, flies, lures, baits, and tackle mentioned will enable the angler to be successful anywhere, as I have been. As they are so narrowed down and simplified in comparison with the usual voluminous list, they will not confuse the beginner, and, if used with skill and confidence, will give the best results anywhere. On broad river, lake, or streamlet better results will be secured with the tackle here mentioned than with the ordinary and often perplexing variety. The five artificial flies and two artificial minnows mentioned have done practically all my artificial-bait fishing in Britain and this country ; the sizes being varied to suit the conditions of weather and water. The tackle for natural-bait fishing is equally simple.

For the convenience of those only wishing to consult the " Guide to the Rivers and Lakes," this has been kept separate from the hints to anglers and sportsmen.

The fishing, shooting, and pig-hunting experiences given are entirely my own, but where I think the experience of others may be useful, I have recommended their books for perusal.

As this book is intended for both the local and visiting sportsman, it is hardly possible to avoid including a description of the country, though such country may be already familiar to the former.

As only some of the articles may be read, some repetition is scarcely avoidable.

In conclusion, my thanks are tendered to His Excellency the Governor, the Earl of Ranfurly; to the Premier, the Right Hon. R. J. Seddon, whose Government has done so much to distribute trout and game in this country, even sending lately an expert to Europe and America to still further advance this work, and the introduction of salmon; also to the Hon. Sir J. G. Ward (Colonial Secretary) and his Department, the officers of the Government Survey Department, Printing Department, Railway Department, Weather Forecast Office, Government Tourist Department, the officers of the numerous acclimatisation societies, and to many others, for their courtesy.

SPORT IN MAORILAND.

CHAPTER I.

GENERAL DESCRIPTION OF THE COUNTRY.

SHAPE AND LATITUDE.

MAORILAND is a long and rather narrow country, extending for about eleven hundred miles in length, between latitudes 34 and 48, lying nearly north and south, and all parts of the country are more or less within moderate distance of the sea. It is divided into three islands by narrow channels, and its total area is nearly that of England, Scotland, and Ireland combined.

CLIMATE.

Owing to the length of the islands north and south, and the great altitude of some of the mountain-ranges, almost every variety of climate can be attained, ranging from the subtropical of the north to the alpine and perpetual glaciers and snow of the high lands of the south. Speaking generally, the climate may be described as a better, brighter British climate—more sunshine and blue sky, longer breezy summers, and milder winters.

Otherwise, everything is grander and greater—the mountains, rivers, fiords, lakes, and waterfalls, some of the latter being over 1,900 ft. in height. Parts of the country are very rich and fertile, and the scenery combines that of Britain, Norway, Holland, Switzerland, and Italy.

VOLCANOES.

Where the hot springs and volcanoes are active, which is over some hundred miles in length, is " Wonderland."

MOUNTAINS, RIVERS, LAKES, AND TROUT.

A mountain-chain runs the greater part of the length of the islands, varying in height from about 3,000 ft. to over 12,000 ft. The highest mountain in the North Island is over 9,000 ft., and the perpetual-snow or glacier line is at about that height above sea-level. The highest mountain in the Middle Island is over 12,000 ft., and the perpetual-snow or glacier line is at about 8,000 ft. above sea-level. Perhaps a third of the country is occupied by mountains, which are mostly forest-clad ranges.

Among the mountains are situated large lakes, some of which, surrounded by forest, are of great beauty; and from these lakes and ranges issue, in all directions, the most magnificent rivers and streams, admirably adapted for salmon and trout, and many of which, although running a course of not more than a hundred and fifty miles, discharge sixteen times as much water as the

English Thames. Hardly any of them are navigable, however, even for small craft, except for a few miles up from the coast; and fine trout are caught right down to and in the salt water.

The water of the glacier and perpetual-snow fed rivers remains very cold down to the sea even in the hottest weather, which increases the flow of ice-water; but in most of them the cold of the water is modified in the lower course by the addition of water from tributaries which rise in the lower country.

Many of the largest rivers have much of the character of mountain-torrents over the whole of their course, whilst others are the very counterpart of the Tweed, in character, length, and volume. Often they are surrounded from source to mouth by highly fertile country, much richer and more fertile naturally than any part of the Tweed's banks or valley, English grasses and clover reaching to the water's edge.

The country is a network of pure-water rivers and streams of all sizes and character, which, with few exceptions, have shingle, boulder, or rock bottom and beds. Nearly all these streams are stocked with trout originally obtained from the English Thames and Loch Leven, and with rainbow trout (*Salmo irideus*) obtained from California. The latter is a very game and handsome fish, and is chiefly found in the North Island, it being able to stand a higher temperature than the British varieties.

The total length of rivers, streams, and burns dealt with by the author in this book amounts to 17,357 miles, and the total length of the lakes to 487¾ miles.

As the New Zealand mountains and rivers are greater and grander than the British, so the New Zealand trout are larger than any British river trout, probably averaging six times as much in weight. They are not infrequently caught by anglers up to 11 lb. and 12 lb. in weight, and a few have been caught weighing up to 30 lb. and 34 lb. Some of these are apparently a variety of the bull trout (*Salmo eriox*). This great increase in size as compared with their ancestors is no doubt owing to the great abundance of feed —mostly of the whitebait description, which come in from the sea, and swarm in the rivers in summer, finding their way almost to the sources. There is also an abundance of fresh-water minnow in lakes not connected with the sea, or separated from it by high waterfalls in the connecting river.

Phenomenal bags of large trout are sometimes made, frequently near the mouths of the larger rivers. It would require a fair-sized book to hold the records of these takes.

The forests do not lose their foliage in winter, and contain some splendid timber.

SHOO'ING, ETC.

There are red and fallow deer, the former better developed than in Scotland, and both are fairly numerous; in some localities they are found in thousands. Moose, sambur, and axis have also been introduced, and in some places wild cattle and wild pigs are plentiful. The latter can be hunted with dogs and knife or spear. Coursing is indulged in to some extent, and there is a sprinkling of pheasants, hares, rabbits, Californian and Virginian quail, wild ducks, and wild pigeons, &c., distributed more or less over the islands.

The Government takes an active interest in the game and also in the trout, both being protected by law.

With the exception of small portions of some of the smaller streams, the trout-fishing is open to the public ; and there is little difficulty in sportsmen obtaining leave to fish or shoot anywhere. Licenses to fish are issued by the acclimatisation societies, a fee of £1 being charged, and on the license being indorsed by the local acclimatisation society the holder may fish all over the country, from the 1st October to the 30th April.

Licenses to shoot are issued by the Government for a small fee.

GUN-MAKERS AND FISHING-TACKLE DEALERS.

Guns, good fishing-tackle, flies, and rods can be got in the large and in many of the smaller towns. There are fly-dressers in some of the towns, and the trout-flies that are produced are not surpassed in Britain. It is advisable to apply to the secretaries or other representatives of the acclimatisation societies for the addresses of these dressers.

SEA FISHING.

There is good sea fishing in all the harbours and tidal rivers. The kahawai (sometimes called the Maoriland salmon) takes a spinning bait or Grilse fly, and makes a good run for it. These fish average from 3 lb. to 4 lb. weight, and are sometimes found in great number.

HACKS AND HUNTERS.

Good useful hacks can be bought for about £15, hunters for about £10 more, both with a good dash of blood; but for heavy weights you might have to pay more.

RACING CLUBS, ETC.

There are some hundred racing clubs in the colony. The highest stake is the New Zealand Cup of 1,500 sovereigns, and there are several other races for which big prize-money is given. There are also about a dozen trotting clubs and a number of hunt clubs, mostly harriers and drag. Polo clubs are scattered over the country, and golf is in great favour in all the towns.

SETTLED COUNTRY.

The country, where occupied, is almost entirely under English grasses, chiefly surface-sown without ploughing or harrowing, and much of it on cleared forest land. Some splendid pasture is obtained in this way, and the crops grown are much the same as those in Britain.

The fruits, which are in considerable abundance, range from the subtropical lemon to the varieties grown in the colder British climate.

The birds, which are very numerous, include the British song and small birds.

The stock grazed are chiefly English long-wool sheep, or crosses from them, and short-horn cattle. There are over 19,000,000 sheep, 1,209,000 cattle, and 250,000 horses in the colony.

A good deal of the lower country is occupied by peasant proprietors of from 50 to 200 acres, and by yeomen farmers. The tenure generally is either freehold or lease in perpetuity—999 years. A large proportion of country is also used as sheep-farms, some of which are of considerable extent.

MINERALS.

The chief minerals are gold and coal. The annual output of gold is about £1,000,000, obtained by dredging the rivers, by sluicing, and by deep sinking.

POPULATION.

The population, including about forty thousand Maoris, is about eight hundred thousand. The people are essentially British, and are guarded by five hundred Civil police—a much less number in proportion to the population than in most countries. There are a thousand clergy, of various denominations. The medical men number five hundred, and the dentists two hundred.

GOVERNMENT SCHOOLS.

Good free Government schools are established everywhere that a class of twenty or so can be got together, and even where there is a less number the Government gives all reasonable assistance. Unless other instruction is obtained by parents, the attendance at these schools is compulsory.

The age at which attendance is required is from five to fifteen years, and from seven to thirteen years attendance is compulsory; so that there is a reasonably well educated population growing up. These schools are also open to Maori children, and are staffed by qualified and certificated teachers.

There are also good private schools and colleges.

RAILWAYS, COASTAL STEAMERS, ROADS.

About 2,300 miles of railway is open for traffic, and, as the lines run mostly north and south, travelling is fairly convenient. The railways are almost entirely Government property, and are being extended in all directions.

The fares per mile by all trains, both first- and second-class, are less than English rates. Return tickets are issued at double rates, with facilities for breaking the journey, and are available for three months from date of issue. There is no third class on the New Zealand railways. Tickets are obtainable also at any time of the year, available over the whole of the railways for six weeks, for about £8, and for twelve months for about £60. If required for one Island only the prices are much less. Tickets of this nature are all first class. The trunk railway-lines are connected by a good and frequent coastal steamer service.

There is a great length of made roads, a good proportion of which are macadamised and in fairly good order for wheel traffic, and bicycles are very much used in all the towns and villages.

POSTAL, ETC.

Communication by post, telegraph, or telephone is regular and easy all over the country. English mails are delivered in thirty-five days from time of despatch from the Old Country.

HOTELS, ETC.

There are about fifteen hundred hotels, and the tariff ranges from 4s. to 12s. 6d. per diem and from £1 to £3 10s. per week.

In the chief towns there are fairly good clubs.

The principal towns are lighted by gas or electricity, and are served by the usual tramway.

OCEAN STEAMERS.

A fleet of fine powerful ocean steamers traverse the various European and American routes to the colony, and there is a frequent steamer service to the chief Australian and Tasmanian ports.

TOURIST AGENCIES.

Intending visitors will find it saves them a great deal of trouble if they put themselves in communication with the New Zealand Government Tourist Department, the chief office of which is in Wellington; and there are also branches in Britain and the Australasian Colonies.

Cook's Tourist Agency also has offices all over this country.

GENERAL.

Visitors who like the sport of the country well enough to remain in it might find an investment in landed property, and possibly situated near the banks of a good river, which would perhaps give a return of 5 per cent. That rate, however, is not generally considered sufficient by the ordinary settler who farms his land.

To those wishing to learn more of the past and present of Maoriland I would recommend a little volume by the Hon. William Pember Reeves, Agent-General for New Zealand. It is one of the " Story of the Empire Series," and contains a great deal of information in a very condensed form. The Official Year-book and the Tourists' Guides issued by the Government also give much information about railways, steamers, fares, hotels, tariffs, guides, accommodation, &c., and contain a number of photographs of scenery, including rivers and lakes.

" The New Zealand Index Annual," published yearly at the New Zealand Index Annual Office, Dunedin, contains descriptions of some three thousand towns, villages, and places, how and where they are situated, and how to get there; hotel and boarding accommodation, charges, fares; particulars of shooting and fishing (if any) at each place; coach times and routes; cycling routes and state of roads, &c.; also general particulars about the gold and other industries.

A time-table is published by the Government for all the railways.

Maps of the country can be obtained at the Government Survey Offices in many of the towns, and at booksellers.

CHAPTER II.

TACKLE AND EQUIPMENT.

RODS—GENERAL.

TAKING it for granted that the fisher will wade wherever required, two lengths of rods are sufficient for fishing ordinary rivers or lakes. With these two lengths—10 ft. single-handed and 14 ft. two-handed—all the different kinds of fishing can be undertaken successfully, and I have used them in Britain and this country for some fifty years, though I have tried others.

To be fully equipped for fishing on rivers, streams, and lakes of various volume and size, three rods are required—one of 10 ft., of medium stiffness, for artificial-fly fishing (for this purpose Hardy's cane with steel centre has the advantage of great additional strength without any perceptible increase of weight, and with fair play will land any trout on fly tackle); one of 14 ft., fairly stiff for minnow fishing; and one of 14 ft., lighter and more supple for artificial- and natural-fly fishing, and for fishing with creeper and worm in clear water. For this Hardy's cane with steel centre has the advantage that a lighter rod with great increase of strength can be used.

On all rods Hardy's Universal winch-fitting is preferable, as it will fit almost any size of reel-plate.

The joints should be either Hardy's lockfast or plain suction. Unnecessarily heavy rods should be avoided. The tendency in this country is to use too heavy rods and too light tackle, a combination that is responsible for the loss of many fish by the breaking of the tackle.

SINGLE-HANDED RODS.

Single-handed rods should be so made that when put together with the reel in its place the rod, when laid across any steady narrow edge, balances a little higher up than where the hand would grasp it. This should be just in front of the reel, and the point of balance should be within 1 ft. of the hand. Unless some care be taken to adjust this balance the rod will tire the wrist. In single-handed rods the reel should be about 3 in. or 4 in. from the butt end.

If made of green heart the 10 ft. rod should not weigh more than 16 oz.; if of cane with steel centre, not more than 14 oz. This may be considered the fly rod proper. If it is likely to be used for large trout the cane with steel centre is most reliable and desirable.

The rod should be moderately stiff, with stiffish top. If there are two tops they should be of equal stiffness. Where there are two tops to the rod in Britain, one is often made finer for artificial-fly fishing with very fine gut.

In this country, where the trout run so much heavier than in Britain, very fine gut should only be used upon rare occasions, as it wastes too much time in playing the fish, even if it does not cause the loss of the fish itself. It is better, generally, to use gut of moderate strength, and the same tops, if moderately stiff at the point, will do on occasion for all the baits dealt with.

The short rod is undoubtedly the best for artificial-fly fishing in any river that can mostly be fished across by wading. This fishing, to be done properly, entails incessant casting, sometimes perhaps twelve casts per minute, and accuracy of casting to the spot desired. Justice cannot be done with a much longer, heavier rod. Instantaneous striking to a rise is necessary : and here the light short rod has all the advantage, also in playing fish held by so slight a hold as a small fly-hook. For casting so light a line as is required for artificial fly, more or less against the wind sometimes, a moderately stiff rod is necessary; a very supple one is quite at a disadvantage.

The preference for long rods sometimes arises from a mistaken idea that the casting-power of a rod is in proportion to its length. Other things being equal, this is not so, because the casting-power is about in proportion to the height of the point of the rod from the ground. A man holds a rod about 5 ft. from the ground, so that the top of a 10 ft. rod will be 15 ft. from the ground, and the top of a 14 ft. rod 19 ft. from the ground. The casting-powers of the 10 ft. and 14 ft. rods will be about in the ratio of 15 to 19, and not of 10 to 14. Thus, if the casting-power of the 10 ft. rod were 20 ft., the casting-power of the 14 ft. rod would be about 25 ft.

Where instantaneous striking is required, as in artificial-fly fishing, the longer the rod the longer the motion of the hand is in reaching the point of the rod and in being conveyed to the line. The extra weight of the longer rod also has a slowing effect. It is more difficult also to use just the amount of strength necessary with a two-handed rod. and beginners in striking are much more apt to tear away the hook or break the tackle.

SINGLE- AND TWO-HANDED RODS COMPARED.

As the height the rod is held from the ground has no effect on striking, the quickness of striking with single- and two-handed rods will be in the ratio of 14 to 10, owing partly to the elasticity of the rod. The same ratio applies to casting.

In Fig. 1 will be seen illustrated by the open space between the rod and line about the proportion of quick striking and casting properties of the two lengths of rods. It will be seen that the 10 ft. rod would strike about one-fourth quicker than the 14 ft. rod. The 10 ft. rod, then, possesses in a greater degree the qualities requisite for light, accurate, and incessant casting, for instantaneous striking, and the delicacy for playing hooked fish required for artificial-fly fishing, as also for fishing with a small minnow when the river is low and clear. The 14 ft. rod possesses all these qualities in moderate degree, and is fairly well suited to fishing with minnow and the other baits and lures mentioned, as well as with the artificial fly where it is needful to throw a longer line.

Fig. 1.

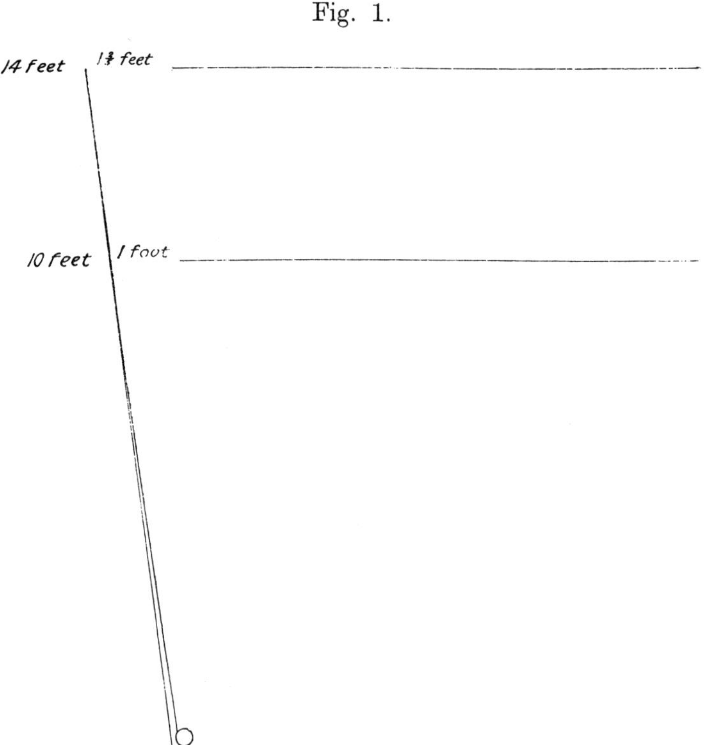

Scale, ¼ in. to 1 ft.

Fig. 2.

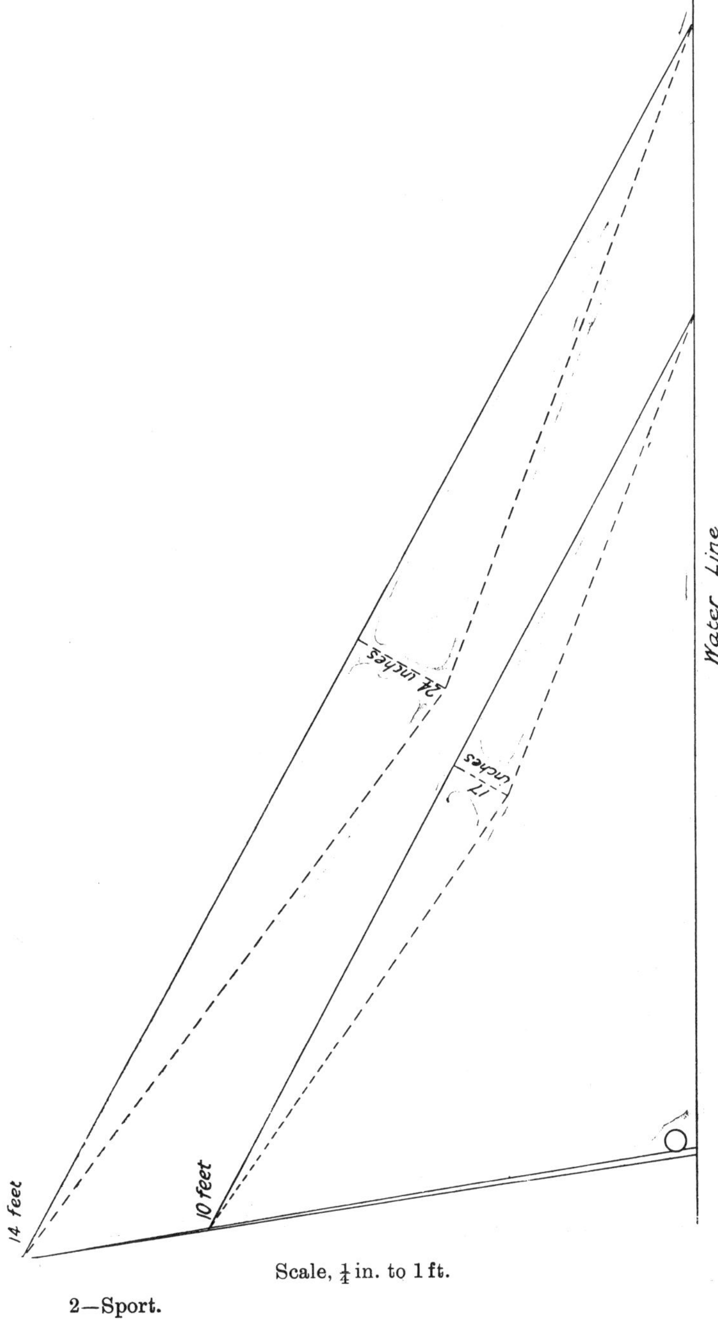

Scale, ¼ in. to 1 ft.

2—Sport.

In Fig. 2 is shown the difference in " sag " to be brought up in striking with a long line and rod as compared with a shorter line and rod. In each case the line out is about twice the length of the rod, and is represented by the dotted line, and the direct line of pull by the black lines, which are parallel. In one case the sag in ratio is $\frac{4}{8}$ in., in the other $\frac{3}{8}$ in. The chances in striking are thus as 4 to 3 in favour of the short line and rod, taking credit for the greater quickness in using owing to its lightness and its being worked by one hand. It will thus be seen that a longer line than necessary should not be used with any rod.

TWO-HANDED RODS.

It has been shown that with the two lengths of rod mentioned all ordinary purposes can be served effectively. The 14 ft. rod is suitable for use on broad rivers or on lakes for all the lures and baits dealt with, more particularly for use with the natural minnow, worm, creeper, cicada, &c., which are apt to be torn if cast with the force required with a short rod.

With the longer rod a relatively shorter line can be used, and the bait can sometimes be dropped almost where required. As with the natural baits such quick striking is not generally required as with the artificial baits, the loss of some of the quick-striking power is not of so much importance. In these rods the reel is so placed as to leave ample room for one hand behind it.

The rod should balance within 2 ft. of the upper hand. The weight is about 25 oz.

It will be seen in comparing these weights with those of single-handed rods that a very little increase of length causes a great increase in weight in proportion to the length gained. Thus the 14 ft. rod is about twice as heavy as the 10 ft. rod. If intended for fishing with either the artificial or natural minnow, the rod should be fairly stiff with stiffish tops.

For those chiefly fishing large rivers or lakes, requiring a two-handed rod, a lighter and more supple 14 ft. rod than the one for minnow fishing is often desirable in addition, but the top should not be weak. This is for artificial- or natural-fly fishing and fishing with creeper, worm, &c., in clear water. Hardy's cane with steel centre is very well suited for this rod, giving great strength with little weight.

Two lengths of rod have been given as sufficient, but to the middle piece of my 14 ft. rods I have an extra handle made about 18 in. long. This converts the two upper pieces into a single-handed rod about 10 ft. 8 in.—a most convenient, light, and pleasant rod for artificial-minnow or any sort of natural-bait fishing in the smaller streams. Being stiff, it will also do good service in the larger rivers with the heaviest fish. It is particularly handy in working up-stream with artificial minnow, in a gale of wind, or in the dark; also, on occasion, for fly fishing with unusually stout tackle.

ROD-HANDLES.

The handles are made of various materials, all of which have their respective advocates. Those made of wood are preferable, as they are less affected by wet. A suitable thickness of handle for most people is 1 in. in diameter.

ROD—NUMBER OF PIECES.

All the rods here mentioned are understood to consist of three pieces. What those composed of more pieces gain in portability they lose in more important qualities.

ROD-RINGS.

These may be Snake, Hardy's Bridge, or Hardy's rust-proof upright steel. I use the last, but they are all good. They all let the line run more freely than the old lie-down rings, but they are more liable to be damaged by coming in contact with trees, stones, &c. For this reason it is well to use the smallest, which is sufficient for the thickest line, and lessens the chance of injury, or of the line clinging to the ring, which is particularly objectionable in a bad light.

ROD-COLOUR.

This is a matter of fancy. Perhaps a dark colour is more suitable, being less conspicuous.

REEL FOR SINGLE-HANDED ROD.

The reel for a single-handed rod is generally large enough if $2\frac{1}{2}$ in. to $2\frac{3}{4}$ in. in diameter, holding from 40 to 60 yards No. 20 Hardy's or Bartlett's braided waterproof silk line. The reel should be metal, and of the best workmanship. The ordinary pillar is the best for winding the line on. Hollow pillars of large diameter take up space that is better occupied by reserve line, which, if ordinary care is used in winding it on, will give off the rest of the line just as well as a thick pillar. My preference is for a reel that lets off the line very easily ; and the speed has often, in playing a fish, to be further quickened by pulling the line off with the disengaged hand. The line is less apt to get tangled on a narrow reel than on a wide one, and it winds in more quickly.

I never use a reel with a multiplier or check, because they are liable to get out of order, and to stick at critical times. The fingers of the right hand—the hand that holds the rod—should be used as a check with the single-handed rod, and the fingers of the uppermost hand as a check with the two-handed rod. This check is perfect ; it gives no trouble when practised a little, and is instantly let go by opening the fingers, and as quickly resumed (see Figs. 3 and 4). The required pressure can be got to a nicety. The line is passed under the fourth and third fingers over the second, and under the first (see Fig. 3). The check-hold is the same for both hands, as shown below, where the line is seen to pass out from the reel above the lowest bar. The tackle is thus firm for striking, and this check prevents the reel line from running out when casting with rather heavy lures, such as minnow, natural or artificial.

Fig. 3.

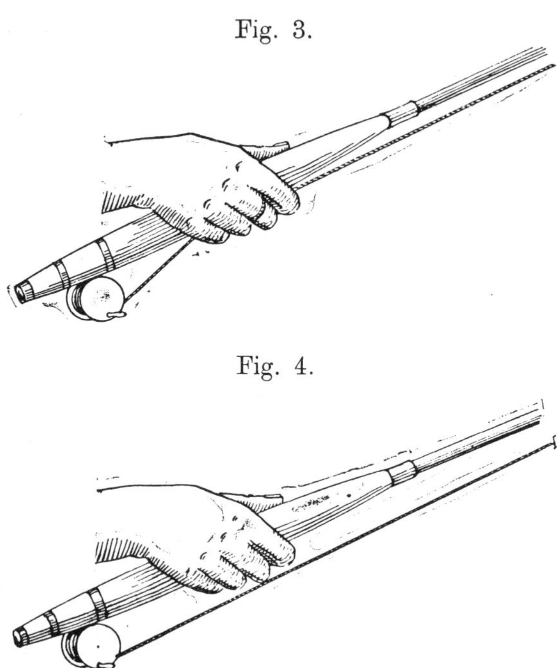

Fig. 4.

If a light line is being thrown, such as for artificial fly, it may be sufficient to simply include the reel line in the grasp of the rod, or of the forefinger only.

REEL FOR TWO-HANDED ROD.

For a two-handed rod of 14 ft., if for fishing on broad, deep rivers, or from the banks of lakes, the reel should be at least 3 in. in diameter, holding not less than 60 to 80 yards of line. This length is necessary where hooked fish cannot be followed, and a long length of line may possibly be required. No. 22 Hardy's or Bartlett's braided waterproof silk line is suitable. If for use on streams of ordinary width, the reel and line for single-handed rods will do for this rod. In other particulars a reel such as described for use with the single-handed rod, using neither check nor multiplier, is suitable, the hand-check hold being the same on the uppermost hand as for the single-handed rod.

REEL LINES FOR SINGLE-HANDED RODS.

The best material is good silk, braided and waterproofed. Twisted lines are apt to get kinked, and are generally unsuitable for minnow, or any spinning bait. Hardy's or Bartlett's No. 20 waterproof braided silk lines are very good. If the No. 20 line, when new, will stand 10 lb. dead-weight it is strong enough, if properly used, to land any trout. These lines break at about 13 lb. Forty to sixty yards have been recommended for single-handed rods, with the expectation that it would not often be necessary to run out more than a third of this length. Commonly some part of the line which is in use beyond the top end-ring of the rod gets worn or injured. It must then be cut off, as a splice or knot might stick in the rings, and is quite inadmissible. If by accident a knot, which would have to be picked open, gets on the reel line it will generally be more prudent to cut the line off there. Sixty yards of line will allow of several such cuttings before it is too short for ordinary use.

A line should be solid, so as to obtain the requisite strength with the least bulk, and allow of the greatest possible length being got on to a reel of a given size.

The wind and water have least effect on the line in casting, striking, or playing a fish—all important matters. On this account, in fine fishing with artificial or natural fly, Nos. 18 and 16 parallel lines have the advantage of lightness for striking or playing a fish. The former breaks at about 9 lb., and the latter at about 7½ lb. Nos. 18 and 16 are hardly strong enough for minnow fishing.

A loop of about 1 in. long should be made on the line, fastened by waxed silk varnished over, to loop the casting-line to. For Nos. 18 and 16 parallel lines it is safer to make the loop by knotting before whipping with the waxed silk. There are various knots which can be used on occasions instead of this loop.

TAPERED LINES.

Hardy's or Bartlett's Nos. 16 to 20 to 16 tapered lines are suitable for light-fly fishing, but are too light for minnow, natural or artificial. It is well to make the loop by knotting before whipping with the waxed silk. Parallel lines I think preferable, because as the taper wears away the line alters to a greater thickness.

REEL LINE FOR TWO-HANDED ROD.

The best material is good silk, braided and waterproofed. The strength of line mentioned for single-handed rods will generally be found sufficient — No. 20 Hardy's or Bartlett's—and the general remarks under that head will apply here. If the line is intended for fishing from the banks of broad rivers or lakes, where hooked fish cannot be followed, 60 to 80 yards of No. 22 Hardy's or Bartlett's line may be required. This line breaks with about 18 lb.

DRYING LINES.

On coming home lines should not be put away wet, or they will soon rot; but they should be wound on a chair-back, or anything that will allow the air free play upon them. When thoroughly dry, at least the part in constant use should be dressed with some such soft unsalted grease as pure raw linseed-oil. This will not stick when wound on the reel, and can be applied with a flannel saturated with the oil and doubled round the line. This will to a great extent replace the dressing worn off the line, which is more or less subject to cracking, and this tends to weaken it.

GUT.

Gut should be round and clear; and for general purposes, if used with the size of reel lines mentioned, a good casting-line for minnow fishing is of very stout Lake gut, with traces a shade lighter. If casting-line, trace, or lower gut line are each about $4\frac{1}{2}$ ft. long, they make the length of gut 9 ft., which is convenient to use with both the lengths of rods given. This length of gut allows of a fish being landed without the knots on the line getting into the rings, which might cause a break. For fine fishing even 13 ft. of gut might be used with the longer rod without the knots on the line getting into the rings when landing a fish.

It should be remembered, as a reason for using a liberal length of gut, that a good deal of the line often falls near and over the fish. The gut on the artificial-minnow or natural-minnow tackle should be in proportion to the trace. If, however, it is intended to fish in rivers near the sea-outlet, or in lakes, it is prudent to have traces of salmon-gut and tackle in proportion.

If tapered reel lines are used for fly fishing, a strength of casting-line to continue the taper should be used.

Very fine gut is unsuitable for any purpose where the fish run heavy. My practice in Britain was to use the finest gut to be had for some fly fishing. Never use doubtful or frayed gut.

TO TINT GUT.

For general purposes gut is best tinted bluish. If left its natural whitish colour it glitters and shows too much in the water. Trout mostly see the gut from below, and against the sky, of which the colour recommended is a fair average representation.

A handful of logwood and a bit of copperas, less than half the size of a pea, which can be got at the chemist's, boiled in a quart of water for a quarter of an hour, will give this tint. The least bit too much copperas will make it too blue. Pour the liquid, free from the chips, into a basin. The gut should be put in the liquor when cold, and left there until it is of the required tint; it should then be rinsed in cold water. If in the hank, shake and hang it up to dry. It is prudent to test the effect on a strand or two before putting in any quantity.

TO SOAK GUT BEFORE KNOTTING.

Before knotting or tying, gut should always be well soaked in cold water. Neglect of this is the cause of many breaks, as gut is very brittle when dry, and cracks easily. The stouter the gut the longer it requires to soak. If the knotting is being done at leisure it is well to have stout gut soaked for an hour or two at least before beginning, and to take care that it is kept wet until the knots are made.

KNOT FOR GUT LINES.

The best knot for general purposes is the double slip-knot. This is made by laying the ends together and knotting one round the other, passing the ends twice through, which makes the double knot, as shown below. When the knots are pulled tight, and together, cut off the super-fluous ends to within about $\frac{1}{16}$ in. Gut is apt to slip, and should be carefully tied.

Fig. 5.

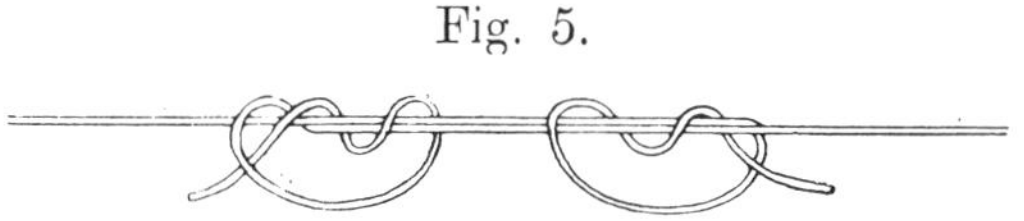

If at first any difficulty should be experienced in making the double knot as shown, the single slip-knot could be used. This is made in the same way, except that the end is passed through once instead of twice. It is not quite so secure as the double slip-knot, and the ends of gut should be left a good ⅛ in.

Thread or other whipping about gut tackle should be avoided; if used instead of knots it is apt to wear and slip off. It makes the knots much more conspicuous, and does not serve any good purpose.

HOOKS.

Dublin Limerick hooks are by me, with few exceptions, taken as a standard of size. When using hooks of other makes, which for certain purposes are sometimes recommended, this must be borne in mind, and the corresponding size chosen, although perhaps of a different number. Different makers use different numbers to denote the size of hook, and they are continually changing this number. This leads to great confusion, and it would save much trouble and misunderstanding if all makers would adopt one standard, as is done by makers of shot. There is, however, a slight difference in size of the shot of corresponding numbers made by different makers.

Fig. 6.

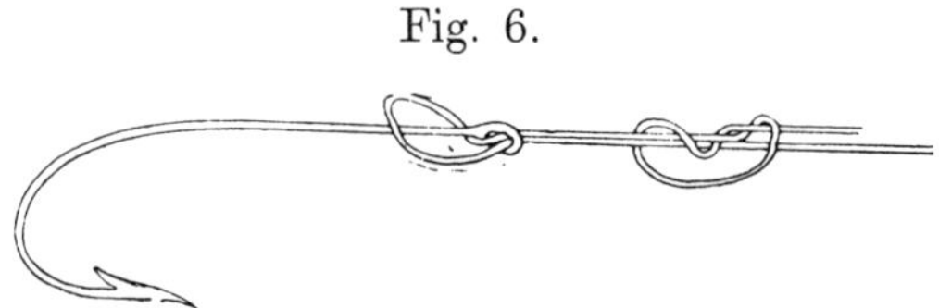

In Fig. 6 a good way is shown to fasten gut to Pennell eyed hooks, either to flies or other tackle. The gut must first be soaked until quite soft. In the case of flies, the loop shown, when pulled tight, fits over the head of the fly. To make the fasten-

ing, pass about 2 in. of the end of the gut through
the eye, then over the back of the hook, and then
back through the eye. The short and long ends
of gut will now be parallel. With the short end
make a single, or, for large flies, a double, knot
round the long end; pull this knot a little tight,
and then, pulling on the long end, work the fastening until the loop fits tightly close above the back
of the eye, with the knot against the eye. Then
pull the knot tight and cut off the end of the gut
to about $\frac{1}{16}$ in.

The eye of the ordinary trout-fly size of hooks
is too small to allow of moderately fine gut being
passed twice through to make the fastening shown
in Fig. 6. In this case what is commonly known
as the "jam knot" may be used. To make this
knot, hold the hook, with the back down, in the
left hand, and with the eye pointing to the right.
With the right hand pass about 2 in. of the gut
through the eye, and with this make a common
knot round the longer end of gut. Leave this
knot sufficiently open to pass quite easily over the
eye, and pull on the longer end of gut until the
knot passes over the eye. After seeing that the
gut of the knot fits close behind the eye, pull on
the longer end until the knot fits tightly. This
knot, if the gut is cut off too short, is liable to
slip. On that account at least $\frac{1}{8}$ in. should be
left, and the fastening looked to occasionally.
When making the knot, if the end of the gut is
passed through twice it will be much less liable
to slip. If needed to complete the fit of the gut,

when the gut is tightened behind the eye, pull on the short end before cutting it off.

LANDING-NET AND FRAME.

My net is made by the Manchester Cotton-twine Spinning Company, Crumpsall, near Marple, England; but it can be made in this country of tanned cord. It is of hard black cord, with a mesh 2 in. on each side, or 8 in. round the mesh. It is laced on to the frame with the cord of which the net is made. The net is 46 in. in circumference at the frame, 12 in. deep when shrunk, and is improved by some lead, like a pistol bullet, fastened to the lower point of the net.

The frame is made of No. 8 spring steel wire, or of $\frac{3}{8}$ in. wide, light, flat spring steel, edge up, brazed together where it is driven into the handle, which is protected by a strong short ferrule, into which the frame is sunk to the depth of its thickness or width; it has a straight side, 20 in. long, and is 12 in. across from this to the handle. The sides of the frame form the segment of a circle.

The handle is of ash or hickory, such as spare pick or hammer handles are made of, about 2 ft. or 3 ft. long, and $\frac{3}{4}$ in. diameter. This should get a coat of raw linseed-oil. When the net is carried on the fishing-bag, as mentioned at page 33, 2 ft. is long enough for a fixed handle; this gives a reach of 3 ft. When it is desired to have the handle longer than this it should be telescopic, otherwise it interferes with the back of the legs

in a very awkward manner when walking. If the
telescopic handle is chosen it should be one that
will not turn round when being used.

Net, frame, and handle weigh about $\frac{3}{4}$ lb.

This net differs from the ordinary landing-net
in having a larger frame, which makes it easier
to get a fish into; and in being half the usual
depth of nets, which makes it more manageable
in every way. There is also much less chance of
the trebles being broken by fish hanging to them.
The large mesh lessens the trouble from hooks
catching, and the hard cord prevents them stick-
ing in it. With common care this net is suitable for landing fish of 6 lb. or 7 lb. weight. It
can be made with stronger frame, up to No. 4
spring steel wire, which is advisable if it is to be
used for catching minnows. For heavier fish
a larger frame and net should be used. The
frame is the proper shape for catching minnows for bait, and for this purpose a scrim net
should be temporarily fitted to it over the cord
net. The frame and handle can be made by gun-
smiths and others.

This net was designed by myself forty-five years
ago, and I still use it in preference to the many
others which have been invented since. The only
advantage of the more recent nets is that they
are more conveniently portable when travelling.
The frame can be made to fold up if desired. A
round frame has the defect that in landing trout
in shallow water it only touches the bottom at one

point, and a fish getting loose is apt to escape round it.

These remarks have been made at considerable length, because the best landing-nets and frames in common use are still so defective that gaffs are often used for trout of a size for which they are quite unsuited. It is almost needless to add that the size of mesh recommended is too large for ordinary British brown trout.

GAFF OR CLIP.

The gaff or clip should be of the best temper and very sharp. If a telescopic handle is used it should be such as will not turn round at an inopportune time.

WADERS.

Waterproof wading-trousers may be useful in cases where deep wading is required. The ordinary waterproof wading-stockings are so well known that it is unnecessary to describe them. Both these and the trousers should be turned inside out to dry after use.

For those who live near a river, or who fish often and only for a short time, rubber wading-boots will be found convenient, being much more quickly put on and off than wading stockings or trousers. They should have leather soles, with a sufficient number of large nails in the heels and soles to prevent slipping. Rubber soles wear quite smooth, and are therefore unsuitable. The uppers should be turned down when the boots are put on and off, and left so to dry after use. It is as well not to turn down the uppers at the place where the stiff and pliant parts of the leg meet, as they are apt to crack there. The rubber can be repaired with the solution and material used to mend bicycle-tires.

FISH BAG AND BASKET.

A bag made of light unbleached (say No. 4) sail - canvas is most suitable. Where much fishing is done it is well to have two bags, so that one can be washed, preferably with the help of a deodoriser. A medium size is 22 in. long by 14 in. deep, with a flap about 4 in. deep, and three metal buttons. The band may be of the same material, about $2\frac{1}{2}$ in. to 3 in. wide, and of length to suit the user.

If a landing-net is used, and the band of the bag worn over the left shoulder, as advised, to leave the right free, a loop of the same material about $2\frac{1}{2}$ in. long, the full width of the band, can be placed on the band where band and bag meet. This loop will take the handle. The net will then be behind the left shoulder. A ring of cord round the band at the place mentioned above will allow of the net being carried in this way on any bag. If the net is top-heavy a cord fastened to the middle of the straight side of the frame, passed over the left shoulder, and fastened by a loop to a front button of the coat, will keep it in position and prevent it from being dropped. My preference is for this style of bag, which can be made by sailmakers or by any one, rather than for

3—Sport.

any of the numerous and more complicated kinds that have been invented. It is much lighter than most of these. Of course, the size must be made to suit requirements. The one I have described will hold 30 lb. to 40 lb. of fish of average length.

Baskets are not suitable where it is necessary to get through rough places or undergrowth. These are so well known as not to require description.

FLY-BOOK AND TACKLE-BOX.

There are so many different designs of these that it is hardly possible to go into the subject in detail. The size will vary according to requirements. If a book is used a broad thin one is preferable to a thick dumpy one.

FLASK FOR CREEPER, CICADA, GRASSHOPPER, ETC.

This should be a japanned zinc flask, 8 in. high, $2\frac{1}{4}$ in. across the bottom, 1 in. across the top, with a strong hinge lid, round in shape, perforated over its whole height, and it should have a zinc handle $\frac{3}{4}$ in. in diameter and $\frac{3}{4}$ in. wide, and fastened $1\frac{1}{2}$ in. from the top edge of flask. It should be hung from a button-hole by putting twine loop round the flask and through the handle.

SCISSORS AND KNIFE.

A pair of small sharp scissors should be kept in the fly-book or elsewhere, and a small sharp knife should be carried.

VARNISH.

Spirit varnish for varnishing rods, the waxed thread of loops on reel lines, the thread on trebles, or other hooks tied on with thread, &c., can be obtained at a tackle-dealer's.

THREAD.

Strong button-hole silk thread is suitable for lacing together the joints of rods, and silk thread not quite so strong for making loops on reel lines. Silk thread is necessary also for putting on uneyed trebles or other hooks.

SWIVELS.

Swivels of moderate size may be useful for making or mending traces.

SPLIT SHOT OR LEAD WIRE.

No. 1 split shot, or lead wire, is sometimes used for minnow tackle.

DISGORGER.

A disgorger is sometimes useful when hooks are swallowed.

WAX.

A piece of shoemaker's wax, for waxing thread for making loops on reel lines, for lacing together the suction-joints of rods, and for general purposes, should be carried in leather or tin box.

BATON.

This is for killing fish by a smart blow on top of the head. A convenient length is 15 in.; diameter, fully $\frac{3}{4}$ in. It can be cut wherever there is undergrowth ; or made of hardwood, and may be carried in the bag. A baton is not required when suitable telescopic gaff is used, as this serves the same purpose.

WEIGHING-MACHINE.

A small machine that will weigh from 15 lb. to 25 lb. is useful—one that will go in the waistcoat pocket for preference.

TENT.

A tent 6 ft. by 8 ft., with a fly, will weigh under 20 lb., and is large enough for two people. Such tents are used by thousands all over the country, and can be bought in any village or town. A larger size can be obtained if required. Where there are growing saplings poles need not be carried. A sheltered place should be selected, and the tent be pitched with the head slightly uphill, with a trench cut round the head and sides to carry off the water.

WATERPROOF SHEETS.

Waterproof sheets to put on the ground under the blankets can be got at sailmakers and elsewhere. A good size is 7 ft. by 3 ft. or $3\frac{1}{2}$ ft.; a sheet of this size would weigh under $3\frac{1}{2}$ lb. They are useful also to cover the pack when shifting camp.

AXE OR HALF-AXE.

This is convenient to cut firewood, tent-poles, or tracks through undergrowth, and can be got anywhere. If carried on pack-horse the axe-head should be provided with a leather cover to guard against possible injury to horse or goods.

PACK-SADDLE.

In country where vehicles cannot be taken a pack-horse may be convenient. The hooks on the saddle which hold the rings of the pack-straps should be just far enough apart to let the ring of the pack - strap between them. This reduces the chance of the ring being thrown off the hook when the horse jumps an obstacle. A tether-rope is often useful.

LANTERN.

A small lantern will be found useful in many ways—by the river-side, when dark, and in the tent; but if carried on the person oil should be burned, as kerosene is dangerous. It is a good plan to hang it in the tent by a copper wire.

CALICO BAG.

Calico bags to hang up the blankets and food in should be provided, as a protection from flies.

COOKING UTENSILS.

These should not be bulky or heavy. A great deal can be done with a frying-pan, a tin billy or two, and some tin pannikins and plates.

PROVISIONS.

Tinned provisions can be got so easily that there should be no difficulty about carrying food. It is well to have the tins of such a size that the contents are likely to be used at one meal, as if left open flies are apt to spoil the contents.

WATERPROOF WAX MATCHES.

The waterproof matches are the best to carry; they are to be had in many grocers' shops. The ordinary wax matches can be kept dry if carried in a corked phial or bottle.

TO TAKE CARE OF RODS.

To put rods out of danger for the night at the camp or water-side, and so as to have them ready for use, tie them perpendicularly securely to a tree if there are any about. It may be worth while bringing a pole some distance, and fixing it firmly in the ground, for this purpose if there are no trees available. The rods will thus be out of the way of the stock, and other risks, and ready for early morning use.

MACKINTOSH.

A short-sleeved mackintosh of such a length as to well cover the tops of the waders, and with sleeves very narrow at the wrists, will be found useful. It should be made so as to hook up for deep wading ; it can be made in the colony.

CHAPTER III.

CASTING AND STRIKING.

———

CASTING WITH A SINGLE-HANDED ROD.

ALTHOUGH I deal with the casting and striking adapted for each kind of lure under separate heads, there are some rules which can be applied to all, and giving them here saves a certain amount of repetition.

In the first place, the object is to cast the lure to some definite spot, and to take aim at that spot. The first thing required in taking aim at anything is to fix the eye steadily on the object aimed at until the missile is discharged, and so it is with casting. Accurate casting and striking in fishing are very much what accurate aiming is in shooting game. The wind is a disturbing element in each case, and allowance must be made for it. Random casting and random shooting are much alike. The knowledge of the habits of game and fish, and where to look for them, is essential to any great success. The power of endurance and the activity of the man affect the results in both cases.

When the beginner is able to cast with accuracy to any desired spot he should practise making his line fall lightly, so as not to disturb the water more than is necessary. This is of importance in all fishing, but more particularly with artificial and natural fly, light minnow, &c. To do this let him aim at an imaginary spot in the air, say a couple of feet over where he wants the lure to alight. The line will then fall more softly than if thrown directly at the spot which it is desired to reach.

Until this accuracy and lightness of casting is attained much success must not be looked for in artificial-fly fishing, where the flies and line should hardly disturb the smooth water, and where casting to rising fish is required. Nor will a dawdling style suit in artificial-fly fishing, where this taking aim and casting may be repeated, say, about twelve times per minute. Hand and eye must be on the alert.

For any sort of fishing never cast a longer line than is absolutely required, so long as the object of keeping out of sight of the trout, as well as reaching their locality, is attained. The directions in some books to fish fine and far off are misleading. The shorter the line the more it is under control for accurate, light, quick casting, as well as for striking. Of course, no fixed rule can be laid down, as it may be desirable sometimes to cast a long line to distant spots which cannot be approached by wading. As a general rule, it is not necessary to use a line, with lures, much over one and a half times the length of the rod.

Written directions for casting are not easy to follow, and practice will be found the best teacher. I would therefore advise the beginner to remember as much of these directions as he can, and to practise them at home on the lawn, or in the yard, in the following manner : Place a mark—piece of paper or suchlike—on the ground, and with about one and a quarter times the length of the rod of reel line out quietly set to work to cast over the right shoulder at the mark. Do not forget to fix the eye on the mark while making the cast, and allow the line to swing its full length behind before bringing it forward. With practice the eye fixes on the mark with a quick involuntary glance. Avoid making the line crack like a whip in casting, as in fishing this would generally mean that the hooks were cracked off. When able to throw accurately and lightly to the mark with the above length of line, lengthen it to twice the length of the rod. This length should be mastered, at any rate, and the learner can please himself about casting a longer line. Having become fairly perfect in casting over the right shoulder, next practise over the left.

The foregoing will be good practice for artificial-fly casting, as the flies are of imperceptible weight. For practice with minnow or suchlike baits it is advisable to tie a bit of wood the size of the minnow lengthways to the reel line, in the same position as the minnow would occupy. It will be found that a less whipping, and a rather more pitching or heaving, style of casting is required, owing to the weight and size of the minnow; and this is much the style of casting for all the natural baits.

The practice at home should be with the reel line only, as it is much easier to practise with at first. For beginners who live at a distance from the river, and whose time there is limited, it is better to learn all they can at home than to learn it at the river-side. This would also afford an opportunity of practising to those who choose to adopt the hand-check for the line mentioned (see Fig. 3, page 22), instead of having a check on the reel.

CASTING WITH A TWO-HANDED ROD.

Owing to two hands being used and to the length and weight of the rod, casting with a two-handed rod will be slower than with the single-handed rod; otherwise the same directions will apply. The learner should practise over the right shoulder until accuracy and lightness have been acquired, and then over the left shoulder, until, at any rate, a line twice the length of the rod can be cast. For those who choose to adopt the hand-check for the line mentioned (see Fig. 3, page 22) this is a good time to master it.

STRIKING.

As the times for striking with the various artificial and natural baits vary, directions will be given for this under the heads of those baits. The following directions apply to all.

STRIKING WITH A SINGLE-HANDED ROD.

Strike by a slight quick motion of the wrist (not by a motion of the arm) in the same direction as the rod is moving. If the rod is raised, or the direction be otherwise altered, the effect will be slower and the chance of hooking much lessened.

STRIKING WITH A TWO-HANDED ROD.

Strike in the same direction as the rod is moving. In using two hands and a powerful rod care must be taken that it is not done too hard. Striking too hard is a common fault with beginners, and leads them to endeavour to counteract the too great force used by " striking from the reel," instead of with the line held firmly by the fingers (see Fig. 3, page 22).

CHAPTER IV.

SYSTEMATIC DIVISION OF THE WATER TO BE FISHED.

THE following remarks show how to secure the greatest possible return of fish from a given area, and show also the loss of opportunity and how chances of catching fish are thrown away by the ordinary haphazard method of fishing a river or stream. The more trout there are in a river the more are lost by want of system.

The fisher will, of course, understand that the following is only a general illustration, which can be altered to suit different circumstances, as, for instance, where the river is too deep and broad to allow of the middle or opposite bank being reached.

FISHING UP BY SECTIONS.

Let the angler divide, in his mind, the rapid, which is, say, 180 yards long and about 40 yards wide, into three sections about 60 yards each, and again divide it up the middle, making six sections, as in Fig. 7 ; or he may vary the number of sections according to the length of the rapid.

Fig. 7.

O   L

Foot of Rapid.	A	C	E	Head of Rapid.
	B	D	F	

The fisher (O) is on the bank at the foot of A. A, B, C, D, E, F, are sections of the rapid where trout are on the feed.

The angler makes the first cast straight up the side on which he is standing of section A, the next partly up and across, the next up and across as far as the centre line, which is about 20 yards from the bank where he stands. Then, taking a step up stream after each three or more casts, he gradually works up stream until, arrived at A, there is a fish hooked. He leads it to the landing-place (L) down stream. If he thinks there is a chance of getting another trout out of the same section (which will depend a good deal upon how far up stream the plunges of the first have disturbed the water) he may cast over it again.

Having finished with the first section, the fisher, wading in far enough to enable him to cast across the lower end of section B, proceeds to fish that portion in the same manner as A, casting up the middle line first, and so working across to the opposite bank. By doing this he will see that, if he stirs up any mud in wading, it goes down through the water he has fished, and does not affect what is not yet fished.

If a trout is hooked in B, the fisher proceeds as in A; when B is done with he takes C; and so on to D, E, and F. By working up stream in this way the trout a few yards higher up will not be disturbed, as the current will carry the disturbed water down to the fisher and to the water in which he has already fished.

I have in Britain, when trout were numerous, by fishing in the above-described manner, sometimes taken a dozen or two out of a rapid of about the length given, where, but for this care, perhaps not half a dozen would have been secured.

FISHING DOWN BY SECTIONS.

The following way of fishing in sections down stream is suitable in very swift, rough, running water with minnow, artificial or natural. If the bank will allow of it, keep well back from the edge of the stream out of sight of the trout until straight opposite to the upper corner of A. Then, while still standing the length of the rod from the edge, make a cast or two at that place.

Fig. 8.

L		O		
Foot of Rapid.	A	C	E	Head of Rapid.
	B	D	F	

Arrived at the edge, at the upper corner of A, take a cast nearly straight down the edge of the stream; then make the second cast to the middle of the section, and the third cast to the middle line. If a trout is hooked in A, follow the direction already given to lead it down stream to the landing at L. If your chances of another trout in A are done for, wade in by degrees until able to cast across the upper end of B. Cast straight down first, then to the middle of the section, and then as near the opposite bank as you can, as trout are often close to the edge, even in shallow water. Then fish the remainder of the sections to the head of the rapid in the order of the letters.

FISHING UP WITHOUT SECTIONS.

In fishing up streams of about half the width, or less, of the first example, and which can be cast right across from the bank, if the bank will not allow fishing from it you must, if possible, wade. In either case you must pull the trout down stream to land them, as already directed. It is even more necessary in small streams to fish up than it is in large rivers, as there is not the volume of water in the former helping to conceal the fisher, and a hooked trout plunging down a narrow stream will completely scare the fish in that part of it.

FISHING DOWN SMALL STREAMS BY SECTIONS.

If you wish to fish down, try, at any rate, to do it in sections the whole width of the stream, instead of a double row as for the broader water, thus :—

Fig. 9.

L	O		
Foot of Rapid.	A	B	C	Head of Rapid.

Beginning at the top corner of section A, fish down to the lower end of that section, landing trout at L; then begin at top corner of B, and fish down to the lower end of that section; next begin at top corner of C, and fish down to lower end of that section.

One object of fishing or casting up or down, beginning from the side where you are standing and so working across to the opposite bank, is that if you hook a fish near the side you are standing on you may get it out without its running across the stream and alarming fish that may be lying more towards the opposite bank. Thus,

Fig. 10.

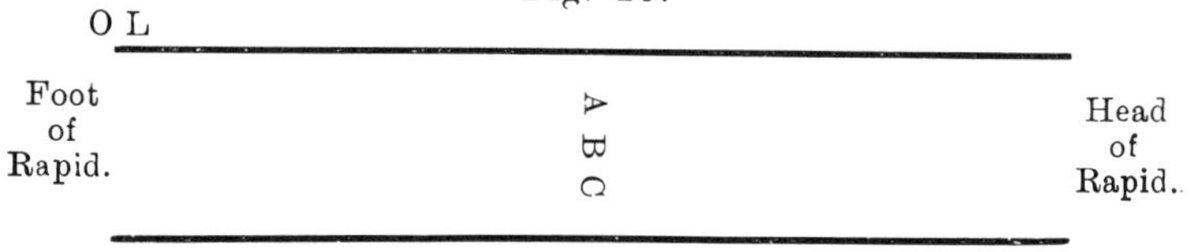

O L

Foot of Rapid.   A B C   Head of Rapid.

A, B, and C are trout, and O the fisher. The fisher hooks A and lands it at L; B and C may be undisturbed. He then hooks B, again landing at L; C may yet be undisturbed, and can be hooked and landed at L But if he hooks C first and it comes plunging across B and A there is little chance of the latter two taking a place in the bag at that time.

SUMMARY.

The following is a summary of the advantages of fishing up stream and in sections, as against the ordinary way of fishing down stream: (1.) The trout do not see you so easily, as they lie head up stream. (2.) You can use a shorter line, and thus have more chance of hooking. (3.) You have much better control of the hooked fish, and there is less chance of losing it. (4.) The trout when hooked do not disturb the unfished water nearly so much. This makes this system of fishing even more desirable in this country than in Britain, as the fish here are so much larger and disturb more water. (5.) The muddy water caused by the wader does not affect the unfished water.

4 –Sport.

CHAPTER V.

HOW TO PROCEED ON ARRIVING AT THE RIVER.

———

THE following directions will answer for fishing with all the lures :—

(1.) It is assumed that you are going to work up stream and intend to begin in the rapid at the head of a pool. On arriving at the part of the river a little below where you intend to begin to fish, look out the best landing-place in the pool, and let it be as near the foot of the rapid as possible. If you cannot get one in the pool try to get one in the rapid as near the foot as possible. The most desirable landing-place is where the water gets shallow so gradually that the trout has to turn on its side before getting to the edge of the dry shingle or bank. If possible, select a place free from roots or such things, round which the line might become entangled, and so possibly cause the loss of the fish. It is better to go some distance to a good landing than to risk losing your fish on a bad one, particularly with a good fish. Many fish are lost and much disappointment caused through neglecting to select, or being unable to find, a good landing-place down the river below where the fish is hooked. These directions take long to tell;

but the experienced fisher will select the best landing-place at a glance, and will continue to do this as he proceeds, so that when a fish is hooked he always knows where to try to lead it.

(2.) Put the gut lines, and hooks or lures with gut attached, without taking them out of the coils, into shallow water, securing them from floating away, and keeping them under water by placing a stone on them. Gut when dry is very brittle and easily cracked, and requires to be handled carefully. It is well to soak a set of spare gut lines and lures at the same time, unless you carry a small flat zinc box with damp flannel or sponge to keep spare casts damp and ready.

(3.) Put together the rod. First put the top and middle pieces together, if plain suction-joints, securing by enlacing and tying a strong waxed silk thread in the joint-catches. Then put the middle piece and butt together. See to the line-rings being in line. Hardy's lockfast joints adjust themselves.

(4.) Attach the reel, which will be on the under-side of the rod, with the handle on the right. Then take the end of the reel line and pass inside the lowest bar of the reel, passing it through the rings and out through the end ring.

(5.) The gut line or trace will now be pretty well softened. Undo the coils and straighten by pulling gently between the fingers; now pass the loop of the thick end of the gut line over the

loop of the reel line, and run it a little way up
the reel line ; then pass the thin end of the gut
line through the loop of the reel line, pulling
them gently into position. Examine the gut
from end to end to ascertain that it is free from
cracks or flaws. If there are any, break there
and retie with the double slip-knot (see Fig. 5,
page 27). Now take the spare gut line or fly
casts which may have been soaking all this time
and wind them round your hat, where, being in
large coils, they will be handy for use. Gut
should only be carried on the hat while it may
be required, as it may so get damaged. For the
same reason it should only be kept damp when
needed for use at the water's side.

It is necessary to attend to these particulars
to prevent loss of time when the trout may be
taking well, which is seldom more than a few
hours at a time.

Unless you have an attendant—who is most
useful where trout run large — your fishing-
bag is slung over the left shoulder to leave the
play of the right free. The landing-net, if used,
can be hung on your back by the loop on the
shoulder-band of the bag, and behind the left
shoulder.

You are now ready to begin with any of the
lures or baits, of which I treat further on.

If the angler intends returning by the river-
side he may find it convenient to hide the trout,
as they are caught, in the shingle or otherwise,
and to pick them up on the way back.

CHAPTER VI.

PLAYING AND LANDING.

I SHALL give under separate heads the proper way to strike with each lure, but the following directions for playing and landing the fish will be found suitable for all the lures employed.

The fish being hooked, instantly, if necessary, give line, and, without using more than the least pressure, raise the rod to a position leaning back rather from the upright, in front of the breast and shoulder, to enable the flexibility of the rod to counteract the strain of the sudden jumps and rushes. Here it is that a light pliant single-handed rod will show its value when light tackle is used. The extent to which the rod is bent, independently of the sense of feeling, will give some indication of the amount of pressure being exerted.

It may be well now to shift the rod to the left hand, to allow the right the free use of the reel, handle, and line. At the instant of hooking the fish, and afterwards, it may be necessary to be quick in the giving-out of line by pulling it from the reel with the disengaged hand, a little above the hand which holds the rod, *outside* of which latter hand the line now runs.

The fish should from the first be treated as though only hooked through some fragile bit of skin, with a hold which will not bear much pulling. The rod must never be allowed to be more than moderately bent, always keeping a gentle pressure on the line, and not allowing it to get slack. This must be managed by letting out line at times, and at others reeling in, helping this sometimes by stepping quickly backward or forward. If the fish leaps out of the water, lower your rod-point quickly, to avoid its striking the line while tight, and so perhaps breaking it.

The usual direction to keep a firm hold on the fish is vague, and is often overdone by beginners, not infrequently resulting in a smash. The trout, if the fishing is being done up stream, will most likely be hooked higher up the stream than where you are standing. Whether hooked above or below, as soon as you have made safe the first rushes by perhaps letting out line and following, keep lower down stream than the fish. If this position is lost, regain it as soon as possible, as in this way the current helps in giving you power to keep the trout from disturbing the unfished sections. Do not by attempting to stop rushes risk losing a hooked fish.

Large trout when hooked often rush down the stream for the pool where they are accustomed to find shelter in the deep water. Guide the fish quietly down stream, and keep as much out of sight as possible, which your position down stream will render comparatively easy. Guide it down the side of the river you are on, if you can, until you arrive at the pool; here allow it to rush about until tired. Never let a fish have a long line, if you can do with moderate length by wading or keeping up with it. A long line is not well under control, and is more likely to get caught on snags.

When the fish is getting tired, guide it to opposite the shallow landing-place selected, either in the rapid or pool. If the ground allows, step back from the water with the object of keeping out of sight, as the fish will not come near the landing-place as long as it can help it if it sees you there. Manœuvre it to the landing, and when it has fairly turned on its side (with its head to the bank is best) reel in until the line is about 1 ft. shorter than the rod; this will allow you to put the net on the river side of the fish, and, drawing the net along the bottom, scoop it out.

After the fish is aground care should be taken to avoid using much force, as if only slightly hooked this is the time when the hold is most likely to give way and the fish perhaps escape into deep water. In shallow water, with the fish aground, if you have no landing-net or gaff, putting both hands under the fish and throwing it out may do. Get in the water on the river side of the fish to do this. If in so doing there is occasion to lay the rod down, let the handle of the reel be uppermost, so that if the fish makes another dash for freedom the line will run out.

If instead of such a landing-place you are obliged to land your fish from deep water the landing operations will be different. Having completely tired the fish, you must shorten the line to a little less than the length of the rod, holding the rod in the left hand, so that the elasticity will ease the jerks. You must then manœuvre to get the net under the fish. In deep water the fish can dive down in every direction, and so care must be taken to keep the hooks clear of the net until the fish is in it. Then lift the fish out smartly and kill at once to prevent it breaking the tackle.

Never, if it can be avoided, pull a fish against the stream, for by so doing you are heavily handicapping your chances of landing it. In any case it is risky to take hold of the line to pull in a fish when landing it.

The foregoing directions are, of course, intended to apply chiefly to good-sized trout. In your landing or other operations you must avoid treading on the line, as this would very likely cut it wholly or partly. If you have any reason to think the line is injured, quickly examine as much of it as passed through the end ring of your rod.

Having seen to all this, get to work again without delay, for trout seldom take freely for more than a few hours at a time.

I entirely condemn the tug-of-war style of playing fish. Rarely is anything gained by using force, as a slightly hooked fish is almost sure to get away

—in fact, the loss of most hooked fish may be put down to using too much force. There is no more excuse for a fisher letting a trout break the line in water that is clear of snags, and where he can follow it, than there is for a man being thrown off a horse. In one case he cannot manage the trout, in the other he cannot manage the horse: bad fisher, bad rider. It is not very unusual to hear fishers say, " The trout took my minnow " or " broke my line," as if the circumstance was owing to having encountered a specially malignant fish. Make it a maxim in this country, where trout run large, but are not always numerous, that a fish on the hook is worth two in the river, and deal with them carefully after they are hooked.

CHAPTER VII.

FACTS FOR TROUT-FISHERS.

EFFECT OF WIND AND WEATHER ON "THE TAKE."

THE information given below will be found correct over the whole of the country, with the slight exceptions that unusual combinations of weather may produce.

When there is "thunder in the air," or during a thunderstorm, trout will not take, though exceptionally they may do so during a thunderstorm with heavy rain. Directly the thunderstorm is spent they often take eagerly.

When the wind has any west in it trout generally take fairly during some part of the day—say, from north-west, changing by the west to south—taking more freely as it works southward. With minnow particularly, a cold, wet, squally south-wester generally gives good sport, and the fish are on the feed more or less throughout the day.

When the wind has any east in it trout are seldom eager to feed; if it works from the south towards the east and north-east they are still less inclined to feed; and when at north-east—a warm wind generally—they seem to be spellbound, and scarcely move at all, even in the early dawn or late in the evening.

If there is a mist on the river or lake, and not on the land, trout do not generally take well. With a river or stream just rising from rain, particularly after being low for some time, trout are always on the alert and take well, unless under the influence of an easterly wind, as already mentioned. When dew is very heavy on the ground trout seldom take freely until it has gone off.

During mild and warm weather, and during the warm part of the season, if the water is clear and low, the earliest dawn and the late evening are the best times to look for sport with any of the lures, and these times generally are worth all the rest of the day. This applies more particularly to the North Island. The trout are on the feed then, and the imperfect light helps to disguise the tackle. If the water is tinted or discoloured sport may often be had during a great part of the day. The discoloured water disguises the tackle and allows of sport in a stronger light.

The effect of the direction of the wind on the state of the rivers can only be learnt locally. The north-west wind, which is in many parts of the country a hot, dry wind, has a shrinking effect on many rivers, though it has quite a contrary effect on some of the rivers that rise among the glaciers and perpetual snow of the Middle Island, where, by causing probably a heavy rainfall on the ranges, it melts the snow and ice, and often brings such rivers down in too heavy flood to be fishable.

Take care that your shadow, or that of the rod, does not fall on the water you are fishing or are about to fish. It is generally best to have the sun or moon in your face when other things suit. Keep out of sight of the trout. If you are seen you are not likely to capture them for an hour or two afterwards, at any rate, and those that have not seen you may be scared by the flight of those that have. A dog is an unsuitable companion.

In running water trout at rest always lie with head up stream, and in back-waters and eddies with head against the current. Fish up stream whenever practicable, as you can thus approach within a comparatively short distance unobserved; whereas if fishing down stream, more especially in clear water, you are seen a long way off. Avoid light-coloured clothing, which is more readily seen than dull or dark coloured. As in most other active exercises, it is well to have all your clothing of wool.

Trout generally come on the feed once every day, sometimes several times. This is known as " the time of the take," and should be watched for and made the most of while it lasts. If the trout are not feeding they cannot be caught, but they generally give some indication when they are on the feed, such as rising at flies and rushing after minnows. " The time of the take " may, among other causes, be sometimes due to a slight and only temporary shift of the wind to a more favourable quarter.

It is seldom of use casting more than a few times over one place, particularly if the water is clear, as, if the trout are on the feed, and see the lure and mean to have it, they almost always take it at once.

In the early part of the season trout are mostly to be found in pools and slow-running water, and should be looked for there. Later on, when they gain strength, they spread all over the river, and should be fished for accordingly. As the season advances, and trout become more shy and difficult of capture in the larger main streams, good sport may often be obtained in the smaller tributaries. Under ordinary conditions the fish are more numerous in the small streams, in proportion to the volume of water, than in the main streams, and are less uncertain in their humour. As the season declines, sport usually improves in the main streams.

In the country commonly known as " papa," a kind of soft stone resembling indurated pipe-clay, and also in clay country, the rivers when once flooded will sometimes remain for weeks too thick and discoloured to be fishable. Clay or papa country streams should generally be fished while they are clear, when rising, and before the water gets too thick (which it does very quickly sometimes), and when tinted after a flood.

The water of the rivers and streams in pumice country is usually very clear, and does not dis-colour much, even in heavy rains. In some of the lighter pumice land, after heavy rains, great quantities of pumice-grit and lumps of pumice are carried into the streams, and it is of little use fishing until this has settled. Such pumice streams should be fished while they are rising, but before the pumice-grit and lumps are disturbed by the rising water. Some of the largest rivers and lakes in the North Island are in pumice country—viz., the Waikato River, Lakes Taupo, Rotorua, and Rotoiti. This part of the country is commonly known as the Taupo, Rotorua, or Waikato country, and the pumice is chiefly confined to it. Both rivers and lakes in pumice country contain large trout; and so also do the rivers in papa and clay country, which have almost invariably shingle beds.

In any of the above-mentioned kinds of country the angler will do well to note the streams in the neighbourhood that are not so much affected by floods, and to fish them when the others are not fit for fishing in. For instance, some of the tributaries may be in a different formation, and so be in first-rate order, while the main stream is unfishable; or the main stream itself may be in good order above a certain point, but be unfishable below that.

In shingle or limestone country the rivers and streams, while rising, generally remain fishable for a considerable time before getting too thick, and the sediment soon settles sufficiently to allow of fishing being resumed.

The conditions of water and weather suited to the different lures are given when dealing with the subject of the lures.

Regarding the few colours and small variety of artificial flies and minnows given in this book : It often happens that, where a great variety of flies and minnows is used, a change in the fly or minnow fished with gets the credit of obtaining better sport, when the credit should be given to the altered humour of the fish— to their coming on to feed. Sometimes special artificial flies or minnows are said to be particularly killing on certain rivers or lakes. It will be found, on examination, that if the water of these rivers or lakes is generally clear the special flies will be black or dull coloured. Should the water be more or less tinted or discoloured the special flies will be reddish or bright coloured.

If the principles laid down for the selection of colour and size of flies (see Chapter VIII.) and minnows (see Chapter IX.) are carried out no special flies or minnows will be required, and a great amount of time and guesswork will be saved. The above remarks relate to brown trout.

Sea-trout (*Salmo trutta*) will sometimes, when fresh from the sea particularly, take fly or minnow of almost any colour or size. My opinion, however, is that in their case the variety of colour and size of flies and minnows generally employed might with advantage be reduced to what is recommended in Chapters VIII. and IX., but with the addition sometimes of tinsel to the brighter-coloured flies.

Rainbow trout (*Salmo irideus*) have a good deal in common with sea-trout in the variety of flies and minnows they will take. My remarks on brown trout likewise apply to the rainbow variety. I have met with great success using the flies and minnows mentioned in Chapters VIII. and IX. Brown and rainbow trout generally occupy the same stream.

The fishing season begins on the 1st October and ends on the 30th April. Any one intending to fish the whole length of the country, beginning with the opening of the season on the 1st October, should commence in the north, as the weather is considerably warmer there than in the south, and, working south as the summer comes on, return to the north for the finish of the season.

CHAPTER VIII.

ARTIFICIAL-FLY FISHING.

THIS perhaps requires more mechanical skill, and is also probably more misunderstood, than any of the other ways of fishing.

For rods, reels, lines, gut, see Chapter II.

For rivers that can be fished across by wading, the light 10 ft. rod is the most suitable; but for rivers too deep to wade, the light 14 ft. rod might be desirable. 9 ft. or 10 ft. is about the length of gut to use with the 10 ft. rod, while with the 14 ft. rod the gut might be about 13 ft. It should taper from the reel line to the tail fly.

The multiplication of the varieties of flies used is one of the ways of making a complicated business of what is really a simple matter. In Fig. 11, facing page 67, are shown nearly the largest size of the five flies, of three colours in all, that have served me well round the world for fifty years. The thing to be careful about is to suit the size and colour of fly to the condition of water and weather. This most important matter being attended to, I have no hesitation in saying that, used by a skilful fly fisher, these five flies will do more execution than the largest variety with their endless list of names.

5—Sport.

By " a skilful fly fisher " is meant not merely one who can throw a fly line fairly well. He must know where to look for the trout in the different seasons, the conditions of water, and how to adapt the size and colour of fly to the constantly changing weather and water. These changes may occur several times in a day, particularly in lake fishing, where the day might begin with a hardly perceptible breeze and ripple, when perhaps the use of the small flies would be judicious. This breeze might increase during the day to half a gale, making rough water, and the use of the largest flies would then be requisite, so as to allow of their being seen by the trout. Should that breeze die away in the latter part of the day, leaving only a slight ripple, then a return to the small flies would be advisable; and if the fishing is continued to a dim light, or dark, the large flies might be again used with advantage. These remarks, with some modification as to size of fly, apply also to fishing the long, almost currentless pools of large rivers, although the waves cannot be as large as in the lakes. Sometimes while fishing long pools it is remunerative to put on a cast of smaller flies than those being used for the rapids.

I allow that a skilful fly fisher might do as much execution with a great variety of flies, but he would be handicapped by the loss of time and useless trouble involved. The credit given for taking trout to the change to some fancy fly is generally due to the change in the humour of the fish, to their beginning to feed more freely, or to the chance change to a fly better suited to the condition of weather and water. Although five flies are here given, there are only three colours of feathers and dubbing used altogether, the fourth colour being the yellow silk with which some of the flies are made. The colours are red, greyish brown, and black. These flies are commonly known as red hackle, hare's-ear, black hackle, black spider, hare's-ear spider.

No. 1, red hackle, light-brown mallard wing, yellow-silk body, is the most easily seen when the water is discoloured, and therefore best for use at that time.

No. 2, turn of brown partridge hackle, hare's-ear body, light woodcock wing, put together with yellow silk : A killing fly when the water is clear and low.

No. 3, black hackle, grouse wing, brown-silk body, put together with brown silk : Easily seen when the water is clear and low, and kills well then.

No. 4, spider, black hackle, tied with brown silk, brown-silk body : Easily seen when the water is clear and low. A good fly to use as a tail fly when the trout are getting into high condition and shy, and when there is bright sunshine.

No. 5, spider, brown partridge hackle, hare's-ear body, put together with yellow silk : Very killing, when the water is clear and low, among high-conditioned and shy trout. Used as a tail fly this is perhaps the most reliable of the whole, particularly among large trout of 2 lb. and upwards.

These flies are improved by a tail, formed of a couple of strands of the hackle used in each, varying in length from ¼ in. to ½ in. in proportion to the size of the fly. Almost any feathers, if of the same colour and suitable texture, would do as well as those named.

The hackles of the spiders should be a little longer than the hooks, but the ends should not be cut off to effect this. Soft hackles, if procurable, should be used in preference to wiry ones, as they have a more life-like appearance in the water.

The greyish-brown flies with hare's-ear body are of a very natural colour, and are generally the best for shy trout. Very fine distinctions of shades of colour are not required. The trout see the flies from below, in which position slight differences of shade cannot be distinguished. Natural specimens of the same fly also differ a good deal in shade.

Bulky flies should be avoided, as they are apt to interfere with the hook getting a good hold, and are not natural in appearance. Nearly all water-flies are slender, and it will be found that sparsely dressed flies are most killing, as they fall more lightly on the water. These were the flies

Fig. II.

1
2
3
4

5

To face page 68.

of my early days on Tweedside, and no local
fisher of that country of hereditary expert trout
and salmon fishermen would use a bulky fly.

The flies in the illustration are on Pennell-eyed
Limerick hooks, equal to No. 8 Dublin Limerick
hooks in size. These hooks are best for sizes
equal to Nos. 11 to 7 Dublin Limerick, or larger,
as the gut is apt to crack at the end of the shank
of uneyed hooks. On this account, if uneyed
hooks are used, the gut next the hook should be
proved by a moderate pull after being in use for a
time. If when holding the gut of an uneyed hook
between the finger and thumb of the left hand,
about $\frac{1}{4}$ in. from the hook, on pressing the hook
downwards with the finger of the right hand, the
gut bends sharply where it joins the hook, it is no
longer reliable. The smaller sizes of flies will do
on rust-proof round-bend hooks, as that shape of
hook takes a bigger hold for its size than any
other. Perhaps the most generally useful sizes of
hooks for flies are No. 10 round-bend and Pennell-
eyed Limerick hooks, equal to Nos. 11, 9, and 8,
Dublin Limerick. The two latter are for use
among large trout, and in late evening and night
fishing or in discoloured water.

This gives four sizes of flies for general fishing,
but sometimes a larger fly does good execution.
The largest size of fly to which the trout will rise
freely at the time should always be used, on
account of the better hold the large hook takes.
Many trout, when it is necessary to use small

flies, are lost through the thin wire of the small hooks cutting through the small hold they take. For this reason, for clear water, the spider flies have an advantage, as they are less bulky than winged flies, and hide the hook better and so allow the use of a rather larger hook.

To guard against it being said that so small a variety of flies might answer among unwary and hungry trout, but would not do so among those in streams much fished, the following instances from among many are given: I met with comparatively marked success, using only the flies mentioned, in the Almond Water, close to Edinburgh, a stream which was unceasingly fished by numbers of the anglers from that town; also on the Tyne, in East Lothian. In both of these streams the trout were exceptionally shy. One size of fly used was the smallest given here, and one a little smaller.

Using the 10 ft. rod, three flies will be enough to use at a time. From the smaller sizes to the size equal to No. 9 Dublin Limerick, they will be far enough apart at about 20 in. for the smaller, and 24 in. for the larger. Above that size they are better further apart—say, 30 in. to 36 in., according to size, and two of these will be sufficient. In any case two flies are enough to use at a time in small streams.

With the 14 ft. rod four of the smaller, up to equal to No. 9 Dublin Limerick, and three of the larger flies can be generally managed at the same distances apart as for the 10 ft. rod. If the flies are not of the same size the largest should be the tail fly, as this will help the casting. As the tail fly takes the most trout, the fly which happens to be the taking one for the time being should be placed as tail fly, and the dropper fly above it may often with advantage be one of the same kind.

Try to have the knots on the gut line at about the distance apart that you want to fasten the droppers. The length of gut connecting the dropper flies with the gut cast should not be more than $2\frac{1}{2}$ in., including the fly, and rather less than this for the smaller flies. A greater length lets the gut of the droppers twist round the gut line, making a most objectionable thick conspicuous place close to the fly. Attach them above, not on, the knots on the gut line, by making a loop, *not knotted*, on the dropper gut at the distance from the fly that you wish the dropper gut to be fastened. Then pass the end the fly is on and the other end through the loop, which is now round the line, and pull tight and close; then make a simple knot with the loose end of the dropper gut round the part of the dropper gut which the fly is on. While still loose, with the thumb-nail of the right hand work the knot close up to the loop round the line before pulling tight; then cut off the end, leaving about $\frac{1}{16}$ in. This fastening is not liable to crack at or wear the line, is secure, and makes little show in the water. (See Fig. 12, page 72.)

Fig. 12.

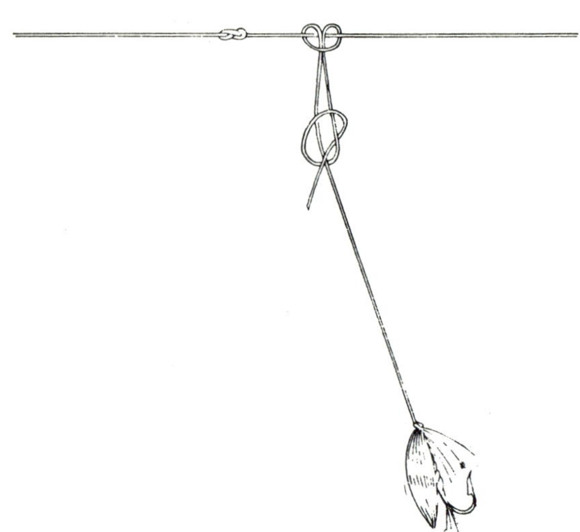

It sometimes slips up the line above the knot, but a little attention will replace it. While attaching the droppers in this way it is most convenient to have the gut line stretched tight, say, by having the tail fly hooked round a tack.

The best way of making up a cast of uneyed flies with fine gut for small trout is by making the gut on the dropper flies form part of the main line, the dropper gut leaving the main line from the up-line side of the knot. This is not suitable for large trout unless tested frequently, because the gut on the dropper flies is liable to crack where it leaves the main line.

The general direction just given for making up a cast with fine gut for clear water refers to eyed flies as well as uneyed. To make it clearer the following direction for a cast of three small-eyed flies is added : Select and well soak a 9 ft. casting-

line of the desired fineness. Cut off the loop at
the thin end and attach an eyed fly. Then cut
the casting-line, preferably at a knot, about 2 ft.
above. Next attach the second fly to the other
end of the 2 ft. of casting-line. Now cut off about
2 ft. more of the casting-line, and, laying the thin
end of this parallel with the gut on which the
second fly is, the fly lying up line, knot them
together, at about 2 in. from the fly, with the
double knot or double slip-knot, as if joining
two ends of gut in the ordinary way. Then
attach the third fly to the other end of the 2 ft.
of casting-line as before, and knot the remainder
of the casting-line 2 in. from the third fly in
the same way.

It is easy to adapt uneyed flies to this plan,
or to have a greater or less number than three,
either eyed or uneyed, taking care that the gut
on the uneyed flies is of the same strength as
the pieces of casting-line. These two ways of
making up a cast of flies minimise the number
of knots.

Loops are out of place on any trout fly cast,
as they show too much, and should not be within
3 ft. of any fly. The plan of putting a knot on
the dropper gut to keep it from slipping through
the slip-knot on the line allows of changing the
fly readily; but it is liable to slip through, which
with heavy fish may cause a serious shortage in
the bag. The tail-fly gut should be attached to
the line by the double slip-knot. (See Fig. 5,
page 27.)

Experience of the weather and the state of the water will enable the fisher to judge which colour and size of fly is likely to be suitable. He can have casts ready made up, with the dull-coloured flies for clear water and fine weather, and with the brighter-coloured flies chiefly for discoloured water and stormy dark weather. The casts should also be made up with at least three sizes of hooks, the hooks on each separate cast to be of the same size, and perhaps the tail fly left to be put on at the waterside. The smaller sizes will generally be the most taking in clear water, fine weather, and in a strong light, because the deception is not so readily seen. To enable the trout to see the flies the size can be increased in proportion as the water is discoloured or the weather dark and stormy.

WHERE TO FIND TROUT.

At the beginning of the season, before they have got into condition, most of the fish will be in the pools and the slow-running water. The foot of the pools is often a good place to fish if there is enough breeze to raise a ripple. As the season advances and the trout gain strength they go more into the quicker water, until they are spread all over the deep water and shallows, and may be got in water just deep enough to cover them.

Trout seldom take the artificial fly freely until their attention is attracted to the surface by the natural fly. It does not by any means always follow that a fly similar in colour and size to the natural fly on the water at the time will be the right artificial fly to use. For instance, with the March brown on the water, if it is very low and clear and the weather fine, an artificial fly the size of the one on the water would very likely be too large, showing its artificial nature too plainly. Here the use of a smaller fly—No. 2, of the hare's-ear sort, or, if there is bright sunshine, No. 4 — would be judicious. On the other hand, if the water is discoloured or the weather stormy, it might be well to put on a larger fly than the natural one, so as to allow it to be seen more readily. In discoloured water an entirely different-coloured fly might do better, such as a red hackle, No. 1, as being more conspicuous.

It has happened to me many times while fishing in the Tweed, the water being well tinted and literally covered with March browns, that the trout were rising so that the whole surface was broken into a continuous rise. Casting among these March browns I hardly got any fish until the fly was changed to a bright-red hackle with yellow body and light wing. Among the multitude of March browns on the water my flies of the same colour and size were only one or two in the crowd, and their chance of being taken was in the same ratio. When the colour was completely changed they became conspicuous in the crowd, and I secured a number of trout.

"TIME OF THE TAKE."

This should be watched for, and the most made of it while it lasts, which is seldom for long at a time; but it sometimes occurs several times in a day. The trout will be seen rising freely at the natural fly. In the deep water of the pools the trout are near the surface while this time lasts, and may be caught there if there is a ripple, or by casting carefully over the splash of the rises. About the edges of pools large trout may sometimes be got in water hardly deep enough to cover them, and where they stir up the mud when they rise. In such places the spider flies are very deadly.

The pools, when there is sufficient ripple, should be carefully fished, as they often give the largest trout and best sport to the fly fisher. They are not generally much fished with the other lures. In some of the best rivers the pools occupy the greater part. Unless the trout are rising very freely the deep water does not give much sport. Where shallow bars in pools merge into the deep water are often good places to fish, as trout lying in the deep water often come out on these to feed.

At night, in warm weather, good sport may sometimes be had. When there are moths and suchlike about a very slight breeze is the best, as it allows of their lighting on the water and attracting the trout to the surface. Casting over the rises will be found satisfactory; but in pools —and at night particularly—trout cruise about more, so that casting a good many times in one place where trout are about may be remunerative. When nearly dark, and in the dark, good-sized flies, rather larger than those used in daylight, and fairly strong gut, are the best.

Two flies are enough, at about 20 in. apart; any more gives trouble. Sizes equal to Nos. 11, 9, or 8, Dublin Limerick hooks, are often suitable; but the size of hook it is advisable to use varies with the conditions of weather and water, as in daylight. Either the No. 2 grey-brown, or No. 1 red hackle, winged fly will do. If the water is low and clear the use of the No. 5 grey spider as a tail fly is frequently judicious. (See Fig. 11, facing page 67.)

At night casting a comparatively short line is often sufficient, as trout are bolder than in the daytime, and often large fish are caught near the edges of rapids and pools in shallow water, close to the fisher, where there would be no chance of success by daylight. Unnecessary disturbance of the water by wading should be avoided. If you can, fish from the shallow side of the river, where probably the best landing-places are.

CONDITIONS OF WATER.

Perhaps the most favourable time is when rain has raised the water a very little, and it is just tinted.

SHADOW.

The fisher must take care that neither his shadow nor that of the rod falls on the water he is fishing or intends to fish. It is well also to remember that his figure is strongly outlined even on a dull day, or at night, with the sunlight or moonlight behind, if there is no bank or suchlike at his back. He is also more conspicuous when standing on a bank than if low down and about the level of the water. On this account it may be well to kneel sometimes to keep out of sight. The same purpose is served while wading.

WIND.

If casting against the wind can be avoided the fishing will be better and more pleasant. If it blows so that the flies cannot be kept in the water, good sport may sometimes be had with a small minnow. For this, when the water is clear, a gale is best.

CASTING.

Casting must be so done that the flies alight on the water first, with as little of the line as possible, and softly. Make the descent of a snow-flake the standard. To accomplish this the rod should not be allowed to get lower than at an angle of about 45° with the water. Just before the flies drop on the water raise the end of the rod slightly, which makes them alight softly. If you cast where there is no ripple, allow any slight disturbance to subside before pulling the flies towards you.

Make a cast or two straight up the side you are on, and so work by degrees as close to the opposite bank as you can, even casting on to it sometimes if it is clear, and allowing the flies to drop off into the water. Trout often lie close to the bank. Cast partly up and partly across, never allowing the flies to be quite so low down the stream as opposite where you are standing.

Incessant casting is necessary. Move a step or two up stream after having covered all the water within reach, so that all the likely water will gradually be cast over. Walk smartly past all water not worth fishing.

Unless the trout are rising it is seldom of much use casting many times over one place, particularly if the water is clear. If a trout sees a fly and means to try for it, it does so at once ; but in rough water or rough weather the fly may not be seen for the first few casts, and therefore it is often worth while to cast over the same place half a dozen times.

In casting to a rise, if in a rapid, let the flies drop a full yard higher up the stream than where the rise appeared to be, as by the time it has caught the eye the circle will probably be lower down the stream than where the trout is.

If a trout rises to your fly, and is missed, cast over it until it ceases to rise.

It is not advisable to try to keep the flies on the surface; they are better sunk, if only a few inches. They must never furrow the surface, neither must the line near them. As they float down stream raise the end of the rod so as to have as little sag in the line and as little line in the water as possible. Unnecessary line in the water in a strong current drags the flies down too fast and interferes with striking. Trout take the sunk flies in a much more certain way, not being so apt to miss them as when on the surface.

In fishing up stream the flies come down with the current, as the natural ones almost always do, and so present a natural appearance. The current also helps to keep the hackles or legs expanded and life-like. Pulled against the stream, the current makes the hackles cling to the hook, and gives a most unnatural appearance to the fly.

STRIKING.

The eye and hand must be on the alert for striking instantly to a rise, or a stoppage of the line, as in rough water a rise cannot always be seen. With the single-handed rod strike in the direction in which the rod is moving, with a quick motion of the wrist—not of the arm. A mere movement of the hand is sufficient. At the moment of taking the fly the trout closes its mouth, and then is the best chance of the hook catching.

Large brown trout, either in Britain or this country, rise more slowly than small ones, sometimes making no perceptible break of the surface. It is sometimes remunerative to strike gently when the gleam of a trout is seen about where the flies are, although there is no stoppage of the line or visible rise. The flies are often taken by large trout when a foot or more under water.

Never cast a longer line than is needed to keep out of sight of the trout and to reach the desired spot. The bad effect of a long line in delaying the effect of the strike by reason of the amount of sag to bring up, and by there being so much of it in the water as well as being affected by the wind, has been shown. (See Fig. 2, page 17.) Strike with the two-handed rod in the direction in which the rod is moving, and with the slightest motion of both hands.

FISHING IN FLOODS AND DISCOLOURED WATER.

As some anglers only like fishing with artificial fly, a few remarks are here given on fishing with fly when the rivers are flooded with rain-water and are discoloured.

In warm summer weather, from early dawn until dark evening, trout may be caught when the direction of the wind, and other conditions of the weather already mentioned, are favourable. They may be caught in shallow pools, in the shallow edges of pools and rapids, where the temporary shallow side streams join the pools and main rapids, and in shallow rippling water generally if sheltered from the strong main current. In such shallow places the trout have a better chance of seeing the flies in the thick water than where it is deeper.

Sometimes large trout and good sport are got when the water is considered too thick for the minnow fisher, and where it is too shallow to work a minnow satisfactorily.

The flies that generally succeed are the No. 5 spider and No. 1 red hackle. If the day is bright, the former, used as a tail fly, will probably, as in clear water, take nine out of ten of the large fish caught. In clear water, when used as a tail fly, the trout mostly take it quietly, without any perceptible rise, and are generally felt before being seen.

Hooks equal to No. 9 Limerick are commonly suitable during the day, but if the light is dull, as in the early morning and late evening, or if the water is very thick, it may be judicious to try a No. 1 tail fly on equal to No. 8 Limerick hook, and the first dropper should be No. 1 on equal to No. 9 Limerick hook. The flies for fishing in this condition of water should be on stout gut.

In fair-sized rivers, while generally following the directions already given for fishing up stream, it is better to adopt a method of casting up, but more nearly at right angles to the current, so as to allow the flies to be spread across the stream, and therefore more likely to be seen by the trout. This modification may sometimes be adopted in large rivers when they are clear, taking care to cast again before the flies are lower down the river than the fisher.

If the bank is of shingle or is low, and will allow of it, the edges may be fished by standing back from the water and casting nearly at right angles to the current.

FISHING DOWN.

If the water is rather thick, fishing down is often most successful, principally because the trout cannot see the fisher so readily as in clear water. Therefore, after fishing over the likely places in the usual way, it may be remunerative to go over them again, fishing down, and by sections, if it is desired to disturb the water as little as possible in landing fish. (See Fig. 8, page 46.) Although I quote Fig. 8, yet for thick water it is not generally requisite to wade in much, as the middle current is commonly too strong to be worth fishing, the trout mostly seeking shelter by keeping nearer the edges.

The object of fishing down when the water is thick is to give the trout a better chance to see the flies, which can be worked more slowly than when casting up stream. While keeping the rod at about the same angle to the water as in fishing up stream, work the flies slowly with a slight jerking motion, which tends to attract attention. The trout in thick water sometimes miss the fly owing to being unable to see it properly, but as a rule they take a bold hold. It is advisable to cast oftener over a likely place when the water is thick than when clear, because the trout may not see the flies for some time. There are very few rises at the natural fly when the water is much discoloured, because it is generally too small and floats too quietly to be readily seen by the trout.

If two large trout are hooked at the same time, either in clear or discoloured water, they are out of the control of the fisher, and the result is generally the loss of one or both of the trout through the tackle giving way. The 10 ft. rod is quite suitable for use when the water is thick.

No attempt has been made at a description of dry-fly fishing, which requires much practice. And, whatever its merits under exceptional conditions, it has the disadvantage that in ordinary circumstances the fly spends most of its time in the air instead of in the water. To those who care to familiarise themselves with this mode of fishing I would recommend, among many others, a newly published book, " Dry-fly Fishing, " by F. M. Halford, where this subject occupies as many pages as are in the whole of this book. I must not, however, be understood to indorse the use of the great number of flies mentioned.

CHAPTER IX.

ARTIFICIAL-MINNOW FISHING.

ARTIFICIAL-MINNOW FISHING IN CLEAR WATER.

A ROD is recommended with stiffish tops and two butts, which will make two rods of different lengths—one of 14 ft., and, by using the short butt, one of about 10 ft. 8 in. (For rods, reels, lines, gut, see Chapter II.) The beginner is recommended to use the shorter rod at first, as it is more easy to manage. Fishing up stream with artificial minnow entails more or less constant casting according as the water at the places fished runs fast or slow. If every likely place for a trout is cast over, this rod by many fishers will be found heavy enough at the end of the day.

A casting-line of stout Lake gut, and a trace a shade lighter, with three swivels, should be joined together, making about 1 ft. shorter than the short rod. This casting-line and trace will also do for the 14 ft. rod, and the 9 ft. of gut will allow the line to be shortened in landing fish without getting the gut into the rod-rings of the shorter rod. A good length of gut is conducive to quick striking, as well as being but little visible. If the trace has no link-spring to hook into the minnow—and for fine fishing it is better without — it should have a loop at least 1 in. long at the bottom, to allow of the easy passage of the minnow and trebles in putting on or changing the minnow. The loop at the head of the strand on which the minnow is should be quite small, say $\frac{1}{2}$ in. Experienced fishers may prefer not to have a loop near the minnow in fine water, as it shows more than a slip-knot does.

When attaching the gut to the minnow, pass the thick end of the strand of gut, doubled like a loop, through the metal loop, one end being about $1\frac{1}{2}$ in. long; then pass the short and long ends through the gut loop, pull tight, and fasten the short end by a simple knot round the long end of gut, working the knot close up to the minnow before pulling tight, and leaving about $\frac{1}{8}$ in. of gut end. In this case the usual order of taper is reversed, to help it to stand the wear next the minnow.

Good-sized swivels are generally best, as they also serve the purpose of leads. For this purpose one is conveniently placed at about 15 in. or 18 in. from the minnow, and above that any split shot can be advantageously put. No. 1 shot is suitable. Unleaded minnows are preferable, as they enable exactly the desired weight to be put on.

In fishing up stream very little if any lead is wanted; while, in fishing down, pulling against the current tends to bring the minnow to the surface, and more weight is required. It is generally best to keep the minnow sunk at least 6 in., if the depth of the water will allow of it.

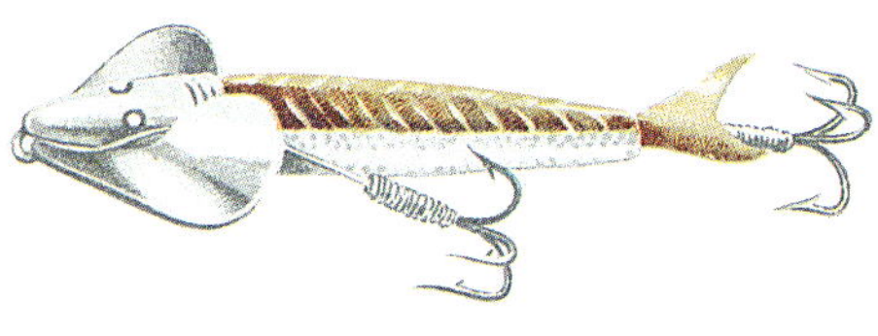

Fig. 13.
1

2

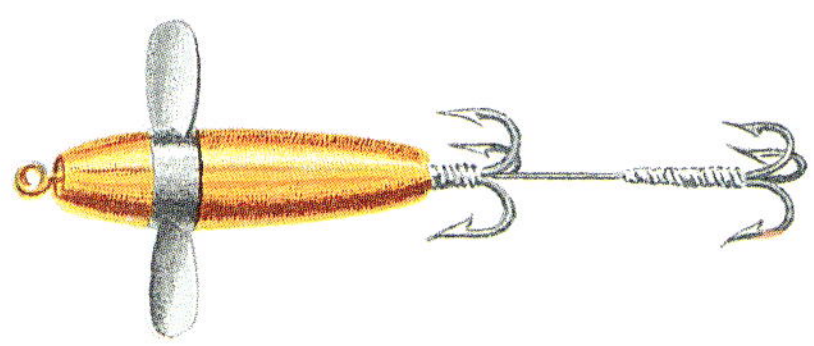

3

To face page 87.

Three sizes and two colours of minnow are sufficient for trout-fishing in any ordinary rivers or lakes in Britain or this country. The sizes are, from tip of nose to tip of tail, $1\frac{3}{4}$ in., 2 in., $2\frac{1}{4}$ in. A small extra minnow for very low clear water is shown in the illustration. The largest size is as big as a salmon fly, and therefore is likely to be easily seen by the trout.

The illustrations shown facing this page are of the smallest size of these minnows, of different colours and kinds.

No. 1 has a silver belly, silver metal fins, and a yellowish-brown back; it is a good minnow, with great hooking-power. For use when the river or lake is full and discoloured or well tinted; when clear and pretty full, in dark, blowy, rough weather; during heavy rain; in the dark or semi-dark of early morning or evening; and in very rough, rapid water.

No. 2 is the same, with a coat of spirit varnish over it, making the metal fins and belly of a duller colour. This can be easily done by the angler, and the varnish is quite dry in an hour, so that only one colour of minnow need be bought. For use when the river or lake is clear, the weather fine, and the light stronger. Minnow No. 1 will also do for minnow No. 2 when the silver is worn off the belly, if the metal fins are coated with spirit varnish.

They are made of soleskin, silk, and other materials, by Hardy Brothers and Bartlett. The first material is perhaps the most useful. The patent M.C. minnow is admirable for fine fishing. If the trebles require renewing, Hardy's double-eyed trebles, which require no silk tying, have many advantages. These trebles can be had of the required sizes. Trebles should always be put on with double gut. A stock of gut which will go double through the eyes of these trebles should be kept. It is of no use to twist the gut, and care should be taken that the two strands are parallel. To put these trebles on, pass the two lengths of gut either singly or together through the eye at the top end of the shank, then once or twice round the shank, then through the second eye; this done, tie a knot on the double gut, which will prevent it slipping back through the eye. Cut off the superfluous end within about $\frac{1}{8}$ in. of the knot. If the gut is rather thin, pass the end through twice to make the knot large enough.

No. 3 is a Devon, 1 in. long, with two tail trebles of best temper, and needle-sharp points. It is transparent, of a yellow-amber colour, with silvered metal fins, which can be varnished if too bright. It spins perfectly. Hardy's, with brass swivel *inside*, suits the purpose well. From the position of the trebles they are not so apt to catch in any weed there may be in the river as those of Nos. 1 and 2. When the river is low, clear, and weedy this is a very suitable and deadly bait; and into shallow water, and places where large trout often lie, this and the smallest size of Nos. 1 and 2 may be thrown with the short or fly rod almost as lightly as a fly.

When the water is discoloured or the weather is dark and stormy it requires a bright minnow, perhaps one of the larger ones, to be readily seen. If the water is clear and the weather fine and the light stronger, a dull-coloured minnow of small size will likely be best. In selecting a minnow the smallest that will serve the purpose of being readily seen at the time should generally be used, for the following reasons: The artificial nature of the bait is less likely to be detected; a small minnow is more readily taken into the fish's mouth, consequently the chances of securing the smaller trout as well as the larger are much increased; the artificial minnow has not the properties of taste or smell—a trout on seizing the minnow will at once discover the artificial fraud, and, unless the hooks catch immediately, will throw it out of its mouth. The importance of using a minnow which can be easily taken into the mouth at the first rush will be evident; also of striking at once, as the trout shuts its mouth on seizing the minnow, and that is the best chance of hooking it.

On feeling the fish, strike instantly, smartly, firmly, but not violently, without altering the direction in which the rod is moving, so as to drive in the hooks. Many fish are lost after playing them for a time because the hooks were only resting, and not driven in.

In rough water a fish often hooks itself, but in comparatively smooth water more udgment is required on the part of the angler. When a fish is seen to rush at the bait do not alter the rate at which the bait is moving, but act just as if you did not see it. Strike when the fish is felt or when it is seen to urn back; it may then have the minnow, or it may not.

After having missed a trout it is often worth while to make half a dozen careful casts, to see if it will come again, which it may do unless it has seen you. It is seldom worth while casting in any place long unless trout come after the minnow, because if they mean to try for it they generally do so at the first few casts.

The nature of the water to be fished also affects the size of minnow it is desirable to use. Thus, in strong-running rough water the largest might be advisable, while on arriving at the slower-running smooth water the smallest might be the only one of any use. Changes in the state of the river, time, and weather also make a temporary change judicious. I have killed as large trout with the smallest minnows as with the larger ones under certain conditions.

The fisher should familiarise himself with the position of the metal fins of the minnow when undamaged, so as to be able to restore them to their proper shape if bent. The metal fins can generally be bent into proper position by pressure with finger and thumb. On these metal fins being in proper position chiefly depends the quick spinning of the minnow, which is of the greatest importance in disguising the tackle. The better a minnow spins the more slowly may it be drawn through the water, a slow rate being a great advantage sometimes. The minnows want constant examination while in use, particularly the gut and trebles of the smaller sizes. A fresh minnow should be put on as soon as any sign of weakness appears. See that the minnow is not caught upside down on the gut, and that the hooks are free.

Let us assume that it is still almost dark in the morning, and that the rod and tackle were made ready over-night, the minnow is known to spin properly, and the whole have been left in a safe place by the river-side all night. The fisher is standing at the foot of the rapid, as shown in Fig. 7, page 45. As soon as he can see at all, he pulls out line to about once and a quarter to once and a half the length of the rod, and, holding the line a little above the minnow with the left hand, he then swings the rod back over the right shoulder, and, simultaneously letting go the line, makes the first cast straight up the side of the stream he is on—this at such a distance from the edge that the water is deep enough to cover a trout. Then pulling the minnow slowly towards him until it is within a yard or two of his feet, he repeats the cast a little further out, and so works across the stream. As the casts reach more nearly straight across from where he is standing, the minnow may be allowed to swing round with the stream and down stream, giving perhaps a slight jerking motion to the rod, until the full length of the line is down stream and close to the edge. Then, with the point lowered to within a yard or so of the water, to counteract the tendency of the minnow to come to the surface, he should pull slowly against the stream, continuing the jerking motion, to where he is standing.

In every case where there is a chance of a fish he should avoid lifting the minnow for a fresh cast before it is close to the edge. Trout often follow the minnow right across the river, and withhold their attack until it is close to the edge in shallow water. This is particularly the case in the imperfect light of the early morning and late evening, when they come at the minnow more boldly than in a stronger light—so boldly sometimes and so close to the fisher that he might think my cautions about keeping out of sight were overdone. It must be remembered, however, that the trout's attention in the rush of pursuit is concentrated on the minnow. Trout frequently have a difficulty in getting back from the shallow water into which they get in this way.

Never allow the minnow to furrow the surface, and take care that the line does not do this either within some yards of the minnow.

If the rapid has now been fished up to the head, turn your attention to the foot of the pool above.

In the strong-running rather smooth water just before it breaks into the rough rapid trout are generally lying, often large ones. Fish this up and across in the same way as the rapid, and if you have a good ripple from a breeze to help you may secure some of them. As soon as you get to the almost stationary deep water of the pool walk smartly on to the next rapid.

Trout are not often caught in deep, still, clear water with minnow, unless there is a gale and big ripple; and if you see them chasing minnows near the surface, particularly in a bad light, then you have a chance of success. It is best to keep the minnow moderately sunk when the water is deep enough—if out of sight, so much the better. Trout are less apt to miss it than when worked near the surface, where the light is stronger. When the minnow is well sunk the attack is generally felt before being seen, and the fisher is not so likely to alter the spinning and so scare the fish, or strike too soon and miss it. If you see a trout rise do not cast right over it, but a few yards from and beyond, and bring the minnow past it, as in this way the line is less likely to scare it.

The time when trout perhaps take the minnow most freely in clear water is when the river is low and rain is raising it. The harder the wind blows the better, particularly if with driving showers—a regular squally wet day, with the wind from north-west to south-west — south-west perhaps best. If the wind gets round to the east success becomes doubtful, and the north-east wind is almost always bad. This wind seems to have a deadening effect on the fish.

Care should be taken that neither the shadow of the fisher nor of his rod falls on the water to be fished either by daylight or moonlight. This applies also to discoloured water.

ARTIFICIAL-MINNOW FISHING IN DISCOLOURED WATER.

When the water begins to discolour from rain the humour of the trout will vary with the winds just mentioned, and the formation of the land through which the river runs will affect the condition of the water. If the formation is gravel, or limestone, or suchlike, the fish will probably take freely until the water is a good deal discoloured; and will do so again as soon as the sediment has settled enough, changing from yellow to brown, the water becoming the colour of strong tea without milk. When of this colour (the minnow water proper) the river will still be pretty full, but it rarely remains at its best for many hours, so it is advisable to catch the first of it if possible.

If there has been a long continuance of flood, the trout, owing to being overfed, sometimes do not take freely when the water is falling. At this time they may be caught with minnow in quite different places from those where they are caught when the water is clear. The pools will now have a good deal of current, and may be fished with success. Fishing on the section plan for fishing down stream (see Fig. 8, page 46) is still advisable, as disturbing less the unfished water in landing fish.

In fishing where, in the low state of the river, the water was still and shallow, but has become a-foot or two deep under the bank, a landing-net is indispensable. In this condition of water much of the fishing can be done without wading. A good deal of the water fishable when the river was low will now perhaps be running too strong, and the trout may have shifted to quieter water.

Owing to the strong current small fish congregate near the bank, where the current is generally less. This attracts the trout to the sides of the river, and even if lying further out they are, owing to the discoloured water, bolder in following the minnow to the edge. It is therefore more than ever advisable to bring the minnow close to the edge before lifting for a fresh cast.

In clay, or what is known as papa formation, a flooded state of the river is very unsatisfactory. The water soon gets thick, and has a lot of clay in solution, and rarely ever becomes of the desirable porter or strong-tea colour. Make the most of the time while the river is rising, and before it gets too thick, as after this little can be done until it is nearly clear again, which may not be for a week or two, or even more. Before the river has risen much, this thick water, if the result of very heavy rain washing down papa cliffs, may be in patches, and by looking you may find stretches of water still clear enough for fishing. Rivers in this sort of country vary a good deal, and local observation is the best guide. The main river may be unfishable below the junction with a clay-country tributary, and quite fishable above it, and so on.

When rivers are too high and muddy to fish in the ordinary way, if you have time watch for trout rising at minnows, flies, &c. This will be mostly in shallows and under the banks. If you cast there you will very likely get them.

CHAPTER X.

NATURAL-MINNOW AND FISH-TAIL FISHING.

EXCEPT in the smaller streams, the 14 ft. rod is the most suitable for natural minnow, because the force required to cast a long line with a short rod would be apt to tear the bait. The 10 ft. 8 in. single-handed part of this rod is suitable for streams, say, not more than about 30 ft. wide. The top should be stiffish. (For rods, reels, lines, gut, see Chapter II.)

A casting-line of stout Lake gut, and a trace a shade lighter, with three good-sized swivels, should be joined together, making about 1 ft. shorter than the short rod, and will then also do for the 14 ft. rod. The swivels serve partly as leads, the lowest being about 15 in. to 18 in. from the hooks. Above the lowest swivel place any split shot (No. 1), if required. In fishing up stream very little, if any, may be required.

Fishing up stream with natural minnow in clear water, particularly in the smaller streams, is very effective ; but, on the whole, fishing up stream with natural minnow is not so suited to large rivers, owing to the slower mode of casting required than with the artificial one. In large rivers, fishing down in sections (see Fig. 8, page 46) will generally be found most convenient and remunerative.

When properly used the natural minnow is a much more deadly bait than the artificial minnow, particularly in the slower water and rivers. A little practice is required in putting the bait on the hooks, and care is also necessary in casting.

The illustrations show the medium size of the tackles and baits, and the simplest and best forms of minnow and fish-tail tackles, with which I am acquainted—the latter for use when small enough fish to use whole cannot be got. These are simple to bait, spin well, and from the large size of the main hook — No. 13 Pennell-eyed Limerick—take a good hold, and are therefore suited to large trout. The lip-hook or treble is small; No. 13 Hardy's double-eyed treble, as a large lip-hook, interferes with the spinning, and shows too much. The side hook of the medium-sized fish-tail tackle is No. 13 Hardy's double-eyed treble.

To attach the side treble to the tackle proceed as follows: Have double gut on the treble in the form of a loop. Pass the loop round the gut between the large hook and the lip-hook; then pass the treble through the loop and pull close. For the medium-sized tackle shown, the gut loop on the treble, including the treble, should be about 1 in. long. Hardy's double-eyed trebles are much the best for this, as by taking only one turn of the gut round the shank of the treble, and not putting the knot on, that keeps the gut from slipping back through the eyes until the last, the length of loop can be adjusted by working the gut through the eyes of the treble. If the gut on the treble is rather too fine, make the knot that prevents the gut slipping back through the eyes by turning the ends through twice, so as to make the knot sufficiently large.

By using hooks in proportion these tackles can be used for a very small or large bait. Fig. 14 gives illustrations of the tackles: No. 1 is a minnow tackle, and No. 2 a fish-tail tackle.

Fig. 14.

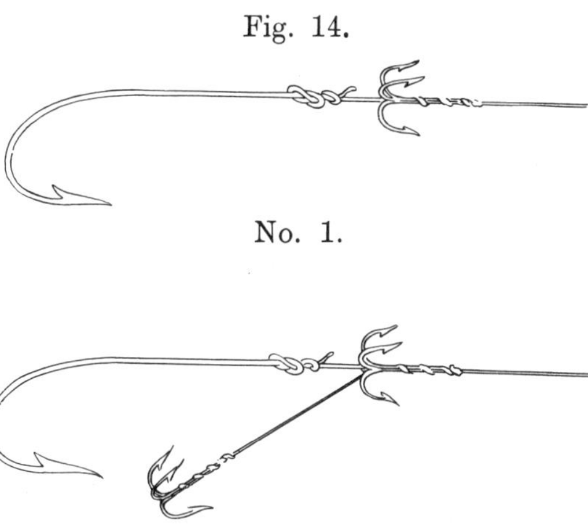

No. 1.

No. 2.

For smaller tackles one of Pennell's small-eyed Limerick hooks, or the ordinary double-eyed lip-hook, may be used for a lip-hook. The combination of large Pennell-eyed Limerick hooks and Hardy's double-eyed trebles is a most suitable one for our large trout.

Fig. 15 gives illustrations of the tackles baited:
No. 1 with small fish (about 2 in.), and No. 2 with
fish cut in half to about that length.

Fig. 15.

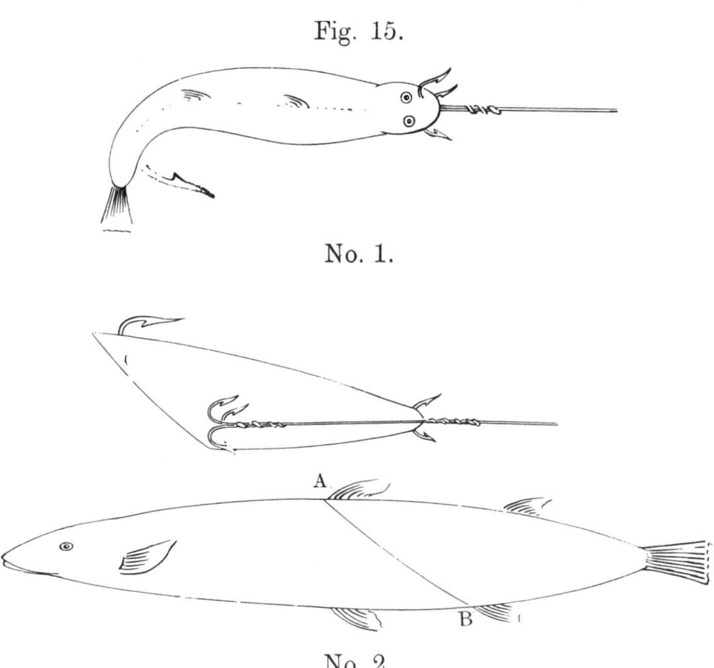

No. 1.

No. 2.

To bait No. 1 tackle, enter the large hook at
the mouth, and run the fish along over the bend
and shank, taking care not to rupture the skin or
belly. When about $\frac{1}{4}$ in. from the tail, more or
less in proportion to the size of the bait and
tackle, bring the barb through clear. The eye
of the hook should now be well inside the mouth,
which should be clear for the lip-hook. Now, if
the length of the tackle is proportioned to the
bait, the lip-hook is in position to be readily
passed through the upper and lower lips, taking
enough not to tear away easily. The mouth

being thus closed greatly helps the spinning. Should the gut between the hooks be a little too long it can be shortened by a turn round the upper hook before passing it through the lips. Care should be taken to properly adjust the bait and regulate the curve. Without attention to this it will not spin well, and will be unattractive. The bend of the large hook gives the curve in the bait just where it is wanted, the shank gives support, and the weight of the large hook is advantageous.

If the bait is allowed to get too straight it will not spin well, nor will it do so if too curved, besides which it will have a most unnatural look. The quicker it spins the greater the chance of trout taking it. Quick spinning is of first importance, and disguises the tackle.

No. 1 tackle is suited to all kinds of small fish of the right size, which for ordinary fishing may be from $1\frac{3}{4}$ in. to $2\frac{1}{2}$ in. In small streams and low clear water the smaller is often best if on a proportionate tackle. Inanga, bullies, the numerous small fish of the estuaries and harbours are suitable ; the bright ones are best.

It often happens that the fish available are too large, when No. 2, the Parr tail tackle of Tweedside (trebles being substituted for plain lip and side hooks), can be used by cutting fish of from 4 in. to 5 in., as shown in Fig. 15, page 100.

Divide the fish with a small sharp pocket-knife, in the direction A to B. Cut off all the fins and tail closely and neatly on the part to be used, rounding off the tail and not breaking the adjoining skin. A pair of small scissors may be found convenient to cut off the fins instead of the knife.

To bait No. 2 tackle, enter the large hook near the tail, and, taking care not to break the skin, bring it out about $\frac{1}{4}$ in. from the other end; then pass the treble or small hook through the tail from top to bottom, not across, letting the side treble hang by the side with one of the hooks stuck into the bait. (See Fig. 15, page 100.)

No. 1 tackle will do for this bait on a pinch, and No. 2 can be used for whole bait. If No. 2 is used for whole bait the side treble is intended to be stuck into the outside curve of the bait. No. 2 is suitable for lake fishing from a boat with whole bait up to 4 in., using hooks in proportion.

This cut bait will last longer than most minnows, as, the end foremost being the tail, it is protected by the skin from the rush of water, and the thick end behind makes it spin well. As with the minnow, the great thing is quick spinning. Reverse the bait with the idea of that being a more natural position, and it will be worn out of shape directly, and will cease to spin. Used in strong-running clear water the fish-tail is much more effective, particularly among large trout, than at first seems likely. It can on occasion be used in the same places and under the same conditions as the minnow proper. A thin bit of board just large enough to cut the fish-tail on, carried in the bag or basket, will be found convenient.

Casting with the natural minnow or fish-tail requires more care than with the artificial minnow, as if the cast ends with a jerk the bait is sure to be broken. On this account a long line is particularly undesirable if it can be avoided. Sometimes the bait may be heaved or pitched forward, sometimes merely dropped from the end of the rod. With a 14 ft. rod it is quite likely that a line about a yard longer than the rod will, in discoloured water, be sufficient for most of the work.

In working the lure, generally keep the rod-point low, to within a yard or so of the water, giving a very slight jerky movement in pulling it towards you, and finishing close to the edge, where often a fish will seize it.

Striking with the natural minnow and this tackle is entirely different from striking with the artificial. With the latter it is hardly possible, on feeling the fish, to strike too quickly. With the natural minnow, on feeling the fish, slacken line for a second or two by allowing the rod-point to go smartly towards the trout for about a yard. Then strike smartly in the direction the rod was moving in. In clear strong-running water the fish will very likely hook itself at the first rush, but in flood-water, when you are fishing the quieter-running water and pools, this moment of slack line and delay gives the fish a chance to get a better hold of the bait and hooks before striking. The difference in the mode of striking is due to the fish's natural desire to eject the fraud and to swallow the real fish. In striking with the fish-tail the procedure is the same.

In discoloured water it is better to work the bait at such a depth that it is not seen by the fisher.

The most favourable weather for clear water is a gale of wind from the north-west to south-west —if with a rising river, dark and raining, so much the better. The most favourable time is generally in the early morning, and after 4 o'clock in the afternoon until dark.

Care should be taken that neither the shadow of the fisher nor of his rod falls on the water to be fished, by daylight or moonlight. This applies also to discoloured water.

In flood-water the most favourable time is when the river is rising and getting discoloured, until it gets too thick. The fisher should try and begin soon enough at any time of day. When the river is falling, and the water changing from yellow to brown, is perhaps the minnow water proper. The fisher should try to catch the very first of this condition, so as not to lose the chance when the trout begin to take, at whatever time of day this may be, as the best of it seldom lasts many hours. In these circumstances most of the fish will be got in water which is almost without current when the

river is clear, where the water is a foot or two
deep, towards the edge of deep pools and under
banks.

When the water is rising and getting discoloured the large trout are often cruising near
the edge; when the water is falling, and of the
right colour, large trout are often close to the
edge seeking the small fry sheltering there from
the stronger current farther out.

The water at the edge where trout have to be
landed is often a foot or two deep, with perhaps a
steep bank, and a landing-net is required. As the
water clears sport will have to be looked for in
the quicker-running water.

One of the drawbacks to natural-minnow fishing is the difficulty experienced by those not
living near a river or brook in catching and pre-
paring a quantity of live minnows for use. When
the water is thick and in flood small fry can
generally be captured by using a net made of
open-mesh scrim, such as is used for wall-paper-
ing. The frame, in shape, size, and handle,
should be the same as for landing (see Chapter II.,
page 30), only the steel frame for this work requires to be rigid and stronger, and the handle
may be 6 ft. in length. Any woman can sew this
scrim into the shape of a landing-net, stitching it
over the frame. It will cost only a few pence,
and is as good while it lasts as the most expen-
sive small-mesh net, and can at a pinch be used
as a landing-net.

In floods work it in the same direction as the current runs, under banks and places where small fry are likely to shelter from the current, generally bringing it lightly along the bottom. If the water is clear it is as well to stir up the mud, when the small fish are more easily caught. Larger nets of the same material can be made for this purpose. Inanga can be caught with small artificial flies or worms, and cut to the required size.

For those who have command of a small stream of clean water the best plan is to have a reservoir made of zinc, with a lid, half of which should be fixed, and the other half to open from a hinge across the middle; the half that opens should be made to fasten securely. The whole lid and about a third down the side from the top should be thickly perforated to allow the water to run through freely when sunk by weights to the bottom of the stream. There should be a strongly fixed arch handle across the top for convenience. This reservoir is better than a wire cage, which when taken out of the water leaves the minnows without water. A reservoir of from 2 to 4 gallons capacity will be useful, but, of course, it can be made any size to suit requirements. A common pint tin pannikin, with the bottom perforated, is a convenient thing for dipping up the minnows when wanted.

A smaller reservoir of the same pattern, holding from half a gallon to a gallon, is a convenient means of taking the minnows from where they are caught to the store reservoir. The perforations are required to admit air, and to facilitate changing the water.

If an attendant is available, this is a convenient way of carrying the minnows while fishing. If they must be carried dead, a clear bottle, large enough to hold sufficient for the day, filled with water to which formalin and glycerine have been added, will enable them to be kept quite fresh for the day. About a teaspoonful of Scherning's formalin, to be obtained at chemists', added to a quart bottle of water, will keep baits quite fresh for that time. In a solution in the proportion of a teaspoonful or two teaspoonfuls of formalin to a quart of water, with a teaspoonful of glycerine added to prevent hardening, they will keep for a year or for an indefinite period. Care must be taken that they are fresh when put in the solution, that they remain covered, and that the bottles are properly corked. The bottleful of formalin solution should not be more than one-third filled with fish if intended to be kept for any time, and the bottle should be moved now and then after the fish are put in, so as to allow the solution to reach them freely. Formalin has not the bad effects on tackle that salt or spirits of wine has.

The general way of preserving minnows for fishing is by dry-salting them. If this is done, slightly larger minnows should be salted than are required when used fresh, as they shrivel up; but at best the salted ones are dull-coloured and easily torn.

There is much in the previous chapter under the head of " Artificial - minnow Fishing " applicable to " Fishing with the Natural Minnow and Fish-tail."

CHAPTER XI.

WORM, GRUB, CREEPER, CICADA, GRASS-HOPPER FISHING.

———

THESE baits are given under one head because the rod to use, mode of casting, manner of working the lure, part of rivers to fish, and conditions of weather and water suitable are much alike for all.

Care should be taken that neither the shadow of the fisher nor of his rod falls on the water to be fished, by daylight or moonlight.

Worms will be dealt with under the head of " Fishing with Worm."

When it is intended to fish with grub, creeper, cicada, or grasshopper, a sufficient quantity should, if possible, be collected the evening before, as even if the fisher has an attendant at the water-side much time may be lost procuring these while trout are on the feed. A small butterfly-net may be found handy for securing cicada and grasshoppers. The use of these baits does not generally begin until the trout are getting tired of the natural water-flies and have given up rising freely at the artificial fly, or until the weather and water have lost the cold of the early part of the season. The trout are then strong, and are spread over all parts of the river and the strongest running water.

The most suitable rod for fairly full-sized rivers and streams is the light 14 ft. rod recommended for artificial-fly fishing in lakes and unusually broad rivers too deep to be waded. (For rods, reels, lines, gut, see Chapter II.) This length is desirable, because with a long line any of these baits is apt to be torn, and the use of the long rod with a comparatively short line allows the bait to be thrown a sufficient distance lightly and ac-curately, without using force, and still enables the fisher to keep well out of sight. For small streams the shorter part of this rod can be used, or one of about that length, at the discretion of the fisher.

The 9 ft. of gut, with stout Lake for the upper half, generally recommended for both rods (see Chapter VIII., page 65), is also suitable here, as it presents little surface to the water, and is not carried down so quickly as a thicker line, and is necessary in clear water. With the 14 ft. rod, when fishing in clear water, about 13 ft. of gut may be used with advantage. In attaching the strand of gut (on which is the tackle for any of these baits) to the casting-line, do so with the slip-knot, and not by loops, which show too much.

Casting should be done lightly, as for artificial fly, and generally over the same places (see Chapter VIII.), but rather more slowly, taking care not to tear the bait by any jerk. It is not often necessary to throw a much longer line than the rod. Cast up stream and across until the bait comes nearly as far down as opposite where you stand. Cast in all likely places, and a couple of yards above where you expect a trout to be.

There should not be more than 4 ft. or 5 ft. of gut in the water when any of these baits are used, as, the fishing being done by casting up stream, more line in the water would bring the bait down stream too fast, and also interfere with striking.

The fisher should endeavour to let the bait move down stream as it would if loose, which is the natural rate, neither hastening nor retarding it, and keeping the rod always a little farther down stream than the bait. He should keep constant watch that the bait is in good order. It generally is best to fish from the shallow side of the river if possible. To use any of these baits properly in clear water requires observation and skill second only to that needed for artificial-fly fishing.

FISHING WITH WORM IN CLEAR WATER.

The first thing that should be done is to lay in a large stock of worms, and, after washing the soil from them, to keep them in a large jar filled with soft wet moss from which the water has been partly squeezed. This jar should be kept in the shade in a cool place. Being in the moss, the worms will be clean and more fit to handle. This will take at least a week. The worms

should be of fairly uniform size—say, 2 in. or
3 in. long. The former are the most suitable for
small streams and trout. The jar should be
examined every two or three days, and any dead
worms picked out and the moss changed or rinsed
in water. Care should be taken that the moss
does not get dry.

A stock of worms can be provided by heavily
manuring a small plot of rather damp ground in
a garden or some shady place. If the soil is
deep and loose they can be brought to the surface by thrusting a strong stick in about 2 ft.,
and then shaking it backwards and forwards
forcibly.

To carry the worms while fishing, a small
flannel bag, large enough to admit the hand,
and containing wet moss, is the best. This
should be kept damp. It should have a loop
to fasten to the button-hole or button of the
coat, and a draw-string to secure the mouth
when required.

A sufficient number of worms should always
be carried to enable a fresh bait to be put on
as soon as the one in use becomes the least
water-logged or injured, as in this state it is
unattractive to the fish : the more lively the
bait the more attractive it is to the fish.

For a long day's fishing it is better to carry in
the fish bag or basket, or otherwise, a larger bag
than the one just described, filled with wet moss,
in which the main supply of worms can be carried

out of the sun and wind. A hundred or two worms may not be found too many for a day's fishing. Care should be taken if these bags are laid down that the mouths are well tied, or the worms will most likely escape.

My preference is for the tackle commonly known as Stewart's, made up with three No. 12 Dublin Limerick hooks. If unusually large trout are expected, it is best made up with three Pennell-eyed Limerick hooks, equal in size to No. 11 Dublin Limerick.

Fig. 16, below, shows the manner of baiting, in which it is perhaps best to have the head nearest the lower hook and the tail to the upper.

Fig. 16.

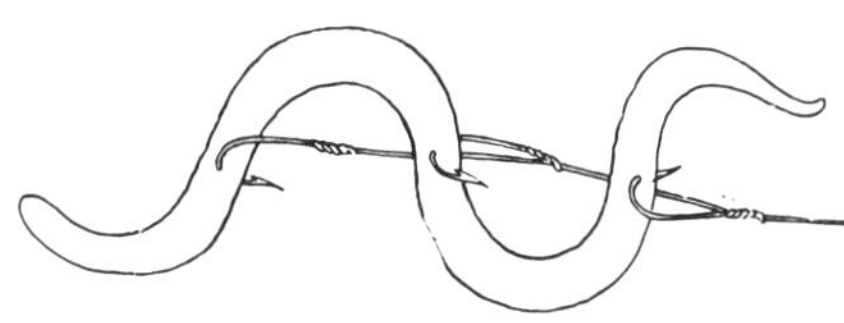

Those who prefer the single-hook tackle will find a No. 6 Dublin Limerick hook, or the same size of a Pennell-eyed Limerick hook, answer well. When using the single hook enter it a little from the head of the worm and run the worm over it until the shank is quite covered, taking care not to bring the point through, and leaving a little of the tail to play about. If the worm is rather large for the hook, bring out the point when partly along, and, missing a little, re-enter the point, bringing the parts where the hook was brought out and re-entered together.

The weather and condition of water which often afford good sport to the worm fisher are a bright sunny day and clear low water.

Cast up stream and across.

Fish with worm whenever trout may be expected to be, but it is not of much use fishing still pools or smooth water unless there is a sufficient breeze to raise a ripple.

Allow the worm to sink as deep as you can without using lead to help. Fishing in this way, in shallow swift-running water particularly, you will find trout occasionally rise at the worm as they would at a fly. In warm weather trout may begin to take the worm as soon as it is light enough to see; in cold weather they will probably not take it until the warmer part of the day.

The stopping of the line is generally the first notice of the bait having been taken. With the three-hook tackle lower the end of the rod down stream gently until the line is straight, then strike down stream. With the single-hook tackle give a little more time before striking. When the line begins to move away steadily is a favourable time to strike.

FISHING WITH WORM IN DISCOLOURED WATER.

If the line is weighted with shot the most suitable rod will be the 14 ft. minnow rod or the short part of it. (See page 85.)

When the river first begins to rise and is discoloured trout will be found in much the same places as when it is low and clear. As the flood rises and the water becomes thicker they will seek the shelter of quiet water under banks, and the shallow side of pools, and such places. It sometimes now answers to fish down stream for a time, as, the water being thick, the trout cannot see the fisher so easily.

If the water runs pretty fast it is often advisable to put on one or two No. 1 split shot. These should be placed not less than 15 in. from the hooks.

If the place fished is the shallow side of a pool it is well to begin at the top, by casting straight out and following the line to the foot, then walk back and begin again. If the pool is long, and the trout fairly plentiful and large, it will be advantageous to fish down in sections. (See Fig. 8, page 46.)

When the water clears sufficiently to enable the trout to see the fisher, fishing up stream should be resumed.

FISHING WITH THE PINE-GRUB.

In decayed pine-trees there is a large grub which is taken greedily by trout. These grubs can be found in the decayed wood by chopping with an axe. They are used with the same tackle, in the same manner and conditions of water and weather, as worm. To carry them at the water-side a worm-bag or tin box is handy.

FISHING WITH THE CREEPER IN CLEAR WATER.

This black and ugly-looking creature is harmless, although it has such an unpleasant appearance. It can be found under good-sized stones near the river's edge and in the shallow water in the early summer. The flask mentioned in Chapter II., page 34, is suitable for carrying them in.

The tackle consists of two hooks of the same size—No. 12 to No. 8, Dublin Limerick—on one piece of gut, so that the point of one may be about $\frac{1}{2}$ in. from the point of the other. For small streams and trout it can be baited with one creeper; for large rivers and trout with two or three.

To bait with one creeper, put the lower hook through the creeper across, a little above the tail, and then the upper hook through at the shoulder. To bait with two creepers, enter the lower hook about the middle, run it along the body and bring it out at the tail; then run the creeper up the shank of the lower hook and put the upper hook through the shoulders; now take the second creeper, and entering the lower hook a little above the middle bring it out a little below.

For large trout a Pennell-eyed Limerick hook of the same size makes a good lower and one of Hardy's small double-eyed trebles a good upper hook.

This bait is of little use in still water, but should be used in swift-running places.

Cast up stream and across into any little eddies in shallow fast-running water, and at the sides of strong-running water.

Strike down stream directly the line stops, or on feeling the trout.

In warm weather trout will take the creeper freely at dawn; but in cold weather it may be later in the day, when the sun is out, before they take it freely.

FISHING WITH CICADA AND GRASSHOPPER.

This mode of fishing lasts from midsummer to autumn, and may be pursued successfully in the rapids, and in pools of rivers if there is sufficient breeze and ripple on the pools.

A suitable flask to carry these baits is described in Chapter II., page 34.

The tackle is the same as for fishing with creeper, and is baited in the same way. It consists of two hooks of the same size—No. 12 to No. 8, Dublin Limerick—on one piece of gut, so that the point of one may be about $\frac{1}{2}$ in. from the point of the other. For small streams and trout it can be baited with one cicada or grasshopper; for large rivers and trout with two or three.

To bait with one cicada or grasshopper, put the lower hook through crosswise, a little above the tail, and then the upper hook through about the shoulder. To bait with two cicada or grasshoppers, enter the lower hook about the middle, run it along the body and bring it out at the tail; then run the bait up the shank of the lower hook and put the upper hook through the shoulders; now take the second bait, and entering the lower hook a little above the middle bring it out a little below. If the hooks are not well covered put on another bait.

For large trout a Pennell-eyed Limerick hook of the same size makes a good lower and one of Hardy's small double-eyed trebles a good upper hook.

As the trout are, at the time these baits are available, in strong condition and scattered all over the river, they may be fished for in all parts, particularly near the edges, when the river is a little up and discoloured.

In warm weather the fisher cannot begin too early in the morning. In the early morning he is likely to find large trout, even when the river is low and clear, feeding close to the bank and in shallow water.

Cast up stream and across.

The cicada or grasshoppers may float on the surface, when the trout will make a distinct rise if the water is not too thick for the fish to see them; but they are not so apt to miss them if a little under water, when they are taken in a very determined way.

Strike down stream the instant you see a rise, or when the line stops.

This is much like the May-fly fishing of the Tweed, in the Old Country. There are many other insects, such as blow-flies, beetles, &c., which may be used successfully in the manner here described.

CHAPTER XII.

LAKE FISHING.

IN the lakes large trout are to be caught, and in some the fish are in great numbers; but, owing to the extreme clearness of the water of most of the lakes, the trout are not easily taken. Natural and artificial minnow and live bait have been used successfully both in fishing from the bank and from boats.

Although these lakes give rather uncertain sport, they are the chief stores of trout for the rivers, and for this reason should be protected.

A good way to learn the habits of the lake trout is to camp close to the edge of the lake, and to commence by fishing the rivers by daylight, watching in quiet weather the movements of the lake trout in the early morning and late evening.

The first thing that should be ascertained, if possible, is where their feeding-places are. These will commonly be in from 4 ft. to 10 ft. of water, where the shallow merges into the deep water; near the mouths of rivers and streams running into the lake, and also where the streams run out of the lake; where large boulders afford shelter; and under trees from which insects drop into the water.

As in rivers, when the fisb are feeding well they may be caught sometimes in much deeper water than that mentioned.

In the lakes trout are affected by the weather and direction of the wind just as they are in the rivers, and the time of day or night most suitable for river fishing is suitable for lake fishing. It is, however. desirable for daylight fishing that there should be a good breeze to ripple the water. On the whole, with clear water and mild weather, it will be found that the time of earliest dawn, and from just before sunset until after dark, are worth the whole of the rest of the day. In a rough south-wester, however, good sport may sometimes be got in the daytime, particularly with minnow.

In river fishing, in the smooth pools with no perceptible current. more skill is required than where there is a swift rippling current, and more depends on a breeze; and the same applies with regard to lake fishing. (See " Artificial-fly Fishing," Chapter VIII., pages 66 to 76; " Artificial-minnow Fishing," Chapter IX., page 85; " Natural-minnow and Fish-tail Fishing," Chapter X., page 97.

In windy weather, streaks of yeasty froth sometimes form towards the shore, in which drifted insects collect, and trout are attracted to take up their position under or near them. The fisher should therefore cast over and near these streaks.

Where the lake is discoloured by flooded streams running into it trout usually congregate, attracted by the food brought down by the streams, and these are favourable spots to fish.

A boat or Maori canoe may be required to reach the places where the water is of the desired tinge during the various stages of the flood. Neither the boat, canoe, nor anything about it should be of light or conspicuous colour.

When fishing from a boat or Maori canoe, if a good fish is hooked not too far from the shore, it may be prudent to get on shore and land the fish there if there is a good landing-place. There is less risk in this course than in trying to get a large trout into a boat or canoe.

If there are moths about on the water in the evening the trout may be rising at them, and can be caught with artificial fly by casting over the rises if the water is smooth, but it is better when there is just enough ripple to hide the fall of the line on the water.

If the trout are seen to be chasing small fish they can be got with minnow, but more ripple is required to hide the fall of the minnow tackle on the water than with fly. Some of the trout will very likely be feeding close to the bank.

The very large brown trout seldom rise freely at artificial fly anywhere, and are chiefly taken with spinning bait. The natural spinning or the live bait gives much better results than the artificial minnow.

Some lakes can be waded in places in the same way as rivers.

When fishing from the bank of a lake it is requisite to throw a longer line than is generally needed in ordinary river or stream fishing, so as to reach the trout some distance out; and when fishing from a boat it should be kept out of sight of the fish. Unlike fishing in a river, where the fish in the current lie head up stream, and so can be approached up stream unseen by means of a comparatively short line, in a lake the fish are heading and roving in all directions, thus making it more difficult for the fisher to keep out of their sight. It is also necessary to avoid letting the shadow of the fisher, tackle, or boat fall on the water that is being fished or is intended to be fished, both in daylight and moonlight. Sometimes the shadows extend a long way, as in the early morning and late evening.

ARTIFICIAL-FLY FISHING.

For artificial-fly fishing from the bank or from a boat the light two-handed 14 ft. rod, reel, and longest reel line mentioned in Chapter II., pages 12 and 25, will be found suitable. For night fishing a shorter rod can be used, at the discretion of the fisher.

The general directions for artificial-fly fishing and flies in Chapter VIII. are applicable here, but a very slight jerking motion may be given to the flies. Tinsel is seldom of advantage on flies intended for brown trout; occasionally, in stormy weather or after dark, it may attract attention. Under such conditions a grilse fly, say on a No. 4 Limerick hook, and fished like a salmon fly, is sometimes successful.

In fishing from a boat with artificial fly the boat is generally allowed to drift slowly, with an occasional quiet dip of the oars, and the casting is done to leeward. If it drifts too quickly in a strong breeze, a drag made of a large stone fastened in a sack or otherwise to a rope can sometimes be used.

NATURAL-FLY FISHING.

Cicada and grasshoppers can be used (see Chapter XI., page 117), and the fishing done from the bank or from a boat or canoe, as with artificial fly.

MINNOW FISHING.

For artificial- or natural-minnow or fish-tail fishing from the bank or from a boat the two-handed 14 ft. minnow rod, reel, and longest and strongest reel-line mentioned in Chapter II. will be found suitable.

For fishing in the dark a shorter rod can be used, at the discretion of the fisher. The general directions for artificial- and natural-minnow and fish-tail fishing in Chapters IX. and X. are applicable here.

In working the minnow when fishing from the bank or a drifting boat a very slight jerking motion is judicious.

TROLLING FROM A ROWED BOAT OR PADDLED MAORI CANOE.

The two-handed 14 ft. minnow rod, reel, and longest and strongest reel line mentioned in Chapter II. are suitable for this sort of fishing. Supple rods are unsuitable, owing to the weight of the long line used.

In trolling for large trout, particularly at night, the minnow, artificial or natural, should be on very strong gut. A casting-line and traces of salmon-gut should be used, or a casting-line of twisted triple gut is perhaps preferable. It is disappointing to lose the largest fish through the insufficiency of the tackle, and this frequently happens.

Trolling from a rowed boat can be done by fixing one or two rods over the stern, at an angle of about 30 degrees with the water. The rods should be fixed, each between two small wooden pegs, where they lie over the stern, and they should be as far apart as the width of the stern will allow. About 25 yards at least of reel line should be run out, so as to keep the bait away from the disturbance caused by the boat. This length of line can be let out by hand while the boat is moving ahead, and taken in by hand and coiled in the boat, where it will not be trodden on, when the baits require to be examined.

As the rods are not held in the hand, more line than desired might run out while the boat is in motion. This can be prevented by leaving a little slack line near the reel, and putting a sufficiently heavy stone on it, care being taken that the stone is smooth and does not cut the line. The stone is readily displaced on a fish seizing the bait or the hooks getting foul of anything.

A close watch should be kept on the rods. When a fish is known to be at the bait, take up the rod and act as directed under the paragraph referring to striking for artificial-minnow fishing (Chapter IX., page 89), or natural-minnow fishing (Chapter X., page 103). When two rods are being used, immediately a fish is hooked on one line take in the other, to prevent complications with the one on which the fish is. The boatman, if he understands his business, can sometimes give assistance by following a hooked fish.

Generally a good depth for the minnow to be under water is about 2 ft. or 3 ft. This can be regulated by the rate at which the boat is rowed and by the split shot on the trace. (See " Artificial-minnow Fishing," Chapter IX., page 86; " Natural-minnow Fishing," Chapter X., page 97.) The boat should be rowed with as little splash as possible, at a rate that will keep the bait spinning, which will be about a mile and a half per hour. It is not necessary to row against a strong wind, as in this manner of trolling the motion of the boat on the waves works the bait sufficiently.

If a Maori canoe is used, the above directions will also apply. Hardly any splash is made in paddling a canoe, and it has other advantages over a boat; but there are disadvantages, in that there is only room for one rod over the stern, and it is not suited for rough water.

In fishing for large trout with two rods it will be well to bait with the largest size of artificial minnow mentioned in Chapter IX., page 87, on one rod, and with a smaller size on the other. The most suitable size for the time being may thus be arrived at if fish are caught. If the natural minnow is used, the largest size mentioned in Chapter X., page 101, on a fish-tail tackle might be used on one rod, and a rather larger bait, up to 4 in., on a proportionate tackle of the same kind (see Chapter X., page 102) on the other rod. Fish will take a larger bait if it is natural than if it is artificial. In clear water, if there is any light, a moderate-sized bait will be found best.

I have not made mention of trolling from a boat under sail, although it is sometimes convenient, because a sailing-boat is not well under control, and even with practised hands this style of fishing is dangerous on lakes subject to sudden squalls. A small steam-launch when driven at a suitably slow rate is more manageable than a sailing-boat.

WORM AND CRAYFISH FISHING.

For worm or crayfish fishing the two-handed 14 ft. minnow rod, reel, and longest and strongest reel line mentioned in Chapter II. are generally the most suitable.

Trout may sometimes be taken with worm in much the same places as with artificial or natural fly (See Chapter XI., Fig. 16). Where the water is discoloured by flood-water from rivers, good-sized worms on a proportionate tackle are suitable. The line seldom needs shot. Sometimes a boat or canoe may be used with advantage, as in the other kinds of fishing.

The crayfish here referred to are a miniature variety found in considerable quantities in the rivers and lakes, and much fed on by the trout.

CHAPTER XIII.

DIRECTIONS AND EXPLANATIONS

FOR USING THE GUIDE TO THE RIVERS AND LAKES.

THERE being about a thousand rivers, streams, burns, and lakes mentioned in this work, it will at once be obvious that there is a good deal of difficulty in classifying the rivers and streams so as to convey in brief form an idea of their size. This difficulty is increased by the great range in size, from rivers that discharge a swift current of water sixteen times as great as that of the English Thames down to the streamlet. To overcome this as far as possible, the length of the course is given. Of lakes, the length, breadth, and, when known, the height above sea-level is stated. On the whole, the lengths given are a little short of the actual lengths.

In Scotland the terms " river," " water," and " burn " convey a fair idea of the character and dimensions of the piece of water they are intended to describe, but to the general reader these terms would often be as Greek. In this Guide all streams up to ten miles in length are called " burn "; those twenty miles in length, " stream "; and those over twenty miles in length, " river." In a few exceptional cases those of short course but great volume, the outlet of lakes or possibly connecting two lakes, are called " rivers "; the smaller streams, when deep and tidal, are called " creeks."

A map has been prepared, and is published separately from this book, and can be obtained from the Government Printing Office, Wellington; it may also be purchased through local booksellers. On the margin of this map a numbered list of the rivers, streams, burns, creeks, and lakes on each coast separately is given, the number on the list corresponding with the number of the same river, stream, burn, creek, or lake on the map. On the list the rivers are marked R.; streams, Stm.; burns, Bn.; creeks, Cr.; lakes, L.

On the ordinary maps, rivers, streams, burns, and creeks will sometimes be found to have different names at different places. This arises from the Maori custom of giving different names to parts, so as to be able to more readily describe a special locality, but these parts so named have no very definite beginning or termination. In the Guide the general name is used, and in giving the length all the parts are included. The aim has been to simplify the Guide as much as possible.

The main rivers are taken in succession as they occur on the coast, beginning at the north in each Island and taking each coast separately. Tributaries of each river, stream, burn, creek, or lake are given before leaving it, commencing with the one nearest the sea or mouth, and going on to the source of the main river, stream, or burn. Rivers discharging into lakes are taken from the foot of the lake, each side separately.

The descriptions of both the main rivers and tributaries begin from the mouths, and generally the distances to reach them are calculated towards the mouths. The distances given in the Guide by roads and tracks are approximately correct. The words " ice-" or " snow-fed " denote perpetual ice or snow. Where the word " bottom " is used in describing rivers it is intended to mean that the water comes right up to the banks. In this case the landing for fish is generally deep. Where the word " bed " is used in describing rivers it is intended to mean that part of the shingle or other matter forming the river-bed is frequently dry. In this case the landing for fish is generally good.

The term " wadeable " is not intended to mean " fordable." Some idea of the nature of the landing is attempted to be given. " Landing deep " means that the water is there too deep to get the fish aground; and " landing good " indicates where fish can be got aground.

Any present description of the banks and surroundings of streams or lakes may in a couple of years be quite inaccurate. In a new country like this, banks that to-day are covered with scrub, fern, or forest may in a few years be quite clear and sown with English grasses and clovers to the water's edge.

The principal kinds of trout in the rivers and lakes are the brown trout (*Salmo fario*), Loch Leven trout (*Salmo levenensis*), and rainbow trout (*Salmo irideus*). Where there are only rainbow trout much estuary fishing should not be expected, as it is not yet known whether these trout go to sea.

To give a more detailed description of each of the rivers and lakes on the list, or to attempt to deal with the quantity or size of trout likely to be caught in them, would swell this book to too great proportions. Streams or lakes that are now only thinly stocked with trout may in a few years be full of fish, and may then contain other varieties besides those mentioned.

Rivers and lakes are in some cases being stocked, by the brown trout from the rivers travelling round the coast by sea running up the unstocked fresh-water rivers to the lakes; and thus rivers and lakes, in country too rugged and inaccessible to allow of its rivers and lakes being stocked in the ordinary way, now in some instances contain large trout.

It may be explained that some of what are known in this country as brown trout (much of the ova for which was obtained from the English Thames, which contains a large breed of trout) are apparently a variety of bull trout (*Salmo eriox*). These—well known in the Tweed and the North of England—take to the sea naturally when they have the opportunity, and in this country they are frequently caught in nets at sea twenty miles from the nearest fresh-water river In common with the British bull trout, they enter the fresh water during the spring and summer scantily, coming into the rivers in great numbers in the late autumn on their way to spawn, sometimes pushing their way into rivulets hardly deep enough to cover them. The salmon proper generally do not ascend so far. It seems not unlikely that some bull-trout ova has inadvertently been imported perhaps among the salmon ova. These fish are known to enter the Scottish Tweed in millions about and after the close of the salmon-fishing season, and attain to much the same weight as those in our rivers do.

I remember being told, perhaps fifty years ago (long before trout were introduced here), that some of the Thames trout, before the sewage at London polluted the river too much, used to go to sea. The ova from Thames trout was brought here, and it therefore seems natural, when no sewage or other pollution intervenes, that they should resume their old sea-going habits. They are caught in this country with the rod in nearly quite salt water, varying in weight from 1 lb. to 20 lb.; and when recently from the salt water they are as bright as a fresh-run salmon.

It may be taken as a rule that all streams with sufficient water contain some exceptionally large trout, up to 8 lb., 9 lb., 10 lb., 11 lb., and 12 lb. in weight. Sea trout (*Salmo trutta*) have been caught up to 11 lb., and rainbow trout (*Salmo irideus*) up to 12 lb. Trout frequenting the brackish water about the mouths of rivers, and some distance above this, owing to the abundance of feed, grow to exceptional size. Trout weighing up to 34 lb. have been caught in both rivers and lakes.

For some distance up from the mouths of rivers that have their outlet directly into the sea or estuaries the trout are rarely caught with any other bait than minnow, natural or artificial. They hardly rise to the ordinary trout-flies at all, but they can be taken with a grilse fly, fished as for salmon.

As is the case in Britain, the trout in each stream and lake in this country vary more or less in appearance and number of spots.

At or near the mouths of rivers, in fishing for fresh sea-run trout, the minnows, either artificial or natural, mentioned in Chapters IX. and X. will be found suitable. Good sport may sometimes be got with a Halcyon spinner of $1\frac{1}{4}$ in. to $1\frac{1}{2}$ in. The minnow rods, reels, and lines mentioned in Chapter II. are suitable, but specially strong gut and traces should be used, and it is well to use salmon-gut, particularly for fishing in the dark.

The weather affects this sort of fishing much as it does that higher up the rivers, and the tide also affects it as far as the rivers are tidal. Generally the trout begin to feed soon after low water, when the tide begins to make. A desirable time to fish is when the tide makes about daybreak. Near the mouths of rivers good sport may sometimes be got when the tide is running out, as this causes a current to spin the minnow.

The heaviest takes are often made in the dark.

The average weight of trout taken near the mouths of rivers discharging into the sea or estuaries is about 5 lb. The average weight of trout throughout the whole country may be put at about 2 lb., which is about six times the average weight of the trout in Britain.

The glacier and perpetual snow-fed rivers are under quite different influences from those affecting rivers rising in lower country. It is common for the former to be at their lowest during the winter, and to be subject to floods when the warmer weather causes partial melting of the glaciers and snow. It is thus difficult to tell what their condition may be at any particular time. Even when at their lowest some of these rivers have a more or less milky tinge, the result of glacier action. How this ice and snow water affects the trout is not known with certainty, but the best fishing is almost always close to the sea. Although the main stream and upper tributaries of these rivers are glacier and snow fed, it is quite common for the lower and most of the tributaries to be free from glacier and perpetual snow influence, and to be under ordinary conditions.

Many of the larger shingle-bed rivers divide into a number of channels, which alter their position more or less during every flood. Some of these shingle-beds are more than a mile across. The railway and road bridge over the Rakaia River, where it is almost a torrent, is a mile and a quarter long. Good fishing may be obtained in the branch channels of these rivers, particularly when the branches are large and have been established for a year or two.

Generally, trout are on the increase in all the rivers and lakes of New Zealand, which are becoming gradually more accessible to the fisher. Previous to 1868 there was not a trout known to be in the country. The difficulty now is, not to find lakes and rivers containing trout, but to find those that have not trout in them; and this in a country the size of England, Scotland, and Ireland combined, and which is a perfect network of ideal trout and salmon rivers and streams.

The list I have given comprises only some of the best-known streams and lakes, and a great number of others are not mentioned.

Some illustrations are given, reproduced from photos, of good takes of fish in all of the provincial districts, including trout caught in the brackish or salt water. Few of the best takes have been photographed, but a book the size of this could be filled with photos and records of takes as good and even better than those given. Some heavy takes have been made by quite inexperienced anglers. Among the photos of takes this season there is one made by a man seventy-eight years of age. The weight of fish was 80 lb., and included a trout of 20 lb.

I have seldom fished for more than a couple of hours at a time in this country. Living, however, always on the bank of a river, and fishing constantly and at all times, I have in half an hour to a couple of hours frequently taken a weight that would be a great day's take of brown trout in Britain. The lowest average size of the trout I have taken in any season has been over $2\frac{1}{2}$ lb. Fishing for half an hour in the morning and evening, with artificial minnow, my take has sometimes been six or seven trout weighing quite 30 lb., and with artificial fly I have taken them as quickly as they could be hooked and landed. This was at a place situated about eighty miles from the sea. Except when fishing near the mouths of rivers with sea outlet, the average size of the trout of my takes with artificial fly has quite equalled that of those taken with minnow, and has also included as heavy fish. During the last seven years I have taken an average of about 400 lb. of trout with artificial fly. These were all taken on a 10 ft. rod, weighing less than 12 oz., made for me by Hardy Brothers.

The stranger who intends to do some fishing should apply in the first instance to the secretaries or other representatives of the acclimatisation societies for up-to-date information about the fishing in their districts, the size of the streams, &c.; also on the subject of fishing licenses, one of which is available for the whole country, but must at present be indorsed by the secretary or other representative of each separate acclimatisation district visited. There are a considerable number of these societies, and the secretaries or other representatives are to be found in all the principal towns.

The Government Tourist Department has representatives in many of the towns, and can afford much useful information. The chief office is in Wellington. This Department, as well as the representatives of acclimatisation societies can afford information about deer-stalking, winged-game shooting, also about the fishing season.

The Guide will facilitate these inquiries by furnishing the names of the rivers and lakes, and the map shows their locality.

Another reason why the secretaries or other representatives of these societies should be consulted is because they can afford information as to the condition of the rivers affected by gold-dredging. There being gold more or less all over the country, dredges are put on some of the rivers to obtain the gold contained in the silt of the bottom. This dredging has sometimes proved very lucrative, one company paying as high a dividend as 55 per cent. per annum a little while ago. The dredge when working makes the water below it too muddy for fishing. Another method of obtaining gold is by sluicing, which has the same effect on the water.

The angler intending to do much fishing is

advised to take a tent, for use when more sub-
stantial accommodation is not available. He will
thus be enabled to visit places he could not well
reach otherwise.

If a fishing tour of the whole country and
season is intended, it will probably be found
satisfactory to begin with the most northerly part
in the North Island, then visit the Middle Island,
returning to the North Island in the latter part
of the fishing season. There are a great many
rivers and streams to choose from, but at present
the most likely places to obtain sport are the
following :—

North Island.

Auckland District.—Waihou River and tributaries; Lakes Rotorua, Roto-iti, and tributaries.
These contain almost entirely rainbow and some
brown trout. (See Chapter XVI., " North Island :
Rivers and Lakes of the East Coast.")

Taranaki District.—Patea River and other
streams in the neighbourhood of Stratford.
Chiefly brown and some rainbow trout. (See
Chapter XVII., " North Island : Rivers and
Lakes of the West Coast.")

Hawke's Bay District.—Ngaruroro River and
tributaries; Tukituki River and tributaries.
(See Chapter XVI., " North Island : Rivers and
Lakes of the East Coast.") Manawatu River
and tributaries. (See Chapter XVII., " North
Island : Rivers and Lakes of the West Coast.")
These contain brown and some rainbow trout.

Wellington District.—From the Manawatu River below the Gorge; all the rivers on the west coast to Wellington. Chiefly brown and some rainbow trout. (See Chapter XVII., "North Island: Rivers and Lakes of the West Coast.") From the Manawatu River above the Gorge; all the rivers through the Forty-mile Bush and Wairarapa Valley to the Wairarapa Lake on the east coast (for Manawatu River and tributaries which contain brown and rainbow trout, see Chapter XVII., "North Island: Rivers and Lakes of the West Coast"). For the rivers of the Wairarapa Valley, which contain chiefly brown and some rainbow trout, see Chapter XVI., "North Island: Rivers and Lakes of the East Coast," beginning at Lake Wairarapa and the rivers discharging into it. Wainui-o-mata Stream contains brown and some rainbow trout. Hutt River and tributaries contain brown and some rainbow trout. (See Chapter XVI., "North Island: Rivers and Lakes of the East Coast.")

Middle Island.

Marlborough District.—Wairau River and tributaries; Clarence River and tributaries. Chiefly brown trout. The central place for accommodation is Blenheim. (See Chapter XIX., "Middle Island: Rivers and Lakes of the East Coast.")

Nelson District.—Wangamoa Stream; Maitai Stream; Waimea River and tributaries; Motueka River and tributaries; Riwaka Stream. Chiefly brown trout. The central place for accommodation is Nelson. (See Chapter XVIII., " Middle Island : Rivers and Lakes of the North Coast.")

Canterbury North District.—Waiau-ua River and tributaries; Waimakariri River and tributaries. Mostly brown trout. The central place is Christchurch. (See Chapter XIX., " Middle Island : Rivers and Lakes of the East Coast.")

Canterbury South District.—Rakaia River and tributaries; Ashburton River and tributaries; Rangitata River and tributaries; Orari River; Opihi River; Waitaki River and tributaries. These contain brown trout, and are chiefly fished near their mouths for sea-run trout. Christchurch is the chief town. (See Chapter XIX., " Middle Island : Rivers and Lakes of the East Coast.")

Otago District.—Some of the tributaries of the Clutha River. Brown trout. Dunedin is the chief town. (See Chapter XIX., " Middle Island : Rivers and Lakes of the East Coast.")

Southland District.—Oreti River and tributaries; Aparima River and tributaries. Brown trout. Invercargill is the chief town. (See Chapter XX., " Middle Island : Rivers and Lakes of the South Coast.")

Westland District.—Buller River and tributaries; Grey River and tributaries; Hokitika River and tributaries. Chiefly brown trout. The central places for accommodation are Westport,

Greymouth, and Hokitika. (See Chapter XXII., "Middle Island : Rivers and Lakes of the West Coast.")

The visitor should provide himself with a time-table for the New Zealand railways. It is not possible in the compass of such a work as this to give much information about distances by railway. Railways may be extended, as is being done in all directions, so that in a few years railways may take the place of many of the roads and tracks now given in the Guide.

CHAPTER XIV.

HINTS FOR APPROACHING GAME IN FIELD AND FOREST, ETC.

THE following hints apply to game in Maori-land and elsewhere :—

Always approach the game "up wind"—*i.e.*, with the wind coming from the game to you. The scent of your approach and that of your dogs is thus carried away from the game instead of to it; and any noise you may make is carried away from the game, and so is less likely to be heard. Animals. mostly graze moving against the wind, so there is less chance of your being seen by them, as you may be able to approach them from behind. Your dogs, also, will have the scent of the game carried to them instead of from them. Working " down wind " the game is disturbed for a long way ahead. Wild animals, particularly deer and pigs, have very keen scent, sight, and hearing; therefore every endeavour should be made to avoid being scented, seen, or heard by the game. Without such caution there is little chance of getting within reasonable shooting distance of deer or wild cattle, unless they are brought to bay by dogs, or driven.

Therefore the first thing is to note the direction of the wind and to arrange a starting-point accordingly. While noting the direction of the wind at starting, it must not be forgotten that the wind may change, when fresh arrangements to meet this contingency must be made. There are also sub-currents of wind to allow for sometimes—*i.e.*, in rather narrow valleys the wind almost always blows up or down. In river-beds, unless the surrounding country is low and the banks low and open, the wind generally blows up or down, and in approaching game in such places this fact must not be lost sight of.

Deer, wild cattle, wild pigs, and all game are made much wilder and more difficult of approach by being hunted and disturbed by dogs than by shooting.

Avoid any clothing or head-covering of light colour, as it is too easily seen.

The sportsman is assumed to have made himself master of the use of the rifle before taking the field against stags or wild cattle, as mistakes or misses might at close quarters be attended with serious results.

Deer or other game should not be shot at at distances that do not afford a fair chance of killing, as from reasons of humanity wounded game should not be allowed to escape; and, besides, it is unsatisfactory and unsportsmanlike. The distance at which it is reasonable to shoot with a rifle varies with the skill of the sportsman, and with a gun to some extent according to

STAG'S HEAD, WELLINGTON DISTRIOT.

its shooting-power. If we must kill, the sportsman should know where to shoot to cause instant death if possible, and to save suffering to the animals and the possible loss of game. On the illustration of the stag's head the spot to aim at the heads of stags and cattle when they are close to and facing you is marked with dotted lines. (See Fig. 17.) These lines are from the ear to the eye; and just *above* where such imaginary lines would cross is the place where a bullet goes through the brain, and the animal falls dead as if struck by lightning. In making this shot it is better to aim a little high than low.

To aim at an animal broadside on, do so as illustrated (see Fig. 18), when the bullet will generally go through the heart and cause death quickly.

When the animal is in a rather different position than square on either for the front head or for the broadside shot, such allowance must be made in aiming as will occur to the sportsman in endeavouring to reach the parts named. In the broadside shot, if the animal is fired at rather from behind, aim at the place marked; but if fired at rather from the front, aim a little in front of the place marked.

If it is desired to shoot for the heart of an animal facing you, aim at the chest at the same level as for the shot at the broadside.

The sportsman who wishes for perfect directions for aiming at winged and small game in

10—Sport.

various positions is recommended to a work, " Illustrated Treatise on the Art of Shooting," by Mr. Charles Lancaster, the London gunmaker.

A loaded gun is a death-dealing weapon, and this fact should not be lost sight of; and it should always be so carried that if accidentally fired the discharge would be harmless. It is prudent to draw the cartridges before getting over or through fences. In rough ground and forest or under-growth, when after deer or wild cattle, or any game, it is as well to defer loading until there is a chance of a shot, and, if the chance passes, to draw the cartridges until another chance occurs. I have, so to speak, had a gun in my hands ever since birth, but I never neglect to act as here advised. If these precautions were always taken a great number of the deplorable accidents that occur would be avoided.

Take care, in cattle-shooting, that your companions or dogs are not in the line of fire.

Wild cattle, if brought to bay in the forest by dogs, often get into very thick undergrowth, and you may have to get within 10 yards or less of them to see to get a shot. As your companions or dogs may also be hidden by the undergrowth, the greatest care is required, and on this account more than one or two companions should not be taken into such places. A bullet from a rifle or smooth bore often goes through the game at close quarters, hardly losing any of its force. I have known of several men, and also many dogs, being

STAG, WELLINGTON DISTRICT.

killed by bullets which have passed right through the objects aimed at.

The forest is usually very dense and dark, which makes it difficult to get dark-coloured rifle-sights quickly on the object. For this reason it is an advantage to have the fore-sight just tipped about 1-16 in. with brass, which shows against a background of almost any colour, and a fine silver or platinum line behind the centre of the notch in the point-blank back-sight. This applies also to rook rifles for shooting wild pigeons, &c.

About the most useful knife to carry for deer-stalking, cattle-shooting, and pig-hunting is a butcher's knife, of good quality, with a blade 7 in. long, and with the back ground sharp for 2 in. from the point. A few notches can be cut in the corners of the handle to give a better hold. It should have a close - fitting sheath, which should cover the handle except about $\frac{1}{2}$ in., to prevent the knife dropping out or being lost by the sheath catching in the undergrowth. It is awkward when you have a boar by the leg to find you have no knife. If the sheath is worn inside the belt the risk of losing the knife is less. Any saddle-maker can make such a sheath, which can be suspended from a saddle-strap for a belt by a strong loop cut in the sheath about 1 in. from the top. Such a knife and fittings is more useful than any of the elaborate *couteau de chasse*.

In using the knife to stab, take care to have the end of the handle resting against the palm of the hand. This is to give accurate direction to the stab, and to prevent injury to the hand by the blade slipping through it.

The bleeding and dressing of deer and cattle can hardly be learnt except by practical instruction, which is easily got. If deer, cattle, or wild pigs are killed in places difficult to get at, and it is desired to take the meat home, it will reduce the weight to be carried by about one-half, and the meat also will be in a more portable form, if, after bleeding and skinning the deer or cattle, or, bleeding, singeing, or skinning the pigs, but without opening them, the meat is cut off, leaving the bones. This can be accomplished by running the knife right along the back down to the backbone and then clearing the meat closely from the bones in one piece, working down both sides. The meat of deer or cattle can then be cut into suitable-sized pieces to roll up, and that of pigs made into one roll. Meat keeps better so treated, and if it cannot be taken home at once it is well to put up some horizontal poles on forked stakes at a sufficient height from the ground for the meat to be safe from the dogs; then hang the meat to or over the horizontal poles, and, if needed, keep a smoky fire close by to keep off flies. Many people think the smoking improves the meat.

When in strange forests it often saves much time and perplexity if the sportsman, in passing through the undergrowth, breaks the tops of the twigs with right and left hand at short intervals, turning the tops of the twigs outwards from the track walked over. This marks the way taken, and there is thus a track to return by, which may be made clearer by the occasional blazing of trees with the axe. Should at any time the way be completely lost in a large forest, it is well to remember that streams, except in the rarer cases of their ending in a lake, if followed down, almost always lead to the main river or sea. In any case I would advise the newcomer not to take to the forest without a practical guide, and one who has local knowledge is best. A good tracker contributes very materially to sport.

For tent, pack-horses, pack-saddle, half-axe, &c., see Chapter II., under " Tackle and Equipment. Some sacks should be taken to carry the meat in.

Waterproof wax matches are the best kind to carry. They are to be had in many grocers' shops. The ordinary wax matches can be protected from wet in a small corked bottle.

Before shooting over private property it is necessary to obtain permission.

CHAPTER XV.

DEER-STALKING; WINGED GAME; CATTLE SHOOTING; PIG-HUNTING.

DEER-STALKING.

THERE are red and fallow deer in many places in both the North and Middle Islands, and in sufficient number to afford good sport. The secretaries of acclimatisation societies and the Government Tourist Department will afford the latest information as to where the best sport is to be obtained, and where to obtain licenses to shoot.

The deer are fine well-grown animals, as can be seen from illustrations in Chapter XIV., and they are increasing in number rapidly.

Any of the rifles in ordinary use for the purpose will do for this sport, but one with the flattest trajectory is most desirable.

In Chapter XIV. attention is called to the necessity of working up wind, and of keeping out of sight, scent, and hearing.

To succeed in getting near enough to a stag to get a shot at a reasonable distance may in the open bare country involve a journey for some way *ventre à terre*, like a snake, and many other more or less unaccustomed positions. The stalker should not forget that he is most conspicuous where he has only a sky background, and avoid such a position. In looking over the top of a ridge or rise the head should be raised and lowered very gradually, so as not to attract attention, which any abrupt movement would most likely do.

WINGED GAME.

Guns.

Perhaps the most generally useful gun for all purposes is a strong shooting No. 12 bore. If intended chiefly for ducks a full chokebore is suitable. The use of a gun over 10 bore is illegal.

Dogs.

The dogs in use are the same kinds as those in Britain, and can be got in the country fairly well bred. On account of the strict quarantine laws it is better for visitors not to bring dogs unless they intend to remain a year or two in the country.

Pheasants.

Pheasants are scattered all over the Islands. In the North Island, in the neighbourhood of Lake Taupo, in the district of the Waikato, and north of Auckland, they are fairly plentiful. The places mentioned afford a good deal of manuka-scrub cover, and good bags are sometimes made. Much of the land where pheasants are most plentiful is pumice or clay, and unimproved—almost unimprovable.

There are none of the barn-door sort of pheasant
that furnishes the material for battues in England; but, leaving out the artificially reared birds,
there are about the same number in this country
as in England.

Quail.

Californian and Virginian quail are to be met
with all over the country, and in places moderate
bags can be made.

Grey Ducks and Teal.

Grey ducks and teal are pretty evenly distributed; in some localities they are plentiful. A
hundred ducks have been killed in a day by one
12-bore gun with seventy-five cartridges. But
this is an altogether exceptional case; they were
shot on a rather small lagoon.

Native Wild Pigeons.

Native wild pigeons are found in the forests
and clumps of native trees all over the country,
sometimes in considerable numbers. They are a
fine, handsome, large bird, as tame as the British
wild pigeon is wild. They are good birds for
the table, and in the shooting season are sometimes full of fat. It is not easy to get many
flying shots at them, as they sit close and seldom
leave the trees, which are in leaf throughout the
year.

On a bright day they are often perched on the
tops of the high pine-trees with their white
breasts turned to the sun. In wet, cold, blowy

weather they must be looked for lower down among the branches.

The trees being in leaf, the pigeons require a good deal of looking for; therefore it is an advantage to have some Maori or other boys looking for them. A retriever will be found useful. With a hard-shooting rook rifle very fair sport can be got.

HARES.

Hares are to be found all over the country, and in some places are plentiful.

RABBITS.

Rabbits are thinly scattered almost everywhere, and here and there are very numerous. They increase so rapidly that they have to be treated as vermin, and destroyed where possible. In the south of the Middle Island rabbits are put up in tins for export, and are also sent to England frozen, in great numbers, some millions being disposed of in this way annually.   ,

WILD CATTLE SHOOTING.

Wild cattle are found chiefly in or near the edges of forests, in out-of-the-way places, all over the country.

When stalked in the open the procedure is the same as for deer. (See Chapter XIV., page 143.)

If, as is generally the case, they are in the forest, where they live chiefly on the under-growth, they may have to be brought to bay by dog before a shot can be got. The dogs generally employed are known as cattle-dogs—a strong dog with a good deal of collie blood, combining a good nose and intelligence.

Owing to the density of the undergrowth the sport has mostly to be followed on foot; and in broken and mountainous country it is sometimes hard work. In such country a light hard-shooting carbine of the repeating sort fitted with a sling will be found satisfactory.

The cattle being brought to bay, on account of the forest growth being thick, and so as to provide for the safety of the dogs, shots may have to be taken at very close quarters, very likely inside of 10 yards. At the same time cattle must be approached with caution. A wild bull, particularly with his blood up, is not to be played with. The hunter has to be alert to take the chance for a shot without injuring the dogs and to avoid being gored. For where to aim see Chapter XIV., Figs. 17 and 18.

Your game grassed and bled, the next thing to do is to see if it is in good enough condition to take home for meat. At any rate, unless in a difficult place to get at, the hide will be worth taking.

WILD PIG HUNTING.

Wild pigs are to be found in all the out-of-the-way places, but chiefly in and about the forests. They live principally on fern-root, and on the berries that fall from the trees. Most of

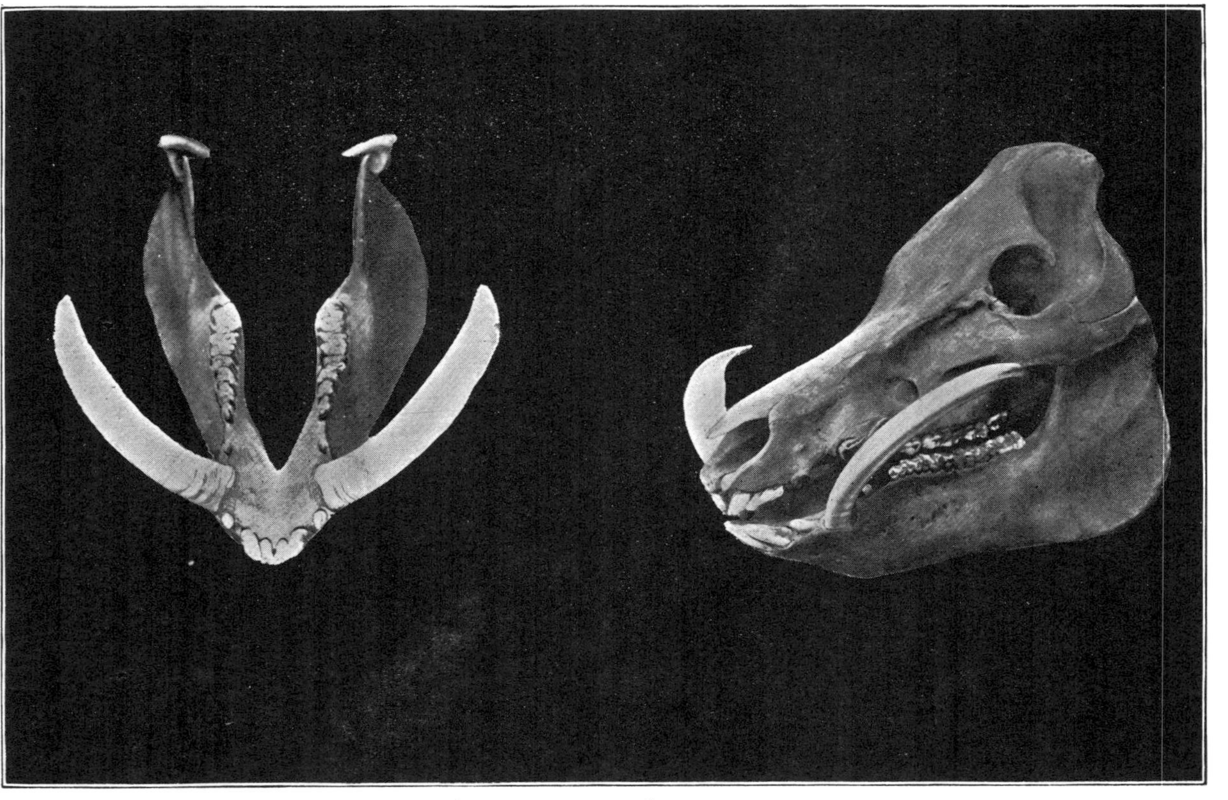

WILD BOAR'S HEAD, HAWKE'S BAY DISTRICT.

the larger trees and many of the shrubs are covered with berries, some the size of small plums.

Owing to the nature of the country the work has mostly to be done on foot, and, as a gun is a heavy burden in such places, a knife is the best weapon to use. With the exception of perhaps half a dozen, the thousands of wild pigs I have grassed have been killed with the knife alone; so only this way of hunting is here dealt with.

Generally the only way to get at the pigs in such country is to bring them to bay with dogs. Where only a little hunting is intended, two dogs will be enough; but, if it is intended to hunt continuously, spare dogs should be left at home to take the place of those that may knock up or get ripped and killed. Useful dogs for the purpose are the cattle-dogs mentioned under " Wild Cattle " (see page 153). One of these with a good nose will find and hunt the pigs, holding a sow or young boar when caught, and bringing an old boar to bay. The fact of either of these things having taken place will generally be made manifest by the squealing remonstrances of the sow or young boar, and by the barking of the dog at the old fellow, who will be gnashing his tusks and watching for a chance to rip the dog open—a consummation which the dog is also watching and dodging to avert.

In Fig. 19 an illustration is given of specimens of tusks, being some of the many I have lying about.

The second or holding dog should be bred
with just enough bull-dog blood to give him pluck
and holding-power, and still allow of some intelligence. Pure bull-dogs get killed directly, because
they seize the pig anywhere about the head.

Generally the best way with the second dog is
to lead him by a strap up to the boar at bay,
and, when quite close, let him go, when, if
properly trained and experienced, he will get a
good hold of the ear, and instantly lay his side
close against the boar's, and try to maintain this
position, and so be out of the way of getting
ripped. The dog, knowing his business, does not
shift his hold, or waste his strength by pulling
the boar about and trying to keep him from
moving, but hampers his movements, which will
be solely and energetically directed to getting at
the dog, or you, or both.

Directly the dog or dogs have a firm hold of
the ear it is your turn to take an active part in
the proceedings, which you can do, among many
other ways, by seizing the boar by the shank of
the hind leg, or, if handier, by the tail first, which
in wild pigs gives a good hold, and afterwards by
the shank. Among other ways of throwing the
pig on his side, the following is generally convenient : Seize the shank of the off hind leg with
the right hand, and, leaning forward, pass the left
hand under the pig's belly and grasp the shank of
the off fore leg with the left hand. Then pull,
with a rather sudden jerk, the two legs from

under him, helping to put him on his side by using your knees or otherwise; this accomplished, kneel on the shoulder to keep him down, holding perhaps the shank of the undermost fore leg in the left hand, and use the knife as is done in bleeding a tame pig. All this should be done smartly and quickly, so as not to exhaust your strength by a long struggle. The dogs sometimes help to embarrass you in these movements.

It is prudent for the novice to practice the throw on small pigs first, or in any other convenient way.

If you cannot throw the pig you must put the knife in its whole length low down close behind the shoulder (see place marked for broadside shot at deer, Fig. 18), and wait until this has killed. To do this, change the grasp of the off hind shank to the left hand, and with the knife in the right put it in behind the right shoulder.

The only proper hold for either dog is by the ear. It gives the safest hold, and does not spoil the meat. If the holding dog is allowed to run loose with the other dog, instead of being led as advised, the chances are that, instead of being fresh, as he is when let loose close to the boar, and so able to keep hold safely for you and himself, when you arrive to his assistance you will find him exhausted. Not having had you to back him up at once, he may be badly ripped, or killed, before you are there to help him, or he may be thrown off just as you are about to take hold. He will, at any rate, most likely have had as much taken out of him as by holding a dozen pigs to which he was led, and may be of little use for the remainder of the day.

My holding - dogs have included a few that could be run singly, because when they came to a boar they barked at him, not taking hold until the hunter was within 10 yards or so, and so were fresh to hold. Such dogs, however, are very rare. These dogs, although cautious, would tackle anything when backed up by the hunter, but knew too much to get uselessly ripped to pieces when by themselves.

A dog soon finds out if he is reliably backed by the hunter. Many dogs are spoilt by the inexperienced hunter shirking closing with the boar, leaving the dog to have it out, in which case the dog generally gets all the worst of it. A boar's tusks are very sharp, and a pig has great strength of neck—it is nearly as thick as its body. These bush-pigs are as active as cats. They turn round sharply, are in good training, and can rip a dog open from end to end at a blow.

When used as advised, a knife is the safest weapon with which to tackle a pig. In thick undergrowth a tomahawk, in making a blow, may get caught overhead; various accidents of this kind have occurred, one of which was the man bringing the tomahawk down on his own head, and getting ripped up by the pig into the bargain. A spear in the same kind of place has the disadvantage that, in drawing it back to make a lunge, before it is far enough back the shaft may strike against something behind. I have seen a Maori get a rip 15 in. long on the inside of the thigh from this cause, and had he been alone he might have been killed.

Boars sometimes get into places where neither man or dog can well tackle them, such as into hollow trees with only their snout and tusks out, their rear and flanks being completely protected, or into the bottom of holes or small streams where the sides are so close together as not to leave room for the dog alongside of the boar. When a boar gets into such a place, if you mean to tackle him it is prudent first to divest yourself of your overshirt or jacket to throw over his head, and so blind him for a moment or two if required. Then jump into the trench behind him, carrying your jacket or shirt in your hand, and quickly seize the hind shank or tail and act as already directed.

Sows are dealt with in the same manner as boars. They give a severe bite.

There are not many accidents except to dogs. Quite a number of mine have been killed. Sometimes horses get ripped when the hunting is done riding in the open.

I was once slightly ripped, owing to the boar getting a sapling between himself and the dog, and so tearing the dog's teeth through the ear.

The dog had him again though at once, and he paid the usual penalty.

Two fatal accidents have come under my notice. Of one of the sufferers, with whom I was well acquainted, no part of the body was recovered, it being eaten and carried away by the pigs; but scraps of the clothing found showed what had happened.

Wild pigs used to be very destructive to lambing flocks, killing and eating the lambs in thousands, and also many sheep.

The skin on the shoulder of old boars is often nearly an inch thick, and so tough that bullets from small sporting rifles fired at a distance of a few feet sometimes fail to go through it.

A pig intended to be eaten should be singed as soon as killed. This is accomplished by the help of burning brushwood or fern, and scraping with the knife in the usual way. Wild pork has little resemblance to the meat of tame pigs. It is darker in colour, and more like dark mutton than tame pork, not so heavy, and when the pig is in condition is good meat.

SHELTER-HUTS.

In places where, from their inaccessibility, it is difficult to take tents, or even simple cooking utensils, very fair shelter may be provided after the Maori manner if the materials are at hand. With manuka-bark, totara-bark, toitoi, raupo, and other materials, a few slight saplings and vines, "supplejacks," or flax, a Maori will make various sorts of shelter in an hour or two that will have some advantages over a tent. No nails are used. I have spent years in such shelters.

The most common kind is a lean-to, open in front to the side sheltered from the wind, with the fire made in the open in front; or the Λ shape, with the fire made in the middle of the floor, the smoke being allowed to escape along the ridge, which is not closed. A half-axe is the only tool required.

The only cooking utensils desirable are a tin billy, pannikin, and sharp sheath-knife. Meat can be cut in thin slices about the size of the hand, and then kept spread out by being stuck on a forked stick, which is then stuck in the ground at an angle over the fire or coals pulled out from it, the meat being turned as required.

Birds can be cooked much more quickly in the same way if the inside is taken out by a hole under the wing, and then a red-hot pebble forced into the inside, just as the bird is going to be put over the fire. It thus cooks from both the inside and outside. Birds are most easily plucked as soon as shot, and if cooked before they are cold will not be tough. The latter also applies to meat.

Fish can be cooked in the same way, and potatoes can be roasted unpeeled by laying them on hot ashes raked from the fire, covering with more hot ashes, and then placing a few hot coals on top.   When done they are removed from the ashes, which can be beaten off with a switch. Damper bread can be cooked in the ashes.

If the camp-fire is not put out while the sportsmen are away, it is prudent to cover it with ashes to keep down the flame, and this will also keep the coals alive for a long time.   When it is desired to make up the fire the ashes are again removed.   I have kept a fire in for many months at a time in this way.

Grey blankets are best for camping.   Sometimes it is convenient to have one end sewn up like a shepherd's plaid, which thus keeps the wind off the head, and at other times to have the blanket sewn up like a sack.

If obliged to camp out without shelter overhead, either with or without blankets, try to lie out of the wind.   Dry fern, scrub, or suchlike, heaped on top of the blankets, or even without the blankets, will keep out much cold, and by this means lives have been saved.   If Maoris form part of the party they will probably prefer, and should have, a separate shelter.

RIVER IN FRONT OF HOUSE.

CHAPTER XVI.

NORTH ISLAND—EAST COAST.

RIVERS AND LAKES FROM DOUBTLESS BAY TO PORT NICHOLSON (BEGINNING AT THE NORTH).

KERIKERI Burn and tributaries have chiefly shingle bottom. Banks moderately high, more or less encumbered with scrub and fern. Wadeable mostly. Landing deep, also good. Course, seven miles. Contains rainbow trout. Reached by steamer from Auckland to Opua, Bay of Islands; thence by train, eight miles, to Kawakawa, from which it is nineteen miles by road: from Kawakawa all parts of the district can be reached. There are several hotels in Kawakawa and hotel accommodation at Kerikeri.

KAWAKAWA River.—The estuary, emptying into the Bay of Islands, has chiefly mud bottom, the river mostly shingle bottom. Banks moderately high, more or less scrub-encumbered. Wadeable partly. Landing deep, also good. Course, twenty-three miles. Contains rainbow trout. Reached by steamer from Auckland to Opua, Bay of Islands; thence by train, eight miles, to Kawakawa: from Kawakawa, which is close to the river, all parts of the district can be reached. There are several hotels in Kawakawa.

TIROHANGA Stream, tributary of Kawakawa River.—Shingle bottom. Banks moderately high, partly scrub - encumbered. Wadeable. Landing deep, also good. Course, twelve miles. Contains rainbow trout. Reached from Kawakawa, which is close by. For approach and accommodation see "Kawakawa River," already mentioned.

Waiomio Burn, tributary of Kawakawa River.— Shingle bottom. Banks moderately high, and more or less scrub - encumbered. Wadeable. Landing deep, also good. Course, eight miles. Contains rainbow trout. Reached from Kawakawa, which is close by. For approach and accommodation see "Kawakawa River," already mentioned.

Ngunguru Stream.—Shingle bottom mostly. Banks moderate height, partly scrub-encumbered. Wadeable partly. Landing deep, also good. Course, fourteen miles. Contains rainbow trout. Reached by nine miles of road from Whangarei, where there are hotels and boardinghouses: Whangarei is reached by steamer from Auckland.

Whangarei River (discharges into Whangarei Harbour).—Mud and shingle bottom. Banks low mostly, and partly encumbered, Wadeable partly. Landing deep, also good. Course, twenty-one miles. Contains rainbow trout. Reached from Whangarei, to which it is close, and where there is hotel accommodation: Whangarei reached by steamer from Auckland.

Wairarohia Burn (discharges into Whangarei Harbour).—Shingle and boulder bottom. Banks fairly clear. Wadeable. Landing chiefly good. Course, four miles. Contains rainbow trout. Reached from Whangarei, to which it is close. For approach and accommodation see "Whangarei River," already mentioned.

Raumanga Burn (discharges into Whangarei Harbour).—Mud and shingle bottom. Banks low and encumbered. Wadeable. Landing deep, also good. Course, five miles. Contains rainbow trout. Reached from Whangarei, to which it is close. For approach and accommodation see "Whangarei River," already mentioned.

Otaika Burn (discharges into the Whangarei Harbour). — Mud and shingle bottom. Banks rather low, and scrub-encumbered. Wadeable

CATCH OF TROUT, AUCKLAND DISTRICT.

partly. Landing deep, also good. Course, eight miles. Contains rainbow trout. Reached from Whangarei, to which it is close. For approach and accommodation see " Whangarei River," already mentioned.

LAKE TAKAPUNA.—Rock bottom mostly, and of great depth. Banks mostly rocky and steep. Wadeable here and there. Landing mostly deep. Length, three quarters of a mile; breadth, three-quarters of a mile. Height above sea-level, 100 ft. Contains rainbow trout. Close to sea-beach. Reached from Auckland by steamer and coach in one hour. There is a hotel on the bank, where boats are kept.

HENDERSON'S Creek (discharges into Waitemata Harbour). — Mud and shingle bottom. Banks moderately high, and not much encumbered. Wadeable partly. Landing deep, also good. Course, ten miles. Contains brown and rainbow trout. Reached from Henderson Station, where there is hotel accommodation, on the Auckland–Makarau Railway.

THAMES or WAIHOU River.—Mud bottom, and estuary of some length Above Te Aroha the bottom is mud, rock, and shingle, and in the upper part there is some pumice. Banks vary from clear and low to high and scrub-encumbered. Wadeable partly in the upper river. Landing chiefly deep. Course, eighty miles. Contains brown and rainbow trout, the latter almost entirely. Reached from the Okoroire Station, on the Auckland–Rotorua Railway, where a coach meets the trains and takes the traveller over the three miles to the Okoroire Hotel and Sanatorium, situated on the bank of the Waihou River.

The chief fish-hatchery of the Auckland Acclimatisation Society is situated on the Waimakariri, a tributary of the Waihou River, on the road, four miles beyond the hotel. Here may be seen the trout in all stages of its growth and existence, from the ova to the vigorous fish of about five pounds. If the visitors find the manager at home, they will have all information freely given, and if bent on fishing they will do well to get his advice about the streams, as the tributaries mentioned are all within easy distance of the hotel.

This will be found admirably adapted for a sportsman's purposes, being well conducted, quiet, and private. Included in the grounds are several well-arranged natural hot mineral baths, which have proved of great efficacy in rheumatic and other affections.

The soil being extremely porous pumice formation, the situation is dry, and remarkably healthy and bracing. All surface water from rains disappears directly. Height above sea-level, about 300 ft.

WAIRERE Burn, tributary of Waihou River.— Pumice bottom. Banks low and high, more or less scrub-encumbered. Wadeable partly. Landing deep, also good. Course, five miles. Contains brown and rainbow trout, mostly the latter. Reached from the Okoroire Station, on the Auckland–Rotorua Railway; thence by nineteen miles of road. For approach and accommodation see " Waihou River," already mentioned.

MANGAWHERO Stream, tributary of Waihou River. —Pumice bottom mostly. Banks low and high, and more or less scrub-encumbered. Wadeable partly. Landing deep, also good. Course, thirteen miles. Contains brown and rainbow trout, chiefly the latter. Reached from the Okoroire Station, on the Auckland–Rotorua Railway; thence to seven miles from the mouth, by eight miles of road from the hotel. For approach and accommodation see " Waihou River," already mentioned.

MANGAWHARA Burn, tributary of Mangawhero Stream.—Pumice bottom mostly. Banks low and high, more or less scrub-encumbered. Wadeable partly. Landing deep, also good. Course, four miles. Contains brown and rainbow trout, chiefly the latter. Reached from the Okoroire Station, on the Auckland–Rotorua Railway; thence by eight miles of road from the hotel. For approach and accommodation see " Mangawhero Stream," already mentioned.

WAIOMOU Stream, tributary of Waihou River.— Pumice bottom mostly. Banks from low to high, more or less scrub-encumbered. Wadeable. Landing deep, also good. Course, thirteen miles. Contains brown and rainbow trout, chiefly the latter. Reached from the Okoroire Station, on the Auckland–Rotorua Railway; thence by two miles of road from the hotel: the road continues down the stream for nine miles, to near the mouth. For approach and accommodation see " Waihou River," already mentioned.

RAPARAPA Burn, tributary of Waiomou Stream. —Pumice bottom chiefly. Banks low, also high, and more or less scrub-encumbered. Wadeable partly. Landing deep, also good. Course, four miles. Contains brown and rainbow trout, chiefly the latter. Reached from the Okoroire Station, on the Auckland–Rotorua Railway; thence by eight miles of road from the hotel. For approach and accommodation see " Waiomou Stream," already mentioned.

KAKAHO Burn, tributary of Waiomou Stream.— Pumice bottom chiefly. Banks from low to high, more or less scrub-encumbered. Wadeable partly. Landing deep, also good. Course, five miles. Contains chiefly rainbow trout. Reached from the Okoroire Station, on the Auckland–Rotorua Railway; thence by road of five miles from the hotel. For approach and accommodation see " Waiomou Stream," already mentioned.

ORAKA River, tributary of Waihou River.— Pumice bottom chiefly. Banks from low to high. partly scrub - encumbered. Wadeable partly. Landing mostly deep. Course, thirty-four miles.

Contains chiefly rainbow trout. Reached from the Okoroire Station, on the Auckland–Rotorua Railway; thence by road of one mile; and two miles further on is the hotel. For approach and accommodation see " Waihou River," already mentioned.

WAIMAKARIRI Burn, tributary of Waihou River. —Pumice bottom mostly. Banks from low to high, partly scrub-encumbered. Wadeable. Landing deep, also good. Course, six miles. Contains brown and rainbow trout, the latter chiefly, in great number. Reached from the Okoroire Station, on the Auckland–Rotorua Railway; thence by road of four miles from the hotel. For approach and accommodation see " Waihou River," already mentioned.

LAKE ROTORUA. — Pumice and shingle bottom and beaches. Banks mostly low and scrub-clad. Wadeable partly. Landing deep, also good. Length, seven miles; breadth, six miles. Height above sea level, 915 ft. Contains brown and rainbow trout. Reached from the Rotorua Station, on the Auckland–Rotorua Railway; also by coach-road from Napier and Wanganui *via* Lake Taupo. The lake contains numbers of brown and rainbow trout; they reach a great size, and numbers have been taken by anglers up to 20 lb. in weight. Trolling and artificial fly are both successful. T. water of the lake and its tributaries is very clear.

The Township of Rotorua partly encircles the southern end of Lake Rotorua, which is connected with Lake Rotoiti by the Ohau Creek, one mile in length. A coach-road runs along the south bank of Lakes Rotorua, Rotoiti, and Rotoehu, which form a chain of twenty-two miles in length. Eleven miles from Rotorua, on this road, is Tiki-tere—boiling mud.

Steam-launches, boats, and canoes can be hired at Rotorua Township, and the trip on Rotorua and Rotoiti can thus be made by water.

CATCH OF TROUT, AUCKLAND DISTRICT.

In Lake Rotorua is the Island of Mokoia, made famous in song and story by the night swim of Hinemoa to it from the mainland to reach her forbidden lover. The distance is variously estimated, but on the map the direct distance is over two miles and a half from the starting-point. There is also on the island the natural hot bath in which the young lady warmed herself after what must have been a rather cooling journey.

Rotorua Township is 171 miles from Auckland by rail. It is 950 ft. above sea-level. The township and neighbourhood may fairly be called not only the wonderland of this country but of everywhere else. Steaming cones and fumaroles, boiling springs and caldrons, geysers and volcanoes, hot rivers, are on all sides, and cover a considerable area of country, extending over some hundreds of miles in length, and there are places where the angler might catch a trout and boil it in a spring within a yard of the margin of the river and of the spot where it was landed. All this, with an occasional earthquake thrown in, and a more or less pervading odour of burning or steaming sulphur, should be more eloquent and suggestive to the evil-doer than many sermons, and might be tried where those fail.

The curative properties of the various hot and mineral baths in Rotorua are great, chiefly for rheumatic and skin affections. The baths are well arranged in suitable buildings. There is a Sanatorium and resident Government medical man, and the whole is under Government control.

The township is well laid out. The soil is extremely porous, and the place is undoubtedly healthy.

There are a number of boardinghouses and well-conducted hotels. Some of the latter compare favourably as regards rooms, table, furnishing, charges, and other things with good English hotels, and the clubs in this country. The visitor will do well to inquire at these hotels about accommodation, routes, guides, &c.

Utuhina Burn, tributary of Lake Rotorua, north side.—Pumice bottom. Banks mostly moderate height, partly scrub - encumbered. Wadeable partly. Landing deep, also good. Course, eight miles. Contains brown and rainbow trout, chiefly the latter. Reached from Rotorua Town, which is at its mouth. For approach and accommodation see " Lake Rotorua," already mentioned.

Ngongataha Stream, tributary of Lake Rotorua, north side.—Pumice bottom. Banks scrub-encumbered except near the mouth, where they are low and clear. Wadeable partly. Landing mostly deep. Course, eleven miles. Contains brown and rainbow trout. Reached (to near the mouth) from Ngongataha Station, on the Auckland-Rotorua Railway, or by coach-road of five miles from Rotorua Town. For approach and accommodation see " Lake Rotorua," already mentioned.

Waitete Burn, tributary of Lake Rotorua, north side.—Pumice bottom. Banks more or less scrub-encumbered. Wadeable partly. Landing deep, also good. Course, eight miles. Contains brown and rainbow trout. Reached to near the mouth from Ngongataha Station, on the Auckland–Rotorua Railway, or by coach-road of six miles from Rotorua Town. For approach and accommodation see " Lake Rotorua," already mentioned.

Awahou Burn, tributary of Lake Rotorua, north side.—Pumice bottom. Banks more or less scrub-encumbered. Wadeable partly. Landing deep, also good. Course, three miles. Contains brown and rainbow trout. Reached (to within a mile of the mouth) by eight miles of road from Rotorua Town. For approach and accommodation see " Lake Rotorua," already mentioned.

Lake Rotoiti, tributary of Kaituna River ; connected with Lake Rotorua by the Ohau Creek, a

TROUT CAUGHT, AUCKLAND DISTRICT.

TROUT CAUGHT, AUCKLAND DISTRICT.

mile long.—Pumice, shingle, and boulder bottom and beaches. Banks high, and partly forest-clad. Wadeable partly. Landing deep, also good. Length, eight miles and a half; breadth, two miles and a half. Height above sea-level, 910 ft. Contains brown and rainbow trout. Running out of the lake on the east side is the part of the Kaituna River known as Okere, discharging on the east coast near Maketu (see " Kaituna River," further on). Reached by road of eleven miles from Rotorua Town, or by boat or steam-launch across Lake Rotorua from the town. For approach and accommodation see " Lake Rotorua," already mentioned.

Lake Rotoehu.—Shingle and pumice bottom and beaches. Banks mostly high, steep, and forest-clad. Wadeable here and there. Landing deep, also good. Length, two miles and a half; breadth, one mile and a half. Height above sea-level, 850 ft. Contains brown and rainbow trout. Reached from Rotorua Town by twenty-two miles of road along the south banks of Lakes Rotorua and Rotoiti. For approach and accommodation see " Lake Rotorua," already mentioned.

Whangapoa Stream, tributary of Waikato River. —Rock, shingle, and pumice bottom. Banks moderately low generally, and fairly clear. Wadeable. Landing deep, also good. Course, seventeen miles. Contains chiefly *S. fontinalis*. Reached from Rotorua in fifteen miles by the coach-road to Lake Taupo, Napier, or Wanganui. At this part there is no accommodation, and unless it is intended to return to Rotorua the same day a tent should be taken. Ten miles further on the road there is a hotel on the bank of the Waikato River, and close to where the Whangapoa runs into it.

Although a tributary of Waikato, a west coast river, I give it here because it is most easily reached by this road.

Waiau Burn (discharges into Tauranga Harbour).—Estuary, sand and mud bottom; shingle, rock, and boulder-bed in upper course. Banks various. Wadeable partly. Landing deep, also good. Course, nine miles. Contains brown and rainbow trout. Reached from the Paeroa Station, where there is hotel accommodation, on the Auckland–Thames Railway; thence by twenty-three miles of the Paeroa–Tauranga Coach-road *via* Waihi, which is half-way, and where there is hotel accommodation. From the burn to Tauranga is thirty-three miles, and ten miles along this road is Katikati, where there is hotel accommodation. Tauranga is reached by various coastal steamers and roads.

Tuapiro Burn (discharges into Tauranga Harbour).—Estuary, sand and mud bottom; shingle, rock, and boulder-bed in upper course. Banks various. Wadeable partly. Landing deep, also good. Course, nine miles. Contains brown and rainbow trout. Reached from Katikati by three miles of the Paeroa--Tauranga Road. For approach and accommodation see " Waiau Burn," already mentioned.

Uretara Burn (discharges into Tauranga Harbour).—Estuary, sand and mud bottom; then shingle and boulder bottom and bed. Banks fairly clear. Wadeable partly. Landing deep, also good. Course, six miles. Contains brown and rainbow trout. Reached from Katikati Township, to which it is close. For approach and accommodation see " Waiau Burn," already mentioned.

Kereatukahia Burn (discharges into Tauranga Harbour).—Mud and shingle bottom; then shingle bottom and bed. Banks mostly low and clear. Wadeable partly. Landing deep, also good. Course, six miles. Contains brown and rainbow trout. Reached from Katikati by two miles of Paeroa–Tauranga Road, or from Tauranga by

twenty miles of the same road. For approach
and accommodation see " Waiau Burn," already
mentioned.

MANIA Burn (discharges into Tauranga Harbour).—Mud and shingle bottom and bed. Banks
mostly low and clear. Wadeable partly. Landing deep, also good. Course, four miles. Contains brown and rainbow trout. Reached from
Katikati by three miles of the Paeroa–Tauranga
Road, or from Tauranga by nineteen miles of the
same road. For approach and accommodation see
" Waiau Burn," already mentioned.

TUAPO Burn (discharges into Tauranga Harbour).—Mud and shingle bottom; then shingle
bottom and bed. Banks mostly low and clear.
Wadeable partly. Landing deep, also good
Course, six miles. Contains brown and rainbow
trout. Reached from Katikati by four miles of
the Paeroa–Tauranga Road, or from Tauranga by
eighteen miles of the same road. For approach
and accommodation see " Waiau Burn," already
mentioned.

WAINUI Burn (discharges into Tauranga Harbour).—Mud and shingle bottom; then shingle
bottom and bed. Banks mostly low and clear.
Wadeable partly. Landing deep, also good.
Course, six miles. Contains brown and rainbow
trout. Reached from Katikati by eight miles of
the Paeroa–Tauranga Road, or from Tauranga by
fourteen miles of the same road. For approach
and accommodation see " Waiau Burn," already
mentioned.

WAIPAPA Burn (discharges into Tauranga Harbour).—Mud and shingle bottom; then shingle
bottom and bed. Banks mostly low and clear.
Wadeable partly. Landing deep, also good.
Course, six miles. Contains brown and rainbow
trout. Reached from Katikati by eleven miles of
the Paeroa–Tauranga Road, or from Tauranga by
eleven miles of the same road. For approach and

accommodation see "Waiau Burn," already mentioned.

TE PUNA Burn (discharges into Tauranga Harbour).—Mud and shingle bottom; then shingle bottom and bed. Banks mostly low and clear. Wadeable partly. Course, six miles. Contains brown and rainbow trout. Reached from Katikati by sixteen miles of the Paeroa–Tauranga Road, or from Tauranga by six miles of the same road. For approach and accommodation see "Waiau Burn," already mentioned.

WAIROA Stream (discharges into Tauranga Harbour).—Estuary, mud and sand bottom for two miles; navigable for boats for nine miles; then shingle bottom and bed. Banks low and fairly clear in lower reaches, steep and partly forest-clad in upper. Wadeable partly. Landing deep, also good. Course, nineteen miles. Contains brown and rainbow trout. Reached from Katikati by eighteen miles of the Paeroa–Tauranga Road, or from Tauranga by four miles of the same road. For approach and accommodation see "Waiau Burn," already mentioned.

OMANAWA Stream, tributary of Wairoa Stream.—Shingle bottom and bed. Banks in lower reaches fairly low and clear; in upper, steep and partly forest-clad. Wadeable partly. Landing deep, also good. Course, eleven miles. Contains brown and rainbow trout. Reached by following up the Wairoa Stream for five miles from where the Paeroa–Tauranga Road crosses it, or (to the mouth) by seven miles of road from Tauranga. For approach and accommodation see "Wairoa Stream," already mentioned.

NGAMUAWAHINE Burn, tributary of Wairoa Stream.—Shingle bottom and bed. Banks fairly clear in lower reaches, then steep, and partly scrub and forest-clad. Wadeable partly. Landing deep, also good. Course, nine miles. Contains brown and rainbow trout. Reached by following up the Wairoa

Stream for nine miles from where the Paeroa–Tauranga Road crosses it, or (to the lower reaches) by thirteen miles of road from Tauranga. For approach and accommodation see " Wairoa Stream," already mentioned.

KAPURERERUA Stream (discharges into Tauranga Harbour).—Mud and shingle bottom ; then shingle bottom and bed. Banks low and fairly clear in lower reaches, steep and partly forest-clad in upper. Wadeable partly. Landing deep, also good. Course, fifteen miles. Contains brown and rainbow trout. Reached from Tauranga, where there is hotel accommodation, and where it discharges into the harbour. Tauranga is reached by coastal steamers, by road from Rotorua and the Auckland–Rotorua Railway, and by road from Paeroa, on the Auckland–Thames Railway.

TAUTAU Burn, tributary of Kapurererua Stream.—Shingle bottom and bed. Banks low and fairly clear in lower reaches, steep and partly forest-clad in upper. Wadeable partly. Course, five miles. Contains brown and rainbow trout. Reached by following up the Kapurererua Stream for seven miles. For approach and accommodation see " Kapurererua Stream," already mentioned.

WAIMAPU Stream (discharges into Tauranga Harbour).—Mud and shingle bottom ; then shingle bottom and bed. Banks low and fairly clear in lower reaches, steep and partly forest-clad in upper. Wadeable partly. Landing deep, also good. Course, sixteen miles. Contains brown and rainbow trout. Reached (to the mouth) from Tauranga), to which it is close. For approach and accommodation see " Kapurererua Stream," already mentioned.

WAIOROHI Burn, tributary of Waimapu Stream.—Shingle bottom and bed. Banks low and fairly clear. Wadeable partly. Landing deep, also good. Course, six miles. Contains brown and rainbow trout. Reached by following up the Waimapu

Stream for three miles. For approach and accommodation see " Waimapu Stream," already mentioned.

Waitao Burn.—Mud and shingle bottom; then shingle bottom and bed. Banks low and fairly clear in lower reaches, steep and partly forest-clad in upper. Wadeable partly. Landing deep, also good. Course, eight miles. Contains brown and rainbow trout. Reached from Tauranga (to near the mouth) by six miles of the Tauranga–Maketu Road. For approach and accommodation see " Kapurererua Stream," already mentioned.

Kaiate Burn, tributary of Waitao Burn.—Shingle bottom and bed. Banks low and fairly clear in lower reaches, steep and partly forest-clad in upper. Wadeable partly. Landing deep, also good. Course, four miles. Contains brown and rainbow trout. Reached by following up the Waitao Burn for two miles from where the Tauranga–Maketu Road crosses it. For approach and accommodation see " Waitao Burn," already mentioned.

Kaituna River.—Estuary, sand and mud bottom; lower part of river slow and deep, with mud and shingle bottom; navigable for fifteen miles; then shingle and pumice bottom and bed. Banks low and clear in lower reaches, steeper and partly forest-clad in upper. Wadeable partly. Landing deep, also good. Course to Lake Rotoiti, out of which it flows, thirty miles. On the part of the river called Okere, and two miles below the lake, there is a waterfall. Contains brown and rainbow trout. Reached from Te Puke, which is near the junction of the Kaituna, Atuaroa, Ohineangaanga, and Waiari, and ten miles from the mouth of the river. Te Puke, where there is hotel accommodation, is on the Paeroa–Tauranga–Maketu Road, sixteen miles from Tauranga and twelve from Maketu, where there is hotel accommodation. Paeroa is a station on the Auckland–Thames Rail-

way. Te Puke is also reached by road from Rotorua *viâ* Lake Rotoiti. This road runs parallel with
the river at a distance of one or two miles nearly
the whole length. For approach and accommodation see " Lake Rotorua," already mentioned.
Maketu is close to the mouth of the river, and is
reached from Rotorua mostly by the same road as
Te Puke, and also by steamer from Tauranga.

ATUAROA Stream, tributary of Kaituna River.—
Shingle and pumice bottom and bed. Banks low
and fairly clear in lower reaches, steeper and partly
forest-clad in upper. Wadeable partly. Landing
deep, also good. Course, eleven miles. Contains
brown and rainbow trout. Reached (to near the
mouth) from Te Puke. For approach and accommodation see " Kaituna River," already mentioned.

OHINEANGAANGA Burn, tributary of Atuaroa
Stream.—Shingle and pumice bottom and bed.
Banks low and fairly clear in lower reaches, steeper
and partly scrub-encumbered in upper. Wadeable
partly. Landing deep, also good. Course, eight
miles. Contains brown and rainbow trout.
Reached (to near the mouth) from Te Puke.
For approach and accommodation see " Atuaroa
Stream," already mentioned.

WAIARI Stream, tributary of Kaituna River.—
Shingle and pumice bottom and bed. Banks low
and fairly clear in lower reaches ; steeper, partly
scrub-encumbered and forest-clad in upper. Wadeable partly. Landing deep, also good. Course,
twenty miles. Contains brown and rainbow trout.
Reached (to near the mouth) from Te Puke. For
approach and accommodation see " Kaituna River,"
already mentioned.

MANGAOREWA River, tributary of Kaituna River.
—Shingle and pumice bottom and bed. Banks
low and fairly clear in lower reaches, steeper and
partly forest-clad in upper. Wadeable partly.
Landing deep, also good. Course, twenty-four

miles. Contains brown and rainbow trout. Reached (to the mouth) from Te Puke, by following up the Kaituna River seven miles, or from Maketu (to the mouth) by seven miles of the Rotorna–Maketu Road. For approach and accommodation see " Kaituna River," already mentioned.

KAIKOKOPU River (discharges into Waihi Estuary).—Mud and shingle bottom in lower reaches, pumice and shingle bottom and bed in upper. Banks low and partly swampy in lower reaches, higher and partly forest-clad in upper. Wadeable partly. Landing deep, also good. Course, which is mostly slow, twenty-one miles. Contains brown and rainbow trout. Reached (to the mouth), across or round Waihi Estuary, in two miles from Maketu, where there is hotel accommodation; from here the Rotorua–Maketu Road runs parallel with the river for nineteen miles, at a distance varying from half a mile to two miles, as far as Lake Rotoiti. For approach and accommodation see " Kaituna River," already mentioned.

PONGAKAWA Stream (discharges into the Waihi Estuary).—Mud, shingle, and pumice bottom in lower reaches; pumice bottom in upper. Banks low and partly swampy in lower reaches; steeper and partly forest-clad in upper. Wadeable here and there. Landing deep, mostly. Course, seventeen miles. Contains brown and rainbow trout. Reached from Maketu. For approach and accommodation see " Kaituna River," already mentioned.

WAITAHANUI Stream.—Estuary, mud and sand bottom; then shingle, pumice, and boulder bottom and bed. Banks low and fairly clear in lower reaches, steeper and partly forest-clad in upper. Wadeable partly. Landing deep, also good. Course, eleven miles. Contains brown and rainbow trout. Reached (to the mouth) by road of twenty miles from Te Puke or Maketu. For approach and accommodation see " Kaituna River," already mentioned.

Rangitaiki River. — Estuary, mud and sand; then the river, dividing, forms an island five miles long and two broad; then shingle, pumice, and sometimes rock bottom, with waterfalls and broken water. Banks low, fairly clear, and mostly pumice. Very little wadeable. Landing almost all deep. Course, 120 miles. Contains brown and rainbow trout. The country from the mouth to the source being mostly rather flat, and pumice, it is generally easy to get over to both the main river and the tributaries. The river is fordable at intervals. Reached (to within fifteen miles of the mouth) from Te Teko, where there is hotel accommodation close to the river. Te Teko is reached from Rotorua Station, on the Auckland–Rotorua Railway; thence by forty-five miles of road *viâ* Lakes Rotorua and Rotoiti: also by fifteen miles of road from Whakatane, where there is hotel accommodation. Thirty miles further up the river is Galatea, where there is accommodation close to the river; and to this point there is a road running parallel to the river at a distance of from half a mile to two miles and a half. Galatea is forty-five miles from Rotorua Township, on the road which continues to Lake Waikaremoana, and thence to the Hawke's Bay Wairoa. Fifty miles further up the river, by road from Galatea, is the Rangitaiki Hotel, situated on the bank of the river, and on the Rotorua – Taupo – Napier Road, seventy-three miles from Lake Rotorua, twenty-three from Lake Taupo, and seventy-eight from Napier. The road from Wanganui to the lower end of Lake Taupo also joins this road twenty-three miles before reaching the Rangitaiki Hotel. The country about the river and tributaries is practically uninhabited, and the most convenient means of reaching the river and tributaries is to make this hotel the headquarters, and to have a tent for camping on the

river and on the many tributaries in the neighbourhood. There are forest tracks to some of the
largest as well as to some of the smaller tributaries, which cannot be given here. Information
about these can be got at the hotel.

WAIKOWHEWHE Burn, tributary of Rangitaiki
River.—Shingle and pumice bottom. Banks low
and fairly clear. Wadeable partly. Landing
deep, also good. Course, nine miles. Contains
brown and rainbow trout. Reached from Te Teko
by sixteen miles of road; from Galatea by fourteen
miles of same road. For approach and accommodation see "Rangitaiki River," already mentioned.

PAHEKEHEKE Burn, tributary of Rangitaiki
River.—Shingle and pumice bottom. Banks low
and fairly clear. Wadeable partly. Landing
deep, also good. Course, eight miles. Contains
brown and rainbow trout. Reached from Te Teko
by twenty miles of road; from Galatea by ten
miles of same road. For approach and accommodation see "Rangitaiki River," already mentioned.

POKAIROA Stream, tributary of the Rangitaiki
River.—Shingle and pumice bottom. Banks low
and fairly clear. Wadeable partly. Landing
deep, also good. Course, twelve miles. Contains
brown and rainbow trout. Reached from Te Teko
by twenty-three miles of road; from Galatea by
seven miles of same road. For approach and
accommodation see "Rangitaiki River," already
mentioned.

MANGAHARAKEKE Stream, tributary of Pokairoa
Stream.—Shingle and pumice bottom. Banks low
and fairly clear. Wadeable partly. Landing deep,
also good. Course, twelve miles. Contains brown
and rainbow trout. Reached from Te Teko by
twenty-three miles of road to the Pokairoa Stream,
then up that stream for two miles and a
half; from Galatea by seven miles of same road,

then following up the Pokairoa Stream. For approach and accommodation see " Pokairoa Stream," already mentioned.

NGATAMAWAHINE Stream, tributary of Rangitaiki River.—Shingle and pumice bottom. Banks low and fairly clear. Wadeable partly. Landing deep, also good. Course, eighteen miles. Contains brown and rainbow trout. Reached from Te Teko by twenty-six miles of road; from Galatea by four miles of same road. For approach and accommodation see " Rangitaiki River," already mentioned.

HOROMANGA Stream, tributary of Rangitaiki River.—Shingle and pumice bottom Banks low and fairly clear. Wadeable partly. Landing deep, also good. Course, fourteen miles. Contains brown and rainbow trout. Reached (to the mouth) from Te Teko by twenty-six miles of road ; from Galatea by four miles of same road. For approach and accommodation see " Rangitaiki River," already mentioned.

WAI-IRO-HIA Burn, tributary of Rangitaiki River. —Shingle and pumice bottom. Banks low and fairly clear. Wadeable partly. Landing deep, also good. Course, six miles. Contains brown and rainbow trout. Reached from Galatea by three miles of road ; from Rangitaiki Hotel by forty-seven miles of same road. For approach and accommodation see " Rangitaiki River," already mentioned.

WHIRINAKI River, tributary of Rangitaiki River. —Shingle, pumice, boulder, and rock bottom and bed. Banks low and fairly clear in lower reaches ; then various and much forest-clad in upper. Wadeable partly. Landing deep, also good. Course, fifty-three miles. Contains brown and rainbow trout. Reached (to the mouth) from Galatea by three miles of road ; from Rangitaiki Hotel by forty-seven miles of same road. For approach and accommodation see " Rangitaiki River," already mentioned.

MANGAWHIRI Burn, tributary of Whirinaki River. —Shingle and pumice bottom and bed. Banks low and clear in lower reaches, steep and partly forest-clad in upper. Wadeable partly. Landing deep, also good. Course, about nine miles. Contains brown and rainbow trout. Reached by following up the Whirinaki River for five miles from the mouth. For approach and accommodation see " Whirinaki River," already mentioned.

OKAHU Burn, tributary of Whirinaki River.— Shingle, pumice, and boulder bottom and bed. Banks various and much forest-clad. Wadeable partly. Landing deep, also good. Course, seven miles. Contains brown and rainbow trout. Reached by following the Whirinaki River for sixteen miles from the mouth. For approach and accommodation see " Whirinaki River," already mentioned.

PEKEPEKE Burn, tributary of Rangitaiki River.— Shingle and pumice bottom. Banks low and fairly clear. Wadeable partly. Landing deep, also good. Course, seven miles. Contains brown and rainbow trout. Reached from Galatea in five miles, by road, and by following up the Rangitaiki River; from the Rangitaiki Hotel in forty-five miles, by road, and by following down the Rangitaiki River. For approach and accommodation see " Rangitaiki River," already mentioned.

WHEAO River, tributary of Rangitaiki River.— Shingle, pumice, boulder, and rock bottom and bed. Banks low and fairly clear in lower reaches, then steep and partly forest-clad in upper. Wadeable partly. Landing deep, also good. Course, twenty-two miles. Contains brown and rainbow trout. Reached (to the mouth) from Galatea in fourteen miles, by road, and by following up the Rangitaiki River; from the Rangitaiki Hotel in thirty-six miles, by road, and by following down the Rangitaiki River. For approach and accommodation see " Rangitaiki River," already mentioned.

Otamatea Stream, tributary of the Rangitaiki River.—Shingle and pumice bottom. Banks low mostly, and fairly clear. Wadeable partly. Landing deep, also good. Course, sixteen miles. Contains brown and rainbow trout. Reached (to the mouth) from Galatea in thirty-six miles, by road, and by following up the Rangitaiki River; from the Rangitaiki Hotel in fourteen miles (to the mouth), by following down the Rangitaiki River; and from the Rangitaiki Hotel in three miles (to the upper half). For approach and accommodation see "Rangitaiki River," already mentioned.

Lake Puarua, Tributary of Rangitaiki River.—Shingle and pumice bottom and beaches. Banks low and fairly clear. Wadeable partly. Landing deep, also good. Length, half a mile; breadth, quarter of a mile. Height above sea-level, 1,000 ft. Rather shallow, with several small feeders. Contains brown and rainbow trout. Reached from the Rangitaiki Hotel by following up the Rangitaiki River for eight miles. For approach and accommodation see "Rangitaiki River," already mentioned.

Whakatane River. — Estuary, mud and sand bottom for three miles; navigable for boats for ten or fifteen miles; then shingle bottom and bed. Banks low and fairly clear in lower reaches, various and partly forest-clad in upper. Wadeable partly. Landing deep, also good. Course, sixty-five miles. Has many feeders. Contains brown and rainbow trout. Reached from Whakatane, at the mouth, where there is hotel accommodation. Whakatane reached from Te Teko by fifteen miles of road. For approach and accommodation see "Rangitaiki River," already mentioned; also by steamer from Tauranga and Opotiki. A track runs nearly the whole course of the river from the mouth, branching off to Lake Waikaremoana on one side and to Ahikereru on the other; then it branches again *via* the Whirinaki River and

Rangitaiki River to Galatea, and *via* the Whiri-naki, Wheao, and down the Waipunga River to the Taupo–Napier Road at Runanga, which is ten miles from the Rangitaiki Hotel.

WAIOEKA River (discharges into Opotiki Harbour).—Tidal for two miles, with mud bottom; then shingle bottom; higher, boulder and rock bottom and bed. Banks for eight miles low and fairly clear; then higher, steep, and forest-clad. Wadeable partly. Landing deep, also good. Course, fifty-two miles. Contains brown and rainbow trout. Reached (to the mouth) from Opotiki, where there is hotel accommodation, and which is reached by various coastal steamers, also by tracks to Tauranga and Gisborne.

KORANGA Stream, tributary of Waioeka River.—Shingle, boulder, and rock bottom and bed. Banks mostly steep and forest-clad. Wadeable partly. Landing deep, also good. Course, fifteen miles. Contains brown and rainbow trout. Reached by following up the Waioeka River forty miles from the mouth. For approach and accommodation see " Waioeka River," already mentioned.

OTARA River (discharges into Opotiki Harbour). —Tidal for two miles, with mud bottom; then mud and shingle bottom for two miles; then shingle, boulder, and rock bottom and bed. Banks low and fairly clear for eight miles, then steep and mostly forest-clad. Wadeable partly. Landing deep, also good. Course, thirty miles. Contains brown and rainbow trout. Reached from Opotiki, to which it is close. For approach and accommodation see " Waioeka River," already mentioned.

WAIANA Stream.—Shingle and boulder bottom and bed. Banks low in lower reaches, higher and fairly clear in upper reaches. Wadeable partly. Landing deep, also good. Course, twelve miles. Contains brown and rainbow trout. Reached by tracks from Opotiki and Gisborne. Accommodation uncertain.

Motu River.—Shingle and boulder bottom and bed. Banks low and partly forest-clad in lower reaches, then high and partly forest-clad in upper. Wadeable partly. Landing deep, also good. Course, seventy miles. Contains brown and rainbow trout. Reached by tracks from Opotiki and Gisborne. Accommodation uncertain.

Manuriki Burn, tributary of Motu River.— Shingle bottom and bed. Banks low and partly clear. Wadeable partly. Landing deep, also good. Course, seven miles. Contains brown and rainbow trout. For approach and accommodation see " Motu River," already mentioned.

Mangatutara Stream, tributary of Motu River. —Shingle bed. Banks partly clear. Wadeable partly. Landing deep, also good. Course, sixteen miles. Contains brown and rainbow trout. For approach and accommodation see " Motu River," already mentioned.

Whahunga Stream, tributary of Motu River.— Shingle bed. Banks various and partly clear. Wadeable partly. Landing deep, also good. Course, thirteen miles. Contains brown and rainbow trout. For approach and accommodation see " Motu River," already mentioned.

Mangakirikiri Burn, tributary of Motu River.— Shingle bottom and bed. Banks partly clear. Wadeable partly. Landing deep, also good. Course, seven miles. Contains brown and rainbow trout. For approach and accommodation see " Motu River," already mentioned.

Takaputahi River, tributary of Motu River.— Shingle bottom and bed. Banks partly clear. Wadeable partly. Landing deep, also good. Course, twenty-two miles. Contains brown and rainbow trout. For approach and accommodation see " Motu River," already mentioned.

Mangaotane Stream, tributary of Motu River.— Shingle and boulder bottom and bed. Banks low and high and partly clear. Wadeable partly.

Landing deep, also good. Course, thirteen miles.
Contains brown and rainbow trout. For approach
and accommodation see " Motu River," already
mentioned.

HAPARAPARA Stream.—Shingle bottom and bed.
Banks low in lower reaches, then high and partly
clear. Wadeable partly. Landing deep, also good.
Course, sixteen miles. Contains brown and rain-
bow trout. Reached by tracks from Opotiki and
Gisborne. Accommodation uncertain.

TE KEREU Stream.—Shingle bottom and bed.
Banks low in lower reaches, higher in upper, and
fairly clear. Wadeable partly. Landing mostly
good. Course, sixteen miles. Contains brown
and rainbow trout. Reached by tracks from Opotiki, Waiapu, and Gisborne. Accommodation uncertain.

RAUKOKORE River. — Shingle bottom and bed,
with rock and boulders in upper reaches. Banks
low and fairly clear in lower reaches, higher and
partly clear in upper. Wadeable partly. Landing
deep, also good. Course, twenty-six miles Contains brown and rainbow trout. Reached by
tracks from Opotiki, Waiapu, and Gisborne. Accommodation uncertain.

WAIKURA Stream, tributary of Raukokore River.
—Shingle bottom and bed. Banks moderate in
lower reaches, high and steep and partly clear in
upper. Wadeable partly. Landing deep, also
good. Course, twelve miles. Contains brown and
rainbow trout. For approach and accommodation
see " Raukokore River," already mentioned.

WHANGAPARAOA Stream. — Shingle bottom and
bed in lower reaches, shingle and boulder bed in
upper. Banks low near the mouth, then higher
and more or less forest-clad. Wadeable partly.
Landing deep, also good. Course, seventeen
miles. Contains brown and rainbow trout.
Reached by tracks from Opotiki, Waiapu, and
Gisborne. Accommodation uncertain.

MOHAU Stream, tributary of Whangaparaoa Stream. — Shingle bottom and bed in lower reaches, shingle and boulder bed in upper. Banks moderate height in lower reaches, steep and high in upper, a good deal forest-encumbered. Wadeable partly. Landing deep, also good. Course, eleven miles. Contains brown and rainbow trout. For approach and accommodation see " Whangaparaoa Stream," already mentioned.

KARAKATUWHERO Stream.—Shingle bottom and bed in lower reaches, shingle and boulder bed in upper. Banks low and clear for two miles, then steep and high and more or less forest-clad. Wadeable partly. Landing deep, also good. Course, fourteen miles. Contains brown and rainbow trout. Reached by tracks from Opotiki, Waiapu, and Gisborne. There is hotel accommodation at Te Araroa, close to the mouth of the Awatere Stream, four miles off.

AWATERE Stream.—Shingle bottom and bed in lower reaches, shingle and boulder bed in upper. Banks low and fairly clear for three miles; then high, broken, and forest-clad. Wadeable partly. Landing deep, also good. Course, nineteen miles. Contains brown and rainbow trout. Reached from Te Araroa, where there is hotel accommodation, at the mouth of the stream. Also reached by tracks from Opotiki, Waiapu, and Gisborne.

TAURANGAKOUTUKU Stream, tributary of Awatere Stream.—Shingle and boulder bottom and bed. Banks broken and mostly forest-clad. Wadeable partly. Landing deep, also good. Course, eleven miles. For approach and accommodation see " Awatere Stream," already mentioned.

WAIAPU River.—Shingle bed in lower and middle reaches and boulder bed in upper. Banks low and fairly clear for a few miles, then various and more or less forest-clad. Wadeable partly. Landing deep, also good. Course, seventy miles. Contains brown and rainbow trout. Reached by tracks from Opotiki and Gisborne. Accommodation uncertain.

Poroporo Stream, tributary of Waiapu River.— Shingle bottom and bed in lower reaches, shingle bed in upper reaches. Banks low and fairly clear for a few miles, then more or less forest-clad. Wadeable partly. Landing deep, also good. Course, fourteen miles. Contains brown and rainbow trout. For approach and accommodation see " Waiapu River," already mentioned.

Mangaoporo Stream, tributary of Waiapu River. —Shingle bottom and bed in lower reaches, shingle and boulder bed in upper. Banks low and fairly clear for two or three miles, then steeper and a good deal forest-clad. Wadeable partly. Landing deep, also good. Course, fourteen miles. Contains brown and rainbow trout. For approach and accommodation see " Waiapu River," already mentioned.

Tapuwaeroa River, tributary of Waiapu River. —Shingle bottom and bed in lower reaches, shingle and boulder bed in upper. Banks moderate in lower reaches, broken and steep in upper, more or less forest-clad. Wadeable partly. Landing deep, also good. Course, twenty-three miles. Contains brown and rainbow trout. For approach and accommodation see " Waiapu River," already mentioned.

Makarika Stream, tributary of Waiapu River.— Shingle bottom and bed. Banks moderate, forest-encumbered here and there. Wadeable partly. Landing deep, also good. Course, fourteen miles. Contains brown and rainbow trout. For approach and accommodation see " Waiapu River," already mentioned.

Ihimgia Stream, tributary of Waiapu River.— Shingle bottom and bed. Banks moderate and fairly clear in lower reaches, steeper and more or less forest-clad in upper. Wadeable partly. Landing deep, also good. Course, eleven miles. Contains brown and rainbow trout. For approach and accommodation see " Waiapu River," already mentioned.

WAITAHAIA Stream, tributary of Waiapu River. —Shingle bottom and bed in lower reaches, shingle and boulder bed in upper. Banks various; steep in upper reaches, and more or less forest-clad. Wadeable partly. Landing deep, also good. Course, eighteen miles. Contains brown and rainbow trout. For approach and accommodation see " Waiapu River," already mentioned.

MANGAMAUNU Burn, tributary of Waiapu River. —Shingle bed. Banks broken, and more or less forest-clad. Wadeable. Landing mostly good. Course, ten miles. Contains brown and rainbow trout. For approach and accommodation see " Waiapu River," already mentioned.

UAWA River.—Estuary, sand and mud bottom; navigable for vessels of light draught for ten miles; then shingle and papa bottom and bed. Banks in lower reaches low and fairly clear; in upper higher, and more or less forest-clad. Wadeable partly. Landing deep, also good. Course, thirty-four miles, contains brown and rainbow trout. Reached from Uawa, where there is hotel accommodation, and which is at the mouth. Uawa is reached by tracks from Opotiki, and is thirty-five miles by coach-road from Gisborne. Reached by coastal steamer from Gisborne to Uawa.

MANGAHEIA Stream, tributary of Uawa River.— Shingle and papa bottom and bed. Banks low and fairly clear in lower reaches, higher and more or less forest-clad in upper. Wadeable partly. Landing deep, also good. Course, sixteen miles. Contains brown and rainbow trout. Reached from Uawa, which is close to the mouth. For approach and accommodation see " Uawa River " already mentioned.

PAKARAE River.—Shingle and papa bottom and bed. Banks low and fairly clear in lower reaches, higher and more or less forest-clad in upper. Wadeable partly. Landing deep, also good. Course, thirty-four miles. Contains brown and rainbow trout. Reached from Pakarae, which is at the mouth, and is eighteen miles from Gisborne by coach-road. Accommodation uncertain.

WAIOMOKU Stream.—Shingle and papa bottom and bed. Banks low and clear in lower reaches, higher and more or less forest-clad in upper. Wadeable partly. Landing deep, also good. Course, eleven miles. Reached from Gisborne by sixteen miles of coach-road, which crosses it a mile from the mouth. Accommodation uncertain.

WAIMATA RIVER.—Mud, sand, and shingle bottom for a few miles ; then shingle and papa bottom and bed. Banks low and fairly clear in lower reaches, higher and more or less forest-clad in upper. Wadeable partly. Landing deep, also good. Course, twenty-six miles. Contains brown and rainbow trout. Reached from Gisborne, which is at the mouth, and where there is hotel accommodation. Gisborne is reached by coastal steamers from Auckland, Napier, and Wellington, and by tracks from Opotiki and Napier.

WAIPAOA River.—Sand and mud bottom for a few miles, then shingle and papa bottom and bed. Banks in lower reaches low and fairly clear ; higher in upper, and more or less forest-clad. Wadeable partly. Landing deep, also good. Course, sixty-five miles. Contains brown and rainbow trout. Reached from Gisborne (to within six miles from the mouth) by six miles of road. Two miles further up the river by road is Patutahi, where is hotel accommodation ; six miles further up the river by road is Ormond, where there is hotel accommodation. Gisborne, where there is hotel accommodation, is reached by coastal steamer from Auckland, Napier, and Wellington, and by tracks from Opotiki and Napier.

Waihora Stream, tributary of Waipaoa River.—
Shingle and papa bottom and bed. Banks in lower
reaches low, and fairly clear; in upper, higher and
more or less forest-clad. Wadeable partly. Landing deep, also good. Course, eighteen miles. Contains brown and rainbow trout. Reached from Te
Karaka (where there is hotel accommodation),
within a mile of the mouth. Te Karaka is twenty
miles by coach-road from Gisborne. For approach
and accommodation see " Waipaoa River," already
mentioned.

Waikohu River, tributary of Waipaoa River.—
Shingle, boulder, and rock bottom and bed. Banks
moderate in lower reaches, and more or less forest-
clad in upper. Wadeable partly. Landing deep,
also good. Course, twenty-three miles. Contains
brown and rainbow trout. Reached from Te Karaka (where there is hotel accommodation), a mile
from the mouth. Te Karaka is twenty miles by
coach-road from Gisborne. For approach and accommodation see " Waipaoa River," already mentioned. The Gisborne–Opotiki track runs close to
the river for its whole length.

Wharekopae River, tributary of Waikohu River.
— Shingle and boulder bottom and bed. Banks
various and partly forest-clad. Wadeable partly.
Landing deep, also good. Course, twenty-five
miles. Contains brown and rainbow trout. For
approach and accommodation see " Waikohu
River," already mentioned.

Totangi Burn, tributary of Wharekopae River.
—Shingle bed. Banks fairly clear. Wadeable.
Landing good. Course, ten miles. Contains
brown and rainbow trout. For approach and accommodation see " Wharekopae River," already
mentioned.

Waingaromia Stream, tributary of Waipaoa
River.—Shingle, boulder, and rock bottom and
bed. Banks various, and more or less forest-clad.
Wadeable partly. Landing deep, also good.

Course, seventeen miles. Contains brown and rainbow trout. Reached (to the mouth) from Te Karaka (where there is hotel accommodation) by ten miles of track. For approach and accommodation see " Waipaoa River," already mentioned.

MANGATU Stream, tributary of Waipaoa River.— Shingle, boulder, and rock bottom and bed. Banks various, more or less scrub-encumbered and forest-clad. Wadeable partly. Landing deep, also good. Course, seventeen miles. Contains brown and rainbow trout. Reached from Te Karaka (where there is hotel accommodation) by track of nine miles to the mouth. For approach and accommodation see " Waipaoa River," already mentioned.

URUKOKOMOKO Burn, tributary of Mangatu Stream.—Shingle and boulder bed. Banks partly clear and partly forest-clad. Wadeable. Landing good. Course, nine miles. For approach and accommodation see " Mangatu Stream," already mentioned.

MARAETAHA Stream.—Shingle and papa bottom and bed. Banks fairly low and clear in lower reaches, partly forest-clad in upper. Wadeable partly. Landing deep, also good. Course, twelve miles. Contains brown and rainbow trout. Reached from Gisborne by road and track of eighteen miles to within a mile of the mouth, and by track from Wairoa. Accommodation uncertain.

KOPUWHARO Stream.—Shingle and papa bottom and bed. Banks fairly clear in lower reaches, more or less forest-clad in upper. Wadeable partly. Landing deep, also good. Course, sixteen miles. Contains brown and rainbow trout. Reached from Gisborne by thirty-eight miles of road and track to within three miles of the mouth, and from Wairoa by thirty miles of track. Accommodation uncertain.

NUHAKA Stream.—Shingle and papa bottom and bed. Banks fairly clear. Wadeable partly. Landing deep, also good. Course, thirteen miles. Contains brown and rainbow trout. Reached from Gisborne by track, and from Wairoa by track of twenty miles, which crosses it a mile from the mouth. Accommodation uncertain.

WAIROA River (Hawke's Bay).—Estuary, mud and sand, navigable for a short distance; rock, shingle, and papa bottom and bed in upper reaches. Banks various. Wadeable partly. Landing deep, also good. Course, eighty miles, including the part called Hangaroa. Contains brown and rainbow trout. Reached by steamer to Wairoa from Napier, forty miles' sail; also by track from Gisborne and Napier. There are several hotels and livery stables in Wairoa.

WAIAU River, tributary of Wairoa River. — Shingle, papa, and rock bottom and bed. Banks low and fairly clear in lower reaches; steeper, with more or less forest, in upper reaches. Wadeable partly. Landing deep, also good. Course, sixty-three miles. Contains brown and rainbow trout. Reached from Frasertown, which is at the mouth, and five miles by road from Wairoa Township. A road from Frasertown runs for ten miles up the bank of the river. For approach and accommodation see " Wairoa River," already mentioned.

TUTAEKURI Burn, tributary of Waiau River.— Shingle bottom and bed. Banks low and clear in lower reaches, forest-clad in upper. Wadeable partly. Landing deep, also good. Course, seven miles. Contains brown and rainbow trout. Reached to the mouth) from Frasertown by three miles of road. For approach and accommodation see " Waiau River," already mentioned.

WAIKARETAHEKE Stream, tributary of Waiau River.—Rock, shingle, and boulder bottom and bed. Banks fairly clear. Wadeable partly. Landing deep, also good. Course, nineteen miles. Contains brown and rainbow trout. Reached (to the mouth) by road of fifteen miles from Wairoa Township, and by ten miles of same road from Frasertown. This road continues for twenty miles up the bank of the stream to its outlet from Lake Waikaremoana. For approach and accommodation see " Waiau River," already mentioned.

Lake Waïkaremoana, tributary of Waikaretaheke Stream.—This is a beautiful sheet of water, mostly wooded to the water's edge, with numerous bays, inlets, islets, and small feeders. Shingle, rock, and papa bottom. Banks mostly wooded, and in places very precipitous. Wadeable here and there. Landing deep, also good. Length, eleven miles; breadth, six miles. Height above sea-level, 2,015 ft. Contains brown and rainbow trout. Reached from Wairoa Township by thirty-five miles of road, which follows up the bank of the Wairoa and Waiau Rivers and the Waikaretaheke Stream. For approach and accommodation see " Waikaretaheke Stream," already mentioned.

Aniwaniwa Burn, tributary of Lake Waikaremoana.—Shingle, rock, and papa bottom and bed. Banks mostly steep and forest-clad. Wadeable partly. Landing deep, also good. Course, seven miles. Contains brown and rainbow trout. Reached (to the mouth) in five miles by boat, canoe, road, or track from the point where the Waikaretaheke leaves the lake. For approach and accommodation see " Lake Waikaremoana," already mentioned.

Mangapuwerawera Burn, tributary of Aniwaniwa Burn.—Shingle, rock, and boulder bottom and bed. Banks steep, broken, and forest-clad. Wadeable partly. Landing deep, also good. Course, one mile. Contains brown and rainbow trout. For approach and accommodation see " Aniwaniwa Burn," already mentioned.

Lake Waikareiti, tributary of Mangapuwerawera Burn.—A beautiful lake, wooded to the water's edge, and with numerous wooded islets. Shingle

CATCH OF TROUT, HAWKE'S BAY DISTRICT.

and rock bottom. Banks undulating and wooded. Wadeable here and there. Landing deep, also good. Length, two miles and a half; breadth, one mile and three-quarters; height above sea-level, 2,500 ft. For approach and accommodation see " Mangapuwerawera Burn," already mentioned.

WAIHI Stream, tributary of Waiau River.— Shingle, rock, and boulder bottom and bed. Banks various, and partly forest-clad in upper reaches. Wadeable partly. Landing deep, also good. Course, twelve miles. Contains brown and rainbow trout. Reached (to the mouth) by following up the Waiau River for twenty miles from Frasertown. For approach and accommodation see " Waiau River," already mentioned.

MANGAONE Stream, tributary of Waiau River.— Shingle and rock bottom and bed. Banks fairly clear in lower reaches, more or less forest-clad in upper. Wadeable partly. Landing deep, also good. Course, thirteen miles. Contains brown and rainbow trout. Reached (to the mouth) by following up the Waiau River for twenty-three miles from Frasertown. For approach and accommodation see " Waiau River," already mentioned.

MANGARUHE River, tributary of Wairoa River.— Rock, shingle, and boulder bottom and bed. Banks broken, and more or less forest-clad. Wadeable partly. Landing deep, also good. Course, twenty-one miles. Contains brown and rainbow trout. Reached (to the mouth) from Wairoa by following up the Wairoa River for eleven miles, and from Frasertown by the same road in six miles. For approach and accommodation see " Wairoa River," already mentioned.

MANGAPOIKE River, tributary of Wairoa River.— Shingle, papa, rock, and boulder bottom and bed. Banks broken and more or less forest-clad. Wadeable partly. Landing deep, also good. Course, twenty-six miles. Contains brown and rainbow trout. Reached (to the mouth) from Wairoa by fifteen miles of road up the bank of the Wairoa River, and from Frasertown by ten miles of the same road. For approach and accommodation see " Wairoa River," already mentioned.

MAKARETU River, tributary of Mangapoike River. —Shingle, papa, and rock bottom and bed. Banks moderately clear. Wadeable partly. Landing deep, also good. Course, twenty-one miles. Contains brown and rainbow trout. For approach and accommodation see " Mangapoike River," already mentioned.

MANGARANGIORA Stream, tributary of Mangapoike River.—Shingle, papa, and rock bottom and bed. Banks broken, and more or less forest-clad. Wadeable partly. Landing deep, also good. Course, thirteen miles. Contains brown and rainbow trout. For approach and accommodation see " Mangapoike River," already mentioned.

RUAKITURI River, tributary of Wairoa River.— Shingle, papa, rock, and boulder bottom and bed. Banks broken, and more or less forest-clad. Wadeable partly. Landing deep, also good. Course, forty-two miles. Contains brown and rainbow trout. Just below where the river joins the Wairoa River there is a high waterfall. Reached (to the mouth) from Wairoa by twenty-two miles of road up the bank of the Wairoa River, and from Frasertown by seventeen miles of the same road. For approach and accommodation see " Wairoa River," already mentioned.

WAIKURA Stream, tributary of Wairoa River.— Shingle and rock bottom and bed. Banks broken, and more or less forest-clad. Wadeable partly. Landing deep, also good. Course, fifteen miles. Contains brown and rainbow trout. Reached (to the mouth) from Tiniroto in twelve miles, by partly following up the Wairoa River. Tiniroto, where there is hotel accommodation, is reached from Wairoa by twenty-seven miles of road which follows up the Wairoa River, and from Frasertown by twenty-two miles of the same road. Tiniroto is also reached from Gisborne by forty-two miles of road. For approach and accommodation see " Wairoa River," already mentioned.

WAIHUA Stream.—Shingle, rock, and papa bottom and bed. Banks fairly clear in lower reaches, forest-clad in upper. Wadeable partly. Landing deep, also good. Course, seventeen miles. Contains brown and rainbow trout. Reached (to within a mile of the mouth) from Wairoa by twelve miles of the Wairoa–Napier track. For approach and accommodation see " Wairoa River," already mentioned.

MOHAKA River.—Estuary, mud and sand; then shingle and boulder bottom and bed. Banks sometimes papa cliffs, but often only on one side, the other being bare shingle. Wadeable partly. Landing mostly good. Course, seventy-six miles. Contains brown and rainbow trout. Reached (to the mouth) by steamer from Napier, a few hours' sail, or from Wairoa (where there is hotel accommodation) by eighteen miles of track. Wairoa is reached by steamer from Napier by forty miles' sail. The greater part of the river and tributaries can be best reached from the Napier–Taupo Coach-road, on which there are hotels at the Mohaka Bridge, forty miles from Napier; at Tarawera, on the Waipunga River, fifty miles from Napier; also at the Rangitaiki River Bridge, seventy-eight miles from Napier.

TEHOE Stream, tributary of Mohaka River.— Shingle and boulder bottom and bed. Banks steep. Wadeable. Landing deep, also good. Course, fifteen miles. Contains brown and rainbow trout. Reached (to the mouth) from the Mohaka Bridge by following down the Mohaka River seventeen miles. For approach and accommodation see " Mohaka River," already mentioned.

Hautapu Burn, tributary to Tehoe Stream.—Shingle and boulder bottom and bed. Banks steep. Wadeable. Landing deep, also good. Course, seven miles. Contains brown and rainbow trout. For approach and accommodation see "Tehoe Stream," already mentioned.

Waipunga River, tributary of Mohaka River.—Shingle, boulder, and rock bottom and bed. Banks mostly high and steep, with some forest and scrub. Wadeable. Landing deep, also good. Course, twenty-five miles. Contains brown and rainbow trout. Reached (to the mouth) from the Mohaka Bridge by following down the Mohaka River seven miles, also from the Napier–Taupo Coach-road, which for many miles runs close to it. There is hotel accommodation at Tarawera, close to the river. For approach and accommodation see "Mohaka River," already mentioned.

Puneketura Burn, tributary of Mohaka River.—Shingle and boulder bottom and bed. Banks rather high and clear in lower reaches, forest-clad in upper. Wadeable. Landing deep, also good. Course, ten miles. Contains brown and rainbow trout. Reached (to the mouth) from the Mohaka Bridge by following up the Mohaka River four miles. For approach and accommodation see "Mohaka River," already mentioned.

Aripia River, tributary of Mohaka River.—Shingle, boulder, and pumice bottom and bed. Banks rather steep, fairly clear, with a little scrub and forest. Wadeable partly. Landing deep, also good. Course, twenty-one miles. Contains brown and rainbow trout. Reached (to the mouth) from the Mohaka Bridge by following up the Mohaka River eight miles ; also (to the upper waters) from the Rangitaiki Bridge Hotel. For approach and accommodation see "Mohaka River," already mentioned.

Taharua Stream, tributary of Mohaka River.—Shingle, boulder, rock, and pumice bottom and bed. Banks fairly clear, rather steep and high. Wadeable partly. Landing deep, also good. Course, twelve miles. Contains brown and rainbow trout. Reached (to the mouth) from the Mohaka Bridge by following up the Mohaka River twenty-five miles; or (to the upper waters) from the Rangitaiki Bridge Hotel. For approach and accommodation see " Mohaka River," already mentioned.

Esk Stream.—Estuary short, with shingle and sand bottom, then shingle bed. Banks rather willow-encumbered in lower reaches, fairly clear in upper. Wadeable partly. Landing deep, also good. Course, twenty miles. Contains brown and rainbow trout. Reached (to the mouth) from Petane, where there is hotel accommodation, within two miles. Petane is seven miles from Napier, on the Napier–Taupo Coach-road. Two miles from the mouth, on the bank, is Eskdale, where there is hotel accommodation, ten miles from Napier on this road. For seven miles above this a road runs close to the stream. Seventeen miles above Eskdale, on the same road, is Pohui, where there is hotel accommodation, and where there are several trout streams.

Tutaekuri River.—Estuary, mud, sand, and shingle. The lower part of this is the old and present Napier Harbour, available for coastal steamers and craft; the upper part is known as the Inner Harbour, has mud and shingle bottom, and is navigable for boats for four miles from the mouth of the river, which is rather slow for the first four miles, with mud and shingle bottom, then shingle bed. Banks low and alluvial for eight miles; then low and open for ten miles; and then steeper, and a little forest-clad in upper reaches. Wadeable. Landing good. Course, forty-three miles. Contains brown and rainbow trout. Reached (to the mouth) from Napier, which is close to it, and where there is hotel accommodation. A road runs from the mouth of the river for twenty-six miles, close to the bank. On this road, two miles from the mouth, is Meanee, where there is hotel accommodation; there is also hotel accommodation at Taradale, two miles further up; at Puketapu, six miles further; and at Waikonini, twelve miles above Puketapu.

MANGAONE Stream, tributary of Tutaekuri River. —Shingle bottom and bed. Banks moderate and fairly clear. Wadeable. Landing mostly good. Course, eighteen miles. Contains brown and rainbow trout. Reached (to the mouth) from Puketapu by six miles of road. For approach and accommodation see "Tutaekuri River," already mentioned.

WAIKONINI Burn, tributary of Tutaekuri River.— Shingle bed. Banks moderate and fairly clear. Wadeable. Landing mostly good. Course, eight miles. Contains brown and rainbow trout. Reached (to the mouth) from Puketapu by ten miles of road. For approach and accommodation see "Tutaekuri River," already mentioned.

MANGATUTU Stream, tributary of Tutaekuri River. —Shingle bed. Banks moderate and fairly clear in lower reaches, partly forest-clad in upper. Wadeable partly. Landing deep, also good. Course, twelve miles. Contains brown and rainbow trout. Reached (to the mouth) by five miles of road from the Waikonini Hotel. A road runs up the stream for nearly its whole length. For approach and accommodation see "Tutaekuri River," already mentioned.

OTUKARARA Burn, tributary to Tutaekuri River.— Shingle bed. Banks moderate and fairly clear. Wadeable. Landing mostly good. Course, six miles. Contains brown and rainbow trout. Reached (to the mouth) by four miles of road from the Waikonini Hotel. For approach and accommodation see "Tutaekuri River," already mentioned.

NGARURORO River.—The main river is sometimes affected by snow until December. Estuary short, with shingle bottom; navigable for boats for a mile or two; then shingle and boulder bed. Banks for first twenty miles low and fairly clear; then partly low, partly cliffs, and fairly clear till towards the source, where they become more or less forest-clad. Wadeable. Landing mostly good. Course, eighty miles. Contains brown and rainbow trout. Reached from Hastings Station (where there is hotel accommodation), on the Napier–Wellington–New Plymouth Railway. From here a coach-road of thirteen miles leads up the river to Maraekakaho, on the bank, where there is accommodation. Twenty-nine miles further up the river is Kuripapanga, where there is hotel accommodation on the bank, and thirty miles from the source. Kuripapanga is thirty-seven miles from Hastings and fifty miles from Napier by road.

OKAWA Stream, tributary of Ngaruroro River.—Shingle bottom. Banks fairly clear. Wadeable partly. Landing deep, also good. Course, twelve miles. Contains brown and rainbow trout. Reached (to the mouth) from Hastings by seven miles of road. For approach and accommodation see " Ngaruroro River," already mentioned.

WAITIO Burn, tributnry of Ngaruroro River.—Shingle bottom. Banks moderate and fairly clear. Wadeable. Landing deep, also good. Course, nine miles. Contains brown and rainbow trout. Reached (to the mouth) from Hastings by eight miles of road. For approach and accommodation see " Ngaruroro River," already mentioned.

MARAEKAKAHO Burn, tributary of Ngaruroro River.—Shingle bottom and bed. Banks fairly clear. Wadeable. Landing mostly good. Course, ten miles. Contains brown and rainbow trout. Reached (to the mouth) from Maraekakaho, which is close by. For approach and accommodation see " Ngaruroro River," already mentioned.

Kikowhero Stream, tributary of Ngaruroro River.—Shingle bottom and bed. Banks fairly clear. Wadeable. Landing mostly good. Course, twelve miles. Contains brown and rainbow trout. Reached (to the mouth) from Maraekakaho, which is on the opposite bank of the Ngaruroro River. For approach and accommodation see " Ngaruroro River," already mentioned.

Poporangi Stream, tributary of Ngaruroro River. — Shingle bottom and bed. Banks in lower reaches fairly clear, in upper forest-clad here and there. Wadeable partly. Landing deep, also good. Course, fourteen miles. Contains brown and rainbow trout. Reached (to within three miles of the mouth) by twelve miles of road from Maraekakaho. For approach and accommodation see " Ngaruroro River," already mentioned.

Ohara Stream, tributary of Poporangi Stream.— Shingle bottom and bed. Banks fairly clear in lower reaches, more or less forest-clad in upper. Course, twelve miles. Contains brown and rainbow trout. For approach and accommodation see " Poporangi Stream," already mentioned.

Taruarau River, tributary of Ngaruroro River.— Shingle and boulder bottom and bed. Banks fairly clear. Wadeable partly. Landing deep, also good. Course, thirty miles. Contains brown and rainbow trout. Reached (to the mouth) by following up the Ngaruroro River for twenty miles from Maraekakaho, or by following the Ngaruroro down for nine miles from Kuripapanga; also reached (to fifteen miles from the mouth) by road of eight miles from Kuripapanga. For approach and accommodation see " Ngaruroro River," already mentioned.

Tukituki River.—Estuary short, with shingle bottom; then shingle bed. Banks mostly low and clear. Wadeable. Landing mostly good. Course seventy miles. Contains brown and rainbow trout. Reached (to the mouth) from East Clive, where there are hotels, and which is two miles from the Farndon Station, on the Napier–Wellington Railway. From Clive roads follow the river nearly up to the source. Also reached (to six miles from the mouth) by six miles of road from the Hastings Station (where there are hotels), on the Napier–Wellington Railway; from the Kaikora Station (where there are hotels), on the Napier–Wellington Railway, and then by seven miles of road to Patangata, which is thirty miles from the mouth, and where there is hotel accommodation on the bank; from the Waipukurau Station, on the Napier-Wellington Railway, where there is a good hotel on the bank, forty-five miles from the mouth, and conveniently situated for going to a number of tributaries, and where vehicles can be obtained. Eleven miles up the river from Waipukurau, and two miles from the bank, is Ongaonga, where there is hotel accommodation.

MAKARA Stream, tributary of the Tukituki River.—Shingle bottom and bed. Banks various, and fairly clear in lower reaches, more or less forest-clad in upper. Wadeable partly. Landing mostly good. Course, twelve miles. Contains brown and rainbow trout. Reached (to the mouth) from Patangata by following down the Tukituki River four miles. For approach and accommodation see "Tukituki River," already mentioned.

MANGARARARA Burn, tributary of Tukituki River.—Shingle bottom and bed. Banks fairly clear. Wadeable. Landing mostly good. Course, seven miles. Contains brown and rainbow trout. Reached (to the mouth) from Patangata in a mile. For approach and accommodation see "Tukituki River," already mentioned.

OMAKARE Stream, tributary of Tukituki River.—Shingle bottom and bed. Banks fairly clear in lower reaches, forest-clad here and there in upper. Wadeable partly. Landing deep, also good.

Course, twelve miles. Contains brown and rainbow trout. Reached (to the mouth) from Patangata by following up the Tukituki River for four miles, or from Waipukurau by following down the Tukituki River ten miles. A road runs near this stream for its whole length. For approach and accommodation see "Tukituki River," already mentioned.

Mangatarata Stream, tributary of Tukituki River.—Mud and shingle bottom. Banks generally low and fairly clear. Wadeable partly. Landing deep, also good. Course, eleven miles. Contains brown and rainbow trout. Reached (to the mouth) from Waipukurau by road of five miles. For approach and accommodation see " Tukituki River," already mentioned.

Makaretu River, tributary of Tukituki River.— Shingle bed. Banks mostly clear, but forest-clad towards source. Wadeable. Landing mostly good. Course, twenty-seven miles. Contains brown and rainbow trout. Reached (to the mouth) by road of four miles from Waipukurau. This road follows the bank of the river nearly to the source. At Takapau Station, on the Napier–Wellington Railway, there is hotel accommodation, three miles from the river and ten from the mouth. For approach and accommodation see " Tukituki River," already mentioned.

Tukipo River, tributary of Makaretu River.— Shingle bed. Banks low and fairly clear for lower half of course, then more or less forest-clad. Wadeable. Landing mostly good. Course, twenty-five miles. Contains brown and rainbow trout. Reached (to the mouth) by five miles of road up the bank of the Tukituki River from Waipukurau. Roads run within moderate distance of the river for twenty miles from the mouth. Accommodation uncertain. For approach and accommodation see " Makaretu River," already mentioned.

MAHARAKEKE Burn, tributary of Makaretu River.
—Shingle and rock bottom. Banks mostly low,
with a little flax. Wadeable partly. Landing
mostly deep. Course, ten miles. Contains brown
and rainbow trout. Reached (to the mouth) by
road of five miles from Waipukurau. For approach and accommodation see "Tukituki River,"
already mentioned.

PORANGAHAU Burn, tributary of Maharakeke
Stream.—Shingle bottom and bed. Banks for the
lower eight miles low, clear, with a little flax;
then forest-clad. Wadeable partly. Landing
deep, also good. Course, ten miles. Contains
brown and rainbow trout. Reached (to the mouth)
by seven miles of road from Waipukurau, and
from the Takapau Station, on the Napier–Wellington Railway. The station is close to the burn
and eight miles from the mouth. For approach
and accommodation sce "Maharakeke Stream,"
already mentioned.

WAIPAWA River, tributary of Tukituki River.—
Shingle bed. Banks low and fairly clear except a
few miles of the upper course, which is forest-clad.
Wadeable. Landing mostly good. Course, thirty
miles. Reached from the Waipawa and Waipukurau Stations (where there are hotels), on the
Napier–Wellington Railway. Waipawa is on the
bank, and three miles from the mouth; Waipukurau is five miles from the mouth. The
Waipawa and Tukituki Rivers are connected at
these places by five miles of railway and also road.
A road runs near the river for nearly the whole
length. Thirteen miles above Waipawa Township
is Ongaonga, where there is hotel accommodation,
which can be reached by going four miles from
the bank. For approach and accommodation see
"Tukituki River," already mentioned.

MANGAONUKU River, tributary of Waipawa River.
—Shingle bottom and bed. Banks fairly clear.
Wadeable partly. Landing deep, also good.

Course, twenty-one miles. Contains brown and rainbrow trout. Reached (to the mouth) by four miles of road from Waipawa Township. A road runs within moderate distance of the stream for the whole length. Accommodation uncertain. For approach and accommodation see " Waipawa River," already mentioned.

Mangamouku Stream, tributary of Mangaonuku River.—Shingle bottom and bed. Banks fairly clear. Wadeable partly. Landing deep, also good. Course, eleven miles. Contains brown and rainbow trout. Reached (to the mouth) by fourteen miles of road from the Waipawa Township. A road runs near this stream for a greater part of the length. Accommodation uncertain. For approach and accommodation see " Mangaonuku River," already mentioned.

Maraetotara Stream.—Shingle and rock bottom. Banks fairly clear and rather high. Wadeable partly. Landing deep, also good. Course, twenty miles. Contains brown and rainbow trout. Reached (to the mouth) by five miles of road from East Clive, where there are hotels, and which is two miles from the Farndon Station, on the Napier–Wellington Railway. The Waimarama Road crosses it seven miles from the mouth, and this road is conveniently reached in six miles from the Hastings Station, where there is hotel accommodation, on the Napier–Wellington Railway.

Porangahau River.—Tidal for three miles, with sand and mud bottom ; then shingle, rock, and mud bottom. Banks mostly clear, with a little forest here and there. Wadeable partly. Landing mostly deep. Course, thirty-five miles. Contains brown and rainbow trout. Reached (to Wanstead, where there is a hotel on the bank of the river) by road of fourteen miles from the Waipukurau Station, on the Napier–Wellington Railway. Wanstead is twenty miles from the mouth, and a road runs within moderate distance of the river the whole way. At Wallingford, six miles further down the river, there is a hotel on the bank ; and at Porangahau, eight miles further down, there is a hotel on the bank.

LAKE PURIMU, tributary of Porangahau River.— Shingle and sand bottom. Banks low and clear. Wadeable here and there. Landing mostly deep. Length, three-quarters of a mile; breadth, a quarter of a mile. Contains brown and rainbow trout. Reached from Wanstead by three miles of road. For approach and accommodation see " Porangahau River," already mentioned.

PURIMU Burn, tributary of Lake Purimu.— Shingle bottom. Banks fairly clear. Wadeable partly. Landing mostly deep. Course, six miles. Contains brown and rainbow trout. Reached from Wanstead by four miles of road. For approach and aceommodation see " Lake Purimu," already mentioned.

WAINUI Stream. — Shingle bottom and bed. Banks fairly clear in lower reaches, more or less forest-clad in upper. Wadeable partly. Landing deep, also good. Course, twelve miles. Contains brown and rainbow trout. Reached from Herbertville, which is at the mouth, and where there is hotel accommodation : Herbertville is the coast terminus of the Dannevirke–Herbertville coaches. This road runs down the bank of the stream most of the length, and at Wimbledon, seven miles from the mouth, there is hotel accommodation.

AKITIO River.—Tidal for a mile ; then mud, shingle, rock, and papa bottom. Banks fairly clear in lower reaches, forest-clad in upper. Wadeable partly. Landing deep, also good. Course, thirty-two miles. Contains brown and rainbow trout. Reached (to the mouth) by horse-track of eleven miles from Herbertville, which is the coast terminus of the coaches from Dannevirke, a station on the Napier–Wellington Railway, where there are hotels. This track continues to Castlepoint.

There is accommodation near the mouth of the river.

WAIHI Stream, tributary of Akitio River.—Shingle, rock, and papa bottom and bed. Banks partly forest clad. Wadeable partly. Landing deep, also good. Course, twelve miles. Contains brown and rainbow trout. Reached (to the mouth) by four miles of road from Weber, where there is hotel accommodation, on the Dannevirke–Herbertville Road. A road runs near the stream a great part of the length. For approach and accommodation see " Akitio River," already mentioned.

AOHANGA River.—Tidal for four miles; then shingle, rock, and papa bottom and bed. Banks fairly clear in lower reaches, more or less forest-clad in upper. Wadeable partly. Landing deep, also good. Course, twenty-nine miles. Contains brown and rainbow trout. Reached (to the mouth) from Akitio by seven miles of the Herbertville–Castlepoint track.

PONGAROA Stream, tributary of Aohanga River.—Shingle, rock, and papa bottom and bed. Banks more or less forest-clad. Wadeable partly. Landing deep, also good. Course, twelve miles. Contains brown and rainbow trout. Reached (to the mouth) by following up the Aohanga River fifteen miles ; also reached by fifteen miles of road from Weber, where there is hotel accommodation, on the Dannevirke–Herbertville Road. For approach and accommodation see " Aohanga River," already mentioned.

MATAIKONA Stream.—Mud, shingle, rock, and papa bottom. Banks fairly clear. Wadeable partly. Landing deep, also good. Course, sixteen miles. Contains brown trout. Reached from Aohanga by ten miles of the Herbertville–Castlepoint track. At Whakataki, seven miles further, there is hotel accommodation. From Whakataki there is a coach-road of forty-two miles to Masterton (where there is hotel accommodation), on the Wellington–Napier–New Plymouth Railway.

WHAREAMA River.—Mud, rock, shingle, and papa bottom. Banks fairly clear. Wadeable partly. Landing deep, also good. Course, thirty miles. Contains brown and rainbow trout. Reached (to Tinui, where there is hotel accommodation) by twelve miles of road from Whakataki. Tinui is close to the bank of the river, on the Castlepoint–Masterton Coach-road, and twenty miles from the mouth.

PAHAOA River.—Mud, rock, shingle, and papa bottom. Banks fairly clear. Wadeable partly. Landing deep, also good. Course, thirty miles. Contains brown trout. Reached (to within ten miles of the mouth) by thirteen miles of road from Martinborough, where there is hotel accommodation. Martinborough is twelve miles by road from Featherston Station (where there is hotel accommodation), on the Wellington–Napier–New Plymouth Railway. Accommodation uncertain.

WAINUIORU River, tributary of Pahaoa River.— Shingle, rock, and papa bottom. Banks fairly clear. Wadeable partly. Landing deep, also good. Course, thirty-seven miles. Contains brown and rainbow trout. Reached (to the mouth) by following up Pahaoa River for ten miles from where the Martinborough Road strikes it ; or from Gladstone (where there is hotel accommodation), by seven miles of road, which crosses the river twenty miles from the mouth. Gladstone is reached by ten miles of road from the Carterton Station (where there is hotel accommodation), on the Wellington–Napier–New Plymouth Railway. For approach and accommodation see " Pahaoa River," already mentioned.

Along the coast from Pahaoa to the outlet of Lake Wairarapa, some fifty miles, there are numerous streams; but of these, as fishing-streams, little is known.

14—Sport.

Lake Wairarapa Mouth, or Lake Onoke, where it runs out to sea, and Lake Wairarapa, contain numbers of splendid sea-run trout, which come and go through a greater part of the year.

LAKE WAIRARAPA (discharges into Palliser Bay by an outlet ten miles long, which includes the lake just mentioned, and part of the Ruamahanga River).—Mud and shingle bottom, and rather shallow. Banks rather low, and fairly clear. Length, twelve miles; breadth, three miles and three-quarters. Height above sea-level, about 50 ft. Contains brown and rainbow trout, some of great size. Several rivers and streams discharge into the lake, of which the Ruamahanga River and Tauherenikau River are the principal. These rivers and numerous tributaries, and a network of feeders, are of the shingle-bed character, abounding in rapids and pools, with generally open banks. They drain the Wairarapa Plain and Valley, which is over fifty miles in length by twelve to twenty in width. The Featherston Station is within four miles of the lake by road, which continues along the whole of the south bank. The rivers running into the lake, and their important tributaries, are conveniently reached from Featherston, Greytown, Carterton, and Masterton Railway-stations (where there is hotel accommodation), and from several flag-stations, on the Wellington–Napier–New Plymouth Railway. Good driving-roads are general in the Wairarapa district. There are also plenty of hotels.

RUAMAHANGA River, tributary of, and passes through the lower end of, Lake Wairarapa.— Shingle bottom where it leaves the lake, opening out some distance up to shingle bed. Banks fairly clear. Wadeable mostly. Landing deep, also good. Course, eighty-six miles. Contains brown and rainbow trout. Reached from the Wellington– Napier–New Plymouth Railway by road of twelve miles from the Featherston Station to Martinborough, which is across and close to the river, and thirty miles from the mouth. A road runs from Martinborough, within a mile or two of the river, to within two miles of the mouth; from Greytown Station, by road of four miles, to forty miles above the mouth; from Carterton Station, by road of eleven miles, to Gladstone, which is across and close to the river, and fifty miles above the mouth; from Masterton Station, by two miles of road, to sixty miles above the mouth. At the stations and townships mentioned there are hotels.

HAUNGARUA River, tributary of Ruamahanga River.—Shingle bottom and bed. Banks fairly clear in lower reaches, more or less forest-clad in upper. Wadeable partly. Landing deep, also good. Course, twenty miles. Contains brown and rainbow trout. Has numerous feeders. Joins Ruamahanga near Martinborough. For approach and accommodation see " Ruamahanga River," already mentioned.

WAIOHINE River, tributary of Ruamahanga River. —Shingle bed; then mountain torrent in upper reaches. Banks fairly clear in lower reaches, forest-clad in upper. Wadeable. Landing mostly good. Course, twenty-seven miles. Contains brown and rainbow trout. Reached (to the lower reaches) in a mile from Woodside Station, on the Wellington–Napier–New Plymouth Railway, and in a mile from Greytown on the Woodside–Greytown Railway. Greytown, where there are hotels, is four miles from the mouth. For approach and accommodation see " Ruamahanga River," already mentioned.

MANGATARIRI Stream, tributary of Waiohine River.—Shingle bed. Banks fairly clear. Wadeable. Landing mostly good. Course, fifteen miles. Contains brown and rainbow trout. Reached (to near the mouth) from the Dalefield or Carterton Stations on the Wellington–Napier–New Plymouth Railway. There is hotel accommodation at Carterton. For approach and accommodation see "Waiohine River," already mentioned.

TAUERU River, tributary of Ruamahanga River. —Shingle, mud, and papa bottom. Banks fairly clear. Wadeable partly. Landing deep, also good. Course, forty-one miles. Contains brown and rainbow trout. Joins the Ruamahanga River near Gladstone, where there is hotel accommodation. For approach and accommodation see "Ruamahanga River," already mentioned.

WAINGAWA River, tributary of Ruamahanga River.--Shingle and rock bed; mountain torrent in upper reaches. Banks fairly clear in lower reaches, forest-clad in upper. Wadeable. Landing good. Course, twenty-five miles. Contains brown and rainbow trout. Reached from Masterton Station (where there is hotel accommodation), on the Wellington–Napier–New Plymouth Railway, from which it is three miles by driving-road. It is also accessible by good roads for a considerable distance up. Masterton is six miles from the mouth. For approach and accommodation see "Ruamahanga River," already mentioned.

MANGATERERA Stream, tributary of Waingawa River.—Shingle bed. Banks low and clear in lower reaches, forest-clad in upper. Wadeable. Landing good. Course, eleven miles. Contains brown and rainbow trout. Reached (to the mouth) by ten miles of road from Masterton. These roads run up and near the bank of the Waingawa River. For approach and accommodation see "Waingawa River," already mentioned.

WANGAEHU Stream, tributary of Ruamahanga River.—Mud and shingle bottom. Banks steep and fairly clear. Wadeable here and there. Landing mostly deep. Course, twenty miles. Contains brown and rainbow trout. Reached from the Masterton Station (where there are hotels), on the Wellington–Napier–New Plymouth Railway, by road of five miles, to within four miles of the mouth. This road continues up the bank of the stream for nearly the whole length. For approach and accommodation see " Ruamahanga River," already mentioned.

WAIPOUA Stream, tributary of Ruamahanga River. —Shingle bed. Banks low and fairly clear. Wadeable. Landing good. Course, twenty miles. Contains brown and rainbow trout. Close to Masterton Station (where there is hotel accommodation, four miles from the mouth), on the Wellington–Napier–New Plymouth Railway. For approach and accommodation see " Ruamahanga River," already mentioned.

KOPUARANGA Stream, tributary of Ruamahanga River.—Shingle bed. Banks low and fairly clear. Wadeable. Landing good. Course, twenty miles. Contains brown and rainbow trout. Reached (to near the mouth) from Masterton Station, on the Wellington–Napier--New Plymouth Railway. Masterton is five miles from the river by road and the railway, both of which then run close to the stream for twelve miles. For approach and accommodation see " Ruamahanga River," already mentioned.

At Masterton is situated the chief fish-hatchery of the Wellington Acclimatisation Society. It has been a great success, has stocked a large proportion of the streams of the colony with trout, and has also supplied Australia with ova. It has for a number of years distributed 1,500,000 trout-fry annually, a total of 10,000,000. The principal sorts kept at the hatchery are the English brown or yellow trout (*Salmo fario*), Loch Leven trout (*Salvo levenensis*), rainbow trout (*Salmo irideus*), American brook char (*Salvelinus fontinalis*). Besides this, the society has bred and distributed with great success red and fallow deer, and many sorts of game and game birds. To the enthusiasm of the chairman, Mr. A. J. Rutherford, a practical fisher, and the experience and painstaking efforts of the expert curator, Mr. L. F. Ayson, must be ascribed most of the great results achieved.

TAUHERENIKAU River, tributary of Lake Wairarapa.—Shingle bed from the lake for fifteen miles, until in the neighbourhood of Featherston it becomes a mountain torrent of the Tararua Ranges. Banks in the lower reaches as far as Featherston low and fairly clear, then deep mountain gorges. Wadeable. Landing mostly good. Course, twenty-five miles. Contains brown and rainbow trout. Reached (to within four miles of the mouth) from Featherston Station, on the Wellington–Napier–New Plymouth Railway, by four miles of road, and also to points six and nine miles from the mouth by roads of two and three miles. There is hotel accommodation at Featherston.

ORONGORONGO Stream.—Shingle and boulder bed. Banks low and clear in lower reaches, high and forest-clad in upper. Wadeable mostly. Landing mostly good. Course, nineteen miles. Contains brown trout. Reached by track of eight miles from the Wainuiomata Stream. Accommodation uncertain. For approach and accommodation see " Wainuiomata Stream," following.

WAINUIOMATA Stream.—Shingle and rock bottom. Banks various and fairly clear. Wadeable. Landing mostly good. Course, eighteen miles. Contains brown and rainbow trout. About fourteen miles from the mouth is situated a reservoir which supplies Wellington with water, and the stream is fishable for three miles above this. Reached from the Lower Hutt Station, on the Wellington–Napier–New Plymouth Railway, where there are hotels and livery stables, and then by road for nine miles. Accommodation sometimes arranged with settlers close by.

HUTT River (discharges into Wellington Harbour).—Tidal for two miles. Shingle, boulder, and rock bed. Banks fairly clear, with gorse and forest here and there. Wadeable. Landing mostly good.

CATCH OF TROUT, WELLINGTON DISTRICT.

Course, thirty miles. Contains brown and rainbow trout. The river and tributaries can be reached by the Wellington–Napier–New Plymouth Railway (to within two miles of the mouth) from the Lower Hutt Station, after which there are seven stations in the next twenty miles more or less close to the river and tributaries. There is also a good road following the river for some twenty miles above the Lower Hutt: on this road there are hotels and accommodation houses at the Lower Hutt, Taita, Wallaceville, Upper Hutt, and Mungaroa, all either close to or within easy distance of the streams.

WHAKATAKI Burn, tributary of Hutt River.— Rock, boulder, and shingle bed. Banks high, rocky, and difficult. Wadeable partly. Landing mostly deep. Course, ten miles. Contains brown and rainbow trout. Reached (to the mouth) in a mile from the Wallaceville or Upper Hutt Railway-stations, where there are hotels. For approach and accommodation see "Hutt River," already mentioned.

AKATARAWA Stream, tributary of the Hutt River. —Shingle and rock bed. Banks steep and rough. Wadeable partly. Landing deep, also good. Course, fifteen miles. Contains brown and rainbow trout. Reached (to the mouth) by three miles of road from the Upper Hutt Railway-station, where there is a hotel. For approach and accommodation see "Hutt River," already mentioned.

MUNGAROA Stream, tributary of Hutt River. Shingle and rock bottom. Banks low and encumbered by forest and scrub. Wadeable. Landing deep, also good. Course, eleven miles. Contains brown and rainbow trout. Reached from Upper Hutt Railway-station by track of a mile and a half to Wallaceville, which is five miles from the mouth, and where accommodation can be got in the village; also from the Mungaroa Railway-station, which is close to the stream and two miles from the mouth.

CHAPTER XVII.

NORTH ISLAND.—WEST COAST.

RIVERS AND LAKES FROM AHIPARA BAY TO PORIRUA HARBOUR (BEGINNING AT THE NORTH).

AWAROA Stream (discharges into Wangape Harbour). — Shingle bottom and bed. Banks partly clear. Wadeable partly. Landing deep, also good. Course, eleven miles. Contains rainbow and brown trout. Reached (to near the mouth) from Kohukohu (where there are hotels) or Rawene by twenty-six miles of tracks. Kohukohu and Rawene reached by steamer from Onehunga; also by coach-road from Kawakawa, Bay of Islands.

ROTOKAKAHI River (discharges into Whangape Harbour). — Shingle bottom and bed. Banks partly clear. Wadeable partly. Landing deep, also good. Course, twenty-two miles. Contains rainbow and brown trout. Reached (to near the mouth) from Kohukohu (where there are hotels) or Rawene by twenty-five miles of track, or (to fifteen miles above the mouth) by eleven miles of road. Kohukohu and Rawene reached by steamer from Onehunga, also by coach-road from Kawakawa, Bay of Islands.

MANGAMUKA Stream (discharges into Hokianga Harbour). — Shingle bottom and bed. Banks partly clear, partly forest-clad. Wadeable partly. Landing deep, also good. Course, fourteen miles. Contains rainbow and brown trout. Reached (to near the mouth) from Kohukohu (where there are hotels) or Rawene by ten miles of tracks; Kohukohu and Rawene reached by steamer from Onehunga. The stream is also reached by coach-road from Kawakawa, Bay of Islands.

WAIPAPA River (discharges into Hokianga Harbour).—Shingle bottom and bed. Banks partly clear, partly forest-clad. Wadeable partly. Landing deep, also good. Course, twenty-two miles. Contains rainbow and brown trout. Reached (to the mouth) from Kohukohu (where there are hotels) or Rawene by boat, twelve miles. A mile up the river is Rangiahua, where there is hotel accommodation. Rangiahua is also reached by coach-road from Kawakawa, Bay of Islands. Kohukohu and Rawene reached by steamer from Onehunga.

WAIMA River (discharges into Hokianga Harbour).—Shingle bottom and bed. Banks partly forest-clad. Wadeable partly. Landing deep, also good. Course, twenty-one miles. Contains rainbow and brown trout. Reached (to the mouth) from Rawene in two miles, and from Taheke, where there is hotel accommodation, in three miles (to a point eleven miles above Rawene). Taheke is sixteen miles from Rawene by coach-road. Rawene is reached by steamer from Onehunga, also by coach-road from Kawakawa, Bay of Islands.

WAIMEA Stream, tributary of Waima River.— Shingle bottom and bed. Banks partly forest-clad. Wadeable partly. Landing deep, also good. Course, twelve miles. Contains rainbow and brown trout. Reached from Taheke, where there is hotel accommodation, near to the stream and five miles from the mouth. For approach and accommodation see "Waima River," already mentioned.

PUNAKITERE River, tributary of Waima River.— Shingle bottom and bed. Banks partly forest-clad. Wadeable partly. Landing deep, also good. Course, twenty-four miles. Contains rainbow and brown trout. Reached from Taheke, where there is hotel accommodation close to the river at three miles from the mouth. For approach and accommodation see " Waima River," already mentioned.

OTAUA Burn, tributary of Punakitere River.— Shingle bottom and bed. Banks partly forest-clad. Wadeable partly. Landing deep, also good. Course, eight miles. Contains rainbow and brown trout. Reached (to the mouth) in a mile from Taheke. For approach and accommodation see " Punakitere River," already mentioned.

WAIRORO Burn, tributary of Punakitere River.— Shingle bottom and bed. Banks partly forest-clad. Wadeable partly. Landing deep, also good. Course, eight miles. Contains rainbow and brown trout. Reached from Taheke by following up the Punakitere River for eleven miles. For approach and accommodation see " Punakitere River," already mentioned.

WHIRINAKI Burn (discharges into Hokianga Harbour).—Shingle bottom and bed. Banks partly forest-clad. Wadeable partly. Landing deep, also good. Course, nine miles. Contains rainbow and brown trout. Reached (to the mouth) from Rawene by eleven miles of road, or from Taheke, where there is hotel accommodation, by fifteen miles of road. Taheke is sixteen miles by road from Rawene. Rawene is reached by steamer from Onehunga, or by coach-road from Kawakawa, Bay of Islands.

WAIMAMAKU River.—Shingle bottom and bed. Banks partly forest-clad. Wadeable partly. Landing deep, also good. Course, twenty-one miles. Contains rainbow and brown trout. Reached (to the mouth) from Opononi, where there is hotel accommodation, by nine miles of track, or (to the upper waters) by ten miles of track from Taheke, where there is hotel accommodation : this track continues near the river to the mouth, near which it joins the track to Opononi. Opononi is reached from Rawene by sixteen miles of track. Taheke is reached from Rawene by sixteen miles of road. Rawene is reached from Onehunga by steamer, or by coach-road from Kawakawa, Bay of Islands.

WAIROA River (Kaipara), (estuary and river).— Sand and mud bottom as far as tidal; then some shingle and rock bottom. Tidal for eighty miles. Navigable for sea-going ships and steamers for fifty miles and for small steamers for eighty miles. The upper waters almost reach the east coast. Eighty miles from the mouth there are falls; also at eighty-six miles. About here the fishing-water begins. Banks mostly low and muddy as far as it is tidal, and then rather steep. Forest-clad here and there. Wadeable partly in the upper reaches. Landing mostly deep. Course, including the parts called Wairua, Whakapara, and Kaimamaku, 120 miles. Contains rainbow and brown trout. Reached (to the mouth) from Auckland to the Helensville Station (where there are hotels), on the Auckland–Makarau Railway, then by river-steamer seventy miles, to Dargaville, where there are hotels; then again by river-steamer for thirty miles to Wharekohe, two miles below the Wairua Falls. Near here there is accommodation; and a track and road of twenty miles leads to Whangarei Town, on the east coast, where there are hotels. There is also a track from Dargaville to Whangarei. The river can be reached (to within ten miles of the source) from Whangarei, from the Whakapara Station, where there is accommodation close to the river, on the Whangarei–Whakapara Railway. Twenty-two miles further is Kawakawa River and Town. There are also streams at Whangarei. See "Rivers and Lakes of the East Coast." Whangarei is reached from Auckland by steamer *viâ* the east coast.

KAIHU River, tributary of Wairoa River.—Mud bottom and partly tidal for five miles; then shingle and boulder bed. Banks of lower part low, then higher; more or less forest-clad. Wadeable above tidal water. Landing deep, also good. Course, twenty-seven miles. Contains rainbow and brown trout. Reached (to the mouth) from Dargaville. The Dargaville-Kaihu Railway has many stations, and runs along the course of the river from Dargaville to Kaihu, eighteen miles. Accommodation can be got at intervals along the river up to Kaihu. For approach and accommodation see " Wairoa River," already mentioned.

MANGAKAHIA River, tributary of Wairoa River. —Joins the Wairoa River eighty miles from the mouth. Boulder and shingle bed. Banks various, and more or less forest-clad. Wadeable partly. Landing deep, also good. Course, forty miles. Contains rainbow and brown trout. Reached (to the mouth) from Dargaville by steamer in thirty miles, or by track of twenty miles. Accommodation can be got not far from the junction of the Wairoa River. There is a track and road from here to Whangarei, about twenty-eight miles. For approach and accommodation see " Wairoa River," already mentioned.

WAIKATO River.—Estuary, shingle and mud bottom. Tidal for twenty-eight miles; navigable for small steamers for twenty-eight miles. Shingle, sand, pumice, and rock bottom. Banks of all kinds, from low, clear, and flax-encumbered, to high, precipitous, and scrub-encumbered. Wadeable in places. Landing mostly deep. Course to Lake Taupo, 200 miles: the lake is 25 miles long; river at south end of lake 33 miles: total, 258 miles. Contains brown and rainbow trout, both below and above the Huka Falls, which are over 30 ft. high, and three miles below Lake Taupo. It is a fine, broad, deep river of clear water; and the water of nearly all its tributary streams and lakes is likewise clear. The river and tributaries flood the banks very little even in the heaviest freshes, and the beds hardly shift at all. There are fine rapids. The country through which it flows is more or less pumice, there being more pumice in the upper reaches and towards the source. Much of the river and upper tributaries are within easy reach of the Auckland–Rotorua Railway and Auckland–Wellington Main Trunk Line, and of the branches from these lines. Hotels are numerous on these railways.

KARAPIRO Stream, tributary of Waikato River.—Shingle, rock, and sand bottom. Banks fairly clear in lower reaches, forest-clad towards the source. Wadeable partly. Landing deep, also good. Course, eleven miles. Contains brown and rainbow trout. Reached (to the mouth) from Cambridge Station (to which it is close, and where there are hotels), on the Frankton Junction–Cambridge Railway. For approach and accommodation see " Waikato River," already mentioned.

POKAEWHENUA River, tributary of Waikato River.—Shingle, rock, and pumice bottom. Banks fairly clear, with some scrub. Wadeable partly. Landing deep, also good. Course, twenty-six miles. Contains brown and rainbow trout. Reached (to the mouth) from Cambridge Station (where there are hotels), on the Frankton Junction–Cambridge Railway, and by fifteen miles of road up the bank of the Waikato River; also from the Putaruru Station (where there is hotel accommodation), on the Frankton Junction–Rotorua Railway, then by five miles of road to Lichfield (where there is hotel accommodation), within three miles of the river, which the road strikes sixteen miles above the mouth. For approach and accommodation see " Waikato River," already mentioned.

NGUTUWERA Stream, tributary of Pokaewhenua River.—Shingle and pumice bottom. Banks fairly clear. Wadeable partly. Landing deep, also good. Course, eleven miles. Contains brown and rainbow trout. Reached (to within four miles of the mouth) from Lichfield by a mile of road. For approach and accommodation see "Pokaewhenua River," already mentioned.

WAIPA No. 2 Stream, tributary of Waikato River. —Shingle, rock, and pumice bottom. Banks fairly clear. Wadeable partly. Landing deep, also good. Course, eighteen miles. Contains rainbow and brown trout. Reached (to the mouth) from Cambridge Station (where there are hotels), on the Frankton Junction–Cambridge Railway, then by eighteen miles of road up the bank of the Waikato River; this road continues within a mile of the stream for twelve miles, when it crosses it, and reaches Lichfield in ten miles; at Lichfield there is hotel accommodation. For approach and accommodation see "Waikato River," already mentioned.

WAIPAPA Stream, tributary of Waikato River.— Shingle, rock, and pumice bottom. Banks fairly clear in lower reaches, more or less forest- and scrub-clad in upper. Wadeable partly. Landing deep, also good. Course, fifteen miles. Contains brown and rainbow trout. Reached (to near the mouth) from opposite the mouth of Waipa No. 2 Stream by tracks of twenty miles, following up the Waikato River. For approach and accommodation see "Waikato River," already mentioned.

WAITETE Stream, tributary of Waipapa Stream. —Shingle, rock, and pumice bottom. Banks fairly clear in lower reaches, forest-clad in upper. Wadeable partly. Landing deep, also good. Course, seventeen miles. Contains brown and rainbow trout. Reached (to the mouth) by tracks that follow up the Waikato River from opposite the mouth of Waipa No. 2 Stream. For approach and accommodation see "Waipapa Stream," already mentioned.

MANGAKINO River, tributary of Waikato River.— Shingle, rock, and pumice bottom. Banks fairly clear in lower reaches, forest-clad in upper. Wadeable partly. Landing deep, also good. Course, twenty-four miles. Contains brown and rainbow trout. Reached (to near the mouth) from opposite the mouth of Waipa No. 2 by track of thirty miles up the Waikato River; the track continues to the Waipapa and Waitete Streams. For approach and accommodation see " Waikato River," already mentioned.

MANGATAHAE Burn, tributary of Mangakino River. —Shingle, rock, and pumice bottom. Banks, lower half fairly clear, upper forest-clad. Wadeable partly. Landing deep, also good. Course, nine miles. Contains brown and rainbow trout. Reached (to the mouth) by following up the Mangakino River for four miles from the mouth. For approach and accommodation see " Mangakino River," already mentioned.

WHANGAPOA Stream, tributary of Waikato River. —Shingle, rock, and pumice bottom and bed. Banks fairly clear. Wadeable partly. Landing deep, also good. Course, eighteen miles. Contains brown and rainbow trout, and *S. fontinalis.* Reached (to the mouth) from the Taupo–Rotorua Coach-road at Atiamuri, where there is a hotel near the mouth, and on the bank of the Waikato River. This is twenty-five miles from Taupo, and twenty-five miles from Rotorua. This road runs parallel with the stream at a mile distant for most of the length, crossing it ten miles from Atiamuri and fifteen from Rotorua, where there is hotel accommodation. For approach and accommodation see " Waikato River," already mentioned; also see Chapter XVI., " Lake Rotorua," under " Rivers and Lakes of the East Coast."

POUTO Stream, tributary of Waikato River.— Shingle, rock, and pumice bottom. Banks mostly low and clear. Wadeable partly. Landing deep, also good. Course, fourteen miles. Contains brown and rainbow trout. Reached (to the upper waters) from the Taupo–Napier Coach-road in five miles from Opepe Wood, the scene of the massacre of troopers during the Maori war. The Lake Taupo Hotel is distant from Opepe by this road twelve miles, and the Rangitaiki Hotel, which is on this road and on the bank of the Rangitaiki River, is distant eleven miles from Opepe. For approach and accommodation see " Waikato River," already mentioned.

Lake Taupo, tributary of Waikato River.— Pumice bottom and beaches mostly. Banks partly low, chiefly pumice and pumice cliffs. Wadeable from the beaches. Landing deep, also good, Length, twenty-five miles ; breadth, seventeen miles ; height above sea-level, 1,211 ft. Contains brown and rainbow trout. Reached generally by the Napier – Taupo – Rotorua Coach-road, which passes the lower end of the lake, where there are hotels. Here is also the Spa Hotel and Sanitorium, which is on the site of hot-spring wonders, and has various natural hot and mineral baths of great curative properties in rheumatic and other complaints. There are also natural hot baths at Waipahihi Hotel and at Wairakei. These places are all a few miles from the lower end of the lake, and on this coach-road. A trout might be landed from the Waikato River within a yard of a boiling spring, and boiled there direct from the landing-net. The lower end of Lake Taupo is connected, by coach-road of thirty-six miles round the eastern side of the lake, with Tokaanu, at the head of the lake, where there is a hotel near where the Waikato River runs into the lake. This coach-road is continued to the Wanganui River, where a steamer completes the journey, amid fine scenery, to Wanganui Town. There are steam-launches, and various boats and canoes for hire on the lake. The streams running into the east side of the lake can be reached from the coach-road which crosses them between the foot of the lake and Tokaanu, or by steam-launch, boat, or canoe from the hotels at the foot of the lake, or at Tokaanu. The streams running into the west side of the lake can be reached by rather uncertain tracks from these hotels, or from the lake by the same means as for the east side.

WAITAHANUI Stream, tributary of Lake Taupo, east side.—Pumice bottom. Banks low, and flax- and scrub-encumbered in the lower part, fairly clear in the upper. Wadeable partly. Landing deep, also good. Course, thirteen miles. Contains brown and rainbow trout. Reached (to the mouth) from the coach-road between the lower end of the lake and Tokaanu. For approach and accommodation see " Lake Taupo," already mentioned.

HINEMAIAI Stream, tributary of Lake Taupo, east side.—Pumice bottom. Banks low and rather flax- and scrub-encumbered. Wadeable partly. Landing deep, also good. Course, fifteen miles. Contains brown and rainbow trout. Reached (to the mouth) from the coach-road between the lower end of the lake and Tokaanu. For approach and accommodation see " Lake Taupo," already mentioned.

WAIPEHI Burn, tributary of Lake Taupo, east side.—Pumice bottom. Banks mostly low, and more or less scrub-encumbered. Wadeable partly. Landing deep, also good. Course, seven miles. Contains brown and rainbow trout. Reached (to the mouth) from the coach-road between the lower end of the lake and Tokaanu. For approach and accommodation see " Lake Taupo," already mentioned.

TAURANGA Stream, tributary of Lake Taupo, east side.—Pumice bottom. Banks mostly low, and more or less scrub-encumbered in lower reaches, forest-clad in upper. Wadeable partly. Landing deep, also good. Course, twenty miles. Contains brown and rainbow trout. Reached (to the mouth) from the coach-road between the lower end of the lake and Tokaanu. For approach and accommodation see " Lake Taupo," already mentioned.

WAIOTAHA Stream, tributary of Lake Taupo, east side.—Pumice bottom. Banks mostly low and more or less scrub-encumbered. Wadeable partly. Landing deep, also good. Course, twelve miles. Contains brown and rainbow trout. Reached (to the mouth) from the coach-road between the lower end of the lake and Tokaanu. For approach and accommodation see " Lake Taupo," already mentioned.

WAIKATO River (upper part), tributary of Lake Taupo, south side.—Pumice, shingle, and rock bottom. Banks various, fairly clear, scrub-encumbered here and there in lower reaches, partly forest-clad in upper. Wadeable partly. Landing deep, also good. Course, thirty-three miles. Contains brown and rainbow trout. Reached (to the mouth) near Tokaanu from the coach-road between the lower end of the lake and Tokaanu. For approach and accommodation see " Lake Taupo," already mentioned.

WAIHORA Burn, tributary of Lake Taupo, west side.—Pumice and rock bottom. Banks more or less scrub-encumbered in lower reaches, forest-clad in upper. Wadeable partly. Landing deep, also good. Course, ten miles. Contains brown and rainbow trout. For approach and accommodation see " Lake Taupo," already mentioned.

WAIHAHA Stream, tributary of Lake Taupo, west side.—Pumice and rock bottom. Banks more or less scrub-encumbered in lower reaches, forest-clad in upper. Wadeable partly. Landing deep, also good. Course, twelve miles. Contains brown and rainbow trout. For approach and accommodation see " Lake Taupo," already mentioned.

WHANGANUI Burn, tributary of Lake Taupo, west side.—Pumice and rock bottom. Banks more or less scrub-encumbered in lower reaches, forest-clad in upper. Wadeable partly. Landing deep, also good. Course, nine miles. Contains brown and rainbow trout. For approach and accommodation see "Lake Taupo," already mentioned.

KURATOU Stream, tributary of Lake Taupo, west side. – Pumice and rock bottom. Banks more or less scrub-encumbered in lower reaches, forest-clad in upper. Wadeable partly. Landing deep, also good. Course, thirteen miles. Contains brown and rainbow trout. For approach and accommodation see "Lake Taupo," already mentioned.

WAIPA River, tributary of Waikato River.— Shingle, rock, and pumice bottom and bed. Banks various, from low and clear to high scrub-encumbered, and in the upper reaches forest-clad here and there. Wadeable partly. Landing deep, also good. Course, eighty-six miles. Contains brown and rainbow trout. Reached (at the mouth) by Ngaruawahia Station (where there is hotel accommodation), on the Auckland – Wellington Main Trunk Line; from Frankton Junction (where there is hotel accommodation), on the Auckland– Wellington Main Trunk Line; and from Hamilton Station (where there is hotel accommodation), on the Frankton Junction – Rotorua Railway. From Frankton Junction the river is reached by seven miles of road to Whatawhata, where there is hotel accommodation, fifteen miles from the mouth; from Hamilton, Whatawhata is reached by eight miles of the same road. From the Te Awamutu Station (where there is hotel accommodation), on the Auckland--Wellington Main Trunk Line, the river is reached by road of eight miles to Pirongia (late Alexandra), where there is hotel accommodation on the bank. Pirongia is thirty-two miles from the mouth. The river is also reached from Otorohanga Station (where there is accommodation on the bank), on the Auckland– Wellington Main Trunk Line: Otorohanga is fifty-two miles from the mouth. Roads from the

mouth run close to or within moderate distance of
the river for four miles above Pirongia. Above
Otorohanga there are only tracks in the neighbourhood of the river. For approach and accommodation see " Waikato River," already mentioned.

Te Pahu Burn, tributary of Waipa River.—
Shingle, pumice, and rock bottom. Banks more
or less forest-clad. Wadeable, partly. Landing
deep, also good. Course, ten miles. Contains
brown and rainbow trout. Reached (to the mouth)
from Whatawhata, where there is hotel accommodation, by four miles of the Whatawhata–Raglan
Road. From the mouth a road runs the greater
part of the way near the burn, and on to Pirongia.
For approach and accommodation see " Waipa
River," already mentioned.

Mangapiko River, tributary of Waipa River.—
Shingle and rock bottom and bed. Banks mostly
clear, but with scrub here and there. Wadeable
partly. Landing deep, also good. Course, twenty-
seven miles. Contains brown and rainbow trout.
Reached at Te Awamutu Station (where there is
hotel accommodation), on the Auckland–Wellington Main Trunk Line. Te Awamutu is on the
bank of the river, and is nine miles from the mouth,
which is reached by eight miles of road to Pirongia,
where there is hotel accommodation. To six miles
above Te Awamutu the river can be reached by a
road which crosses it; above this there are only
tracks. For approach and accommodation see
" Waipa River," already mentioned.

Puniu River, tributary of Waipa River.—Shingle
bottom and bed. Banks mostly low and clear,
with some scrub in lower reaches, forest-clad towards the source. Wadeable partly. Landing
deep, also good. Course, thirty-six miles. Contains
brown and rainbow trout. Reached from Te Puni
Station, on the Auckland–Wellington Main Trunk
Line, which is near the river; and six miles from
the mouth there is Pirongia, where there is hotel

accommodation. At Te Awamutu, three miles along the railway-line from Te Puni, there is hotel accommodation, and three miles up the river from Te Puni Station there is Kihikihi, where there is hotel accommodation a mile from the river; above this there are only tracks. For approach and accommodation see " Waipa River," already mentioned.

MANGATUTU Stream, tributary of Puniu River.— Shingle bottom and bed. Banks fairly clear, with some scrub, in lower reaches; forest-clad in upper. Wadeable partly. Landing deep, also good. Course, twenty miles. Contains brown and rainbow trout. Reached (to the mouth) from Te Puni Station, on the Auckland–Wellington Main Trunk Line, by following up the Puniu River for six miles, or from Kihikihi, where there is hotel accommodation, for five miles. For approach and accommodation see " Puniu River," already mentioned.

OWAIRAKA Stream, tributary of Puniu River.— Shingle bottom and bed. Banks fairly clear, with some scrub. Wadeable partly. Landing deep, also good. Course, thirteen miles. Contains brown and rainbow trout. Reached (to the mouth) from Te Puni Station, on the Auckland–Wellington Main Trunk Line, by following up the Puniu River for nine miles, or from Kihikihi, where there is hotel accommodation, eight miles away. For approach and accommodation see " Puniu River," already mentioned.

WAIPARI Stream, tributary of Puniu River.— Shingle bottom and bed. Banks fairly clear, with some scrub, in the lower half; forest-clad in the upper. Wadeable partly. Landing deep, also good. Course, fifteen miles. Contains brown and rainbow trout. Reached (to the mouth) from Te Puhi Station, on the Auckland–Wellington Main Trunk Line, by following up the Puniu River fifteen miles, or from Kihikihi, where there is hotel accommodation, fourteen miles distant. For approach and accommodation see " Puniu River," already mentioned.

MANGAKEMUA Burn, tributary of Waipari Stream. —Shingle bottom and bed. Banks fairly clear, with some scrub; forest-clad towards the source Wadeable partly. Landing deep, also good Course, ten miles. Contains brown and rainbow trout. Joins the Waipari Stream close to the mouth. For approach and accommodation see " Waipari Stream," already mentioned.

MOAKURARUA Stream, tributary of Waipa River. — Shingle bottom and bed. Banks fairly clear, with some scrub, in lower reaches; forest-clad in upper. Wadeable partly. Landing deep, also good. Course, sixteen miles. Contains brown and rainbow trout. Reached (to the mouth) by four miles of road from Pirongia, where there is hotel accommodation. This is the Pirongia–Kawhia Road, and keeps near the stream for five miles. For approach and accommodation see " Waipa River," already mentioned.

TURITEA Burn, tributary of Moakurarua Stream. —Shingle bottom and bed. Banks fairly clear, with some scrub, in lower reaches; forest-clad towards source. Wadeable partly. Landing deep, also good. Course, ten miles. Contains brown and rainbow trout. Reached (to the mouth) by following up the Moakurarua Stream three miles. For approach and accommodation see " Moakurarua Stream," already mentioned.

MANGAORONGA River, tributary of Waipa River. —Shingle bottom and bed. Banks fairly clear, with some scrub; forest-clad towards source. Wadeable partly. Landing deep, also good. Course, twenty-three miles. Contains brown and rainbow trout. Reached from the Kiokio Station, on the Auckland–Wellington Main Trunk Line, which is on the bank, and two miles from the mouth. Two miles away by railway is Otorohanga, where there is accommodation. For approach and accommodation see " Waipa River," already mentioned.

WAITOMO Stream, tributary of Waipa River.—Shingle and rock bottom and bed. Banks fairly clear, with some scrub, in lower reaches; then forest-clad. Wadeable partly. Landing deep, also good. Course, eleven miles. Contains brown and rainbow trout. Reached (to the mouth) from the Otorohanga Station (where there is accommodation), on the Auckland–Wellington Main Trunk Line, and thence it is a mile down the bank of the Waipa River. Near here are the Waitomo limestone caves, which are worth seeing. For approach and accommodation see " Waipa River " already mentioned.

MANGAOKEWA River, tributary of Waipa River.—Shingle bottom and bed. Banks more or less scrub- and forest-clad. Wadeable partly. Landing mostly good. Course, thirty-five miles. Contains brown and rainbow trout. Reached (to the mouth) at the Otorohanga Station (where there is accommodation), on the Auckland – Wellington Main Trunk Line. From there the railway follows the river closely for eighteen miles, with stations at short intervals. At Te Kuiti Station, thirteen miles above Otorohanga, there is accommodation, with the river a few yards distant. For approach and accommodation see " Waipa River," already mentioned.

HANGATIKI Stream, tributary of Mangaokewa River.—Shingle bottom and bed. Banks more or less scrub- and forest-clad. Wadeable partly. Landing deep, also good. Course, twelve miles. Contains brown and rainbow trout. Reached (to near the mouth) from the Hangatiki Station, on the Auckland–Wellington Main Trunk Line. Otorohanga, where there is accommodation, is six miles along the railway. For approach and accommodation see " Mangaokewa River," already mentioned.

Mangapu Stream, tributary of Mangaokewa River. — Shingle bottom and bed. Banks more or less scrub- and forest-clad. Wadeable partly. Landing deep, also good. Course, fifteen miles. Contains brown and rainbow trout. Reached (to the mouth) from the Hangatiki Station, on the Auckland–Wellington Main Trunk Line, in half a mile. Otorohanga, where there is accommodation, is six miles along the railway. For approach and accommodation see "Mangaokewa River," already mentioned.

Mangawhero Stream, tributary of Waipa River. —Shingle bottom and bed. Banks more or less scrub- and forest-clad. Wadeable partly. Landing deep, also good. Course, twelve miles. Contains brown and rainbow trout. Reached (to the mouth) by following up the Waipa River half a mile from Otorohanga Station (where there is accommodation), on the Auckland – Wellington Main Trunk Line. For approach and accommodation see "Waipa River," already mentioned.

Waitetuna Stream (discharges in Whangaroa Harbour).—Shingle bottom and bed. Banks partly clear, also partly scrub- and forest-clad. Wadeable partly. Landing deep, also good. Course, eleven miles. Contains brown and rainbow trout. Reached from Raglan, where there is hotel accommodation. Raglan is reached by steamer from Auckland and by a coach-journey of thirty miles from Hamilton Station, on the Frankton Junction–Rotorua Railway. This road reaches the stream seven miles from Raglan and one mile from the mouth, running along the bank for four miles. About half-way between the Waitetuna and Hamilton, some eighteen miles, the road crosses the Waipa River, at Whatawhata, where there is hotel accommodation.

Awakino River.—Sand, mud, shingle, clay, rock, and papa, with little bed. Banks scrub- and forest-clad here and there. Wadeable partly. Landing deep, also good. Course, thirty-five miles. Contains brown and rainbow trout. Reached (to the mouth) from Mokau, at the mouth of the Mokau River, by three miles of track. For approach and accommodation see " Mokau River," further on.

MANGANUI Stream, tributary of Awakino River. —Mud, shingle, and clay bottom. Banks more or less scrub- and forest-clad. Wadeable partly. Landing deep, also good. Course, thirteen miles. Contains brown and rainbow trout. For approach and accommodation see " Awakino River," already mentioned.

MOKAU River.—Estuary short. Navigable for steamers for twenty-five miles. Sand, mud, shingle, clay, rock, and papa bottom, with little bed. Fifty miles from the mouth there are waterfalls. Banks various, with forest to water's edge for a long distance. Wadeable partly on upper reaches. Landing mostly deep. Course, eighty-eight miles. Contains brown and rainbow trout. Reached (to the mouth) by steamer from New Plymouth *via* Waitara. At Mokau, at the mouth of the river, there is accommodation. Reached also (to the mouth) from Waitara Station (where there is hotel accommodation), on the New Plymouth–Waitara Railway, by coach-road, which continues on to Te Kuiti Station, on the Auckland–Wellington Main Trunk Line. Reached also from the Mokau Station, on the Auckland–Wellington Main Trunk Line, which crosses it sixteen miles from the source.

MANGAOTAKI Stream, tributary of Mokau River.— Shingle, boulder, and rock bottom and bed. Banks more or less forest-clad. Wadeable partly. Landing deep, also good. Course, fourteen miles. Contains brown and rainbow trout. Reached (to the mouth) by following up the Mokau River forty-four miles from Mokau. For approach and accommodation see " Mokau River," already mentioned.

Mokau-iti Stream, tributary of Mokau River.—
Shingle and rock bottom and bed. Banks more
or less forest-clad. Wadeable partly. Landing
deep, also good. Course, eighteen miles. Contains
brown and rainbow trout. Reached (to the mouth)
by following up the Mokau River for forty-six
miles above Mokau. For approach and accommodation see "Mokau River," already mentioned.

Mapiu Stream, tributary of Mokau River.—
Shingle and rock bottom and bed. Banks more or
less forest-clad. Wadeable partly. Landing deep,
also good. Course, seventeen miles. Contains
brown and rainbow trout. Reached (to the mouth)
by following up the Mokau River fifty-four miles
above Mokau. For approach and accommodation
see "Mokau River," already mentioned.

Mapara Stream, tributary of Mapiu Stream.—
Shingle and rock bottom and bed. Banks more or
less forest-clad. Wadeable partly. Landing deep,
also good. Course, seventeen miles. Contains
brown and rainbow trout. Joins the Mapiu Stream
near the mouth. For approach and accommodation see "Mapiu Stream," already mentioned.

Mangapehia Stream, tributary of Mokau River.—
Shingle and rock bottom and bed. Banks more or
less forest-clad. Wadeable partly. Landing deep,
also good. Course, twenty miles. Contains brown
and rainbow trout. Reached (to the mouth) by
following up the Mokau River for sixty miles above
Mokau, or from the Mokau Station, on the Auckland–Wellington Main Trunk Line, and then following the Mokau River down twelve miles. It
can also be reached (to the upper waters) in four
miles from several railway-stations south of Mokau,
on the Auckland–Wellington Main Trunk Line.
For approach and accommodation see "Mokau
River," already mentioned.

Waitara River.—Estuary about a mile, with
mud and sand bottom; navigable for small steamers
for a mile; tidal for two miles and a half; then

mud, shingle, and boulder bottom and bed. Banks partly clear, with some forest. Wadeable partly. Landing deep, also good. Course, seventy miles. Contains brown and rainbow trout. Reached (to near the mouth) at Waitara Station (where there are hotels), on the New Plymouth–Waitara Railway.

MANGANUI River, tributary of Waitara River.— Shingle and boulder bottom and bed. Banks partly forest-clad in lower reaches, then partly clear. Wadeable partly. Landing deep, also good. Course, twenty-four miles. Reached (to the mouth) from Sentry Hill Junction, on the Wellington–Wanganui–New Plymouth Railway, and then by six miles of road to Manganui. Accommodation uncertain. Also reached from Inglewood Station (where there is hotel accommodation), on the same railway, and then by three miles of road, which crosses the river seven miles from the mouth. Inglewood is also conveniently situated for reaching a number of tributaries of the Manganui River that are near the township. Also reached from Midhirst Station (where there is hotel accommodation close to the river), on the same railway, which crosses it here, seventeen miles from the mouth and seven from the source. For approach and accommodation see " Waitara River," already mentioned.

NGATORONUI Stream, tributary of Manganui River.—Boulder and shingle bottom and bed. Banks fairly clear, but with scrub here and there. Wadeable partly. Landing deep, also good. Course, eleven miles. Contains brown and rainbow trout. Reached from Inglewood Station (where there is hotel accommodation), on the Wellington–Wanganui–New Plymouth Railway, by two miles of road, which crosses it two miles from the mouth. A road from Inglewood also crosses it a mile and a half from the township and five miles from the mouth. For approach and accommodation see " Manganui River," already mentioned.

NGATOROITI Burn, tributary of Ngatoronui Stream.—Boulder and shingle bottom and bed. Banks fairly clear, with scrub here and there. Wadeable partly. Landing deep, also good. Course, nine miles. Contains brown and rainbow trout. Reached from Inglewood Station (where there is hotel accommodation), on the Wellington–Wanganui–New Plymouth Railway, by two miles of road, which crosses it about the junction with the Ngatoronui. A road from Inglewood also crosses it a mile and a quarter from the township and two miles from the mouth. For approach and accommodation see " Ngatoronui Stream," already mentioned.

WAITEPUKE Stream, tributary of Manganui River.—Shingle and boulder bed. Banks mostly low and fairly clear. Wadeable partly. Landing deep, also good. Course, eleven miles. Contains brown and rainbow trout. Reached from Inglewood Station (where there is hotel accommodation), on the Wellington–Wanganui–New Plymouth Railway, by four miles of road, which crosses it four miles from the mouth ; or it can be reached from the Norfolk Road Station, on the same railway, and then by a mile of road to the same place. For approach and accommodation see " Manganui River," already mentioned.

WAIPUKU Burn, tributary of Manganui River.— Shingle bottom and bed. Banks fairly clear, with some scrub. Wadeable partly. Landing deep, also good. Course, nine miles. Contains brown and rainbow trout. Reached from Midhirst Station (where there is hotel accommodation), on the Wellington–Wanganui–New Plymouth Railway, and then by two miles of road, which crosses it two miles from the mouth ; or from Waipuku Station, on the same railway, which crosses it beside the road. For approach and accommodation see "Manganui River," already mentioned.

WAIONGONA River.—Sand, shingle, and boulder bottom and bed. Banks fairly clear, with some scrub towards the mouth, then more or less forest-clad, then fairly clear with some scrub in upper reaches. Wadeable partly. Landing deep, also good. Course, twenty-one miles. Contains brown and rainbow trout. Reached (to the mouth) from Waitara Station (where there are hotels), on the New Plymouth–Waitara Railway, from which it is two miles away; also from Sentry Hill Junction, on the same railway, which is close to the river and four miles from the mouth; it is also reached from a number of stations between Sentry Hill and Inglewood Station (where there are hotels), on the Wellington–Wanganui–New Plymouth Railway. From Sentry Hill Junction to Inglewood Station the river runs near the railway. Inglewood is a mile from the river by road, which crosses it twelve miles from the mouth.

WAIWAKAIHO Stream.—Shingle and boulder bottom and bed. Banks fairly clear towards the mouth, then a little forest-clad, then fairly clear with some scrub. Wadeable partly. Landing deep, also good. Course, nineteen miles. Contains brown and rainbow trout. Reached (to near the mouth) from New Plymouth (where there are hotels) by a mile of road; also from Inglewood Station (where there are hotels), on the Wellington–Wanganui–New Plymouth Railway, thence by four miles of road, which crosses the stream at Egmont Village, ten miles from the mouth; this road then runs at a moderate distance from the stream to New Plymouth, eight miles.

From New Plymouth to the next-mentioned stream, sixty miles round the coast, there is a perfect network of burns and streams, probably thirty, all more or less containing trout. A road runs from New Plymouth at a maximum distance of three miles from the coast-line, crossing the stream near the mouth, and continuing on to Hawera Station (where there are hotels), on the Wellington–Wanganui–New Plymouth Railway, a total distance of seventy miles. In addition to this road, a great number of these streams are easily accessible to the upper waters by roads and cross-roads leading from it. A good deal of the country along the road is forest, and Mount Egmont, 8,260 ft. high, and on which most of the streams take their rise, forms the centre of a radius to the road of sixteen miles. Starting from New Plymouth, on this road there are hotels at the following places, and at the distances apart given : Okato, seventeen miles ; Rahotu, thirteen miles; Opunake, ten miles; Otakeho, fifteen miles; Manaia, five miles ; and Hawera, ten miles.

Manaia Burn.—Shingle bottom and bed. Banks low and fairly clear in lower reaches, partly forest-clad in upper. Wadeable partly. Landing deep, also good. Course, ten miles. Contains brown trout. Reached from Manaia, where there is accommodation close to the burn, two miles from the mouth and ten miles by road from the Hawera Station (where there are hotels), on the Wellington–Wanganui–New Plymouth Railway.

Inaha Stream.—Shingle bottom and bed. Banks rather low and fairly clear in lower reaches, partly forest-clad in upper. Wadeable partly. Landing deep, also good. Course, seventeen miles. Contains brown trout. Reached from the New Plymouth–Hawera Road, which crosses it two miles from the mouth, three from Manaia (where there is accommodation), and seven from Hawera Station (where there are hotels), on the Wellington–Wanganui–New Plymouth Railway.

Waingongoro River. — Shingle and boulder bottom and bed. Banks various, fairly clear in lower reaches, partly forest-clad in upper. Wadeable partly. Landing deep, also good. Course,

CATCH OF TROUT, TARANAKI DISTRICT.

twenty-six miles. Contains brown and rainbow trout. Reached (to within a mile of the mouth) from the New Plymouth–Hawera Road, which crosses it five miles from Manaia (where there is accommodation), and five miles from the Hawera Station (where there are hotels), on the Wellington–Wanganui–New Plymouth Railway; reached also from the Normanby Station (where there are hotels), on the same railway, by two miles of road, which crosses it six miles from the mouth; then from Te Roti Station, on the same railway, which is close to the river and nine miles from the mouth; also from Eltham Station (where there are hotels), on the same railway, near the river, and fourteen miles from the mouth. The river can also be reached from Stratford Station (where there are hotels), on the same railway, by four miles of road, which crosses it twenty miles from the mouth. Near here is Mount Egmont, 8,260 ft. high, and which is a forest reserve and park of over 78,000 acres.

Patea River.—Navigable for small steamers for a mile, and for canoes for thirty miles. Sand and mud bottom in lower reaches, shingle and boulder bottom in upper. Banks mostly moderate, fairly clear, with a little forest. Wadeable partly. Landing deep, also good. Course, sixty-five miles. Contains brown and rainbow trout. Reached (to near the mouth) from Patea Station (where there are hotels), on the Wellington–Wanganui–New Plymouth Railway. From here up to Stratford, fifty-four miles, the river may be followed, but with uncertain accommodation. At Stratford Station (where there are hotels), on the Wellington–Wanganui–New Plymouth Railway, the river runs through the town, which is ten miles from the source. There are a number of burns accessible from Stratford by good roads.

Mangaehu River, tributary of Patea River.— Shingle and boulder bottom and bed. Banks mostly low and fairly clear. Wadeable partly. Landing deep, also good. Course, twenty-three miles. Contains brown and rainbow trout. Reached (to the mouth) by following up the Patea River forty-one miles from Patea Station (where there are hotels), on the Wellington–Wanganui – New Plymouth Railway; or from Stratford Station (where there are hotels), on the same railway, and thence by thirteen miles of road. For approach and accommodation see " Patea River," already mentioned.

Te Popo Burn, tributary of Patea River. — Shingle bottom and bed. Banks fairly clear. Wadeable partly. Landing deep, also good. Course, eight miles. Contains brown and rainbow trout. Reached (to the mouth) from Stratford Railway-station, and thence by three miles of road. For approach and accommodation see " Patea River," already mentioned.

Kahouri Burn, tributary of Te Popo Burn.— Shingle bottom and bed. Banks fairly clear. Wadeable partly. Landing deep, also good. Course, six miles. Contains brown and rainbow trout. Reached (to the mouth) from Stratford Railway-station, and thence by three miles of road. For approach and accommodation see " Te Popo Burn," already mentioned.

Whenuakura River.—Shingle bottom and bed. Banks fairly clear, with a little scrub and forest. Wadeable partly. Landing deep, also good. Course, thirty-one miles. Contains brown trout. Reached (to within two miles of the mouth) from the Whenuakura Station (where there is hotel accommodation), on the Wellington–Wanganui– New Plymouth Railway. A road from between Patea and the Whenuakura runs for twenty miles up the river, the upper ten miles being close to the river.

Waitotara River.—Sand and mud bottom in lower reaches, shingle and boulder bottom and bed in upper. Banks low and fairly clear, with forest here and there. Wadeable partly. Landing deep, also good. Course, fifty-five miles. Contains brown trout. Reached (to within four miles of the mouth) from the Waitotara Station (where there are hotels), on the Wellington–Wanganui–New Plymouth Railway. A road from Waitotara Railway-station runs up the river, and on reaching Kaimanuka, twenty-five miles from the mouth, keeps fairly near the river for twenty-two miles. Kaimanuka is also reached by whaleboat from the mouth of the river. Accommodation above Waitotara uncertain.

Kai-iwi River.—Shingle and boulder bottom and bed. Banks various, with some scrub and forest here and there. Wadeable partly. Landing deep, also good. Course, twenty-three miles. Reached (to within three miles of the mouth) from the Kai-iwi Station, on the Wellington–Wanganui–New Plymouth Railway. Accommodation uncertain nearer than Aramoho Junction (where there is hotel accommodation), on the same railway.

Wanganui River.—Tidal for thirty miles. Navigable for steamer of light draught to Pipiriki, sixty miles up, and for boats for eighty, to Taumaranui. There are some rapids to negotiate before reaching either of these places. Mud, sand, and shingle bottom in the lower reaches; shingle, rock, papa, boulder, and pumice bottom and bed in the upper. Banks in lower reaches mostly low, and willow-encumbered here and there, then partly low, partly cliffs, and a good deal scrub- and forest-clad. Wadeable partly. Landing deep, also good. Course, including the parts called Ongaruhe and Waimeha, 180 miles. Contains brown and rainbow trout. Reached (to within four miles of the mouth) at Wanganui (where there are hotels), on the Wellington–Wanganui–New Plymouth Railway, and through which the river flows; also (to the mouth, at Castlecliff) by the Wanganui–Castlecliff Railway, or by four miles of road from Wanganui. There is hotel accommodation at Castlecliff. The upper river is conveniently reached by steamer from Wanganui to Pipiriki, sixty miles, where there is accommodation, and where general information can be got about the river and tributaries. From Pipiriki a coach runs to Tokaanu, at the head of Lake Taupo, connecting with a coach service to Napier from the foot of the lake, and with a coach service to Lake Rotorua. Between the foot of Lake Taupo and on to Lake Rotorua is a chain of hot springs and baths. The Main Trunk Railway, Auckland to Wellington, is planned to reach the upper river from Auckland at about twenty-two miles from the source, and then to run for twenty-three miles down and close to the river.

MANGANUI-A-TE-Ao River, tributary of Wanganui River.—Snow-fed. Shingle, rock, and boulder bottom and bed. Banks partly low, partly cliffs, and a good deal forest-clad. Wadeable here and there. Landing deep, also good. Course, thirty-three miles. Contains brown and rainbow trout. Reached from Pipiriki, where there is accommodation, by tracks to various points, and (to the mouth) by canoe up the Wanganui River, seven miles from Pipiriki. For approach and accommodation see "Wanganui River," already mentioned.

WANGAMOMONA River, tributary of Wanganui River.—Shingle, rock, papa and boulder bottom and bed. Banks partly low, partly cliffs, and partly scrub and forest-clad. Wadeable partly. Landing deep, also good. Course, twenty-one miles. Contains brown and rainbow trout. Reached (to the mouth) from Pipiriki, where there is accommodation, by following up the Wanganui River twenty-four miles. For approach and accommodation see "Wanganui River," already mentioned.

TANGARAKAU River, tributary of Wanganui River. —Shingle, rock, boulder, and papa bottom and bed. Banks low and partly cliffs, a good deal forest-clad. Wadeable partly. Landing deep, also good. Course, fifty-five miles. Contains brown and rainbow trout. Reached (to the mouth) by following up the Wanganui River twenty-seven miles above Pipiriki, where there is accommodation; reached also from Stratford Station (where there are hotels), on the Wellington–Wanganui–New Plymouth Railway, thence by roads and tracks for forty-six miles, to a point fourteen miles from the mouth. For approach and accommodation see "Wanganui River," already mentioned.

RETARUKE River, tributary of Wanganui River.—Shingle, rock, and boulder bottom and bed. Banks, some low, some cliffs, a good deal forest-clad. Wadeable partly. Landing deep, also good. Course, twenty-six miles. Contains brown and rainbow trout. Reached (to the mouth) by following up the Wanganui River forty-eight miles above Pipiriki, where there is accommodation. For approach and accommodation see "Wanganui River," already mentioned.

OHURA River, tributary of Wanganui River.—Shingle, rock, boulder, and sand bottom and bed. There is a waterfall at the mouth, and another a quarter of a mile above. Banks from low to cliffs, and from forest-clad to fairly clear. Wadeable partly. Landing deep, also good. Course, fifty-three miles. Contains brown and rainbow trout. Reached (to the mouth) by following up the Wanganui River for fifty-one miles above Pipiriki, where there is accommodation. The Main Trunk Railway, Auckland to Wellington, is planned to run within five miles of the source, and then to run in the direction of the river for thirteen miles at a distance of five miles. For approach and accommodation see "Wanganui River," already mentioned.

TURAKINA River.—Shingle bottom and bed; some rock and several high waterfalls in upper reaches.

Banks chifly low and fairly clear in lower reaches, then some cliffs with forest here and there, and mostly forest towards the source. Wadeable. Landing mostly good. Course, sixty miles. Contains brown and rainbow trout. Reached (to the mouth) from the Turakina Station (where there are hotels) on the Wellington–Wanganui–New Plymouth Railway, thence five miles. Turakina is on the bank of the river. From Turakina roads run up near and in the immediate neighbourhood of the river for forty miles. The river can also be reached (to the middle and upper part) from the Marton–Hunterville Railway (the proposed Auckland–Wellington Main Trunk Railway). From the Hunterville Station, where there is hotel accommodation, the river can be reached by seven miles of road at thirty miles from the mouth. This road continues up the river for ten miles, and down the river thirty miles.

Mangapapa Stream, tributary of Turakina River. —Shingle and rock bottom and bed. Banks forest-clad here and there. Wadeable partly. Landing deep, also good. Course, twenty miles. Contains brown and rainbow trout. Reached (to the mouth) by following up the Turakina River thirty miles above Turakina ; or from the Hunterville Station, on the Marton–Hunterville Railway, and thence by twelve miles of road to the mouth. For approach and accommodation see " Turakina River," already mentioned.

Rangitikei River. — Shingle bed chiefly, with papa and sandstone in the upper reaches. Banks various, from fairly low to papa and sandstone cliffs of from 200 ft. to 400 ft. ; from twenty miles from the mouth they are more or less forest-clad, with clear intervals. Wadeable. Landing good, mostly. Course, 123 miles. Contains brown and rainbow trout. With the exception of thirty miles nearest the source, the greater part of the river is easily accessible by good roads and railways.

Reached (to the mouth), among several other ways, from Greatford Station (where there is accommodation), on the Wellington–Wanganui--New Plymouth Railway, and thence by fifteen miles of road near the bank. Three miles from Greatford on this road is Bulls, where there are hotels. At the mouth there is a ferry. Greatford is a mile from the river and twenty from the mouth. From Greatford up the river can be reached at short intervals from the railway for twenty-five miles, as far as Mangaonoho Station—the Marton–Hunterville Railway (the proposed Auckland–Wellington Main Trunk Railway) running at two or three miles distance from the river. At Hunterville Station there is hotel accommodation, forty-three miles from the mouth. From Mangaonoho, the present end of the line, there is a road within a short distance of the river for twenty miles up. At Ohingaiti, four miles along this road, there are hotels near the bank and fifty-four miles from the mouth. At Mangaweka, seven miles further on this road, there is accommodation close to the bank, sixty-two miles from the mouth. After passing Mangaweka the accommodation is uncertain at present.

Tutaenui Stream, tributary of Rangitikei River. —Shingle bottom and bed. Banks mostly low, and fairly clear. Wadeable partly. Landing deep, also good. Course, nineteen miles. Contains brown and rainbow trout. Reached (to the mouth) from the Greatford Station, on the Wellington–Wanganui–New Plymouth Railway, and thence by six miles of road, through Bulls (where there are hotels) two miles from the mouth and close to the stream. This road runs up and close to the stream its whole length. The stream passes close to the Greatford Station, six miles from the mouth, and close to the Marton Station, on the same railway (where there is hotel accommodation) twelve miles from the mouth. For approach and accommodation see "Rangitikei River," already mentioned.

POREWA River, tributary of Rangitikei River.— Shingle bottom and bed. Banks low and fairly clear. Wadeable partly. Landing deep, also good. Course, twenty-four miles. Contains brown and rainbow trout. Reached (to the mouth) from Marton Junction (where there is hotel accommodation), on the Marton–Hunterville Railway, then at short intervals from the railway, which is close to the stream, as far as Hunterville, where there is hotel accommodation, thirteen miles from the mouth. For approach and accommodation see "Rangitikei River," already mentioned.

MANGAMAKO Burn, tributary of Rangitikei River. Shingle bottom and bed. Banks various, with some scrub and forest. Wadeable partly. Landing deep, also good. Course, ten miles. Contains brown and rainbow trout. Reached (to the mouth) from Mangaonoho Station, on the Marton–Hunterville Railway, and thence by two miles. For approach and accommodation see "Rangitikei River," already mentioned.

MAKOHINE Stream, tributary of Rangitikei River. —Shingle bottom and bed. Banks mostly high and steep, and mostly forest-clad. Wadeable partly. Landing deep, also good. Course, thirteen miles. Contains brown and rainbow trout. Reached (to the mouth) from Mangaonoho Station, on the Marton–Hunterville Railway, thence by two miles of road, which crosses it at the mouth. Two miles further on this road is Ohingaiti, where there are hotels. For approach and accommodation see "Rangitikei River," already mentioned.

KAWHATAU River, tributary of Rangitikei River. —Shingle bottom and bed. Banks partly high and steep cliffs, more or less forest-clad. Wadeable partly. Landing deep, also good. Course, twenty-six miles. Contains brown and rainbow trout. Reached (to the mouth) from the Mangaonoho Station, on the Marton–Hunterville Railway, by thirteen miles of road *viâ* Mangaweka. A road runs up the bank of the river from the mouth for ten miles. For approach and accommodation see "Rangitikei River," already mentioned.

HAUTAPU River, tributary of Rangitikei River.— Shingle, rock, and papa bottom and bed. Banks low and cliffs, and forest-clad in lower and middle reaches, low and clear in upper. Wadeable partly. Landing deep, also good. Course, thirty-six miles. Contains brown and rainbow trout. Reached (to the mouth) from the Mangaonoho Station, on the Marton–Hunterville Railway; thence by seventeen miles of road *viâ* Mangaweka. This road runs close up the bank of the river for seven miles, to Otaihape, where it crosses the river; nine miles further on, the road again reaches the river, twenty miles from the mouth, and continues close up the bank for eight miles. For approach and accommodation see "Rangitikei River," already mentioned.

MOAWHANGO River, tributary of Rangitikei River. —Shingle and rock bottom and bed. Banks various; partly forest-clad for a third of the course, then fairly low and clear. Wadeable partly. Landing deep, also good. Course, forty-two miles. Contains brown and rainbow trout. Reached (to the mouth) from the Mangaonoho Station, on the Marton–Hunterville Railway; thence by seventeen miles of road to the mouth of the Hautapu River, and thence by following up the Rangitikei River for eight miles. For approach and accommodation see "Rangitikei River," already mentioned.

MANGAMAIRE Stream, tributary of Rangitikei River.—Shingle bottom and bed. Banks low and fairly clear. Wadeable. Landing mostly good. Course, sixteen miles. Contains brown and rain-bow trout. Reached (to the mouth) by following up the Rangitikei River for nineteen miles from where it is crossed by the West Coast–Kuripapanga

Road. For approach and accommodation see "Rangitikei River," already mentioned.

Manawatu River.—Estuary about three miles. Tidal for some twelve miles; navigable for small steamers for that distance. Sand, shingle, rock, and papa bottom and bed. Banks chiefly low and alluvial with some flax and forest for forty-four miles; then rock gorge for four miles, dividing the Ruahine and Tararua Ranges; then partly low, partly gravel and papa cliffs, more or less forest-clad, to the source. Wadeable partly. Landing deep, also good. Course, 113 miles. Contains brown and rainbow trout. It rises on the eastern side of the Ruahine Range, and passes through good and settled country.

The greater part of the river and most of the tributaries are within moderate distance of railway-stations by good driving-roads.

There are thirty fishable tributaries, a number of which are generally in good order when the main river is too much discoloured. It was first stocked by the author with ova obtained from Otago in 1872.

Reached (to within four miles of the mouth) from the Foxton Railway-station (where there are hotels), on the Palmerston–Foxton line, and thence by four miles of road. At the Shannon Station (where there is hotel accommodation), on the Wellington and Manawatu Company's Railway, close to the river, sixteen miles from the mouth. From Longburn Junction (where there is hotel accommodation), on the Wellington and Manawatu Company's Railway, close to the river, thirty-nine miles from the mouth. At Palmerston North Station (where there are hotels), on the Wellington–Wanganui–New Plymouth and Wellington–Palmerston–Napier Railways. Palmerston North is a mile from the river, and forty-three miles from the mouth. At several stations between Palmerston North and Ashhurst, nine miles, the railway

CATCH OF TROUT, HAWKE'S BAY DISTRICT.

and road are a mile from the river. From Ashhurst Station (where there are hotels close to the river), on the Palmerston North–Napier Railway, and fifty-three miles from the mouth: from Ashhurst to Woodville there is a road of nine miles; four miles of this runs through the gorge on the river-bank. From Woodville Junction, where there are hotels; thence by road or rail, four miles, to the river, at sixty-four miles from the mouth. Woodville is conveniently situated for getting to several good tributaries in the neighbourhood. Here also useful information about the river and tributaries can be obtained. At several stations between Woodville and Dannevirke (seventeen miles) the railway and road are three miles from the river by roads. There is also a road of twenty-one miles from Woodville to Dannevirke: eleven miles of this road is up the bank of the river; ten miles from Woodville on this road is Kumeroa, where there is hotel accommodation near the river; Kumeroa is seventy miles from the mouth. From Dannevirke (where there are hotels), on the Wellington–Napier Railway, the river is reached by road of three miles; this is eighty-three miles from the mouth. Above here for fifteen miles the river is not so easily got at, the banks being a good deal forest-clad. From the Makotuku Station (where there are hotels), on the Wellington–Napier Railway, the river is reached in a mile and a half; this is ninety-eight miles from the mouth. From Ormondville Station (where there is hotel accommodation), on the Wellington–Napier Railway, the river is reached by a mile and a half of road; this is one hundred miles from the mouth. At Kopua Station, which is near the river, on the Wellington–Napier Railway; this is one hundred and three miles from the mouth. Accommodation near the river above here is uncertain, except by returning to Ormondville; or Takapau may be reached from the river in seven miles by road or railway. Here are several rivers and streams discharging on the east coast, this being the watershed. For these see Chapter XVI., "North Island—Rivers and Lakes of the East Coast: Tukituki River."

Otauru Burn, tributary of Manawatu River.—Shingle bed. Banks various and fairly clear. Wadeable. Landing deep, also good. Course, ten miles. Contains brown and rainbow trout. Reached (to the mouth) from Shannon Station (by which it flows, and where there is hotel accommodation), on the Wellington and Manawatu Company's Railway. For approach and accommodation see "Manawatu River," already mentioned.

Tokomaru Stream, tributary of Manawatu River.—Shingle and mud bottom in lower reaches, shingle bed in upper. Banks mostly low and fairly clear. Wadeable partly. Landing deep, also good. Course, thirteen miles. Contains brown and rainbow trout. Reached (to the mouth) at Tokomaru Station (to which it is close), on the Wellington and Manawatu Company's Railway. Nearest hotel is at Longburn Junction, eight miles by railway or road. For approach and accommodation see "Manawatu River," already mentioned.

Oroua River, tributary of Manawatu River.—Shingle bottom in lower reaches; shingle bed in upper, rock towards the source. Banks in lower reaches low, with some willows; fairly clear in upper until near the source, where there is some forest. Wadeable partly. Landing deep, also good. Course, seventy miles. Contains brown and rainbow trout. Reached (to within a mile of the mouth) at the Oroua Bridge Station (which is close to the bank), on the Palmerston North–Foxton Line. The nearest hotel is at Longburn Junction, seven miles off by railway or road. Fourteen miles up the river from

the mouth there is a hotel, at Awahuri, half a mile
from the river and eight miles by road from the
Palmerston North Railway-station (where there
are hotels), on the Wellington–Wanganui–New
Plymouth and Napier Railways. Five miles up the
river from Awahuri by road is Feilding Station
(which is close to the river, and where there are
hotels), on the Palmerston North–Wanganui–New
Plymouth Railway; this is eighteen miles from
the mouth. Eight miles up the river by road from
Feilding Station is Cheltenham, where there is
hotel accommodation within a mile of the river;
this is twenty-eight miles from the mouth. Ten
miles up the river by road from Cheltenham is
Fowler's, where there is hotel accommodation
within a mile of the river; this is forty miles
from the mouth. Ten miles up the river by road
from Fowler's is Apiti, where there is hotel accommodation within a mile of the river; this is
fifty-one miles from the mouth. Five miles above
Apiti is Rangiwahia, where there is hotel accommodation a mile and a half from the river; this is
fifty-six miles from the mouth. For approach and
accommodation see " Manawatu River," already
mentioned.

TAINUI Stream, tributary of Oroua River.—
Shingle bottom and bed. Banks mostly low, with
some willows in lower reaches, fairly clear in
upper. Wadeable partly. Landing deep, also
good. Course, sixteen miles. Contains brown
and rainbow trout. Reached (to the mouth) at
the Oroua Bridge Station, on the Palmerston
North–Foxton Line. The nearest hotel is at
Longburn Junction, seven miles off by railway
or road. Ten miles up the stream is Awahuri,
where there is hotel accommodation. Awahuri
can be reached by three miles of road ; or Palmerston North Station (where there are hotels),
on the Wellington – Wanganui – New Plymouth
Railway, can be reached by five miles of road.

For approach and accommodation see "Oroua River," already mentioned.

KIWITEA River, tributary of Oroua River.—Shingle bottom and bed. Banks low and fairly clear in lower reaches, forest-clad towards the source. Wadeable partly. Landing deep, also good. Course, thirty-two miles. Contains brown and rainbow trout. Reached (to the mouth) from Feilding Station (where there are hotels), on the Palmerston North – Wanganui – New Plymouth Railway, by a mile of road. Eight miles up the river by road from Feilding Station is Cheltenham, where there is hotel accommodation within half a mile of the river by road: this is about seven miles from the mouth. Twenty-six miles up the river by road from Cheltenham is Pemberton, where there is hotel accommodation two miles from the river; this is thirty miles from the mouth. For approach and accommodation see " Oroua River," already mentioned.

TIRITEA Stream, tributary of Manawatu River. Shingle bottom and bed. Banks various and fairly clear. Wadeable partly. Landing deep, also good. Course, thirteen miles. Contains brown and rainbow trout. Reached (to the mouth) from Palmerston North Station (where there are hotels), on the Wellington–Wanganui – New Plymouth and Napier Railway, thence two miles of road to the Manawatu River, then a mile up the bank. For approach and accommodation see " Manawatu River," already mentioned.

POHANGINA River, tributary of Manawatu River. —Shingle bed. Banks various, low and alluvial in the lower reaches, high and steep towards the source, with scrub and forest here and there. Wadeable. Landing mostly good. Course, seventy-seven miles. Contains brown and rainbow trout. Reached (to the mouth) from the Ashhurst Station (where there are hotels), on the Palmerston–Napier Railway, thence by a mile. From Ashhurst a road runs up the bank of the river for eight miles to Pohangina, which is on the bank of the river : this is ten miles from the mouth.

MAKIEKIE Stream, tributary of Pohangina River. —Shingle bed, rock towards the source. Banks rather steep, more or less scrub- and forest-clad. Wadeable partly. Landing deep, also good. Course, fourteen miles. Contains brown and rainbow trout. Reached (to the mouth) from the Ashhurst Station (where there are hotels), on the Palmerston–Napier Railway, thence by eight miles of road to Pohangina, and by following up the Pohangina River for six miles. For approach and accommodation see " Pohangina River," already mentioned.

MANGAATUA Stream, tributary of Manawatu River. —Shingle bottom and bed. Banks low, fairly clear, with some scrub. Wadeable partly. Landing deep, also good. Course, thirteen miles. Contains brown and rainbow trout. Reached (to the mouth) from Woodville Junction, where there are hotels, thence by four miles of road; four miles from the mouth it runs close to Woodville. For approach and accommodation see " Manawatu River," already mentioned.

MANGAHAO River, tributary of Manawatu River.— Shingle, rock, and boulder bottom and bed. Banks low, high, precipices and rock gorges. Fairly clear with some scrub in lower reaches, forest-clad in upper. Wadeable partly. Landing deep, also good. Course, forty-four miles. Contains brown and rainbow trout. Rises among the snow-clad peaks of the Tararua Ranges. It is second only to the Manawatu River in importance. Maori tradition says that it rises in the famous Lake Hapuakorai, where water-fowl are very plentiful. It runs to within six miles of Shannon; then, turning sharp to the east, cuts a deep gorge, one of the finest in this country, through the Tararua Ranges, emerging at the Kakariki clearing. Reached (to within a mile and a half of the mouth) from the

Mangatainoka Station (where there is hotel accommodation), on the Wellington–Napier Railway, thence by four miles of road. Ballance, where there is accommodation, is three miles from the mouth and on the banks. It is also reached from the Pahiatua Station (where there are hotels), on the Wellington–Napier Railway, thence by a mile; this is about eight miles from the mouth. From Makakahi Station, on the same railway, thence by a mile : this is fourteen miles from the mouth. From Tutaekara Station, on the same railway, thence a mile and a half; this is seventeen miles from the mouth. From Hukanui Station, thence two miles; this is twenty-one miles from the mouth. Above this it becomes less easy of access. For approach and accommodation see " Manawatu River," already mentioned.

Makaretu Burn, tributary of Mangahao River.—Shingle bottom and bed. Banks fairly clear, with some scrub. Wadeable partly. Landing deep, also good. Course, seven miles. Contains brown and rainbow trout. Reached (to the mouth) in a mile from Ballance. For approach and accommodation see " Mangahao River," already mentioned.

Matarua Burn, tributary of Mangahao River.—Shingle bottom and bed. Banks fairly clear, with some scrub. Wadeable partly. Landing deep, also good. Course, six miles. Contains brown and rainbow trout. Reached (to the mouth) from Pahiatua Station, thence four miles; or from Ballance, thence by four miles of road up the bank of the Mangahao River. For approach and accommodation see " Mangahao River," already mentioned.

Tiraumea River, tributary of Manawatu River.—Shingle, papa, and rock bottom. Banks mostly steep, with papa cliffs and some scrub. Landing deep, also good. Course, forty-three miles. Contains brown and rainbow trout. Reached (to the mouth) from the Ngawapurua Station, on the Wellington–Napier Railway. Mangatainoka Station (where there is hotel accommodation), on the same railway, is three miles from the river and three miles from the mouth. It is also reached from Pahiatua Station, on the same railway, thence by six miles of road to Kaitawa, where there is accommodation on the bank; this is twelve miles from the mouth. Twelve miles up the river from Kaitawa is Alfredton, where there is accommodation, two miles and a half by road from the bank; this is twenty-four miles from the mouth. Alfredton is also reached from the Eketahuna Station, on the same railway, and thence by twelve miles of road. From Alfredton a road runs up the bank of the river for thirteen miles. For approach and accommodation see "Manawatu River," already mentioned.

MANGATAINOKA River, tributary of Tiraumea River.—Shingle bed. Banks mostly low and fairly clear except towards the source. Wadeable. Landing deep, also good. Course, thirty-four miles. Contains brown and rainbow trout. Reached (to the mouth) from Ngawapurua Station, on the Wellington–Napier Railway, thence in a mile; also from the Mangatainoka Station (where there is hotel accommodation on the bank), on the same railway; this is three miles from the mouth. A road from here runs to Eketahuna Railway-station, twenty miles. Sixteen miles of this road is within half a mile of the river, with hotel and other accommodation at intervals. It is also reached from Pahiatua Station (where there are hotels near the river), on the same railway; this is six miles from the mouth. From Makakahi Station (where there is hotel accommodation) a mile from the river, on the same railway; this is twelve miles from the mouth. From Eketahuna Station (where there are hotels), on the same railway, thence by eight miles of road; this is twenty-five miles from the mouth. For approach and accommodation see " Tiraumea River," already mentioned.

MAKAKAHI River, tributary of Mangatainoka River.—Shingle bottom and bed. Banks low and fairly clear, with some scrub. Wadeable partly. Landing deep, also good. Course, twenty-six miles. Contains brown and rainbow trout. Reached (to the mouth) from the Pahiatua Station (where there are hotels), on the Wellington–Napier Railway, thence by following up the Mangatainoka River for three miles. From the mouth a road runs close to the river for twenty-one miles. At Eketahuna Station, on the same railway, there are hotels close to the river. This is fifteen miles from the mouth. For approach and accommodation see " Mangatainoka River," already mentioned.

MAKAIRO Burn, tributary of Tiraumea River.— Shingle bed. Banks fairly clear. Wadeable. Landing mostly good. Course, nine miles. Contains brown and rainbow trout. Reached (to the mouth) from the Mangatainoka Station (where there is hotel accommodation), on the Wellington–Napier Railway, thence by six miles of road. For approach and accommodation see " Tiraumea River," already mentioned.

MAKURI Stream, tributary of Tiraumea River.— Shingle and rock bottom and bed. Banks in lower reaches high, with rocky gorge seven miles from mouth for two miles; then lower, and fairly clear in upper. Wadeable partly. Landing deep, also good. Course, sixteen miles. Contains brown and rainbow trout. Reached (to the mouth) from Pahiatua Station, on the Wellington – Napier Railway, thence by six miles of road to Kaitawa, where there is accommodation, then two miles down the Tiraumea River. Nine miles by road up the river-bank from Kaitawa is Makuri, where there is hotel accommodation. For approach and accommodation see " Tiraumea River," already mentioned.

Iʜᴜʀᴀɴᴀ Stream, tributary of Tiraumea River.—
Shingle bottom and bed. Banks fairly clear.
Wadeable partly. Landing deep, also good.
Course, thirteen miles. Contains brown and rainbow trout. Reached from the Eketahuna Station,
on the Wellington – Napier Railway, thence by
twelve miles of road to Alfredton, where there is
accommodation, and which is half a mile from the
bank and three from the mouth. For approach
and accommodation see " Tiraumea River," already
mentioned.

Aᴡᴀᴘɪᴋᴏᴘɪᴋᴏ Burn, tributary of Manawatu River.
Shingle bottom and bed. Banks fairly clear, with
some scrub. Wadeable partly. Landing deep,
also good. Course, six miles. Contains brown
and rainbow trout. Reached (to the mouth) from
Kumeroa, where is hotel accommodation, thence
by two miles of road. For approach and accommodation see " Manawatu River," already mentioned.

Rᴀᴘᴀʀᴀᴘᴀᴡᴀɪ Burn. — Shingle bottom and bed.
Banks low, more or less scrub-encumbered and
forest-clad. Wadeable partly. Landing deep, also
good. Course, ten miles. Contains brown and
rainbow trout. Reached (to the mouth, opposite
Kumeroa, where there is hotel accommodation) by
the Woodville–Kumeroa–Dannevirke Road. Also
at the Matahiwi Station, on the Wellington–Napier
Railway, and by the Woodville–Dannevirke Road,
which crosses it at the same place. This is four
miles from the mouth. For approach and accommodation see " Manawatu River," already mentioned.

Oᴛᴀᴡᴀ Burn, tributary of Manawatu River.—
Shingle bottom and bed. Banks partly forest-clad
in lower reaches, with some scrub in upper. Wadeable. Landing deep, also good. Course, six miles.
Contains brown and rainbow trout. Reached (to
near the mouth) from Kumeroa, where there is
hotel accommodation, thence by a mile and a half

of road. For approach and accommodation see
" Manawatu River," already mentioned.

OTOPE Burn, tributary of Manawatu River.—
Shingle bottom and bed. Banks mostly high, and
more or less scrub-encumbered and forest-clad.
Wadeable partly. Landing deep, also good.
Course, six miles. Contains brown and rainbow
trout. Reached (to the mouth) from Kumeroa,
where there is hotel accommodation, thence by
four miles of the Woodville–Kumeroa–Dannevirke
Road. A road runs up the burn for the whole
length. For approach and accommodation see
" Manawatu River," already mentioned.

ORUAKERITAKI Burn, tributary of Manawatu
River.—Shingle bottom and bed. Banks mostly
high, and more or less scrub- and forest-clad.
Wadeable partly. Landing deep, also good.
Course, nine miles. Contains brown and rainbow
trout. Reached (to the mouth) from the Woodville–Kumeroa–Dannevirke Road, six miles from
Kumeroa, where there is hotel accommodation;
also (a mile above the mouth) from the Tahoraite
Station, on the Wellington–Napier Railway, thence
by a mile of road. The Woodville–Dannevirke
Road crosses it at the same place. There are
hotels in Dannevirke, which is five miles by road
from this crossing. For approach and accommodation see " Manawatu River," already mentioned.

TAMAKI Stream, tributary of Manawatu River.
—Shingle bed. Banks mostly low gravel, partly
clear and partly scrub- and forest-clad. Wadeable
mostly. Landing mostly good. Course, thirteen
miles. Contains brown and rainbow trout.
Reached (to within two miles of the mouth) from
the Tahoraite Station, on the Wellington–Napier
Railway, thence by track down the stream. The
Tahoraite Station is half a mile from the banks.
The Woodville – Dannevirke Road crosses the
stream near the same place as the railway, three
miles from Dannevirke, where there are hotels.

RIVER AT SIDE OF HOUSE.

For approach and accommodation see "Manawatu River," already mentioned.

KAKAIWHANGA Burn, tributary of Tamaki Stream. —Shingle bottom and bed. Banks chiefly low gravel, partly scrub - encumbered. Wadeable. Landing mostly good. Course, five miles. Contains brown and rainbow trout. Reached (to the mouth) by following up the Tamaki Stream for three miles from the Tahoraite Railway-station or Woodville–Dannevirke Road. For approach and accommodation see "Tamaki Stream," already mentioned.

MANGATERA Stream, tributary of Manawatu River.—Shingle bottom and bed. Banks partly high and steep, partly low, more or less scrub- and forest-clad. Wadeable partly. Landing deep, also good. Course, eleven miles. Contains brown and rainbow trout. Reached (to the mouth) from the Dannevirke Station (where there are hotels), on the Wellington–Napier Railway, thence by three miles and a half of the Dannevirke–Tahoraite– Weber Road; also crossed by the Dannevirke– Weber Road a mile from Dannevirke and two from the mouth. From the Mangatera Station, where there is hotel accommodation a quarter of a mile from the stream. This is the end of the main street of Dannevirke, and five miles from the mouth. For approach and accommodation see " Manawatu River," already mentioned.

TAPUATA Burn, tributary of Mangatera Stream. —Shingle bottom chiefly. Banks steep, and more or less scrub- and forest-clad. Wadeable partly. Landing mostly deep. Course, seven miles. Contains brown and rainbow trout. Reached (to the mouth) by a mile of the Dannevirke–Weber Road, where it crosses the Mangatera Stream. Also crossed by the Dannevirke–Tahoraite Road two miles from the mouth, and at Dannevirke. For approach and accommodation see " Mangatera Stream," already mentioned.

MANGATORO Stream, tributary of Manawatu River.
—Shingle bottom and bed. Banks in lower reaches
high precipices of papa and gravel, and forest-clad;
lower, papa and gravel, and partly scrub- and
forest-clad in upper. Wadeable partly. Landing
deep, also good. Course, twenty miles. Contains
brown and rainbow trout. It is reached (to the
mouth) from the Dannevirke Station (where there
are hotels), on the Wellington–Napier Railway,
by roads and forest-tracks for eight miles; also
by the Dannevirke–Weber Road, which crosses
it ten miles from Dannevirke and five from the
mouth. There is no accommodation nearer than
Dannevirke. For approach and accommodation
see " Manawatu River," already mentioned.

This was probably the first stream to contain
trout in the North Island, being stocked by the
author, on whose property it was, in the early
seventies, with ova obtained as a present from
Otago, and also with ova from his private hatchery.
The ova had to be carried more than fifty miles on
packhorses over rough forest tracks, as the termination of a long sea and land journey. The ven-
ture was a great success. Trout of large size and
in considerable number were soon to be seen.
Later, the hatchery owed its success to the care of
Mr. Robert Smith, the manager of the property,
and to that of his wife, Mrs. Smith, who in Mr.
Smith's absence on one occasion left her bed in
the middle of the night, and, without any prepara-
tion, waded the rising river in a violent thunder
and rain storm, and so rescued twenty thousand
hatched ova, a large number in those days.

MANGAMAIRE Burn, tributary of Mangatoro
Stream.—Shingle bottom mostly. Banks high, and
precipices, of papa; forest-clad in lower reaches;
lower, and forest - clad in upper. Wadeable
partly. Landing deep, also good. Course, seven
miles. Contains brown and rainbow trout.
Reached (to the mouth) from Dannevirke by

RIVERS AT BACK OF HOUSE—MEETING OF THE MANAWATU AND MANGATORO.

ten miles of the Dannevirke–Weber Road, to the Mangatoro Stream, then one mile. For approach and accommodation see " Mangatoro Stream," already mentioned.

MANGAPAPATEA Burn, tributary of Mangatoro Stream. — Shingle and rock bottom. Banks mostly steep and high papa, scrub-encumbered. Wadeable partly. Landing mostly deep. Course, five miles. Contains brown and rainbow trout. Reached (to the mouth) from Dannevirke by the Dannevirke–Weber Road to the Mangatoro Stream, then up the bank of the Mangatoro for a mile and a half. For approach and accommodation see " Mangatoro Stream," already mentioned.

MANGATAKOTO Burn, tributary of Mangatoro Stream. –– Shingle, boulder, and rock bottom. Banks high, steep, and forest-clad in lower reaches; lower, with some scrub, in upper. Wadeable partly. Landing mostly deep. Course, five miles. Contains brown and rainbow trout. Reached (to the mouth) from Dannevirke by the Dannevirke – Weber Road to the Mangatoro Stream, then up the bank of the Mangatoro for four miles. For approach and accommodation see " Mangatoro Stream," already mentioned.

WAITAHORA Burn, tributary of Mangatakoto Burn. — Shingle and rock bottom. Banks low, with some scrub. Wadeable partly. Landing mostly deep. Course, three miles. Contains brown and rainbow trout. Reached (to the mouth) by following up the Mangatakoto Burn for a mile and a half from the mouth. For approach and accommodation see " Mangatakoto Burn," already mentioned.

MANGAPUAKA Stream, tributary of Manawatu River. — Shingle, boulder, and rock bottom. Banks high, steep, and forest-clad in lower reaches; lower and partly clear in upper. Wadeable partly. Landing mostly deep. Course eleven miles. Contains brown and rainbow trout.

Reached (to the mouth) from Dannevirke by eleven miles of roads and forest tracks. It cannot well be reached by a stranger without a guide. For approach and accommodation see " Manawatu River," already mentioned.

MANGATEWAINUI Stream, tributary of Manawatu River.—Shingle bed. Banks high, and more or less forest-clad. Wadeable mostly. Landing deep, also good. Course, sixteen miles. Contains brown and rainbow trout. Reached from the Makotuku Station (where there are hotels), on the Wellington–Napier Railway, thence by two miles along the railway, which crosses it four miles from the mouth. Also reached from the Dannevirke – Norsewood Road, which crosses it nine miles from Dannevirke and eight from the mouth : there are hotels at Matamau, four miles by road from here. For approach and accommodation see " Manawatu River," already mentioned.

MANGATEWAI-ITI Burn, tributary of Mangatewainui Stream.—Shingle bottom and bed. Banks high and mostly forest-clad. Wadeable partly. Landing deep, also good. Course, nine miles. Contains brown and rainbow trout. Reached from the Dannevirke – Norsewood Road, which crosses it eight miles from Dannevirke and two from the mouth ; also (to the mouth) from the Mangatewainui Stream, half a mile above the railway. For approach and accommodation see " Mangatewainui," already mentioned.

OHAU Stream.—Shingle bed. Banks low and fairly clear. Wadeable. Landing good. Course, twenty miles. Contains brown and rainbow trout. Reached at the Ohau Station, on the Wellington and Manawatu Company's Railway, which is five miles from the mouth. The nearest hotels are at Levin, three miles off by road and railway.

WAIKAWA Stream. — Shingle bottom mostly. Banks high and fairly clear, with some scrub and willows. Not much wadeable. Landing mostly deep. Course, twelve miles. Contains brown and rainbow trout. Reached from the Manakau Station (where there is hotel accommodation), on the Wellington and Manawatu Company's Railway, a mile by road from the stream and four from the mouth, to which a road runs from the station.

MANAKAU Burn, tributary of Waikawa Stream. —Mud and shingle bottom. Banks fairly clear. Wadeable partly. Landing deep, also good. Course, six miles. Reached (to the mouth) by two miles of road from the Manakau Station. For approach and accommodation see " Waikawa Stream," already mentioned.

WAITOHU Stream. — Shingle bottom. Banks fairly clear, with some scrub. Wadeable partly. Landing deep, also good. Course, fourteen miles. Contains brown and rainbow trout. Reached (to the mouth) from the Otaki Station (where there are hotels), on the Wellington and Manawatu Company's Railway, thence by three miles of road; also from the station by a mile of road, to three miles from the mouth.

OTAKI River.—Shingle bottom and bed, with rock in upper reaches. Banks low and fairly clear in lower reaches, rock gorges and forest-clad in upper. Wadeable partly. Landing deep, also good. Course, thirty miles. Contains brown and rainbow trout. Reached from the Otaki Station (where there are hotels), on the Wellington and Manawatu Company's Railway; this is half a mile from the bank and two miles from the mouth, to which there is a road.

WAIKANAE Stream.— Shingle bottom and bed. Banks low and fairly clear. Wadeable partly. Landing deep, also good. Course, twelve miles. Contains brown and rainbow trout. Reached from the Waikanae Station (where there is accommodation), on the Wellington and Manawatu Company's

Railway. This is on the bank, and three miles from the mouth.

PORIRUA HARBOUR.—Running into this are the Horokiwi, Pahautanui, and Porirua Burns, which contain brown and rainbow trout. Reached from the Porirua Station, where there is hotel accommodation. The Horokiwi, which is the furthest away, is reached (to the mouth) in three miles.

CHAPTER XVIII.

MIDDLE ISLAND—NORTH COAST.

RIVERS FROM CAPE KOAMORU TO CAPE FAREWELL
(BEGINNING AT THE EAST).

WAITOHI Burn.—Shingle bed and bottom. Banks in lower reaches fairly clear ; high, steep, and forest-clad in upper. Wadeable. Landing deep, also good. Course, four miles. Contains brown trout. Runs through Picton (where there are hotels), which is reached by steamer, or from Blenheim by rail.

KAITUNA Stream. — Estuary short, with mud bottom ; mud and shingle bottom higher. Banks low and partly forest-clad. Wadeable. Landing deep, also good. Course, twelve miles. Contains brown trout. Reached by Blenheim–Nelson Coach-road, which runs close to the stream for the whole length. There are hotels at Havelock, four miles from the mouth, and accommodation further up.

PELORUS River. — Estuary a mile, with mud bottom ; then boulder and shingle bottom. Tidal for short distance. Banks mostly high and forest-clad. Wadeable partly. Landing deep, also good. Course, thirty-two miles. Contains brown trout. Reached (to the mouth) by the Blenheim–Nelson Coach-road at Havelock, twenty-eight miles from Blenheim and fifty from Nelson. There are hotels at Havelock.

WAKAMARINA Stream, tributary of Pelorus River. —Shingle bottom ; boulder gorges in upper reaches. Banks mostly high, steep, and forest-clad. Wadeable mostly. Landing deep, also good. Course, eleven miles. Contains brown trout. For approach and accommodation see " Pelorus River," already mentioned.

Rai Burn, tributary of Pelorus River.—Shingle and mud bottom. Banks low and almost entirely forest-clad. Wadeable partly. Landing mostly deep. Course, nine miles. Contains brown trout. For approach and accommodation see " Pelorus River," already mentioned.

Tinline Burn, tributary of Pelorus River.— Boulder and shingle bottom. Banks hilly and forest-clad. Wadeable. Landing deep, also good. Course, seven miles. Contains brown trout. For approach and accommodation see " Pelorus River," already mentioned.

Wangamoa Stream. — Boulder and shingle bottom. Banks fairly clear towards the mouth; forest-clad in upper reaches. Wadeable. Landing deep, mostly. Course, eleven miles. Contains brown trout. Reached from the Nelson–Blenheim Coach-road, which runs within four miles of the mouth and crosses it twelve miles from Nelson, where there are hotels.

Collins Burn, tributary of Wangamoa Stream. —Rock and boulder bottom. Banks partly forest-clad. Wadeable. Landing deep, mostly. Course, four miles. Contains brown trout. For approach and accommodation see " Wangamoa Stream," already mentioned.

Wakapuaka Burn.—Shingle and rock bottom. Banks steep and partly forest-clad towards source. Wadeable. Landing mostly deep. Course, nine miles. Contains brown trout. Crossed by the Nelson–Blenheim Coach-road, eight miles from Nelson, and from this crossing there is a road close to the burn to its mouth. There are hotels at Nelson.

Maitai Stream. — Shingle bottom for first few miles, then rock and boulder for five miles, then shingle bed. Banks steep and fairly clear for six

CATCH OF TROUT, NELSON DISTRICT.

miles, then scrub- and forest-clad. Wadeable mostly. Landing deep, also good. Course, eleven miles. Contains brown and rainbow trout. Reached from Nelson, through which it runs into the sea. Nelson, where there are hotels, is approached by steamer, railway, and coach-road from Westport, and by coach from Blenheim.

Waimea River.—Estuary short, with sand and shingle bottom. Tidal for about a mile, then shingle bed and bottom, then rock and boulder gorges. Banks mostly low and clear for ten miles, then steep and forest-clad. Wadeable partly. Landing mostly good. Course, including the part called Wairoa, twenty-three miles. Contains brown trout. Reached from Brightwater Railway-station, on the Nelson–Motupiko Railway, where there is hotel accommodation, six miles from the mouth.

Roding Stream, tributary of Waimea River.—Boulder and rock gorge. Banks steep and forest-clad. Wadeable partly. Landing mostly deep. Course, fifteen miles. Contains brown trout. For approach and accommodation see " Waimea River," already mentioned.

Lee Stream, tributary of Roding Stream.—Boulder, shingle, and rock bottom. Banks steep and forest-clad. Wadeable partly. Landing mostly deep. Course, twelve miles. Contains brown trout. For approach and accommodation see " Roding Stream," already mentioned.

Hackett Burn, tributary of Roding Stream.—Boulder and shingle bed. Banks close and confined, partly clear and partly forest-clad. Wadeable. Landing deep, also good. Course, four miles. Contains brown trout. For approach and accommodation see " Roding Stream," already mentioned.

Wai-iti Stream, tributary of Waimea River.—Shingle bottom and bed. Banks low and clear in lower reaches, partly scrub-encumbered in upper.

Wadeable. Landing mostly good. Course, nineteen miles. Contains brown trout. Reached from Brightwater Railway-station, where there is hotel accommodation, two miles from the mouth; from Spring Grove Railway-station; from Wakefield Railway-station, where there is hotel accommodation; from Wai-iti Railway-station; from Foxhill Railway-station, where there is hotel accommodation; from Belgrove Railway-station, where there is hotel accommodation. All these stations are on the Nelson–Motupiko Railway, and close to the stream. A coach-road from Nelson also runs for some miles close to the stream.

MOTUEKA River.—Shingle bed and bottom for twenty miles, then rock and boulder gorges for ten miles, then shingle bed to source. Banks various, mostly clear, with patches of forest and scrub. Wadeable partly. Landing mostly good. Course, sixty miles. Contains brown trout. Reached from Motueka, which is about a mile from the mouth, and where there are hotels. Motueka is sixteen miles by sea from Nelson, from which small steamers run almost daily. The river is also reached by railway from Nelson to Motupiko, on the Nelson–Motupiko Railway, where there is hotel accommodation close to the bank, at a point thirty-six miles from the mouth and close to the junction of the Motueka River and Motupiko River, which are here crossed by a bridge. From Motueka to this bridge a road runs for thirty-three miles, from which the river and some of the tributaries are fairly accessible.

GRAHAM Burn, tributary of Motueka River.— Rock bottom. Banks high, partly clear, partly forest-clad. Wadeable. Landing deep, also good. Course, six miles. Contains brown trout. Reached from the Motueka–Motupiko Road at a point twelve miles from Motueka. For approach and accommodation see "Motueka River," already mentioned.

Pearse Burn, tributary of Motueka River.—
Boulder and shingle bottom. Banks steep and
forest-clad. Wadeable partly. Landing mostly
deep. Course, six miles. Contains brown trout.
Reached from the Motueka–Motupiko Road at a
point fourteen miles from Motueka; partly by a
branch road from Thorpe. For approach and accommodation see " Motueka River," already mentioned.

Dove Stream, tributary of Motueka River.—
Rock and shingle bottom. Banks steep and partly
clear. Wadeable. Landing good. Course, eleven
miles. Contains brown trout. Reached from the
Motueka–Motupiko Road at Thorpe, fourteen miles
from Motueka, where the road crosses it, and where
a branch road runs close to it for three miles to its
junction with the Motueka River. For approach
and accommodation see " Motueka River," already
mentioned.

Baton Stream, tributary of Motueka River.—
Boulder and rock bottom. Banks steep, forest and
scrub-clad. Wadeable. Landing deep mostly.
Course, thirteen miles. Contains brown trout.
For approach see " Dove Stream," already men-
tioned, and for approach and accommodation see
" Motueka River," already mentioned.

Sherry Stream, tributary of Motueka River.—
Shingle, boulder, and rock bottom and bed.
Banks low in lower reaches, and partly clear;
forest-clad in upper. Wadeable partly. Landing
deep, also good. Course, fifteen miles. Contains
brown trout. Reached (to the mouth) from the
Motueka-Motupiko Road at a point twenty-two
miles from Motueka and eleven from Motupiko,
where there is hotel accommodation. For approach and accommodation see " Motueka River,"
already mentioned.

Wangapeka Stream, a tributary of Sherry
Stream. — Boulder, shingle, and rock bottom.
Banks low in lower reaches and partly clear;

forest-clad in upper. Wadeable partly. Landing deep, also good. Course, fifteen miles. Contains brown trout. For approach and accommodation see " Sherry Stream," already mentioned.

Tadmor Stream, tributary of Motueka River.— Shingle bed and bottom. Banks mostly low, partly clear, also scrub- and forest-clad. Wade-able. Landing deep, also good. Course, twenty miles. Contains brown trout. Reached from the Motueka–Motupiko Road at a point twenty-six miles from Motueka and seven from Motupiko, where there is hotel accommodation. For approach and accommodation see " Motueka River," already mentioned.

Motupiko River, tributary of Motueka River.— Shingle bed in lower reaches, rock bottom in upper. Banks mostly low and clear, higher up gorge. Wadeable. Landing deep, also good. Course, twenty-eight miles. Contains brown trout. Reached fram Motupiko Railway-station, where there is hotel accommodation, and which is close to the mouth. For approach and accommodation see " Motueka River," already mentioned.

Riwaka Stream. Shingle bed lower half, then boulder and rock. Banks low and fairly clear in lower reaches, forest-clad in upper. Wadeable. Landing mostly good. Course, eleven miles. Contains brown trout. Reached from Riwaka, where there is hotel accommodation within a mile of the mouth. Riwaka is four miles by road from Motueka, already mentioned, which see for further approach and accommodation.

Takaka River. — Short estuary; then shingle bed for ten miles; then rock and boulder for five miles; then shingle, boulder, and rock. Banks fairly clear for fourteen miles, then mostly forest-clad. Wadeable partly. Landing deep, also good. Course, thirty-five miles. Contains brown trout. Reached by steamer from Nelson to Port Waitapu, in the estuary, from which Takaka Township is three miles by coach-road. The township is also three miles from the mouth. Connected also with Riwaka, Motueka, and Nelson by coach-road. There is hotel accommodation in Takaka and at Upper Takaka, which is sixteen miles up the bank by road. There are some limestone caves of interest near by, also springs.

ANATOKI Stream, tributary of Takaka River.— Shingle, boulder, and rock bed. Banks fairly clear in lower reaches, a good deal forest-clad in upper. Wadeable partly. Landing deep, also good. Course, nineteen miles. Contains brown trout. Reached (to the mouth) at Takaka. For approach and accommodation see " Takaka River," already mentioned.

WAINGARO Stream, tributary of Takaka River.— Shingle, rock, and boulder bottom and bed. Banks fairly clear in lower reaches, a good deal forest-clad in upper. Wadeable partly. Landing deep, also good. Course, seventeen miles. Contains brown trout. Reached (to the mouth) from Takaka by two miles of road. For approach and accommodation see " Takaka River," already mentioned.

WAITUHI Burn, tributary of Takaka River.— Shingle, boulder, and rock bottom and bed. Banks more or less forest-clad. Wadeable partly. Landing deep, also good. Course, nine miles. Contains brown trout. Reached (to the mouth) from Takaka by thirteen miles of road. There is accommodation two miles from the mouth. For approach and accommodation see " Takaka River," already mentioned.

PARAPARA Stream.—Tidal for three miles ; then rock, boulder, and shingle bed for five miles ; then rock, boulder, and shingle bottom. Banks, lower half fairly clear, upper forest-clad. Wadeable partly. Landing deep, also good. Course, twelve miles. Contains brown trout. Reached (to the mouth) from Collingwood, from which it is three miles by road. For approach and accommodation see " Aorere River," following.

AORERE River.—Boulder and rock bottom, in the upper part rock gorge. Banks steep, high, and much forest-clad. Wadeable partly. Landing deep mostly. Course, thirty-five miles. Contains brown trout. Reached from Collingwood, which is close to the mouth, and where there is hotel accommodation, and which is reached by steamer and by coach-road from Nelson.

KAITUNA Burn, tributary of Aorere River.—Rock and boulder bottom. Banks mostly forest-clad, some cleared. Wadeable. Landing deep mostly. Course, five miles. Contains brown trout. Reached (to the mouth) from Collingwood by track of three miles. For approach and accommodation see " Aorere River," already mentioned.

SLATE Stream, tributary of Aorere River.— Shingle, rock, and boulder bottom and bed. Banks more or less forest-clad. Wadeable partly. Course, twelve miles. Contains brown trout. Reached (to the mouth) from Collingwood by road of seven miles. For approach and accommodation see " Aorere River," already mentioned.

CHAPTER XIX.

MIDDLE ISLAND—EAST COAST.

RIVERS AND LAKES FROM CAPE KOAMORU TO LONG POINT (IRIHUKA), (BEGINNING AT THE NORTH).

WAIRAU River.—Estuary of four miles, mud and shingle bottom; tidal for six miles; then open shingle bed and bottom for sixty miles; then rock and boulder bottom and bed for thirty miles. Banks low for the first seventy miles, except a few miles on the left bank; then steep and rocky in the upper reaches. Mostly clear, except twenty miles towards the source, which are forest-clad. Wadeable partly. Landing deep, also good. Course 100 miles. Contains brown trout. Accessible from Blenheim, which s reached by railway from Picton, and which is reached by steamer from various ports. Blenheim is also reached by coach from Nelson, and from the south by coach from the east coast. There are hotels in Blenheim. The Picton–Blenheim Railway crosses and is near the river at the Spring Creek Station, four miles from Blenheim, and eight miles from the mouth; also at the Tuamarina Station, where there is hotel accommodation, six miles from Blenheim. The river is reached by roads near the banks from Blenheim, as far as the ford on the Nelson Coach-road, eight miles from Blenheim. Here is Renwicktown, on the coach-road, where there is hotel accommodation, seven miles from Blenheim. From Renwicktown a road follows the river for some eighty miles; accommodation uncertain.

TUAMARINA Burn, tributary of Wairau River.—
Mud and shingle bottom. Banks low mostly, and
scrub-encumbered. Wadeable partly. Landing
deep, also good. Course ten miles. Contains
brown trout. For approach and accommodation
see " Wairau River," already mentioned.

WAIKAKAHO Burn, tributary of Wairau River.—
Shingle bed and bottom. Banks low, open, and
mostly clear. Wadeable. Landing mostly good.
Course, eight miles. Contains brown trout.
Reached by four miles of road from Tuamarina
Railway-station, where is a hotel. For approach
and accommodation see " Wairau River," already
mentioned.

WAIHOPAI River, tributary of Wairau River.—
Shingle bed and bottom. Banks low and fairly
clear. Wadeable. Landing mostly good. Course,
forty-one miles. Contains brown trout. Reached
by six miles of road from Renwicktown. For
approach and accommodation see " Wairau River,"
already mentioned.

TIMMS Burn, tributary of Wairau River.—
Shingle bed and bottom. Banks various, and
forest-clad in upper reaches. Landing deep, also
good. Course, nine miles. Contains brown trout.
Reached by nineteen miles of road from Renwicktown. For approach and accommodation see
" Wairau River," already mentioned.

TOP VALLEY Burn, tributary of Wairau River.—
Shingle bed and bottom. Banks clear in lower
reaches, partly forest-clad. Wadeable. Landing
deep, also good. Course, six miles. Contains
brown trout. Reached by twenty-four miles of
road from Renwicktown. For approach and
accommodation see " Wairau River," already
mentioned.

WYE Stream, tributary of Wairau River.—
Shingle bed and bottom. Banks partly clear and
partly scrub-encumbered. Wadeable. Landing
deep, also good. Course eleven miles. Contains

brown trout. Reached from Renwicktown by twenty-nine miles of road, which crosses it. For approach and accommodation see " Wairau River," already mentioned.

GOULTER Stream, tributary of Wairau River.— Shingle and boulder bed and bottom. Banks clear for three miles, then forest-clad to the source. Wadeable. Landing deep, also good. Course, eleven miles. Contains brown trout. Reached by thirty-six miles of road from Renwicktown. For approach and accommodation see " Wairau River," already mentioned.

BRANCH River, tributary of Wairau River.— Shingle and boulder bed and bottom. Banks clear in lower reaches, and forest-clad in upper. Wadeable. Landing deep, also good. Course, twenty-four miles. Contains brown trout. Reached from Renwicktown by thirty-six miles of road, which crosses the river. For approach and accommodation see " Wairau River," already mentioned.

LEATHAM River, tributary of Branch River.— Shingle and boulder bed and bottom. Banks clear in lower reaches, and forest-clad in upper. Wadeable. Landing deep, also good. Course, twenty-two miles. For approach see " Branch River," already mentioned.

RAINBOW Burn, tributary of Wairau River.— Boulder and rock bottom. Banks steep and clear. Wadeable partly. Landing deep, also good. Course, nine miles. Contains brown trout. Reached by seventy miles of road from Renwicktown. For approach and accommodation see " Wairau River," already mentioned.

OPAWA River (an overflow from the Wairau River).—Estuary, two miles. Tidal for ten miles, mud and shingle bottom for twelve miles, then shingle bed for eight miles. Banks in lower reaches high and willow-encumbered, in upper reaches low and fairly clear. Wadeable for eight miles in upper reaches. Landing in lower reaches deep, in upper reaches good. Course, eighteen miles. Contains brown trout. Accessible easily by good roads from Blenheim, which is on the river, and where there is hotel accommodation.

TAYLOR Burn, tributary of Opawa River.— Shingle bed and bottom. Banks in the upper reaches high and scrub-encumbered. Wadeable. Landing deep, also good. Course, nine miles. Contains brown trout. For approach and accommodation see "Opawa River," already mentioned.

OMAKA River, tributary of Opawa River.— Shingle bottom and bed. Banks low and open. Wadeable. Landing mostly good. Course, twenty-five miles. Contains brown trout. For approach and accommodation see "Opawa River," already mentioned.

AWATERE River.—Shingle bed. Banks some distance above mouth low and clear ; then for a number of miles high papa cliffs on right bank, left bank mostly low, both banks pretty clear ; banks more contracted in upper reaches, with occasional rock and boulder gorges. Wadeable. Landing chiefly good. Course, sixty-eight miles. Contains brown trout. Accessible from Blenheim by good roads, which follow the river for sixty miles ; but accommodation uncertain. At Awatere there is hotel accommodation, twelve miles by road from Blenheim. This is twelve miles from the mouth of the river.

BLAIRICH Burn, tributary of Awatere River.— Shingle and boulder bed. Banks low, and scrub-encumbered in places. Wadeable. Landing good. Course, eight miles. .Contains brown trout. Reached by six miles of road from Awatere. For approach and accommodation see "Awatere River," already mentioned.

MEDWAY Burn, tributary of Awatere River.— Shingle and boulder bed. Banks low, and scrub-encumbered in places. Wadeable. Landing good. Course, ten miles. Contains brown trout. Reached

TROUT CAUGHT, MARLBOROUGH DISTRICT.

by ten miles of road from Awatere. For approach and accommodation see " Awatere River," already mentioned.

HODDER Burn, tributary of Awatere River.—Boulder and shingle bed. Banks low, and partly scrub-encumbered. Wadeable. Landing good. Course, nine miles. Contains brown trout. Reached by twenty - four miles of road from Awatere. For approach and accommodation see " Awatere River," already mentioned.

GREY Burn, tributary of Awatere River.—Shingle and boulder bed. Banks high, and a good deal scrub-encumbered. Wadeable. Landing good. Course, nine miles. Contains brown trout. Reached by twenty - eight miles of road from Awatere. For approach and accommodation see " Awatere River," already mentioned.

WINTERTON Burn, tributary of Awatere River.—Boulder bed. Banks steep, high, and partly scrub-encumbered. Wadeable. Landing mostly good. Course, seven miles. Contains brown trout. Reached by thirty-two miles of road from Awatere. For approach and accommodation see " Awatere River," already mentioned.

CASTLE Burn, tributary of Awatere River.—Boulder and shingle bed. Banks low, and partly scrub-encumbered. Wadeable. Landing mostly good. Course, nine miles. Contains brown trout. Reached by thirty-six miles of road from Awatere. For approach and accommodation see " Awatere River," already mentioned.

TONE Stream, tributary of Awatere River.—Boulder and shingle bed. Banks low, and partly scrub-encumbered. Wadeable. Landing mostly good. Course, eleven miles. Contains brown trout. Reached by forty miles of road from Awatere. For approach and accommodation see " Awatere River," already mentioned.

FLAXBOURNE Stream.—Shingle bed. Banks low and fairly clear. Wadeable. Landing good.

Course, sixteen miles. Contains brown trout. Reached by coach-road from Blenheim, twenty-five miles. Accommodation uncertain.

URE Stream.—Limestone, boulder, and shingle bed. Banks low, and partly scrub-encumbered. Wadeable. Landing mostly good. Course, seventeen miles. Contains brown trout. Reached by coach-road from Blenheim, thirty - two miles. Accommodation uncertain.

KEKERANGU Burn. — Shingle bed and bottom. Banks low and fairly clear. Wadeable. Landing mostly good. Course, eight miles. Contains brown trout. Reached by fifty miles of coach-road from Blenheim to Kekerangu, where there is hotel accommodation.

CLARENCE River.—Boulder and shingle bed in lower reaches for ten miles; rock gorges for ten miles; then shingle bed to Lake Tennyson. Banks chiefly low and clear, a good deal flat. Wadeable mostly. Landing good. Course, 115 miles to Lake Tennyson. Contains brown trout. Reached (to the mouth) from Blenheim by coach-road, sixty-three miles. Accommodation uncertain here; and for many miles up—perhaps ninety—the angler must rely on his own resources. At this distance from the mouth the coach-road from Culverden to the Hanmer Springs is reached.

PUHIPUHI Burn, tributary of Clarence River.— Boulder torrent. Banks high. Course, six miles. Contains brown trout. Four miles from mouth of Clarence River. For approach and accommodation see " Clarence River," already mentioned.

MILLER Burn, tributary of Clarence River.— Shingle bed. Banks low, and partly scrub-encumbered. Wadeable. Landing good. Course, seven miles. Contains brown trout. Four miles from mouth of Clarence River. For approach and accommodation see " Clarence River," already mentioned.

GEORGE Burn, tributary of Clarence River.—
Boulder torrent. Banks, lower part low, higher
high and rugged, partly scrub-encumbered. Wadeable. Landing mostly good. Course, five miles.
Contains brown trout. Four miles from mouth of
Clarence River. For approach and accommodation
see " Clarence River," already mentioned.

McLEAN Burn, tributary of Clarence River.—
Boulder torrent. Banks, lower part low, higher up
high and rugged, partly scrub-encumbered. Wadeable. Landing mostly good. Course, four miles.
Contains brown trout. Nine miles from mouth of
Clarence River. For approach and accommodation see " Clarence River," already mentioned.

OUSE Burn, tributary of Clarence River.—
Boulder and shingle bed. Banks mostly high and
partly scrub-encumbered. Wadeable. Landing
deep and good. Course, five miles. Contains
brown trout. Twenty miles from mouth of Clarence River. For approach and accommodation
see " Clarence River," already mentioned.

MEAD Burn, tributary of Clarence River.—Limestone shingle bed. Banks low and clear. Wadeable. Landing good. Course, seven miles. Contains brown trout. Twenty-four miles from mouth
of Clarence River. For approach and accommodation see " Clarence River," already mentioned.

DEE Burn, tributary of Clarence River.—Boulder
and shingle bed. Banks low for two miles; then
steep gorge, clear. Wadeable. Landing deep,
also good. Course, six miles. Contains brown
trout. Twenty-seven miles from mouth of Clarence
River. For approach and accommodation see
" Clarence River," already mentioned.

BRANCH Burn, tributary of Clarence River.—
Shingle and boulder bed. Banks low for two miles;
then steep gorge more or less scrub- and forest-
encumbered. Wadeable partly. Landing deep,
also good. Course, six miles. Contains brown
trout. Thirty-one miles from mouth of Clarence

River. For approach and accommodation see "Clarence River," already mentioned.

JAM Burn, tributary of Clarence River.—Boulder torrent. Banks high, rugged, and partly scrub-encumbered. Wadeable. Course, four miles. Contains brown trout. Thirty-four miles from mouth of Clarence River. For approach and accommodation see "Clarence River," already mentioned.

DART Burn, tributary of Clarence River.— Boulder torrent. Banks high, rugged, and partly scrub-encumbered. Wadeable. Landing deep, also good. Course, five miles. Contains brown trout. Thirty-seven miles from mouth of Clarence River. For approach and accommodation see "Clarence River," already mentioned.

MUZZLE Burn, tributary of Clarence River.— Boulder torrent. Banks high, rugged, and partly scrub - encumbered. Wadeable. Landing deep, also good. Course, six miles. Contains brown trout. Forty-one miles from mouth of Clarence River. For approach and accommodation see "Clarence River," already mentioned.

FIDGET Burn, tributary of Clarence River.— Shingle and boulder bed. Banks low for two miles, then steep gorge. Fairly clear. Wadeable. Landing good mostly. Course, four miles. Contains brown trout. Forty - five miles from mouth of Clarence River. For approach and accommodation see "Clarence River," already mentioned.

DUBIOUS Burn, tributary of Clarence River.— Boulder and shingle bed. Banks for first mile low, then high and clear. Wadeable. Landing good mostly. Course, eight miles. Contains brown trout. Forty-eight miles from mouth of Clarence River. For approach and accommodation see "Clarence River," already mentioned.

BLUFF Burn, tributary of Clarence River.— Shingle bed. Banks steep, high, and partly scrub-encumbered. Wadeable. Landing mostly good. Course, five miles. Contains brown trout. Fifty miles from mouth of Clarence River. For approach and accommodation see " Clarence River," already mentioned.

LIMESTONE Burn, tributary of Clarence River.— Limestone, boulder, and shingle bed. Banks for first mile low; then high, rugged, and clear. Wadeable. Landing deep, also good. Course, five miles. Contains brown trout. Fifty-six miles from mouth of Clarence River.

GORE Burn, tributary of Clarence River.— Mountain torrent. Banks high, rugged, and clear. Wadeable. Landing mostly good. Course, seven miles. Contains brown trout. Sixty-two miles from mouth of Clarence River. For approach and accommodation see " Clarence River," already mentioned.

ELLIOTT Burn, tributary of Clarence River.— Shingle bed. Banks high and steep for first mile and a half, then low and clear all through. Wadeable. Landing good. Course, seven miles. Contains brown trout. Sixty-four miles from mouth of Clarence River. For approach and accommodation see " Clarence River," already mentioned.

TWEED Burn, tributary of Clarence River.— Shingle and boulder bed. Banks high and partly scrub-encumbered. Wadeable. Landing mostly good. Course, five miles. Contains brown trout. Sixty-seven miles from mouth of Clarence River. For approach and accommodation see " Clarence River," already mentioned.

PALMER Burn, tributary of Clarence River.— Boulder and shingle bed. Banks for three miles low, then high. Wadeable. Landing good. Course, four miles. Contains brown trout. Seventy-two miles from mouth of Clarence River. For approach and accommodation see " Clarence River," already mentioned.

DILLON Stream, tributary of Clarence River.—
Boulder and shingle bed. Banks high and partly
scrub-encumbered. Wadeable. Landing mostly
good. Course, fifteen miles. Contains brown
trout. Eighty-four miles from mouth of Clarence
River. For approach and accommodation see
" Clarence River," already mentioned.

HOSSACK Burn, tributary of Clarence River.—
Boulder and shingle bed. Banks high and partly
scrub-encumbered. Wadeable. Landing mostly
good. Course, ten miles. Contains brown trout.
Eighty-four miles from mouth of Clarence River.
For approach and accommodation see " Clarence
River," already mentioned.

ACHERON River, tributary of Clarence River.—
Shingle and boulder bed. Banks generally low,
open, and clear. Wadeable. Landing mostly
good. Course, forty-two miles. Contains brown
trout. Ninety miles from mouth of Clarence
River; also ten miles by road from a hotel near
Jollie's Pass, which is on the road to Hanmer
Springs, Upper Wairau, and Culverden Railway-
station, at all of which there are hotels. The
distance by road from Acheron River to Culverden
Railway-station is thirty-six miles. For approach
and accommodation see also " Clarence River,"
already mentioned.

GUIDE Stream, tributary of Acheron River.—
Shingle and boulder bed. Banks generally low,
open, and clear. Wadeable. Landing mostly
good. Course, twelve miles. Contains brown
trout. For approach and accommodation see
" Acheron River," already mentioned.

SEVERN Stream, tributary of Acheron River.—
Shingle and boulder bed. Banks generally low,
open, and clear. Wadeable. Landing mostly
good. Course, nineteen miles. Contains brown
trout. For approach and accommodation see
" Acheron River," already mentioned.

ALMA Stream, tributary of Severn Stream.—

Shingle and boulder bed. Banks generally low, open, and clear. Wadeable. Landing mostly good. Course, sixteen miles. For approach and accommodation see "Acheron River," already mentioned.

SAXTON Stream, tributary of Acheron River.—Shingle and boulder bed. Banks generally low, open, and clear. Wadeable. Landing mostly good. Course, fifteen miles. Contains brown trout. For approach and accommodation see "Acheron River," already mentioned.

LAKE TENNYSON, tributary of Clarence River.—Shingle bottom. Banks partly shelving shingle. Wadeable here and there. Landing mostly deep. Length, two miles; breadth, three-quarters of a mile. Height above sea level, 3,000 ft. Contains brown trout. Reached by track, almost entirely, of twenty-four miles from the Jollie's Pass Hotel. For approach and accommodation see "Acheron" and "Clarence" Rivers, already mentioned.

CLARENCE Burn, tributary of Lake Tennyson.—Rock and boulder bottom. Banks mostly clear. Wadeable. Landing deep, also good. Course, six miles. Contains brown trout. Reached from Lake Tennyson. For approach and accommodation see "Lake Tennyson," already mentioned.

HAPUKU Burn.—Shingle and boulder bed. Mountain torrent. Banks for first four miles low, then forest-encumbered. Wadeable. Landing mostly good. Course, seven miles. Contains brown trout. Reached by eight miles of road from Kaikoura, where there is hotel accommodation, and which is on the coach-road from Blenheim to Culverden Railway-station, on the Christchurch line. Culverden Station is distant from Kaikoura fifty-eight miles.

PUHIPUHI Burn, tributary of Hapuku Burn.—Boulder and shingle bed. Banks high, steep, and mostly forest-encumbered. Wadeable. Landing mostly good. Course, nine miles. Contains brown trout. For approach and accommodation see "Hapuku Burn," already mentioned.

KOHAI Stream.—Shingle and boulder bed. Banks for first four miles low, and then high and rugged and partly scrub- and forest-encumbered. Wadeable. Landing mostly good. Course, twelve miles. Contains brown trout. Reached by three miles of road from Kaikoura. For approach and accommodation see " Hapuku Burn," already mentioned.

KAHAUTARA Stream.—Shingle and boulder bed. Banks open in lower part, steep in upper. Wadeable. Landing deep, also good. Course, sixteen miles. Contains brown trout. Reached by six miles of road from Kaikoura. For approach and accommodation see " Hapuku Burn," already mentioned.

LINTON Burn, tributary of Kahautara River.— Boulder and shingle bed. Banks, steep mountain banks. Wadeable. Landing mostly good. Course, seven miles. Contains brown trout. For approach and accommodation see " Kahautara Stream," already mentioned.

CONWAY River. — Shingle and boulder bed for twenty-five miles. Banks generally clear, with patches of scrub here and there. Wadeable mostly. Landing mostly good. Course, thirty miles. Contains brown trout. Reached by track of sixteen miles from near mouth of Kahautara River, or from the Culverden–Kaikoura Coachroad, which crosses it twenty-four miles from the mouth, twenty-six miles from Kaikoura, and thirty-two miles from Culverden Railway-station. Accommodation uncertain.

LIMESTONE Burn, tributary of Conway River.— Rock and shingle bottom. Banks mostly clear and steep, with rock gorges. Wadeable partly. Landing deep, also good. Course, four miles. Contains brown trout. For approach and accommodation see " Conway River," already mentioned.

SPEY Burn, tributary of Conway River.—Shingle

and rock bottom. Banks fairly clear, and steep in places. Wadeable. Landing deep, also good. Course, eight miles. Contains brown trout. For approach and accommodation see " Conway River," already mentioned.

CHARWELL Stream, tributary of Conway River.— Shingle bed. Banks open and partly clear. Wadeable. Landing mostly good. Course, thirteen miles. Contains brown trout. For approach and accommodation see " Conway River," already mentioned.

WAIAU-UA River.—Snow-fed. Shingle bed for four miles; then rocky gorge with partly shingle bed for twelve miles; then twelve miles of shingle bed; then six miles of rocky gorge with shingle bottom; then shingle, rock, and boulder bed for sixty-two miles. Banks clear for forty miles, then partly clear and partly forest. Wadeable mostly. Course, ninety-six miles to Lake Thompson. Landing deep, also good. Contains brown trout. Approached by track of eight miles from the Conway River, at a point leaving that river at eight miles from the mouth, and reaching the Leader Stream and Waiau-ua River eight miles from the mouth; also reached from Waiau Township, where there is hotel accommodation, twenty-six miles from the mouth of the river, and fourteen by coach-road from the Culverden Railway-station, where there is hotel accommodation. The river is also reached from Rotherham, where there is hotel accommodation, and which is thirty-four miles from the mouth, and seven by coach-road from Culverden Railway-station. At Upper Waiau, sixteen miles further up the river from Rotherham, accommodation can be obtained. Upper Waiau is sixteen miles on the coach-road from Culverden Railway-station to Hanmer Springs. The river runs close to this road for twelve miles, and past Upper Waiau continues to run close to a road leading to Hopefield for another twelve miles, then there is only a

track for thirty miles up the bank of the river:
this track connects with the Clarence River near
Lake Tennyson, the rivers being here four miles
apart, and surrounded by mountains of from
6,000 ft. to nearly 8,000 ft. high.

LEADER Stream, tributary of Waiau-ua River.—
Shingle bed. Banks open and clear. Wadeable.
Landing mostly good. Course, sixteen miles.
Contains brown trout. For approach and accom-
modation see "Waiau-ua River," already men-
tioned.

GOWER Stream, tributary of Waiau-ua River.—
Shingle bed for four miles, then rocky bottom to
its source. Banks open for four miles, then more
rocky and steep. Wadeable. Landing deep, also
good. Course, sixteen miles. Contains brown
trout. For approach and accommodation see
" Waiau-ua River," already mentioned.

STANTON Burn, tributary of Waiau-ua River.—
Shingle bed. Banks clear and fairly open. Wadeable. Landing mostly good. Course, nine miles.
Contains brown trout. Reached from Waiau
Township, where there is hotel accommodation,
on the Culverden–Kaikoura Coach-road. For approach and accommodation see " Waiau-ua River,"
already mentioned.

MASON Stream, tributary of Waiau-ua River.—
Shingle bed. Banks steep generally, and fairly
clear in lower reaches. Wadeable. Landing
mostly good. Course, fifteen miles. Contains
brown trout. Reached from Waiau Township, to
which it is close, and where there is hotel accommodation, on the Culverden–Kaikoura Coach-road.

LOTTERY Stream, tributary of Mason River.—
Shingle bed in lower part, rocky in places higher
up. Banks steep and mostly clear, also partly
burnt forest. Wadeable. Landing deep, also
good. Course, seventeen miles. Contains brown
trout. For approach and accommodation see
" Mason Stream," already mentioned.

HANMER Stream, tributary of Waiau-ua River.—
Shingle bed. Banks open in lower reaches, burn
forest in upper parts. Wadeable. Landing deep,
also good. Contains brown trout. Course, fifteen
miles. Reached from Upper Waiau, to which it
is close, and which is on the Culverden–Hanmer
Coach-road, sixteen miles from Culverden. For
approach and accommodation see "Waiau-ua
River," already mentioned.

CHATTERTON Burn, tributary of Waiau-ua River.—
Shingle bed, and boulders in upper part. Banks
open and clear in lower reaches, burnt forest in
upper parts. Wadeable. Landing mostly good.
Course, seven miles. Contains brown trout. For
approach and accommodation see "Hanmer
Stream," and "Waiau-ua River," already mentioned.

HOPE River, tributary of Waiau-ua River.—
Shingle bed. Banks open and mostly clear in
lower reaches, partly open and partly forest in
upper. Wadeable. Landing mostly good. Course,
twenty - eight miles. Contains brown trout.
Reached by twelve miles of road up the Waiau-ua
River bank from Upper Waiau. For approach
and accommodation see "Waiau-ua River," already
mentioned.

KAKAPO Stream, tributary of Hope River.—
Shingle bed. Banks mostly clear. Wadeable.
Landing mostly good. Course, fifteen miles.
Contains brown trout. For approach and accom-
modation see "Hope River," already mentioned.

BOYLE River, tributary of Hope River.—Shingle
bed in lower reaches, rock gorges and boulders
higher up. Banks generally low and open. Wadeable. Landing deep, also good. Course, twenty-
one miles. Contains brown trout. For approach
and accommodation see "Hope River," already
mentioned.

DOUBTFUL Burn, tributary of Boyle River.—
Shingle and boulder bed. Banks more or less

rough, scrub- and forest-encumbered. Wadeable. Landing mostly good. Course, nine miles. Contains brown trout. For approach and accommodation see "Boyle River," already mentioned.

Lewis Burn, tributary of Boyle River.—Boulder and shingle bed and bottom. Banks various, with forest in places. Wadeable. Landing deep, also good. Course, ten miles. Contains brown trout. For approach and accommodation see "Boyle River," already mentioned.

Edwards Burn, tributary of Waiau-ua River.— Rock and shingle bed. Banks open and clear. Wadeable. Landing mostly good. Course, nine miles. Contains brown trout. Reached by twenty-four miles of road and track up the bank of the Waiau-ua River from Upper Waiau. For approach and accommodation see "Waiau-ua River," already mentioned.

Stanley Burn, tributary of Waiau-ua River.— Shingle bed. Banks steep and rough. Wadeable. Landing deep, also good. Course, ten miles. Contains brown trout. Reached by twenty-eight miles of road and track from Upper Waiau. For approach and accommodation see "Waiau-ua River," already mentioned.

Henry Burn, tributary of Waiau-ua River.— Rocky in lower part, shingle and rock in upper part. Banks rocky and steep. Wadeable. Landing deep mostly. Course, nine miles. Contains brown trout. Reached by thirty-two miles of road and track from Upper Waiau. For approach and accommodation see "Waiau-ua River," already mentioned.

Ada Burn, tributary of Waiau-ua River.—Shingle bed. Banks open, low, and clear, backed by forest. Wadeable. Landing good. Course, six miles. Contains brown trout. Reached in thirty-four miles of road and track from Upper Waiau. For approach and accommodation see "Waiau-ua River," already mentioned.

LAKE THOMPSON, tributary of Waiau-ua River.—
Shingle bottom. Banks fairly clear. Wadeable
partly. Length, one mile and three-quarters;
breadth, half a mile. Contains brown trout.
Reached by ninety-six miles from the mouth of
the Waiau-ua River. For approach and accommodation see "Waiau-ua River," already mentioned.

HURUNUI River.—Snow-fed. Shingle, boulder,
and rock bed, with rock gorges at intervals. Banks
generally open, but in places precipitous. Wadeable. Landing deep, also good. Course, including Lake Sumner, eighty-six miles. Contains
brown trout. Reached by the Christchurch–Culverden Railway, which crosses it near the Hawarden and Medway Stations thirty-three miles from
the mouth. At Hurunui Township, distant five
miles by road from these stations, there is hotel
accommodation. From Hurunui a road runs close
to the river to the mouth, and also up the river for
twenty miles; then the river has to be followed.

GRETA Burn, tributary of Hurunui River.—
Shingle and clay bottom. Banks steep. Wadeable partly. Landing deep, also good. Course,
nine miles. Contains brown trout. Reached
from Hurunui, from which it is twenty miles by
road. For approach and accommodation see
"Hurunui River," already mentioned.

KAIWARA Burn, tributary of Hurunui River.—
Shingle bed. Banks open and clear mostly. Wade-
able. Landing deep, also good. Course, ten
miles. Contains brown trout. Reached from
Hurunui, from which it is eighteen miles by road.
For approach and accommodation see "Hurunui
River," already mentioned.

WAIKARI River, tributary of Hurunui River.—
Shingle bed. Banks open. Wadeable. Landing
mostly good. Course, twenty-one miles. Contains brown trout. Reached from Hurunui, from
which it is sixteen miles by road; also from the

Waikari Railway-station (where there is hotel accommodation), on the Christchurch–Culverden Railway. For approach and accommodation see "Hurunui River," previously mentioned.

Pahau River, tributary of Hurunui River.— Shingle bed, then rock towards source. Banks mostly open. Wadeable. Landing deep, also good. Course, thirty miles. Contains brown trout. Reached from Hurunui, from which it is nine miles by road. For approach and accommodation see "Hurunui River," already mentioned.

Waitohi River, tributary of Hurunui River.— Shingle bed up to rocky gorge, eight miles from mouth; then gorge and steep banks. Banks mostly clear. Wadeable. Landing deep, also good. Course, twenty - seven miles. Contains brown trout. Reached from Hurunui, which is close to the junction with the Hurunui River, also from the railway, which crosses it near the Medbury and Hawarden Stations. For approach and accommodation see "Hurunui River," already mentioned.

Mandamus Burn, tributary of Hurunui River. —Shingle bed, with rocky gorges in upper part. Banks low in places, with rocky cliffs here and there. Wadeable. Landing mostly good. Course, ten miles. Contains brown trout. Reached by nine miles of road from the Hawarden or Medbury Railway-stations. For approach and accommodation see "Hurunui River," already mentioned.

Dove Burn, tributary of Mandamus Burn.— Shingle bed, with rocky gorges in upper part. Banks steep, and a good deal of burnt bush in upper part. Wadeable. Landing mostly good. Course, ten miles. Contains brown trout. For approach and accommodation see "Mandamus Burn," already mentioned.

Mytholm Stream, tributary of Hurunui River. —Shingle bed. Banks rough, with burnt forest.

Wadeable. Landing deep, also good. Course, twelve miles. Contains brown trout. Reached by twelve miles of road from the Hawarden or Medbury Railway-stations. For approach and accommodation see " Hurunui River," already mentioned.

SEAWARD Burn, tributary of Hurunui River.— Mountain torrent. Shingle, boulder, and rock bed. Banks open for four miles, then forest-clad. Wadeable partly. Landing deep, also good. Course, nine miles. Contains brown trout. Reached by eighteen miles of road from the Hawarden or Medbury Railway-stations. For approach and accommodation see " Hurunui River," already mentioned.

LAKE SUMNER, tributary of Hurunui River.—A good deal of deep water round edges. Both boulder and shingle beaches here and there. Banks forest-clad all round north side, open and partly scrub-covered round south side. Wadeable here and there. Landing mostly deep, except on west and south-west side. Length, six miles and a quarter; breadth, one mile. Height above sea-level, 1,727 ft. For approach and accommodation see " Hurunui River," already mentioned.

LAKE KATRINE, tributary of Lake Sumner.—Connected with Lake Sumner by half a mile of stream. Length, one mile; breadth, half a mile. Banks vary from shelving shingle to rocky. Wadeable partly. Landing deep, also good. Contains brown trout. For approach and accommodation see " Hurunui River," already mentioned.

HURUNUI River (South Branch).—Shingle bed in lower part, and rock bottom in upper. Banks partly rock, generally clear. Wadeable. Landing deep, also good. Course, thirty miles. Contains brown trout. Reached in twenty miles from the Hawarden or Medbury Stations. For approach and accommodation see " Hurunui River," already mentioned.

BLYTHE Stream.—Shingle and clay bed. Banks low and fairly clear. Wadeable. Landing deep, also good. Course, eleven miles. Contains brown trout. Reached by road of five miles from Lower Hurunui River. For approach and accommodation see " Hurunui River," already mentioned.

MOTANAU Stream.—Estuary of about two miles. Limestone and shingle bed. Banks open and fairly clear. Wadeable. Landing deep, also good. Course, ten miles. Contains brown trout. Reached by fifteen miles of road from the Waipara Station (where there is hotel accommodation), on the Christchurch–Culverden Railway.

WAIPARA River. — Lagoon estuary, brackish water. Shingle bed to gorge, twelve miles from mouth ; then rock, boulder, and shingle bed, with rocky gorges. Twenty-three miles from the mouth it divides into three branches. Wadeable. Landing deep, also good. Course, thirty-five miles. Contains brown trout. Reached from Waipara Station, where there is hotel accommodation, and where the Christchurch–Culverden Railway crosses it, eight miles from the mouth ; also from several stations between Waipara and Amberley, where there is hotel accommodation. From Waipara a road runs to where the river forks, fifteen miles up.

KOWHAI Stream (North Branch).—Divides a mile from the mouth. Shingle bed for twelve miles from mouth, then boulder bed. Banks mostly open. Wadeable. Landing deep, also good. Course, fourteen miles. Contains brown trout. Reached from Amberley Station, where there is hotel accommodation close to the stream, and where the Christchurch–Culverden Railway crosses it, four miles from the mouth. The lower part can be reached by a road of three miles from Amberley to Leithfield, where there is hotel accommodation ; the upper part can be reached from Amberley by road, which runs near the stream for eight miles.

Kowhai Stream (South Branch).—Shingle bed for eleven miles from junction, then boulder bed. Banks mostly open. Wadeable. Landing deep, also good. Course, thirteen miles. Contains brown trout. Reached from Balcairn Station, where there is hotel accommodation, and near which the Christchurch–Culverden Railway crosses it, three miles from the junction with the North Branch: from Balcairn there is a road of four miles to Leithfield, where there is hotel accommodation. See "North Branch." The upper part must be reached by following the stream from near Balcairn.

Ashley River.—Lagoon mouth, of brackish water. Shingle bed to gorge, thirty miles; then for three or four miles rocky gorge; then shingle bed for ten miles. Banks generally clear except in gorge, where partly forest-clad. Wadeable. Landing mostly good. Course, fifty miles. Contains brown trout. Reached from Ashley Station, which is close to the river and where the Christchurch–Culverden Railway crosses it, eight miles from the mouth, between Ashley and Rangiora Stations, two miles apart, and where there is hotel accommodation. From Ashley and Rangiora roads run for some twenty-five miles near the river and tributaries, and above those places.

Makerikeri Burn, tributary of Ashley-River.— Shingle bed. Banks open and clear. Wadeable. Landing mostly good. Course, eight miles. Contains brown trout. Reached from the Ashley Station by roads, three miles. For approach and accommodation see " Ashley River," already mentioned.

Okuku River, tributary of Ashley River.— Shingle bed for first five miles, then rocky and boulder. Banks low and fairly clear for first five miles, then steep and rocky. Wadeable. Landing deep, also good. Course, twenty-nine miles. Contains brown trout. Reached from the Ashley

Railway-station by roads that run near it. For approach and accommodation see " Ashley River," already mentioned.

GREY Burn, tributary of Okuku River.—Shingle and boulder bed. Banks open and clear for first three miles, then forest-clad. Wadeable. Landing deep and good. Course, seven miles. Contains brown trout. For approach and accommodation see " Okuku River," already mentioned.

KARETU Burn, tributary of Okuku River.—Shingle and boulder bed. Banks open and clear for first three miles, then forest-clad. Wadeable. Landing deep, also good. Course, six miles. Contains brown trout. For approach and accommodation see " Okuku River," already mentioned.

GARRY Stream, tributary of Ashley River.—Shingle and boulder bed. Banks clear for first three miles, then forest-clad. Wadeable. Landing deep, also good. Course, eleven miles. Contains brown trout. For approach and accommodation see " Ashley River," already mentioned.

TOWNSEND Burn, tributary of Ashley River.—Shingle and boulder bed. Banks partly open and partly forest-clad. Wadeable. Landing deep, also good. Course, eight miles. Contains brown trout. For approach and accommodation see " Ashley River," already mentioned.

WHISTLER Burn, tributary of Ashley River.—Shingle and boulder bed. Banks clear and low for first five miles, then steep and forest-clad. Wadeable. Landing mostly good. Course, ten miles. Contains brown trout. For approach and accommodation see " Ashley River," already mentioned.

DUCK Burn, tributary of Ashley River.—Shingle bottom near mouth, clay and shingle higher up. Banks low and open. Wadeable. Landing deep, also good. Course, seven miles. Contains brown trout. For approach and accommodation see " Ashley River," already mentioned.

Waimakariri River.—Snow-fed. Tidal for three miles, with sand and clay bottom; then shingle bed for forty miles; then rock gorge with shingle and rock bottom for twelve miles; then shingle bed for thirty miles; then boulder and rock to source. Banks low and mostly clear except in gorge and towards the source, where they are forest-clad. Wadeable mostly. Landing deep, also good. Course, 100 miles. Contains brown trout. Reached from Kaiapoi Station (where there are hotels), on the Christchurch–Culverden Railway, which crosses it here four miles from the mouth; also from several stations between this and Christchurch, as the river runs close to the line here for four miles; also from the Harewood Road, which runs near the river for seven miles, and which crosses it ten miles from Papanui, which is five miles by rail from Christchurch—this crossing is twenty miles from the mouth; also by the Lower Waimakariri Road, which runs near the river from Courtenay up for eight miles. Courtenay is thirty miles from the mouth of the river, and accommodation can be arranged; or Courtenay can be reached from Christchurch to Kirwee Station on the Christchurch–Springfield Railway, and thence by two miles of road to Courtenay; also from Sheffield Station (where there is hotel accommodation), on the same railway; this is two miles from the river and forty from the mouth. The river can also be reached from Springfield Station (where there is hotel accommodation), on the same railway; this is two miles from the river and forty.six from the mouth. Springfield is the present railway terminus, from which coaches start for the west coast *viâ* the Otira Gorge, and is conveniently situated to several tributaries of the Waimakariri. From Springfield up, the river must be followed for thirty miles, with uncertain accommodation, when it nears the road to the West Coast, near which it runs for ten miles. The coach can be taken on this road from Springfield to Bealey, fifty miles, where there is hotel accommodation. _ This road crosses, and is near several tributaries and tributary lakes. Bealey is eighty-five miles from the mouth, and over 2,000 ft. above sea-level. By continuing this coach-road for seventeen miles through the Otira Gorge, where there is hotel accommodation, the Otira Burn, a tributary of the Teremakau River, is reached; and this river leads to its outlet on the west coast between Greymouth and Hokitika.

Styx Stream, tributary of Waimakariri River.—Shingle and clay bottom. Banks low and clear. Not wadeable. Landing deep. Course, twelve miles. Contains brown trout. Reached in a mile or two from several railway-stations between Christchurch and Kaiapoi. At Christchurch, Belfast, and Kaiapoi there are hotels. For approach and accommodation see " Waimakariri River," already mentioned.

Cust River, tributary of Waimakariri River.—Shingle and clay bottom. Banks low and clear. Wadeable partly. Landing mostly deep. Course, twenty-four miles. Contains brown trout. Reached from several stations between Kaiapoi and Cust Stations, at both of which there is hotel accommodation. For approach and accommodation see " Waimakariri River," already mentioned.

Eyre River, tributary of Waimakariri River.—Shingle bed. Banks clear, low, and open for ten miles above Oxford; then forest-clad. Wadeable. Landing good. Course, thirty-eight miles. Contains brown trout. Reached within a mile or two from a number of railway-stations between Kaiapoi and Oxford, at both of which places there are hotels. Oxford is twenty-five miles from the mouth. For approach and accommodation see " Waimakariri River," already mentioned.

Kowai Stream, tributary of Waimakariri River.—Shingle and boulder bed. Banks low, also clear. Wadeable. Landing mostly good. Course, fourteen miles. Fishable only above the dam generally. Contains brown trout. Reached from Springfield Station (where there is hotel accommodation), on the Christchurch–Springfield Railway ; also from the coach-road to the west coast, on which accommodation can be obtained. For approach and accommodation see " Waimakariri River," already mentioned.

LITTLE KOWAI Burn, tributary of Kowai Stream. —Shingle bed. Banks various, with forest towards the source. Wadeable. Landing mostly good. Course, seven miles. Contains brown trout. Reached from Springfield Station (where there is hotel accommodation), on the Christchurch–Springfield Railway. For approach and accommodation see " Kowai Stream," already mentioned.

RUBICON Burn, tributary of Kowai Stream.— Shingle and boulder bed. Banks for first two or three miles low and clear, and then forest-clad. Wadeable. Landing deep, also good. Course, six miles. Contains brown trout. For approach and accommodation see " Kowai Stream," already mentioned.

LAKE RUBICON part of Rubicon Burn.—Shingle bottom. Banks partly forest-encumbered. Wadeable partly. Landing deep, also good. Length, one mile ; breadth, half a mile. Contains brown trout. For approach and accommodation see " Kowai Stream," already mentioned.

BROKEN Stream, tributary of Waimakariri River. —Rock and boulder bottom. Banks generally steep, and partly clear. Wadeable partly. Landing mostly deep. Course, seventeen miles. Contains brown trout. Reached (to the mouth) by following the Waimakariri River for twelve miles above Springfield ; higher up (where accommodation may be obtained), from the Springfield–West Coast Road, which crosses it, and runs near it and several feeders. For approach and accommodation see " Waimakariri River," already mentioned.

PORTER Burn, tributary of Broken Stream.—
Shingle, boulder, and rock bottom. Banks various,
and partly clear. Wadeable partly. Landing
deep, also good. Course, nine miles. Contains
brown trout. For approach and accommodation
see upper part of "Broken Stream," and "Waimakariri River," already mentioned.

WINDING BURN, tributary of Broken Stream.—
Shingle and boulder bottom and bed. Banks
mostly clear. Wadeable partly. Landing mostly
good. Course, including Lake Pearson, ten
miles. Contains brown trout. For approach
and accommodation see upper part of "Broken
Stream," and "Waimakariri River," already mentioned.

LAKE PEARSON, part of Winding Burn.—Shingle
bottom and beaches, with water of moderate depth
near sides in places. Banks mostly open. Wadeable in places. Landing mostly deep. Length,
two miles ; breadth, quarter of a mile. Contains
brown trout. For approach and accommodation
see upper part of "Broken Stream" and "Waimakariri River," already mentioned.

ESK Stream, tributary of Waimakariri River.—
Shingle bed mostly. Banks mostly clear, partly
forest-clad. Wadeable. Landing mostly good.
Course, twenty miles. Contains brown trout.
Reached by following the Waimakariri River for
twenty-two miles above Springfield. For approach
and accommodation see "Waimakariri River,"
already mentioned.

POULTER River, tributary of Waimakariri River.
—Shingle and rock bed. Banks partly steep,
partly low, chiefly clear within a few miles of the
mouth, and then forest-clad. Wadeable mostly.
Landing mostly good. Course, twenty-three miles.
Contains brown trout. Reached by following the
Waimakariri River for twenty-five miles above
Springfield. For approach and accommodation
see "Waimakariri River," already mentioned.

Cass Burn, tributary of Waimakariri River.—
Shingle and boulder bed. Banks open for two or
three miles, then steep and forest-clad. Wadeable.
Landing mostly good. Course, eight miles. Contains brown trout. Reached by following the
Waimakariri River for thirty-seven miles above
Springfield, or from the coach-road which crosses
it eleven miles from Bealey, where there is hotel
accommodation. For approach and accommodation see " Waimakariri River," already mentioned.

Lake Grassmere, tributary of Cass Burn. —
Shingle bottom and beach on south side. Banks
generally low and clear; on north side is some
scrub. Wadeable partly. Landing deep, also good.
Length, one mile; breadth, half a mile. Contains
brown trout. Reached from the Springfield–West
Coast Road, which runs near it thirteen miles from
Bealey, where there is hotel accommodation. For
approach and accommodation see " Cass Burn,"
already mentioned.

Hawdon Burn, tributary of Waimakariri River.
—Shingle and boulder bed. Banks forest-clad
after the first mile. Wadeable. Landing deep,
also good. Course, ten miles. Contains brown
trout. Reached from the Springfield–West Coast
Road nine miles from Bealey, where there is
hotel accommodation. For approach and accommodation see " Waimakariri River," already mentioned.

Bealey Stream, tributary of Waimakariri River.
—Shingle and boulder bed. Banks partly clear,
partly forest-clad. Wadeable. Landing deep, also
good. Course, nine miles. Contains brown trout.
Reached from the Bealey Hotel, to which it is
close, on the Springfield–West Coast Road. For
approach and accommodation see " Waimakariri
River," already mentioned.

Avon Stream. — Shingle and clay bottom.
Banks low and clear mostly. Wadeable partly.
Landing mostly deep. Course, sixteen miles.

Contains brown trout. Reached from Christchurch, through which it runs, and where there is hotel accommodation.

HEATHCOTE Stream.—Tidal for about two miles, with mud bottom, banks low; then mud and shingle bottom, banks low, with willow groves. Not wadeable. Landing deep. Course, seventeen miles. Contains brown trout. Reached from Christchurch, to which it is close, aud where there is hotel accommodation.

LAKE ELLESMERE. —Discharges into the sea, from which it is separated by a shingle bank. Mud bottom, shingle beach on south, rather shallow generally. Wadeable partly. Landing deep, also good. Length, fifteen miles ; breadth, seven miles. Contains brown trout. Reached from several stations between Ellesmere and South-bridge Stations on the Christchurch–Southbridge Railway. Ellesmere is five miles from the lake. Accommodation may be had at Irwell, which is two miles from the lake. At Doyleston, which is three miles from the bank, there is hotel accom-modation. At Leeston, which is four miles from the lake, there is hotel accommodation ; and at Southbridge, which is seven miles by road from the outlet, there is hotel accommodation.

SELWYN River, tributary of Lake Ellesmere.— Shingle bed ; banks low and clear. Wadeable partly. Landing mostly good. Course, fifty miles. Contains brown trout. Fishable for thirty miles. Reached from the Ellesmere Station, on the Christ-church–Southbridge Railway, which is six miles from the lake. Near this station, down the river, accommodation may be obtained. There is hotel accommodation at the Springston Station, four miles off; also at the Selwyn Station, which is fifteen miles from the lake. In dry seasons the river gets very low or disappears altogether for twenty miles above Selwyn. The river is also reached from the Coalgate, Glentunnel, South

Malvern, and White Cliffs Stations (which are close to the river), on the Christchurch–White Cliffs Railway. At Glentunnel and South Malvern there are hotels.

HAWKINS River, tributary of Selwyn River.— Shingle bed for fourteen miles, then shingle bottom for six miles. Banks low and clear. Wadeable. Landing mostly good. Course, thirty miles. Contains brown trout. Reached by seven miles of road from the Brookside and Selwyn Stations (where accommodation may be got), on the Christchurch–Dunedin Railway; also from the Darfield Station (where there is hotel accommodation), on the Christchurch–White Cliffs Railway.

HORORATA River, tributary of Selwyn River.— Shingle bottom for five miles, then shingle bed for twelve miles. Banks low and mostly clear. Landing deep, also good. Course, twenty-two miles. Contains brown trout. Reached by ten miles of road from the Brookside or Selwyn Stations, on the Christchurch–Dunedin Railway, thence by roads near the Selwyn River for eighteen miles to Hororata, which is close to the Hororata Stream, and where there is hotel accommodation. Or the river may be reached from the Coalgate Station, on the Christchurch–White Cliffs Railway, from which Hororata is distant four miles by road.

WAIANIWANIWA Stream, tributary of Selwyn River. —Shingle bed in lower reaches, and then shingle and clay bottom. Banks low and clear. Wadeable partly. Landing deep, also good. Course, twenty miles. Contains brown trout. For approach and accommodation see " Hawkins River " and " Selwyn River," already mentioned.

IRWELL Stream, tributary of Lake Ellesmere.— Mud and shingle bottom. Banks low and willow-grown. Not wadeable Landing deep. Course, ten miles. Contains brown trout. Reached from the Irwell Station (to which it is close, and where accommodation may be had), on the Christchurch–Southbridge Railway.

HALL's Creek, tributary of Lake Ellesmere.—Mud and shingle bottom. Banks low and willow-grown. Not wadeable. Landing deep. Course, four miles. Contains brown trout. Reached from the Leeston Station (where there is hotel accommodation), on the Christchurch–Southbridge Railway.

RAKAIA River.—Snow-fed. Shingle bed. Banks fairly low and clear. Landing mostly good. Course, 100 miles. Contains brown trout. Receives no tributaries of importance for fifty miles from the mouth. Reached from Southbridge Station (where there is hotel accommodation), on the Christchurch – Southbridge Railway; this is six miles from the mouth of the river. Also reached from the Rakaia Station (which is close to the river, and where there is hotel accommodation), on the Christchurch–Dunedin Railway; this is fifteen miles by road from the mouth. The railway-bridge over the Rakaia is a mile and a quarter long. From Rakaia a driving-road runs up and along the north bank for thirty-eight miles, at a mile or two distant from the river. Reached also from Glentunnel Station, on the Christchurch–White Cliffs Railway, from which there is a coach-road to Lake Coleridge. Windwhistle, which is sixteen miles on this road, is two miles from the river and fifteen above the Rakaia Railway-bridge. There are also other roads approaching Windwhistle and the river from the south, from Methven (where there are hotels), on the Rakaia–Methven Railway.

ACHERON Stream, tributary of Rakaia River.—Shingle bed. Banks steep and clear. Wadeable. Landing deep, also good. Course, twelve miles. Contains brown trout. Reached by the roads already mentioned from Rakaia up that river, and from Glentunnel Station, on the Christchurch–

White Cliffs Railway. Also from Springfield Station, on the Christchurch–Springfield Railway, and then by thirteen miles of the West Coast Road from Springfield and by Lake Lyndon. For approach and accommodation see " Rakaia River," already mentioned.

LAKE LYNDON, tributary of Acheron River.— Shingle bottom and beaches. Wadeable in places. Length, three miles; breadth, half a mile. Height above sea-level 2,730 ft. Contains brown trout. Reached from Springfield Station, on the Christchurch–Springfield Railway, and thence by thirteen miles along the West Coast Road. For approach and accommodation see " Acheron Stream," already mentioned.

HARPER River, tributary of Rakaia River. — Shingle bed. Banks low and clear in lower reaches, forest-clad in upper reaches. Wadeable. Landing mostly good. Course, twenty-four miles. Contains brown trout. Reached by road of thirty-five miles from the Springfield Station, on the Christchurch–Springfield Railway; also by following up the Rakaia River and the road from Windwhistle. For approach and accommodation see " Rakaia River," already mentioned.

LAKE COLERIDGE, tributary of Harper River.— Shingle bottom and some shingle beaches. Banks mostly clear. Wadeable here and there. Landing mostly deep. Length, ten miles; breadth, two miles. Height above sea-level, 1,667 ft. Contains brown trout. Reached from Springfield Station, on the Christchurch – Springfield Railway, by road of twenty-two miles, partly by the West Coast Road and Lake Lyndon; also by road from Windwhistle and by following up the Rakaia and Harper Rivers. For approach and accommodation see " Harper River" and "Rakaia River," already mentioned.

MATHIAS River, tributary of the Rakaia River.— Shingle bed. Banks mostly low, and a good deal scrub-encumbered. Wadeable. Landing mostly good. Course, twenty - five miles. Contains brown trout. Reached by following the Rakaia River, or by roads from Windwhistle. For approach and accommodation see " Rakaia River," already mentioned.

LAKE Stream, tributary of Mathias River.— Shingle bottom. Banks low and clear. Wadeable. Landing deep, also good. Course, nineteen miles. Contains brown trout. For approach and accommodation see " Mathias River," already mentioned.

LAKE HERON, tributary of Lake Stream.—Shingle bottom. Some shingle beaches. Banks steep partly, and clear. Wadeable partly. Landing deep, also good. Length, seven miles; breadth, one mile. Height above sea-level, 2,276 ft. Contains brown trout. For approach and accommodation see " Lake Stream " and " Mathias River," already mentioned.

ASHBURTON River.—Snow-fed. Shingle bed for thirty-five miles; then more confined, with boulder and rock in places, for twelve miles; then shingle bed for a few miles. Banks generally low and clear. Wadeable. Landing mostly good. Course, seventy miles. Contains brown trout. Reached from Ashburton Station (which is close to it, and where there are hotels), on the Christchurch–Dunedin Railway. The river divides just above Ashburton, which is twelve miles from the mouth, and can be reached by driving-road. A road from Ashburton runs for twenty miles up the north bank. It can also be reached from Mount Somers Station, on the Ashburton–Springburn Railway, where there is hotel accommodation close to the river.

ASHBURTON River (North Branch).—Shingle bed for twenty miles, then boulders and rock for fifteen miles. Banks generally low and clear for twenty miles; then steeper, and partly forest - clad. Wadeable. Landing mostly good. Course, forty-four miles. Contains brown trout. Reached from Ashburton by a road up the south bank for twenty miles. This road is also convenient for the South Branch. For approach and accommodation see " Ashburton River," already mentioned.

Taylor's Stream, tributary of Ashburton River. —Shingle bed for eight miles, then boulder and shingle bed. Banks low and clear for eight miles, then steeper and forest-clad for eight miles. Wadeable. Landing deep, also good. Course, twenty miles. Contains brown trout. Reached from Ashburton by road of twenty miles; also from the Springburn Station (where there is hotel accommodation), on the Ashburton–Springburn Railway. For approach and accommodation see " Ashburton River," already mentioned.

Bowyer's Stream, Tributary of Taylor's Stream. —Shingle bed for six miles, then boulder and shingle bottom for five miles. Banks low and clear for six miles, then steeper and forest-clad. Wadeable mostly. Landing mostly good. Course, fourteen miles. Contains brown trout. For approach and accommodation see "Taylor's Stream," already mentioned.

Stour Burn, tributary of Ashburton River.— Shingle and boulder bottom. Banks generally open and clear. Wadeable. Landing deep, also good. Course, twelve miles. Contains brown trout. Reached by following the Ashburton River for eight miles above the Mount Somers Station (where there is hotel accommodation), on the Ashburton–Springfield Railway. For approach and accommodation see " Ashburton River," already mentioned.

Hind's River.—Ten miles through drained swamp now under grain-cultivation. Shingle bottom for ten miles, then shingle bed for twenty miles. Banks low and clear. Wadeable partly. Landing deep, also good. Course, forty-two miles. Contains brown trout. Reached from Hind's

20—Sport.

Station (where accommodation may be had), on the Christchurch–Dunedin Railway. This is ten miles from the mouth, and fifteen to where the river divides. From Hind's Station a road runs up and near the river for twenty miles. Reached also by road of fifteen miles (to near the fork) from the Valetta and Anama Stations, on the Ashburton–Springburn Railway.

Hind's River (South Branch). — Shingle bed and bottom. Banks low and clear. Wadeable partly. Landing deep, also good. Course, twelve miles. Contains brown trout. Reached by road of fifteen miles from Hind's Station. For approach and accommodation see " Hind's River," already mentioned.

Rangitata River. — Snow-fed. Shingle bed. Banks generally low, open, and clear to gorge, thirty miles from mouth, when it becomes more contracted and rocky for eight miles, then opens out again. Wadeable. Landing good. Course, seventy-six miles. Contains brown trout. Has no considerable tributary for fifty miles. Reached from the Rangitata Station, which is on the river and twelve miles from the mouth. At Temuka Station, on the Christchurch–Dunedin Railway, there are hotels ; and, if the assistance of Mr. C. Nicholas, who is an authority, and keeps a livery stable, can be obtained, the chances of sport are at their best, as he is well acquainted with the great number of surrounding rivers and streams.

Forest Stream, tributary of Rangitata River.— Shingle and boulder bed, then mountain torrent. Banks fairly open, and low. Wadeable. Landing deep, also good. Course, seventeen miles. Contains brown trout. Reached by fifty miles of roads and tracks from the Orari Station (where there is hotel accommodation), on the Christchurch–Dunedin Railway ; or from Geraldine, where there are hotels, five miles from Orari

CATCH OF TROUT, CANTERBURY DISTRICT.

Station, on the road mentioned. For approach and accommodation see " Rangitata River," already mentioned.

BUSH Stream, tributary of Rangitata River.— Shingle and boulder bed, then mountain torrent. Banks fairly open and low. Wadeable. Landing deep, also good. Course, sixteen miles. Contains brown trout. Reached by fifty-six miles of roads and tracks. For approach and accommodation see " Forest Stream," and " Rangitata River," already mentioned.

POTTS' Stream, tributary of Rangitata River.— Boulder and shingle bed, then mountain torrent. Banks low and clear. Wadeable. Landing mostly good. Course, sixteen miles. Contains brown trout. Reached by fifty-six miles of roads and tracks. For approach and accommodation see " Forest Stream " and " Rangitata River," already mentioned.

HAVELOCK River, tributary of Rangitata River. —Boulder and shingle bed, then mountain torrent. Banks open and clear. Wadeable partly. Landing deep, also good. Course, thirteen miles. Contains brown trout. Reached by sixty-two miles of roads and tracks. For approach and accommodation see " Forest Stream " and " Rangitata River," already mentioned.

LAWRENCE Stream, tributary of Rangitata River. —Boulder and shingle bed, then mountain torrent. Banks open and clear. Wadeable partly. Landing deep, also good. Course, twelve miles. Contains brown trout. Reached by sixty-seven miles of roads and tracks. For approach and accommodation see " Forest Stream " and " Rangitata River," already mentioned.

ORARI River.—Shingle and rock bed for twenty miles from mouth, when after twelve miles of gorge the river opens out into shingle bed. Banks open to gorge, where they are steep and rocky; above gorge low. Wadeable. Course, forty-seven miles. Landing mostly good, except in gorge, where partly deep. Contains brown trout. Reached from the Orari Station (where there is hotel accommodation) on the Christchurch–Dunedin Railway. Orari is near the river, and ten miles from the mouth. The mouth and lower reaches are most easily reached from Temuka Station (where there are hotels), on the same railway. The river can also be conveniently reached by three miles of road from Geraldine, where there are hotels. Geraldine is five miles by coach-road from the Orari Railway-station.

HEWSON Stream, tributary of the Orari River. Rock and shingle bed, then mountain torrent. Banks various. Wadeable partly. Landing deep, also good. Course, sixteen miles. Contains brown trout. Reached by thirty miles of road and tracks from the Orari Railway-station. For approach and accommodation see " Orari River," already mentioned.

PHANTOM Stream, tributary of Orari River.— Rock and shingle bed, then mountain torrent. Banks various. Wadeable partly. Landing deep, also good. Course, twelve miles. Contains brown trout. Reached by thirty miles of road and tracks from the Orari Railway-station. For approach and accommodation see " Orari River," already mentioned.

OPIHI River.—Shingle bed for twenty miles, then rock gorge of seven miles. Banks open. Wadeable. Landing mostly good. Course, forty-six miles. Contains brown trout. Reached from the Temuka Station (to which it is close, and where there are hotels), on the Christchurch–Dunedin Railway; Temuka is four miles from the mouth. It is also reached by roads which follow the river up for twenty miles above Temuka. At Pleasant Point Station, on the road and railway eight miles above Temuka, there are hotels. Also accessible from Fairlie Station (where there are

CATCH OF TROUT, CANTERBURY DISTRICT.

hotels), on the Temuka–Fairlie Railway : Fairlie is thirty miles up the river from Temuka.

HAEHAE-TE-MOANA River, tributary of Opihi River.—Shingle bed. Banks open. Wadeable. Landing mostly good. Course, twenty-seven miles Contains brown trout. Reached from Temuka Station (where there are hotels), on the Christchurch–Dunedin Railway. For approach and accommodation see "Opihi River," already mentioned.

WAIHI River, tributary of Haehae-te-Moana River.—Shingle bottom, then shingle bed. Banks chiefly clear and low. Wadeable. Landing deep, also good. Course, twenty-five miles. Contains brown trout. Reached from Winchester Station (where there is hotel accommodation), on the Christchurch–Dunedin Railway ; also from Geraldine (where there is hotel accommodation), which is eight miles from Winchester, by road ; also from Temuka Station (where there are hotels), on the Christchurch–Dunedin Railway, and which is close to the river. For approach and accommodation see "Haehae-te-Moana River," already mentioned.

KAKAHU Stream, tributary of Haehae-te-Moana River.—Shingle bottom. Banks low and various, fairly clear. Wadeable partly. Landing deep, also good. Course, eighteen miles. Contains brown trout. Five miles by road from Temuka. For approach and accommodation see "Haehae-te-Moana River," already mentioned.

TENGAWAI River, tributary of Opihi River.— Shingle bed for twenty miles, then rocky and confined. Banks low, open, and fairly clear. Wadeable mostly. Landing chiefly good. Course, thirty-five miles. Contains brown trout. Reached by eight miles of road from the Temuka Station (where there are hotels), on the Christchurch–Dunedin Railway, or for twenty miles further from the same road, which is close to the Temuka–Fairlie Railway. The Temuka–Fairlie Railway is close to the river, which can be reached at Pleasant Point Station, where there are hotels; at Sutherland's Station; at Cave Station, where there is hotel accommodation; at Coal Creek Station; at Albury Station, where there is hotel accommodation; and at Tengawai Station. For approach and accommodation see " Opihi River," already mentioned.

Opuha River, tributary of Opihi River.—Shingle bed with rocky gorges, some of four or five miles. Banks open and clear except in gorges, where they are rocky and precipitous but clear. Wadeable partly. Landing mostly good. Course, thirty miles. Contains brown trout. Reached by sixteen miles of road from Temuka Station (where there are hotels), on the Christchurch–Dunedin Railway. This road keeps within a mile or two of the river for twenty-five miles further up. For approach and accommodation see " Opihi River," already mentioned.

Pareora River.—Shingle bed for twelve miles, then rocky and shingle for five miles; seventeen miles from sea it becomes rocky and confined. Banks mostly low and clear in the lower reaches, some forest in gorge. Wadeable mostly. Landing mostly good, except in gorge. Course, thirty-three miles. Contains brown trout. Reached by two miles of road from St. Andrew's Station (where there is hotel accommodation), on the Christchurch–Dunedin Railway; the station is two miles by road from the mouth of the river. From this point the road runs up and near the river for eighteen miles.

Pareora Stream, tributary of Pareora River.— Shingle and rock bottom. Banks open and fairly clear. Wadeable. Landing deep, also good. Course, fourteen miles. Contains brown trout. Reached from mouth of river by road of ten miles. For approach and accommodation see " Pareora River," already mentioned.

MOTUKAIKA Burn, tributary of Pareora River.—Shingle and rocky bottom, upper part mountain torrent. Banks on lower reaches low and clear; on upper, forest-clad and difficult of access. Wadeable. Landing deep, also good. Course, ten miles. Contains brown trout. Reached by thirteen miles of road from mouth of river. For approach and accommodation see " Pareora River," already mentioned.

WHITE ROCK Stream, tributary of Pareora River. Shingle and rock bottom to foot of hills; then rock, and mountain torrent. Banks, lower part, low and clear; upper, rock, and forest-clad. Wadeable. Landing deep, also good. Course, eleven miles. Contains brown trout. Reached by eighteen miles of road from mouth of river. For approach and accommodation see " Pareora River," already mentioned.

OTAIO River. — Shingle bed for twelve miles; then more confined, ‹n shingle and rock bottom. Banks, lower reaches, low and open; upper reaches, more or less scrub-encumbered and confined. Wadeable. Landing mostly good. Course, twenty-two miles. Contains brown trout. Reached from St. Andrew's Station (where there is hotel accommodation), on the Christchurch–Dunedin Railway; the station is two miles by road from the mouth of the river, and a road from St. Andrew's runs up and near the river for fourteen miles.

MAKIKIHI Stream.—Shingle bed to foot of hills, two miles; then rocky and confined. Banks of lower reaches low and open, higher more confined and forest-clothed. Wadeable. Landing mostly good. Course, eleven miles. Contains brown trout. Reached from Makikihi Station (where there is hotel accommodation), on the Christchurch–Dunedin Railway. The station is a mile from the mouth of the stream, and a road runs along the stream for four miles above the station.

Hook Stream.—Shingle bottom. Banks open and fairly clear for eight miles; then more confined, and partly forest-clad. Wadeable mostly. Landing deep, also good. Course, eleven miles. Contains brown trout. Reached from Makikihi Station (where there is hotel accommodation) on the Christchurch–Dunedin Railway. The station is two miles by road and three by railway from the stream.

Waihao River. — Shingle bed for eight miles, then more rocky and confined for thirty miles. Banks low and clear in the lower reaches, more scrub-encumbered and precipitous in upper reaches. Wadeable. Landing deep, also good. Course, forty-six miles. Contains brown trout. Reached from the Willow Bridge or Morven Stations (which are a mile from the river) on the Christchurch–Dunedin Railway; or from Waimate Station (where there is hotel accommodation), on the Studholme–Waimate–Waihao Downs Railway. From Waimate to the river, near the railway, is by road five miles. It can also be reached by rail from Waimate to Waihao Forks Station, seven miles, and from several intermediate stations. A road runs near the river for twenty-four miles above Waimate.

Waihao River (South Branch). — Shingle and rock bottom. Banks rather steep, and fairly clear. Wadeable. Landing deep, also good. Course, twenty-one miles. Contains brown trout. Reached by rail from Waimate to Waihao Forks Station; from here a road runs up and near the river for sixteen miles. This road can also be taken from Waimate. For approach and accommodation see " Waihao River," already mentioned.

Waitaki River. — Snow-fed. Shingle bed. Banks open. Wadeable partly. Landing deep, also good. Course to Lake Te Kapo, and including the Te Kapo River, 110 miles. Contains brown trout. Reached from the Glenavy Station (where there is hotel accommodation), on the Christchurch–Dunedin Railway. Glenavy is two miles from the mouth. From Glenavy a road runs up near the north bank for thirty-six miles. Twelve miles along this road is opposite Georgetown, where there is hotel accommodation. At Hakataramea, which is also a railway-station, and thirty-six miles by road from Glenavy, there is hotel accommodation: Hakataramea is close to the river, and is on the Oamaru–Duntroon–Hakataramea Railway, which runs up the south bank, as also does a road. The river, which runs near this railway for twenty-six miles, can be reached from eleven stations in that distance. At Uxbridge and Kurow Stations there is hotel accommodation. A road from Uxbridge Station follows up the Waitaki River and beside the railway for twenty-five miles, crossing the tributaries as far as Hakataramea.

AWAMOKO River, tributary of Waitaki River.—Shingle bed in lower reaches and rock higher up. Banks open. Wadeable. Landing good. Course, twenty-two miles. Contains brown trout. Reached from Georgetown by the Uxbridge Station (where there is hotel accommodation), on the Oamaru–Duntroon and Hakataramea Railway. For approach and accommodation see " Waitaki River," already mentioned.

MAEREWHENUA River, tributary of Waitaki River.—Shingle and rock bed. Banks fairly clear. Wadeable. Landing good. Course, twenty-four miles. Contains brown trout. Reached from Duntroon Station, on the Oamaru–Duntroon and Hakataramea Railway. A road runs for eighteen miles up the stream and the North Branch from Duntroon. For approach and accommodation see " Waitaki River," already mentioned.

OTEKAIKE Stream, tributary of Waitaki River.—Shingle and rock bed. Banks fairly clear. Wadeable. Landing good. Course, nineteen miles. Contains brown trout. Reached from the Otekaike Station, on the Oamaru – Duntroon and Hakataramea Railway. For approach and accommodation see " Waitaki River," already mentioned.

OTIAKE Stream, tributary of Waitaki River.— Shingle bed. Banks fairly clear. Wadeable. Landing mostly good. Course, eleven miles. Contains brown trout. Reached from Strachan Station, on the Oamaru-Duntroon and Hakataramea Railway. For approach and accommodation see " Waitaki River," already mentioned.

KUROW Stream, tributary of Waitaki River.— Shingle bed. Banks various and clear. Wadeable. Landing good. Course, eleven miles. Contains brown trout. Reached from Kurow Station (where there is hotel accommodation), on the Oamaru–Duntroon and Hakataramea Railway. For approach and accommodation see " Waitaki River," already mentioned.

AWAKINO Stream, tributary of Waitaki River.— Shingle and rock bottom. Banks various and clear. Wadeable mostly. Landing deep, also good. Course, twelve miles. Contains brown trout. Reached by a mile of road from Hakataramea and Kurow Stations (where there is hotel accommodation), on the Oamaru–Duntroon and Hakataramea Railway. For approach and accommodation see " Waitaki River," already mentioned.

HAKATARAMEA River, tributary of Waitaki River. —Shingle bottom and bed. Banks various and fairly clear. Wadeable. Landing good. Course. thirty-seven miles. Contains brown trout. It is reached from Hakataramea, which is at the mouth, and where there is hotel accommodation. A road from Hakataramea follows up and close to the stream for thirty-seven miles. For approach and accommodation see " Waitaki River," already mentioned.

OTEMATATA River, tributary of Waitaki River.— Shingle bed low down, rock above. Banks open. Wadeable. Landing good. Course, twenty-nine miles. Contains brown trout. Reached by sixteen miles of road that follows up the Waitaki River from Hakataramea River. For approach and accommodation see " Waitaki River," already mentioned.

AHURIRI River, tributary of Waitaki River.— Boulder and shingle bed. Banks fairly clear. Wadeable partly. Landing deep, also good. Course, sixty-one miles. Contains brown trout. Reached by the Waitaki River and from Hakataramea (where there is hotel accommodation), by a road which follows up the Waitaki River for twenty-five miles. For approach and accommodation see " Waitaki River," already mentioned.

OTAMATAPAIO Stream, tributary of Ahuriri River. —Shingle bed and rock. Banks open. Wadeable. Landing good. Course, fifteen miles. Contains brown trout. For approach and accommodation see " Ahuriri River," already mentioned.

OMARAMA River, tributary of Ahuriri River.— Shingle and boulder bottom, rock in upper part. Banks various and clear. Wadeable partly. Landing deep mostly. Course, twenty-two miles. Contains brown trout. Reached by thirty-three miles of coach-road from Kurow or Hakataramea, at Omarama, where there is hotel accommodation. For approach and accommodation see " Waitaki River," already mentioned.

OHAU River, tributary of Waitaki River.—Shingle bed. Banks mostly open and clear, but partly rocky. Wadeable partly. Landing mostly good. Course, sixteen miles. Contains brown trout. Reached by following up the Waitaki River thirty-six miles above Hakataramea. For approach and accommodation see " Waitaki River," already mentioned.

Twizel Stream, tributary of Ohau River.— Shingle bed. Banks open, low, and clear. Wadeable. Landing mostly good. Course, nineteen miles. Contains brown trout. Reached by following up the Waitaki and Ohau Rivers thirty-eight miles above Hakataramea. For approach and accommodation see " Ohau River," already mentioned.

Lake Ohau, tributary of Ohau River.—Shingle and rock bottom and beaches. Banks mostly open, but forest-clad in places. Wadeable partly. Landing deep, also good. Length, twelve miles ; breadth, two miles and three-quarters. Contains brown trout. Reached by following up the Waitaki and Ohau Rivers for fifty-two miles above Hakataramea. For approach and accommodation see " Ohau River," already mentioned. The lake is also connected by roads and tracks with Fairlie Station (where there are hotels), on the Timaru–Fairlie Railway.

Lake Middleton, tributary of Lake Ohau.— Shingle bottom and beaches. Banks low and clear. Wadeable partly. Landing deep. Length, half a mile ; breadth, quarter of a mile. Contains brown trout. For approach and accommodation see " Lake Ohau," already mentioned.

Otao River, tributary of Lake Ohau.—Shingle bed. Banks low, clear, and swampy in places in lower reaches ; forest-clad in upper reaches. Wadeable. Landing mostly good Course, twenty-eight miles. Contains brown trout. For approach and accommodation see " Lake Ohau," already mentioned.

Dobson River, tributary of Lake Ohau.—Shingle bed. Banks low and open in lower reaches, forest-clad in upper. Wadeable. Landing mostly good. Course, twenty-two miles. Contains brown trout. For approach and accommodation see " Lake Ohau," already mentioned.

Pukaki River, tributary of Waitaki River.—

Shingle and boulder bed, with rock bars. Banks generally low and open. Wadeable. Landing deep, also good. Course, ten miles. Contains brown trout. Reached by following up the Waitaki River for forty miles above Hakataramea. For approach and accommodation see " Waitaki River," already mentioned.

LAKE PUKAKI, tributary of Pukaki River.— Shingle and rock bottom. Shingle and rocky beaches. Banks low and open. Wadeable. Landing deep, also good. Length, ten miles; breadth, four miles and a half. Contains brown trout. Reached by following up the Waitaki and Pukaki Rivers for fifty miles above Hakataramea. For approach and accommodation see " Pukaki River," already mentioned. The lake is also connected by roads (which lead to the Hermitage and Mount Cook) with Fairlie Station (where there are hotels), on the Timaru–Fairlie Railway.

TASMAN River, tributary of Lake Pukaki.— Shingle bed. Banks generally low, open, and clear; swampy in places. Wadeable. Landing good. Course, twenty-three miles. Contains brown trout. Reached in sixty miles by following up the Waitaki and Pukaki Rivers, and thence by road on south side of Lake Pukaki. For approach and accommodation see " Lake Pukaki," already mentioned.

TEKAPO River, tributary of Waitaki River.— Shingle and boulder bed. Banks open. Wadeable partly. Landing mostly good. Course, twenty-nine miles. Contains brown trout. Reached by following up the Waitaki River for thirty-six miles above Hakataramea. For approach and accommodation see " Waitaki River," already mentioned.

LAKE TEKAPO, tributary of Tekapo River.— Shingle and rock bottom and beaches. Shallow at lower and upper end. Banks fairly clear. Wadeable partly. Landing deep, also good. Length, fifteen miles ; breadth, three miles. Height above sea-level, 2,321 ft. Contains brown trout. Reached by sixty-six miles of road and track, partly following up the Waitaki River from Hakataramea. For approach and accommodation see " Tekapo River," already mentioned. The lake is also connected by roads (which lead also to the Hermitage and Mount Cook) with Fairlie Station (where there are hotels), on the Timaru–Fairlie Railway.

MacGregor's Lagoon, tributary of Lake Tekapo connecting Lake Alexandrina and Lake Tekapo.— Shingle bottom and beaches. Banks mostly clear. Wadeable partly. Landing deep, also good. Length, three-quarters of a mile ; breadth three-quarters of a mile. Contains brown trout. Reached by seventy-two miles of road from Hakataramea by partly following up the Waitaki River. For approach and accommodation see " Lake Tekapo," already mentioned. The lake is also connected by roads with Fairlie Station (where there are hotels), on the Timaru–Fairlie Railway.

Lake Alexandrina, tributary of MacGregor's Lagoon.—Shingle bottom and beaches. Banks mostly clear. Wadeable partly. Landing deep, also good. Length, four miles and a half ; breadth half a mile. Contains brown trout. For approach and accommodation see " MacGregor's Lagoon," already mentioned.

Godley River, tributary of Lake Tekapo.— Shingle and boulder bed. Banks low, open, and clear. Wadeable mostly. Landing mostly good. Course, twenty-two miles. Contains brown trout. For approach and accommodation see " Lake Tekapo," already mentioned.

Macauley River, tributary of Lake Tekapo.— Shingle and boulder bed. Banks low, open, and clear. Wadeable. Landing mostly good. Course, twenty-two miles. Contains brown trout. For approach and accommodation see " Lake Tekapo," already mentioned.

KAKANUI River. — Shingle and rock bottom. Banks various, and generally clear. Wadeable. Landing deep, also good. Course, forty miles. Contains brown trout. Reached from Maheno Station, on the Christchurch–Dunedin Railway. The station is four miles from the mouth of the river. The Maheno Station is four miles by road to Kakanui, which is near to the mouth, and where there is hotel accommodation. From Maheno Station a road runs up the river for eighteen miles.

WAIRAREKA River, tributary of Kakanui River.— Rock and shingle bed. Banks open. Wadeable. Landing good. Course, twenty-one miles. Contains brown trout. Reached from the Totara Station, on the Christchurch–Dunedin Railway; also from a number of stations on the Oamaru–Tokarahi Railway. For approach and accommodation see " Kakanui River," already mentioned.

KAUROO Stream, tributary of Kakanui River.— Shingle and rock bottom. Banks various. Wadeable. Landing deep, also good. Course, nineteen miles. Contains brown trout. Reached by seven miles of road from Maheno Station, on the Christchurch – Dunedin Railway. For approach and accommodation see " Kakanui River," already mentioned.

KAKANUI River (South Branch).— Shingle and rock bottom. Banks fairly clear. Wadeable partly. Landing deep, also good. Course, eight miles. Contains brown trout. Reached from Maheno Station by road of eight miles, and then by following up the Kakanui River four miles. For approach and accommodation see " Kakanui River," already mentioned.

WAIANAKARUA River.—Shingle bed and bottom. Banks various, and clear in lower reaches. Wadeable. Landing deep, also good. Course, twenty-two miles. Contains brown trout. Reached from the Waianakarua Station (where there is hotel accommodation), on the Christchurch–Dunedin Railway. The station is four miles from the mouth of the river, which divides into two branches three miles from the mouth.

WAIANAKARUA Stream (South Branch). — Shingle bed and bottom. Banks partly clear and partly forest-clad. Wadeable mostly. Landing deep, also good. Course, fifteeu miles. Contains brown trout. For approach and accommodation see " Waianakarua River," already mentioned.

SHAG River. — Shingle bed. Banks open. Wadeable. Landing good. Course, forty-two miles. Contains brown trout. Reached from Shag Point Station (where there is hotel accommodation), from Bushy Station, and from Palmerston Station (at the latter there is hotel accommodation), on the Christchurch – Dunedin Railway : Shag Point and Bushy Stations are two and three miles respectively from mouth of river. Reached also from the Palmerston–Dunback Branch line, which runs near the river for nine miles, with several intermediate stations ; at Dunback there is hotel accommodation. Reached also by road from Palmerston or Dunback : this road is within a moderate distance of the river for thirty miles above Palmerston ; there is accommodation at intervals along this road for nearly the whole distance.

COAL Burn, tributary of Shag River.—Shingle and rock bottom and bed. Banks mostly clear. Wadeable partly. Landing deep, also good. Course, five miles. Contains brown trout. For approach and accommodation see " Shag River," above Palmerston, already mentioned.

SHINGLY Burn, tributary of Shag River.— Shingle and boulder bottom and bed. Banks mostly clear. Wadeable partly. Landing deep, also good. Course, four miles. Contains brown trout. For approach and accommodation see " Shag River," above Palmerston, already mentioned.

WAIKOUAITI River. — Shingle and rock bed. Banks various, and mostly clear. Wadeable. Landing mostly good. Course, thirty-six miles. Contains brown trout. Reached from the Waikouaiti Station (where there is hotel accommodation), on the Christchurch – Dunedin Railway: Waikouaiti Station is close to the mouth of the river. A road runs from Waikouaiti for twenty miles up, and within a moderate distance of the river.

WAIKOUAITI River (South Branch). — Shingle and rock bed. Banks various, and mostly clear. Wadeable. Landing mostly good. Course, fourteen miles. Contains brown trout. Reached by six miles of road, which continues twelve miles within a moderate distance of the river. For approach and accommodation see "Waikouaiti River," already mentioned.

DEEP Burn, tributary of Waikouaiti River.— Rock and shingle bottom. Banks open. Wadeable partly. Landing deep, also good. Course, seven miles. Contains brown trout. For approach and accommodation see "Waikouaiti River," already mentioned.

BACK Burn, tributary of Waikouaiti River.— Rock and shingle bottom. Banks open. Wadeable partly. Landing deep, also good. Course, eight miles. Contains brown trout. For approach and accommodation see "Waikouaiti River," already mentioned.

WAITATI Burn. — Boulder bed, partly open. Banks clear in lower parts, overgrown with forest in upper parts. Wadeable. Landing deep, also good. Course, seven miles. Contains brown trout. Reached from the Waitati Station (where there is hotel accommodation), on the Christchurch– Dunedin Railway. The station is close to the mouth of the burn.

WATER OF LEITH.—Shingle, boulder, and rock bottom. Banks partly open, upper portions forest.

Wadeable. Landing mostly good. Course, six miles. Contains brown trout. Runs into the Harbour of Dunedin. There is hotel accommodation at Dunedin.

TAIERI River.—Estuary, about one mile. Sixteen miles sandy bottom, then rocky gorge for thirty miles, and then mostly shingle bottom. Banks various. Some bare shingle, some high, some scrub-encumbered. Wadeable partly. Landing deep, also good. Course, 140 miles. Contains brown trout. Reached from the Allanton, Otakia, Henley, and Titri Stations, on the Dunedin–Invercargill Railway. At Allanton and Henley there are hotels. Henley is six miles from the mouth of the river. The Otago Central Railway also runs for fifty-four miles close to the river. Towards the far end of the line, where it leaves the river, there is hotel accommodation.

AKATORE Burn. — Shingle and rock bottom. Banks mostly scrub - encumbered. Wadeable. Landing deep, also good. Course, nine miles. Contains brown trout. Reached from the Waihola Station (where there is hotel accommodation), on the Dunedin–Invercargill Railway. A road from the station runs close to the burn to the mouth, which is eight miles from the station.

TOKOMAIRIRO River.—Shingle bottom. Banks low, and more or less willow-encumbered. Wadeable partly. Landing mostly deep. Course, twenty-three miles. Contains brown trout. Reached from Milton Station (where there is hotel accommodation), on the Dunedin–Invercargill Railway: Milton is close to the river, and ten miles by driving-road from the mouth. A road from Milton runs for eight miles within a moderate distance nearly up to the source.

TOKOMAIRIRO River (West Branch). — Shingle bottom. Banks low, and more or less willow-encumbered. Wadeable partly. Landing deep, also good. Course, eighteen miles. Contains

CATCH OF TROUT, OTAGO DISTRICT.

brown trout. The mouth is close to Milton. The road from Milton to Lawrence and the Milton–Lawrence Railway run close to the river for six miles, to Glenore, where there is hotel accommodation. For approach and accommodation see "Tokomairiro River," already mentioned.

CLUTHA River.—Tidal for seven miles; navigable by small steamers for forty miles. It discharges more water than any other river in the country, averaging about 1,690,400 cubic feet per minute. The English Thames discharges about 102,000 cubic feet per minute; so that the Clutha discharges sixteen times as much as the Thames. It also discharges about 300,000 cubic feet per minute more than the African Nile. The explanation of a river with such a comparatively short course discharging so much water is that it is chiefly snow-fed, and drains Lakes Wakatipu, Wanaka, and Hawea, three deep lakes of a combined area of 240 square miles, and also receives numerous considerable tributaries. Shingle, rock, and boulder bed and bottom. Banks mostly clear, and for eight miles below Balclutha chiefly low and alluvial; further up, partly low and partly rock-bound. The river in the lower reaches is from 200 to 300 yards wide, with a current of two to five miles an hour. In the upper reaches, where it is more or less confined in rock gorges, it has a current in places of ten miles an hour. Wadeable partly. Landing deep, also good. Course to Lake Wanaka, 150 miles. Contains brown and rainbow trout. Reached from Balclutha Station (where there are hotels), on the Dunedin–Invercargill Railway. This is within eight miles of the mouth, which can be reached by rail and road on the south bank to Port Molyneux, where there is hotel accommodation; and on the north bank the shingle-bank forming the mouth can be reached by road of three miles from Kaitangata, which is reached by railway or road from Balclutha. At Kaitangata there is hotel accommodation.   Just below Balclutha the river divides, forming the low Island of Inch Clutha, which is seven miles long and two wide.   This is reached by ferry-punt from Kaitangata.

PUERUA River, tributary of Clutha River.—Tidal in lower reaches.   Boulder and shingle bottom. Banks steep, forest- and scrub-covered.   Wadeable partly.   Landing deep, also good.   Course, twenty-three miles.   Contains brown trout.   Reached from the Otanomomo and Romahapa Stations, on the Balclutha–Owaka Railway.   These stations are five and three miles respectively from the mouth of the stream.   Accommodation uncertain.   For approach and accommodation see " Clutha River," already mentioned.

KAITANGATA Creek, tributary of Clutha River.— Muddy bottom.   Banks high and steep.   Not wadeable.   Landing deep.   Course, one mile.   Contains brown trout.   Reached from Kaitangata Station (where there are hotels), on the Balclutha–Kaitangata Railway.   For approach and accommodation see " Clutha River," already mentioned.

KAITANGATA LAKE, tributary of Clutha River.— Shingle and mud bottom.   Banks low and fairly clear.   Wadeable partly.   Landing deep, also good. Length, three-quarters of a mile; breadth, half a mile.   Contains brown trout.   Reached from Kaitangata.   For approach and accommodation see " Clutha River," already mentioned.

KAIHIKU Stream, tributary of Clutha River.— Shingle and boulder bottom and bed.   Banks mainly clear.   Wadeable.   Landing deep, also good.   Course, seventeen miles.   Contains brown trout.   Reached from Balclutha by road up the Clutha of seven miles.   For approach and accommodation see " Clutha River," already mentioned.

WAITAHUNA River, tributary of Clutha River.— Shingle and rock bed.   Banks open and clear. Wadeable.   Landing deep, also good.   Course, thirty-three miles.   Contains brown trout. Reached from Balclutha by eleven miles of road. For approach and accommodation see " Clutha River," already mentioned.

WAIWERA Stream, tributary of Clutha River.— Shingle, boulder, and rock bed. Banks open and clear. Wadeable. Landing deep, also good. Course, nineteen miles. Contains brown trout. Reached from Balclutha by twelve miles of road For approach and accommodation see " Clutha River," already mentioned.

POMAHAKA River, tributary of Clutha River.— Rock and partly shingle bottom for the lower half, more shingle in the upper half. Banks fairly clear. Wadeable partly. Landing in lower half mostly deep, the upper half good. Course, seventy-four miles. Contains brown trout. Reached from Balclutha by thirteen miles of road to the mouth. Also reached from the Waipahi–Heriot Railway, which runs close to the river for fourteen miles. There is hotel accommodation at Waipahi, Tapanui, and Heriot Railway-stations. For approach and accommodation see " Clutha River," already mentioned.

WAIPAHI River, tributary of Pomahaka River.— Shingle and rock bottom. Banks low, a good deal flax-encumbered. Wadeable here and there. Landing almost entirely deep. Course, twenty-seven miles. Contains brown trout. Reached from the Waipahi Station (which is close to the river, and where there is hotel accommodation), on the Dunedin–Invercargill Railway ; also from the Arthurton Station, four miles further up the river on the same line. For approach and accommodation see " Pomahaka River," already mentioned.

OTARAIA Stream, tributary of Waipahi River.— Shingle and rock bottom. Banks low, and partly flax-encumbered. Wadeable partly. Landing deep, also good. Course, twelve miles. Contains brown trout. Reached from the Arthurton Station, on the Dunedin–Invercargill Railway. For approach and accommodation see " Waipahi River," already mentioned.

CROOKSTON Stream, tributary of Pomahaka River.—Shingle bottom. Banks high, and mostly flax-encumbered. Wadeable partly. Landing chiefly deep. Course, twelve miles. Contains brown trout. Reached from Heriot Station (where there is hotel accommodation within a mile), on the Waipahi–Heriot Railway. For approach and accommodation see " Pomahaka River," already mentioned.

HERIOT Stream, tributary of Pomahaka River.— Shingle bottom mostly. Banks rather steep, and partly flax-encumbered. Wadeable partly. Landing mostly deep. Course, thirteen miles. Contains brown trout. Reached from Heriot Station (where there is hotel accommodation close to the stream), on the Waipahi–Heriot Railway. For approach and accommodation see " Pomahaka River," already mentioned.

LEITHEN Stream, tributary of Pomahaka River. —Shingle bottom. Banks mostly high, open, and grass. Wadeable partly. Landing mostly deep. Course, twelve miles. Contains brown trout. Reached by eleven miles of road, or by following up the Pomahaka River from the Kelso Station (where there are hotels), on the Waipahi–Heriot Railway. For approach and accommodation see " Pomahaka River," already mentioned.

SPYLAW Stream, tributary of Pomahaka River.— Shingle bottom mostly. Banks rather steep, and partly flax-encumbered. Wadeable partly. Landing deep, also good. Course, fifteen miles. Contains brown trout. Reached by thirteen miles of road, and then by following up the Pomahaka River for two miles from the Heriot Station (where there is hotel accommodation), on the Waipahi–Heriot Railway. For approach and accommodation see " Pomahaka River," already mentioned.

LITTLE POMAHAKA Burn, tributary of Pomahaka River.—Rock bottom. Banks partly open. Wadeable partly. Landing deep, also good. Course, eight miles. Contains brown trout. Reached by following up the Pomahaka River from Spylaw Stream. For approach and accommodation see " Spylaw Stream " and " Pomahaka River," already mentioned.

TUAPEKA Stream, tributary of Clutha River.— Shingle bottom. Banks low and clear. Wadeable. Landing deep, also good. Course, eighteen miles. Contains brown trout. Reached (to the upper part) by three miles of road from the Lawrence Station (where there are hotels), on the Milton–Lawrence Railway; also from Lawrence by sixteen miles of coach-road to Tuapeka Mouth, where there is hotel accommodation; also by following up the Clutha River and road for twenty-two miles above Balclutha. For approach and accommodation see " Clutha River," already mentioned.

BLACKCLEUGH Burn, tributary of Clutha River.— Shingle and boulder bottom. Banks forest-clad. Wadeable. Landing deep, also good. Course, ten miles. Contains brown trout. Reached by thirteen miles of road from Lawrence Station (where there are hotels), on the Milton–Lawrence Railway, or by following up the Clutha River for four miles above Tuapeka Mouth. For approach and accommodation see " Tuapeka Stream," and " Clutha River," already mentioned.

BEAUMONT Stream, tributary of Clutha River.— Shingle and rock bed. Banks mainly open. Wadeable. Landing deep, also good. Course, thirteen miles. Contains brown trout. Reached from Dunkeld, to which it is close, and where there is hotel accommodation : Dunkeld is reached by twelve miles of coach-road from the Lawrence Station (where there are hotels), on the Milton– Lawrence Railway. The stream is also reached by following up the Clutha River for twelve miles above Tuapeka Mouth. For approach and accommodation see "Tuapeka Stream," and "Clutha River," already mentioned.

Talla Burn, tributary of Clutha River.—Shingle and rock bed. Banks mostly open and clear. Wadeable. Landing deep, also good. Course, ten miles. Contains brown trout. Reached by three miles from Rae's Junction, where there is hotel accommodation; Rae's Junction is reached by seventeen miles of coach-road from Lawrence Station (where there are hotels), on the Milton–Lawrence Railway. The burn is also reached by following up the Clutha River for forty-two miles above Balclutha. For approach and accommodation see "Clutha River," already mentioned.

Fruid Burn, tributary of Talla Burn.—Shingle and rock bed. Banks mostly open and clear. Wadeable. Landing deep, also good. Course, eight miles. Contains brown trout. For approach and accommodation see "Talla Burn," already mentioned.

Minzion Burn, tributary of Clutha River.—Shingle and rock bed. Banks mostly open and clear. Wadeable. Landing deep, also good. Course, eight miles. Contains brown trout. Reached by seven miles of road from Rae's Junction. For approach and accommodation see "Talla Burn," and "Clutha River," already mentioned.

Tima Burn, tributary of Clutha River.—Shingle and rock bed. Banks mostly open and clear. Wadeable. Landing deep, also good. Course, seven miles. Contains brown trout. Reached in a mile from Ettrick Township, where there is hotel accommodation. Ettrick is reached by thirty miles of coach-road from Lawrence Station (where there are hotels), on the Milton–Lawrence Railway. For approach and accommodation see "Clutha River," already mentioned.

BENGER Stream, tributary of Clutha River.—
Shingle and rock bed. Banks mostly open and
clear. Wadeable. Landing deep, also good.
Course, eleven miles. Contains brown trout.
Runs through Ettrick Township. For approach
and accommodation see " Tima Burn," and
" Clutha River," already mentioned.

TEVIOT River, tributary of Clutha River. —
Shingle, rock, and boulder bottom. Banks clear.
Wadeable. Landing deep, also good. Course,
twenty-six miles. Contains brown trout. Reached
from Roxburgh, where there are hotels, and to
which it is close : Roxburgh is reached by coach-
road of forty miles from Lawrence Station (where
there are hotels), on the Milton–Lawrence Railway. For approach and accommodation see
" Clutha River," already mentioned.

MANUHERIKIA River, tributary of Clutha River.—
Shingle bed. Banks open. Wadeable. Landing
mostly good. Course, fifty-five miles. Contains
brown trout. Reached (close to the mouth) from
Alexandra, where there are hotels : Alexandra is
reached by seventy miles of coach-road from Lawrence Station (where there are hotels), on the
Milton–Lawrence Railway. For approach and
accommodation see " Clutha River," already mentioned.

MANOR River, tributary of Manuherikia River.—
Shingle bed. Banks open. Wadeable. Landing
mostly good. Course, twenty-eight miles. Contains brown trout. Reached in a mile from Alexandra. For approach and accommodation see
" Manuherikia River," already mentioned.

EARNSCLEUGH River, tributary of the Clutha
River.—Shingle bed. Banks open. Wadeable.
Landing mostly good. Course, twenty-five miles.
Contains brown trout. Reached at Alexandra, to
which it is close. For approach and accommoda-
tion see " Manuherikia River," and " Clutha
River," already mentioned.

KAWARAU River, tributary of Clutha River.—
Rock and shingle bed. Banks open. Wadeable
partly. Landing deep, also good. Course, thirty-
three miles. Contains brown trout. Reached at
the junction with Clutha River at Cromwell, where
there are hotels : Cromwell is reached by eighty-
six miles of coach-road from the Lawrence Station
(where there are hotels), on the Milton–Lawrence
Railway. The river is also reached by six miles of
road from Queenstown (where there are hotels), on
Lake Wakatipu : Queenstown is reached by railway from Dunedin and Invercargill to Kingston,
where there is hotel accommodation : From Kingston to Queenstown is twenty-five miles by steamer.
For approach and accommodation see " Clutha
River," already mentioned.

NEVIS Stream, tributary of Kawarau River.—
Shingle bed. Banks open. Wadeable. Landing
deep, also good. Course, thirty miles. Contains
brown trout. Reached by sixteen miles of road
and tracks from Cromwell, and by six miles more of
this road to Nevis Township, which is fifteen miles
from the mouth of the river. Also reached by
twenty miles of coach-road from Queenstown
(where there are hotels), on Lake Wakatipu. Not
far from the mouth of the river there is hotel
accommodation ; also at Gibbston, four miles away
on the road to Queenstown. For approach and
accommodation see " Kawarau River," already
mentioned.

LAKE HAYES, tributary of Kawarau River.—
Shingle beaches. Banks fairly clear. Wadeable
partly. Landing deep, also good. Length, two
miles ; breadth, three-quarters of a mile. Contains
brown trout. Reached by eight miles of road from
Queenstown. For approach and accommodation
see " Kawarau River," already mentioned.

SHOTOVER River, tributary of Kawarau River.—
Rock and shingle bed. Banks open, and fairly
clear. Wadeable partly. Landing deep, also good.

Course, forty-three miles. Contains brown trout. Reached from Queenstown by road of four miles to Frankton, where there is hotel accommodation; also by road of twenty-five miles from Cromwell. For approach and accommodation see " Kawarau River," already mentioned.

LAKE WAKATIPU, tributary of Kawarau River.— Shingle bottom, and in places beaches. Banks mostly steep and clear—the bases of high clear ranges. Wadeable here and there. Landing mostly deep, but some good. Length, fifty-four miles; breadth, from one to four miles. Height above sea-level, 1,069 ft. Contains brown trout. Reached from Kingston, on the bank, where there is hotel accommodation : Kingston is reached by railway from Dunedin or Invercargill. From Kingston to Queenstown, where there are hotels, is twenty-five miles by steamer. From Queenstown to Glenorchy, at the head of the Lake, where there are hotels, is thirty-five miles by steamer. There are also tracks round the Lake from Kingston to Queenstown and Glenorchy. Reached also from Cromwell, by coach. For approach and accommodation see " Kawarau River," already mentioned.

LOCKY Stream, tributary of Lake Wakatipu, west side.—Shingle and boulder bed. Banks steep and clear mostly. Wadeable partly. Landing deep, also good. Course, sixteen miles. Contains brown trout. Reached in about ten miles by steamer or boat from Kingston, or from Queenstown. For approach and accommodation see " Lake Wakatipu," already mentioned.

GREENSTONE Stream, tributary of Lake Wakatipu, west side.—Shingle and boulder bed. Banks steep and partly clear. Wadeable partly. Landing deep, also good. Course, seventeen miles. Contains brown trout. Reached by boat or steamer from Queenstown in twenty-five miles; from Glenorchy in ten miles. For approach and accommodation see " Lake Wakatipu," already mentioned.

DART River, tributary of Lake Wakatipu, north side.—Shingle bed in lower reaches; shingle, boulder, and rock bottom and bed in upper reaches. Banks low and clear in lower reaches; partly high, steep, and scrub-encumbered in upper part. Wadeable partly. Landing deep, also good. Course, thirty-six miles. Contains brown trout. Reached by boat or bank in a mile or two from Glenorchy. For approach and accommodation see "Lake Wakatipu," already mentioned.

REES River, tributary of Lake Wakatipu, north side.—Shingle bed in lower reaches; shingle and boulder and rock bottom and bed in higher reaches. Banks in lower reaches low, alluvial, and clear; in upper reaches partly steep, and scrub-encumbered. Wadeable partly. Landing deep, also good. Course, twenty-two miles. Contains brown trout. Reached from Glenorchy, which is at the mouth, and where there are hotels. For approach and accommodation see "Lake Wakatipu," already mentioned.

LINDIS River, tributary of Clutha River.— Shingle bed and bottom. Banks fairly clear and open. Wadeable partly. Landing deep, also good. Course, forty miles. Contains brown trout. Reached by road of four miles from Bendigo, where there is accommodation; also, accommodation may be had on the same road near the mouth of the stream. Bendigo is reached by coach-road from Lawrence Station, on the Milton–Lawrence Railway; also reached by road from Cromwell and from Queenstown. For approach and accommodation see "Lake Waka- tipu," and "Clutha River," already mentioned.

CARDRONA Stream, tributary of Clutha River.— Shingle bed. Banks open and fairly clear. Wadeable partly. Landing deep, also good. Course, twenty-five miles. Contains brown trout. Reached from Pembroke in a mile. Pembroke is two miles from the mouth, and is reached by rail from Dunedin and Invercargill to Kingston, then by steamer to Queenstown, then by coach from Queenstown. Reached also by coach up the Clutha Valley from Lawrence Station, on the Milton–Lawrence Railway; from Kurow Station, on the Oamaru–Duntroon and Hakataramea Railway, and by coach *via* Omaramara and Lindis Valley; also from Kokonga (where there is hotel accommodation), on the Otago Central Railway, and by coach through Central Otago.

LAKE WANAKA, tributary of Clutha River.— Shingle bottom mostly. Banks chiefly steep and clear, with deep water, but with shingle beaches here and there at the north end; and there is shallow water extending a mile across, with mud and shingle bottom. Banks low for some distance back. Length, thirty-five miles; breadth, three miles. Height above sea-level, 928 ft. Wadeable here and there. Landing deep, also good. Contains brown trout. Small steamers ply on the lake from Pembroke, on the bank. Reached from Queenstown by coach-road of forty miles *via* Arrow and the Crown Range : Queenstown, where there are hotels, is reached from Kingston by steamer in twenty-five miles : Kingston reached by railway from Dunedin and Invercargill.

MATUKITUKI River, tributary of Lake Wanaka, west side.—Shingle and rock bed. Banks open and clear mostly. Wadeable. Landing deep, also good. Course, thirty miles. Contains brown trout. Reached from Pembroke (to near the mouth) by eleven miles of road. For approach and accommodation see "Lake Wanaka," already mentioned.

WILKIN Stream, tributary of Lake Wanaka, west side.—Shingle bed. Banks mostly forest, but first five miles on south bank clear. Wadeable. Landing deep, also good. Course, nineteen miles. Contains brown trout. Reached by track of thirty-eight miles from Pembroke, or by steamer from the same place. For approach and accommodation see "Lake Wanaka," already mentioned.

MAKARORA Stream, tributary of Lake Wanaka, north side.—Shingle and rock bed. Banks open and clear mostly, through forest. Wadeable. Landing deep, also good. Course, seventeen miles. Contains brown trout. For approach and accommodation see "Wilkin Stream," already mentioned.

YOUNG Burn, tributary of Makarora Stream.— Shingle bed. Banks low and forest-clad. Wadeable. Landing deep, also good. Course, nine miles. Contains brown trout. Reached by following up the Makarora Stream for five miles from the mouth. For approach and accommodation see "Makarora Stream," already mentioned.

BLUE Burn, tributary of Makarora Stream.— Shingle bed. Banks low and forest-clad. Wadeable. Landing deep, also good. Course, six miles. Contains brown trout. Reached by following up Makarora Stream eight miles from the mouth. For approach and accommodation see "Lake Wanaka," already mentioned.

HAWEA River, tributary of Clutha River.— Shingle, rock, and boulder bottom. Banks various and clear. Wadeable partly. Landing deep, also good. Course, eight miles. Contains brown trout. Reached (to the junction with the Clutha) by four miles of road from Pembroke. For approach and accommodation see "Lake Wanaka," already mentioned.

LAKE HAWEA, tributary of Hawea River.— Shingle bottom mostly; shingle beaches here and there. Banks chiefly steep and clear, with forest here and there. Wadeable in places. Landing deep, also good. Length, eighteen miles; breadth, three miles. Height above sea-level, 1,062 ft. Contains brown trout. Reached by way of Hawea River. For approach and accommodation see that river, and "Lake Wanaka," already mentioned.

DINGLE Stream, tributary of Lake Hawea, east side.—Shingle bed. Banks various, clear for two miles, then forest-clad chiefly for eight miles, then clear. Wadeable. Landing deep, also good. Course, twenty miles. Contains brown trout. Reached by thirteen miles of track from Gladstone, which is ten miles from Pembroke. For approach and accommodation see "Lake Hawea" and "Lake Wanaka," already mentioned.

HUNTER River, tributary of Lake Hawea, north side.—Shingle bed. Banks partly low, and for first fourteen miles open and clear, then forest-covered. Wadeable. Landing mostly good. Course, thirty-three miles. Contains brown trout. Reached by Lake Hawea in eighteen miles from the foot of the lake at Gladstone, or by track of twenty miles round the lake. For approach and accommodation see "Lake Hawea" and "Lake Wanaka," already mentioned."

CATLIN'S River.—Estuary of about five miles; tidal for about two miles. Rock and boulder bottom. Banks steep, forest-covered. Wadeable partly. Landing deep, also good. Course, twenty-seven miles. Contains brown trout. Reached from Owaka Station (where there is hotel accommodation), on the Balclutha–Owaka Railway; Owaka is four miles from the mouth of the river.

OWAKA Stream, tributary of Catlin's River.—Shingle and rock bed. Banks partly open, partly forest-covered. Wadeable. Landing good. Course, nineteen miles. Contains brown trout. For approach and accommodation see "Catlin's River," already mentioned. Roads from Owaka run up and near the river for fourteen miles.

PURAKAUNUI Burn.—Rock and shingle bottom. Banks steep and partly forest-covered. Wadeable partly. Landing mostly deep. Course, seven miles. Contains brown trout. Reached by ten miles of road from the Owaka Station (where there is hotel accommodation) on the Balclutha–Owaka Railway.

CHAPTER XX.

MIDDLE ISLAND.—SOUTH COAST.

RIVERS AND LAKES FROM LONG POINT (IRIHUKA) TO
CHALKY INLET.

TAHAKOPA River. — Estuary of two miles. Sand, rock, and shingle bottom. Tidal for seven miles. Banks steep, partly forest - clad, and encumbered with scrub and flax. Wadeable partly. Landing mostly deep. Course twenty-one miles. Contains brown trout. Reached by rail to Owaka, on the Balclutha–Owaka Railway, thence by driving-road, twenty miles, to Tahakopa. Accommodation uncertain.

McLennan's Creek, tributary of Tahakopa River. —Tidal for three miles. Rock and shingle bottom. Banks steep and forest-clad. Wadeable partly. Landing mostly deep. Course, six miles. Contains rainbow trout. For approach and accommodation see " Tahakopa River," already mentioned.

Back Creek, tributary of Tahakopa River.—Mud bottom. Sluggish. Banks forest - clad. Wadeable partly. Landing deep. Course, nine miles. Contains brown trout. For approach and accommodation see " Tahakopa River," already mentioned.

Tautuku Burn. — Estuary, two miles. Sandy bottom, then boulder and shingle bottom. Banks steep and forest-clad. Wadeable partly. Landing mostly deep. Course, eight miles. Contains brown trout. For approach and accommodation see " Tahakopa River," already mentioned.

Waipati Stream.—Rock and shingle bottom. Banks high, mostly forest-clad. Wadeable partly.

Landing deep. Course, eleven miles. Contains brown trout. For approach and accommodation see "Tahakopa River," already mentioned, and from which it is nine miles by driving-road.

WAIKAWA Stream. — Estuary of three miles. Rock and shingle bottom. Banks high, partly forest-clad. Wadeable partly. Landing deep. Course, fourteen miles. Contains brown trout. Reached by driving-road of forty miles from Owaka Railway-station, to Waikawa, where there is accommodation. For approach and accommodation see "Tahakopa River," already mentioned.

TOKANUI Stream. — Mud bottom. Sluggish. Banks high and flax-encumbered. Wadeable. Landing deep. Course, eleven miles. Contains brown trout. Reached by railway to Wyndham Station, on a branch line of the Dunedin–Invercargill Railway, thence twenty miles by coach-road to Fortrose (where there are hotels), and then by driving-road, seven miles, to Tokanui. Accommodation uncertain.

TITIROA Stream.—Mud bottom with a little reef rock. Banks steep, grassy, mostly flax-encumbered. Wadeable partly. Landing deep. Course, seventeen miles. Contains brown trout. Crossed by the Wyndham–Fortrose Coach-road ten miles from Wyndham ; this road then continues within two miles of the stream to near Fortrose, which is a mile from the mouth. For approach and accommodation see "Tokanui Stream," already mentioned. There are hotels at Fortrose.

WAIMAHAKA Stream, tributary of Titiroa Stream. Mud bottom. Banks mostly steep, and a good deal scrub-encumbered. Not much wadeable. Landing deep. Course, eleven miles. Contains brown trout. Crossed by the Wyndham–Fortrose Coach-road, fifteen miles from Wyndham and five from Fortrose. For approach and accommodation see "Tokanui Stream," already mentioned. There are hotels at Fortrose.

22—Sport.

MATAURA River. — Shingle bottom in lower reaches, and shingle bed in upper part. Banks clear all the way above Wyndham. Wadeable. Landing good above Wyndham. Course, 120 miles. Contains brown trout. Reached (to the mouth) from Fortrose, distant four miles, where there are hotels: Fortrose is reached by coach-road of twenty-five miles from Wyndham Railway-station, where there are hotels, and which is at the junction of the Mataura and Mimihau Stream. The river is also reached from the Mataura and Gore Stations, on the Dunedin–Invercargill Railway, where there are hotels; and from the Mandeville, Riversdale, Athol, and Garston Stations, on the Gore–Kingston Railway. These are all fairly close to the river, and have hotels.

MOKORETA River, tributary of Mataura River.— Rock bottom. Banks high, mostly clear. Wadeable partly. Course, thirty-three miles. Contains brown trout. Reached from Wyndham Station, on a branch of the Dunedin–Invercargill Railway, to which it is close, and where there are hotels.

MIMIHAU Stream, tributary of Mataura River.— Rock and shingle bottom. Banks partly high and partly encumbered. Wadeable partly. Landing good generally. Course twenty miles. Contains brown trout. For approach and accommodation see Mokoreta River, already mentioned.

MARAIRUA Burn, tributary of Mataura River.— Shingle bottom. Banks open. Wadeable. Landing good. Course, six miles. Contains brown trout. Reached by three miles of road from Wyndham Station (where there are hotels), on a branch of the Dunedin–Invercargill Railway.

WAIMUMU Burn, tributary of Mataura River.— Shingle bottom. Banks medium, partly flax-encumbered. Wadeable partly. Landing deep, also good. Course, nine miles. Contains brown trout. Reached from the Mataura Station, on the Dunedin–Invercargill Railway, where there are hotels.

Waikaka River (West Branch), tributary of Mataura River.—Shingle bottom. Banks high. Wadeable partly. Landing mostly deep. Course, thirty miles. For approach and accommodation see " Waikaka River," already mentioned.

Waikaka River (East Branch).—Shingle bottom. Banks various, and partly flax-encumbered. Wadeable partly. Landing mostly deep. Course, ten miles. Reached from Gore, a station on the Dunedin–Invercargill Railway, where there are hotels.

Otamita Stream, tributary of Mataura River.—Shingle and rock bottom. Banks low, clear, grassy. Wadeable partly. Landing deep, also good. Course, seventeen miles. Contains brown trout. Reached easily from the Mandeville Station, on the Gore – Kingston Railway, where there are hotels.

Waimea River, tributary of Mataura River.—Shingle and mud bottom. Banks partly high and flax encumbered, partly low shingle. Wadeable partly. Landing deep, also good. Course, thirty-two miles. Contains brown trout. Reached easily from the Mandeville Station, on the Gore–Kingston Railway, where there are hotels.

McKellar Burn, tributary of Waimea River.—Shingle bottom. Banks high and flax-encumbered. Wadeable partly. Landing deep mostly. Course, seven miles. Contains brown trout. Reached easily from Mandeville, on the Gore–Kingston Railway, where there are hotels.

Waikaia River (East Branch), tributary of Mataura River.—Shingle bottom. Banks open. Wadeable partly. Landing deep, also good. Course, fifty-two miles. Contains brown trout. Reached from Riversdale Station, on the Gore–Kingston Railway, where there are hotels, and from which it is four miles by road.

Dome Stream, tributary of Waikaia River.—Shingle bottom. Mountain stream. Banks mostly low and clear. Wadeable partly. Landing deep, also good. Course, seventeen miles. Contains brown trout. For approach and accommodation see "Waikaia River," already mentioned.

WAIKAIA River (West Branch).—Shingle bed. Banks open. Wadeable. Landing good. Course, thirteen miles. Contains brown trout. For approach and accommodation see "Waikaia River," already mentioned.

TOMOGALAK Stream, tributary of Mataura River. —Shingle and boulder bottom. Mountain stream. Banks high and flax-encumbered. Wadeable. Landing deep, also good. Course, thirteen miles. Contains brown trout. Reached by road from Lumsden Station, on the Gore–Kingston Railway, where there are hotels.

EYRE Stream, tributary of Mataura River.— Shingle bed in lower half, boulder and rock in upper half. Banks low. Wadeable. Landing mostly good. Course, sixteen miles. Contains brown trout. Reached from the Athol Station (to which it is close), on the Invercargill–Kingston Railway : there is a hotel at Athol.

ORETI River.—Has an estuary of thirteen miles and is tidal for six miles. Shingle bottom and bed. River banks more or less forest for twenty miles from the mouth, above that open and clear to the head-waters. Wadeable partly. Landing deep aud good chiefly. Course, 116 miles. Contains brown trout. Reached by road from Invercargill to near the mouth in the Otatara Bush ; by coach to Wallacetown, where there are hotels, seven miles from Invercargill ; from Makarewa, Winton, Dipton, and Lumsden Stations, on the Invercargill–Kingston Railway, at all of which there are hotels at easy distance from the river ; and at Mossburn Station (where there are hotels) on the Lumsden– Mossburn Branch Railway. Also reached from many intermediate stations.

MAKAREWA River, tributary of Oreti River.— Shingle and mud bottom in the lower half, upper

CATCH OF TROUT, SOUTHLAND DISTRICT.

(Otapiri) half, shingle and rock bottom. Banks high, much flax- and forest-encumbered. Wadeable partly. Landing deep. Course, sixty miles. Contains brown trout. Reached by two miles of road from the Wallacetown Station (where there are hotels), on the Invercargill–Kingston Railway.

Tussocks Burn, tributary of Makarewa River.— Mud and shingle bottom. Banks high and more or less encumbered. Wadeable partly. Landing deep. Course, ten miles. Contains brown trout. Reached from the Lochiel Station, on the Invercargill–Kingston Railway.

Titipua River, tributary of Makarewa River.— Mud bottom. Banks high. Not wadeable. Landing deep. Course, twenty-two miles. Contains brown trout. Reached from Edendale Station (where there are hotels), on the Dunedin–Invercargill Railway, thence five miles' walk, or by following up the Makarewa River from Makarewa Junction, on the Invercargill-Kingston Railway.

Hedgehope River, tributary of Titipua River.— Mud and shingle bottom. Banks partly high and flax - encumbered. Wadeable partly. Landing deep. Course, twenty-two miles. Contains brown trout. Reached by following up the Makarewa River from Makarewa Junction, on the Invercargill–Kingston Railway, eight miles' walk.

Lora Stream, tributary of Makarewa River.— Rock and boulder bottom. Banks high and fairly clear. Wadeable partly. Landing deep. Course, twelve miles. Contains brown trout. For approach and accommodation see " Otapiri Stream," already mentioned.

Winton Stream, tributary of Oreti River.— Shingle and mud bottom. Banks high, encumbered with forest, scrub, and flax. Wadeable. Landing deep. Course, twenty miles. Contains brown trout. Reached from Winton Station (by which it flows, and where there are hotels), on the Invercargill–Kingston Railway.

TERRACE Burn, tributary of Oreti River.—Mud and shingle bottom. Banks high, more or less flax-encumbered. Wadeable partly. Landing deep. Course, ten miles. Contains brown trout. For approach and accommodation see " Winton Stream," already mentioned.

BOG Stream, tributary of Oreti River.—Mud and shingle bottom. Banks high and flax-encumbered. Wadeable partly. Landing deep. Course, fourteen miles. Contains brown trout. For approach and accommodation see " Winton Stream," already mentioned.

HILLEND Burn, tributary of Oreti River.—Mud and shingle bottom. Banks high and more or less flax-encumbered. Wadeable partly. Landing deep. Course, seven miles. For approach and accommodation see " Winton Stream," already mentioned.

DIPTON Stream, tributary of Oreti River.— Shingle bottom. Banks fairly clear. Wadeable partly. Landing deep, also good. Course, seventeen miles. Contains brown trout. Reached (to near the mouth) in two miles from Harrington Station (near which there is hotel accommodation), on the Invercargill–Kingston Railway ; also in three miles from Dipton Station (where there is hotel accommodation), on the same railway.

STAG Burn, tributary of Oreti River.—Shingle bottom. Banks more or less flax-encumbered. Wadeable. Landing good mostly. Course, nine miles. Contains brown trout. Reached from Dipton Station (where there is a hotel), on the Invercargill-Kingston Railway.

MURRAY Stream, tributary of Oreti River.— Shingle bottom. Banks high and flax-encumbered. Wadeable. Landing deep, also good. Course, eleven miles. Contains brown trout. Reached from Lumsden Station (where there are hotels), on the Invercargill–Kingston Railway.

ACTON Stream, tributary of Oreti River.—Shingle bed. Banks low and fairly clear. Landing good.

Course, twenty miles. Contains brown trout. For approach and accommodation see " Murray Stream," already mentioned.

Oswald Burn, tributary of Acton Stream.— Shingle bottom. Banks rather high and clear. Wadeable partly. Landing deep. Course, eight miles. Contains brown trout. For approach and accommodation see " Murray Stream," already mentioned.

Cromel Stream, tributary of Acton Stream.— Shingle bottom for the lower half, the upper half boulder bottom. Banks, the lower half high and fairly clear, the upper half forest and scrub-covered. Wadeable. Landing mostly deep. Course, fifteen miles. Contains brown trout. For approach and accommodation see " Murray Stream," already mentioned.

Irthing Stream, tributary of Acton Stream.— Shingle bed and bottom. Banks low mostly. Wadeable. Landing mostly good. Course, eighteen miles. Contains brown trout. For approach and accommodation see " Murray Stream," already mentioned.

Weydon Burn, tributary of Oreti River.— Shingle bottom. Banks rather flax-encumbered. Wadeable. Landing mostly deep. Course, ten miles. Contains brown trout. Reached by eight miles of road from Mossburn Station (where there are hotels), on the Lumsden–Mossburn Branch Railway.

Windley Burn, tributary of Oreti River.— Shingle and rock bottom and bed. Banks low, the upper part forest. Wadeable. Landing good. Course, ten miles. Contains brown trout. Reached by ten miles of road from Mossburn Station (where there are hotels), on the Lumsden–Mossburn Branch Railway.

Aparima River.—Has an extensive estuary, with sand, mud, and rock bottom. Is tidal for four miles; above this it has almost entirely an open shingle bed. Banks low and clear. Wadeable. Landing good. Course, sixty-five miles. Contains brown trout. Reached (to near the estuary mouth) from Riverton Station (where there are hotels), on the Invercargill – Orepuki Railway. Large sea-run trout up-to 13 lb. weight have lately been caught with artificial minnow in front of and not more than 30 yards from the Aparima Hotel, which is situated on the banks of the estuary, and a mile from the Riverton Station. The river is also reached from Thornbury Junction (where there is a hotel), on the same railway, and from Fairfax and Otautau Stations on the Riverton–Nightcaps Railway, where there are hotels that are all at easy distances from the river.

OTAUTAU Stream, tributary of Aparima River.— Shingle and mud bottom. Banks high and grassy, partly scrub-encumbered. Wadeable partly. Landing deep. Course, twelve miles. Contains brown trout. Reached from Otautau Station (where there are hotels), on the Riverton-Nightcaps Railway.

OPIO Stream, tributary of Otautau Stream.— Shingle and mud bottom. Banks high and grassy, more or less flax-encumbered. Wadeable a little. Landing deep. Course, eighteen miles. Contains brown trout. For approach and accommodation see " Otautau Stream," already mentioned.

WAICOLO Stream, tributary of Otautau Stream.— Shingle and mud bottom. Banks high and grassy. Hardly wadeable. Landing deep. Course, eleven miles. Contains brown trout. For approach and accommodation see " Otautau Stream," already mentioned.

WAIRIO Stream, tributary of Otautau Stream.— Shingle and mud bottom. Banks high, clear, and grassy. Hardly wadeable. Landing deep. Course, thirteen miles. Contains brown trout. For approach and accommodation see " Otautau Stream," already mentioned.

ETAL Burn, tributary of Aparima River.—
Shingle bed and bottom. Mountain stream.
Banks high and clear. Wadeable. Landing good
mostly. Course, seven miles. Contains brown
trout. Reached from Nightcaps Station by twelve
miles of the Nightcaps–Mossburn Road. There
are hotels at Nightcaps.

HAMILTON Stream, tributary of Aparima River.
—Shingle bottom. Banks high and partly flax-
encumbered. Hardly wadeable. Landing deep.
Course, seventeen miles. Contains brown trout.
Reached from Nightcaps Station, where there are
hotels, by twenty miles of the Nightcaps–Mossburn Road, or from Mossburn Railway-station by
five miles of road. There are hotels at Mossburn,
which is on the Lumsden–Mossburn Branch Railway.

MOSS Burn, tributary of Hamilton Stream.—
Shingle bottom. Banks steep. Wadeable partly.
Landing deep. Course, eight miles. Contains
brown trout. Reached by road of two miles from
Mossburn Station (where there are hotels), on the
Lumsden–Mossburn Railway.

CENTRE Burn, tributary of Hamilton Stream.—
Shingle bottom. Banks grass and partly clear.
Wadeable. Landing good mostly. Course, nine
miles. Contains brown trout. For approach and
accommodation see " Moss Burn," already mentioned.

POURAKINO River.—Has a long estuary, and is
tidal for some distance. Banks steep and more
or less encumbered. Wadeable partly. Landing
deep, also good. Course, seventeen miles. Is
frequented by sea-run trout. Reached from Riverton Station, on the Invercargill–Orepuki Railway.
The Aparima Hotel, a mile from the station, is
conveniently situated for this river.

WAIAU River.—Snow-fed. The second river in
size in this country, unfordable up to Lake Manapouri. It drains Lakes Monowai, Manapouri, Te

Anau, South and North Mavora; it and the lakes receiving numerous feeders. A rapid, deep river of clear cold water, carrying the fresh water right out into the surf at the mouth. Boulder and shingle bed from the mouth up to the lakes. Banks mostly forest-clad up to Clifden; above that the east bank is nearly clear of forest. Wadeable partly. Mostly fishable from the mouth upwards from one side or the other from the shingle bed, but not fordable up to the lakes. There is a boat ferry near the mouth, and a bridge sixteen miles further up. Landing deep, also good. Course, fifty-five miles to Lake Manapouri; passing through seven miles of the lake, it then runs a course of thirteen miles up to Lake Te Anau, which is the chief source. Reached (to the mouth) by eight miles of driving-road from Orepuki (where there are hotels and livery stables), a station on the Invercargill–Orepuki Railway; or by driving-road from Orepuki to the bridge, twenty miles. A great part of this road runs parallel to and at no great distance from the river, but a belt of forest intervenes for a considerable way. From the bridge this road continues to Lake Manapouri, some forty miles, keeping within a few miles of the river. The river can also be reached by a driving-road of twenty-five miles to the bridge; from Otautau (where there are hotels), on the Riverton–Nightcaps Railway, or from Lumsden Station (where there are hotels), on the Invercargill–Kingston Railway. From here a coach runs to Lake Manapouri, fifty miles, and part of this road runs near the upper Waiau, also crossing the Mararoa River, a chief tributary of the Waiau. There is hotel accommodation at Manapouri. The angler intending to fish the Waiau and its tributaries should be provided with a tent.

ALTON Burn, tributary of Waiau River.—Shingle bed. Banks forest-covered. Wadeable. Landing deep, also good. Course, six miles. Contains brown trout. Reached from the ferry near Waiau mouth. For approach and accommodation see ' Waiau River," already mentioned.

ORAWIA River, tributary of Waiau River.—Shingle bed. Banks shingle and clay; clear of forest except towards the lower part. Wadeable partly. Landing deep, also good. Course, twenty-two miles. Contains brown trout. Reached by track from the road from Orepuki to the Waiau Bridge. For approach and accommodation see "Waiau River," already mentioned.

MERTON Burn, tributary of Waiau River.—Shingle bottom. Banks fairly clear. Wadeable partly. Landing deep, also good. Course, nine miles. Contains brown trout. Reached from the Waiau Bridge, to which it is near. For approach and accommodation see "Waiau River," already mentioned.

LILL Stream, tributary of Waiau River.—Shingle bottom. Banks high, and more or less encumbered with scrub. Wadeable. Landing deep, also good. Course, sixteen miles. Contains brown trout. Reached from the Waiau Bridge, to which it is near. For approach and accommodation see "Waiau River," already mentioned.

DEAN Burn, tributary of Waiau River.—Shingle bottom. Banks encumbered. Wadeable. Landing deep, also good. Course, eleven miles. Contains brown trout. Reached from the Waiau Bridge in seven miles. For approach and accommodation see "Waiau River," already mentioned.

WAIRAKI River, tributary of Waiau River.—Partly snow-fed. Open shingle bed. Banks various. Wadeable partly. Landing mostly good. Course, twenty-five miles. Contains brown trout. Reached from Waiau Bridge by road of eight miles. For approach and accommodation see "Waiau River," already mentioned; or from Otautau, on the Riverton-Nightcaps Railway. At Otautau there are hotels, and the Wairaki is reached by mail-cart to Eastern Bush, twenty-one miles from Otautau, and thence four miles by road to the Wairaki River.

GRASSY Stream, tributary of Wairaki River.— Shingle bottom. Banks partly encumbered. Wadeable partly. Landing deep. Course, twelve miles. Contains brown trout. Joins the Wairaki River towards the mouth. For approach and accommodation see " Wairaki River," already mentioned.

LIGAR Burn, tributary of Waiau River.—Shingle bottom. Banks partly encumbered. Wadeable partly. Landing deep, also good. Course, eight miles. Contains brown trout. Twenty miles by road from Waiau Bridge. For approach and accommodation see " Waiau River," already mentioned.

MONOWAI River, tributary of Waiau River.— Boulder and shingle bottom and bed. Banks much forest-clad. Not wadeable. Landing deep, also good. Course, six miles. Contains brown trout. Reached from Waiau River (to Lake Monowai) by forest tracks, chiefly from the Waiau Bridge, from which it is twenty-four miles. For approach and accommodation see " Waiau River," already mentioned.

LAKE MONOWAI, tributary of Monowai River.— Rock, boulder, and shingle bottom. Banks almost entirely forest. Wadeable here and there. Landing mostly deep, also good. Length, thirteen miles and a half; breadth, three-quarters of a mile. Contains brown trout. Reached from the Monowai River. For approach and accommodation see " Monowai River," already mentioned.

MARAROA RIVER, tributary of Waiau River.— Snow-fed. Shingle and boulder bed. Banks open on both sides until within a mile of Lake Mavora, when they are forest-clad on both sides. Wadeable partly. Landing mostly good. Course, including the South and North Mavora Lakes, sixty-three miles. Contains brown trout. Reached from the Lumsden Station (where there are hotels), on the Invercargill–Kingston Railway: from Lumsden there is a coach-road of fifty miles to Manapouri, where there are hotels; the Mararoa River is reached by the road five miles before reaching Manapouri.

WHITESTONE River, tributary of Mararoa River. —Snow-fed. Shingle bed. Banks clear. Easily fishable and got at. Wadeable partly. Landing deep, also good. Course, twenty-eight miles. Contains brown trout. Reached by thirteen miles of road from Manapouri. For approach and accommodation see "Mararoa River," already mentioned.

LAKE MAVORA, South (Mararoa River passes through it).—Shingle bottom and beaches nearly the whole way on both sides. Banks forest-clad. Wadeable here and 'there. Landing deep, also good. Length, one mile and three-quarters; breadth, three-quarters of a mile. Contains brown trout. Reached by twenty-five miles of track from Lake Wakatipu *via* the Von River; also from Lake Manapouri by road and track *via* the Mararoa River, forty miles. For approach and accommodation see "Lake Manapouri," further on.

LAKE MAVORA, North (Mararoa River passes through it).—Shingle bottom, and beaches nearly the whole way on both sides. Banks forest-clad. Wadeable partly. Landing deep, also good. Length, seven miles; breadth, one mile. Height above sea-level, 2,073 ft. Contains brown trout. For approach and accommodation see "Mavora Lake, South," already mentioned.

LAKE MANAPOURI, tributary of Waiau River, which runs through it. — Snow-fed. A beautiful lake of clear water. Shingle bottom and some shingle beaches. Banks forest-clad to the water's edge, except on east side, where it is open country. Containing numerous forest-clad islands. Wadeable partly. Landing deep, also good. Length, sixteen miles; breadth, eight miles: area 132 square miles. Has four large arms. Height above sea-level, 597 ft. Contains brown trout. Reached from Lumsden Station (where there are hotels), on the Invercargill or Dunedin–Kingston Railway: from Lumsden there is a coach-road of fifty miles to Manapouri, where there is hotel accommodation. Manapouri is thirteen miles by coach-road from Lake Te Anau, and eighteen miles from the Key of the Lakes Hotel, Mararoa. There is a small steamer on Lake Manapouri for use of tourists.

WAIAU River (Upper), running into north side of Lake Manapouri, and connecting with Lake Te Anau.—Shingle, boulder, and rock bottom. Banks mostly forest-clad on west side, and fairly clear after first mile on east side. Wadeable partly. Landing deep mostly. Course, thirteen miles. Contains brown trout. For approach and accommodation see "Lake Manapouri," already mentioned.

IRIS Burn, tributary of Lake Manapouri on north side.—Shingle, boulder, and rock bed and bottom. Banks forest-clad. Wadeable partly. Landing deep, also good. Course, seven miles. Contains brown trout. For approach and accommodation see "Lake Manapouri," already mentioned.

FREEMAN Burn, tributary of Lake Manapouri on north side.—Shingle, boulder, and rock bed and bottom. Banks forest-clad. Wadeable partly. Landing deep, also good. Course, five miles. Contains brown trout. For approach and accommodation see "Lake Manapouri," already mentioned.

AWE Burn, tributary of Lake Manapouri on north side.—Shingle, boulder, and rock bed and bottom. Banks forest-clad. Wadeable partly. Landing deep, also good. Course, six miles. Contains brown trout. For approach and accommodation see "Lake Manapouri," already mentioned.

Spey Burn, tributary of Lake Manapouri on south side. Shingle, boulder, and rock bed and bottom. Banks forest - clad. Wadeable partly. Landing deep, also good. Course, eight miles. Contains brown trout. For approach and accommodation see " Lake Manapouri," already mentioned.

Grebe Stream, tributary of Lake Manapouri on south side.—Shingle, boulder, and rock bed and bottom. Banks fairly clear on east side for seven miles, the rest forest - clad. Wadeable partly. Landing deep, also good. Course, sixteen miles. Contains brown trout. For approach and accommodation see " Lake Manapouri," already mentioned.

Lake Te Anau, tributary of Waiau River.—The largest lake in Maoriland. Shingle bottom and beach for nearly the whole way on east side. Banks mostly forest-clad, and numerous forest-clad islands. Wadeable here and there. Receives numerous feeders. Landing deep, also good. Length, thirty-eight miles; breadth, from one to six miles ; has three great fiords, one about sixteen miles long. Height above sea-level, 694 ft. Contains brown trout. Reached from the Lumsden Station (where there are hotels), on the Invercargill or Dunedin Railway to Kingston, and then fifty miles by coach. There is a small steamer on the lake for the use of tourists. A driving-road of thirteen miles up the bank of the Waiau River connects Lakes Manapouri and Te Anau. There is a hotel at Te Anau, where boats, vehicles, and horses can be obtained. For further approach and accommodation see " Lake Manapouri," already mentioned.

Upokororo River, tributary of Lake Te Anau on east side.—Snow-fed. Shingle bed. Banks low and clear for twelve miles, then forest-covered. Wadeable. Landing deep, also good. Course, twenty-six miles. Contains brown trout. For approach and accommodation see " Lake Te Anau," already mentioned.

EGLINGTON River, tributary of Lake Te Anau, east side. — Snow-fed. Shingle bed in lower reaches, rocky in upper. Banks low and clear for ten miles, then forest-clad. Wadeable partly. Course, thirty-two miles. Contains brown trout. For approach and accommodation see " Lake Te Anau," already mentioned.

CLINTON Burn, tributary of Lake Te Anau, north side.—Snow-fed. Shingle bed in lower reaches, then rocky gorge. Banks low and mostly forest-covered. Wadeable partly. Landing deep, also good. Course, nine miles. Contains brown trout. For approach and accommodation see " Lake Te Anau," already mentioned.

DOON Burn, tributary of Lake Te Anau, west side.—Rock and boulder bed. Mountain torrent. Banks forest-clad. Wadeable partly. Landing deep, also good. Course, nine miles. Contains brown trout. For approach and accommodation see " Lake Te Anau," already mentioned.

To the following rivers there is a good beach from the Waiau River Mouth and lower ferry to Blue Cliff, ten miles; then a 10 ft. track to Preservation Inlet, with some attempt at temporary bridges, all through forest, for sixty-five miles. This track also crosses some sixteen burns, not mentioned, averaging five miles in length.

WAIRAURAHIRI River.—Shingle and rock bottom. Banks steep and forest-covered. Not much wadeable. Landing deep mostly. Course, fifteen miles to Lake Hauroto. Contains brown trout. Reached from Orepuki Station (where there are hotels), on the Invercargill–Orepuki Railway, thence by eight miles of driving-road to lower Waiau ferry, and then by thirty miles broad forest track.

LAKE HAUROTO, tributary of Wairaurahiri River. —Some sand beaches. Wooded almost to water's edge. Length, twenty-one miles; breadth, one mile. Height above sea-level, 611 ft. Contains brown trout. For approach and accommodation see " Wairaurahiri River," already mentioned.

Hauroto Burn, tributary of Lake Hauroto, north end.—Shingle, boulder, and rock bottom and bed. Banks, forest chiefly, except three miles on east side. Wadeable partly. Landing mostly deep. Course, ten miles. Contains brown trout. For approach and accommodation see " Wairaurahiri River," already mentioned.

Hay Burn, tributary of Lake Hauroto, north end.—Rock, boulder, and shingle bottom. Banks steep, forest-clad. Wadeable partly. Landing deep. Course, seven miles. Contains brown trout. For approach and accommodation see " Wairaurahiri River," already mentioned.

Waitutu River.—Estuary of about seven miles into Lake Poteriteri. Rock and shingle bottom. Banks steep and forest-covered. Landing deep. Course, seven miles. Contains brown trout. Reached by thirty-six miles of broad forest track from lower Waiau ferry. For approach and accommodation see " Wairaurahiri River," already mentioned.

Lake Poteriteri, tributary of Waitutu River.—Some sand beaches. Forest almost to the water's edge. Length, eighteen miles ; breadth, one mile and a quarter. Height above sea-level, 120 ft. Contains brown trout. For approach and accommodation see " Waitutu River," already mentioned.

Mouat Burn, tributary of Lake Poteriteri, passing also through Lake Mouat.—Shingle, boulder, and rock bottom and bed. Banks forest-clad. Wadeable partly. Landing deep, also good. Course, including Lake Mouat, ten miles. Contains brown trout. For approach and accommodation see " Waitutu River," already mentioned.

Lake Mouat, tributary of Mouat Burn.—Shingle bottom. Banks forest-clad. Length, one mile and a quarter; breadth, quarter of a mile. Contains brown trout. For approach and accommodation see "Waitutu River," already mentioned.

KAKAPO Burn, tributary of Lake Poteriteri.— Shingle and rock bottom and bed. Banks forest-clad. Wadeable partly. Landing deep, also good. Course, including Lake Kakapo, through which it passes, seven miles. Contains brown trout. For approach and accommodation see "Waitutu River," already mentioned.

LAKE KAKAPO, tributary of Kakapo Burn.— Shingle bottom. Banks forest-clad. Length, one mile; breadth, quarter of a mile. Contains brown trout. For approach and accommodation see "Waitutu River," already mentioned.

PRINCESS Burn, tributary of Kakapo Burn.— Shingle and rock bottom and bed. Banks forest-clad. Wadeable partly. Landing deep, also good. Course, nine miles. Contains brown trout. For approach and accommodation see "Waitutu River," already mentioned.

AAN River. — Shingle bottom. Banks steep, and forest-clad. Wadeable partly. Landing deep chiefly. Course, six miles. Contains brown trout. Reached by forty miles of broad forest track from Waiau lower ferry. For approach and accommodation see "Wairaurahiri River," already mentioned.

LAKE INNES, tributary of Aan River.—Shingle bottom. Forest banks. Length, one mile; breadth, half a mile. Contains brown trout. For approach and accommodation see "Aan River," already mentioned.

PATUPO River.—Estuary for about four miles, to Lake Hakapoua. Mud bottom chiefly, and tidal. Banks forest-clad. Not wadeable. Landing deep mostly. Course, four miles. Contains brown trout. Reached by forty-three miles of broad forest track. For approach and accommodation see "Wairaurahiri River," already mentioned.

Lake Hakapoua, tributary of Patupo River.—
Shingle bottom. Forest to water's edge. Length,
four miles and a half; breadth, three-quarters of a
mile. Contains brown trout. For approach and
accommodation see " Patupo River," already mentioned.

Cavendish Stream.— Shingle and rock bottom.
Banks steep and forest-clad. Wadeable partly.
Landing deep. Course, fourteen miles. Contains
brown trout. Reached by forty-five miles of broad
forest track from the Waiau lower ferry. For approach and accommodation see " Wairaurahiri
River," already mentioned.

Kiwi Stream.—Rock and shingle bottom. Banks
steep and forest-covered. Wadeable partly. Landing deep. Course, fourteen miles. Contains brown
trout. Reached by fifty-two miles of broad forest
track. For approach and accommodation see
" Wairaurahiri River," already mentioned.

Coal Burn.—Shingle and rock bottom. Banks
steep and forest-covered. Wadeable partly. Landing deep. Course, nine miles. Reached by fifty-
five miles of broad forest track from the Waiau
lower ferry. For approach and accommodation
see " Wairaurahiri River," already mentioned.

Wilson Burn. — Rock and shingle bottom.
Banks steep, forest-covered. Wadeable partly.
Landing deep. Course, five miles. Contains
brown trout. Reached by sixty miles of broad
forest track from the Waiau lower ferry. For
approach and accommodation see " Wairaurahiri
River," already mentioned.

CHAPTER XXI.

SOUTH, OR STEWART ISLAND.

——

STREAMS OF THE NORTH AND EAST COAST, BEGINNING AT THE NORTH.

STEWART Island is situated twenty - five miles from the main land, and is reached by sailing-craft or coastal steamer from the Bluff Harbour to Oban, about that distance : the Bluff is reached by seventeen miles of railway from Invercargill. The island contains 425,000 acres, and has 130 miles of coast-line. It is very mountainous, a great part being also forest-covered. It has only 260 inhabitants, whose chief occupation is sea-fishing. Owing to the broken and forest-clad nature of the country, the rivers containing trout are most readily reached from Oban by boat round the coast. Oban is a small township situated in a sheltered bay, and has several accommodation houses or hotels. Trout are caught occasionally off the coast in nets by fishermen, but whether these have come from the main land rivers or those of the island is uncertain.

MURRAY BURN.—Rock, sand, and shingle bottom. Banks more or less forest-covered. Wadeable partly. Landing deep, also good. Course, five miles. Contains brown trout.

MAORI Creek.—Rock, sand, and shingle bottom. Banks more or less forest-covered. Wadeable partly. Landing deep, also good. Course, four miles. Contains brown trout.

FRESHWATER Stream.—Muddy bottom in the lower part, shingle and rock higher up. Banks partly clear, partly manuka scrub. Wadeable partly. Landing deep, also good. Course, thirteen miles. Contains brown trout.

SCOTT Burn, tributary of Freshwater Stream.— Shingle and rock bottom. Banks more or less scrub-encumbered. Wadeable partly. Landing deep, also good. Course, eight miles. Contains brown trout.

HERON Burn.—Rocky, sand, and shingle bottom. Banks more or less forest-clad. Wadeable partly. Landing deep, also good. Course, four miles. Contains brown trout.

LORD's Burn. –Estuary, with muddy bottom; then rock, sand, and shingle bottom. Banks more or less forest-clad. Wadeable partly. Landing deep, also good. Course, seven miles. Contains brown trout.

FRASER Burn, Port Pegasus.--Rock, sand, and shingle bottom. Banks more or less forest-clad. Wadeable partly. Landing deep, also good. Course, six miles. Contains brown trout.

There is fair wild-pigeon and duck shooting on the island.

CHAPTER XXII.

MIDDLE ISLAND—WEST COAST.

RIVERS AND LAKES FROM CAPE FAREWELL TO CHALKY
INLET (BEGINNING AT THE NORTH).

MANGAMANGARAKAU Burn. — Shingle bottom and bed. Banks forest-clad mostly. Wadeable partly. Landing deep, also good. Course, seven miles. Contains brown trout. Reached from Collingwood (where there are hotels) by sixteen miles of track. For approach and accommodation see Chapter XVIII., " Middle Island—Rivers and Lakes of the North Coast: Aorere River."

PATURAU Burn. — Shingle bottom and bed. Banks forest - clad mostly. Wadeable partly. Landing deep, also good. Course, nine miles. Contains brown trout. There is a lake—length, one mile; breadth, half a mile—three miles from the Junction. Reached from Collingwood by twenty-four miles of track. For approach and accommodation see " Mangamangarakau Burn," already mentioned.

TURIMAWIWI Burn.—Shingle bed and bottom. Banks forest - clad mostly. Wadeable partly. Landing deep, also good. Course, nine miles. Contains brown trout. Reached from Collingwood by thirty-three miles of track. For approach and accommodation see " Mangamangarakau Burn," already mentioned.

BIG Stream.—Shingle and rock bed and bottom. Banks forest-clad in lower half, fairly clear in upper. Wadeable partly. Landing deep, also good. Course, sixteen miles. Contains brown trout.

Reached from Collingwood by thirty-seven miles of track. For approach and accommodation see "Mangamangarakau Burn," already mentioned.

HEAPHY Stream.—Shingle bed and bottom. Banks low and forest-clad. Wadeable partly. Landing deep, also good. Course, eighteen miles. Contains brown trout. Reached by track of twenty miles from Karamea River. For approach and accommodation see "Karamea River," further on.

WEKAKURA Burn.—Shingle bed and bottom. Banks forest-clad. Wadeable partly. Landing deep, also good. Course, ten miles. Contains brown trout. Reached by track of thirteen miles from Karamea River. For approach and accommodation see "Karamea River," further on

KOHAIHAI Stream.—Shingle bed and bottom, then rock gorges. Banks low for short distance, then high, all forest-clad. Wadeable. Landing deep, also good. Course, eleven miles. Contains brown trout. Reached by ten miles of track from Karamea River. For approach and accommodation see "Karamea River," further on.

OPARARA Burn.—Estuary half a mile, sand and mud bottom. Tidal for one mile. Shingle bed for six miles, then limestone gorges. Banks low to gorges, then high, all forest-clad. Wadeable partly. Landing deep, also good. Course, six miles. Contains brown trout. Reached (to the mouth) by two miles of track from Karamea River. For approach and accommodation see "Karamea River," further on.

KARAMEA River.—Estuary two miles and a half, mud bottom. Tidal for two miles. Shingle bed for three miles, then rock gorges for some distance. Banks low for seven miles, then various, all forest-clad. Wadeable partly. Landing deep, also good. Course, fifty-one miles. Contains brown trout. Reached (to the mouth) by twenty-four miles of bush track from Mokihinui Station (where there are hotels), on the Westport–Mokihinui Railway. The head-waters can also be reached by the same track from Ngatimoti, on the Motueka Inland Road.

UGLY Burn, tributary of Karamea River.—Rock and boulder bed. Banks forest-clad. Wadeable partly. Landing deep, also good. Course, seven miles. Contains brown trout. Reached from the mouth of the Karamea River by track up the bank of the river for twenty miles. For approach and accommodation see "Karamea River," already mentioned.

ROARING LION Burn, tributary of Karamea River. —Rock and boulder bed. Banks forest-clad. Wadeable partly. Landing deep, also good. Course, eight miles. Contains brown trout. Reached from the mouth of the Karamea River by track up the bank of the river for twenty-six miles. For approach and accommodation see "Karamea River," already mentioned.

LESLIE Burn, tributary of Karamea River.— Rock and boulder bed. Banks forest-clad. Wadeable partly. Landing deep, also good. Course, nine miles. Contains brown trout. Reached from the mouth of the Karamea River by track up the bank of the river for thirty-two miles. For approach and accommodation see "Karamea River," already mentioned.

CROW Stream, tributary of Karamea River.— Rock and boulder bed. Banks forest-clad. Wadeable partly. Landing deep, also good. Course, sixteen miles. Contains brown trout. Reached from the mouth of the Karamea River by track up the bank of the river for thirty-two miles, then up the river for four miles. For approach and accommodation see "Karamea River," already mentioned.

LITTLE WANGANUI Stream. — Tidal for three miles. Shingle and sand bottom, then shingle bed for ten miles, then rock gorges. Banks low, and all forest-clad. Wadeable partly. Landing deep, also good. Course, twenty miles. Contains brown trout. Reached by twelve miles of forest track from the Mokihinui. For approach and accommodation see " Mokihinui River," further on.

MOKIHINUI River.—Shingle bed for four miles, then rock gorges for ten miles. Banks low and forest-clad. Wadeable partly. Landing deep, also good. Course, thirty-four miles, including North Branch. Contains brown trout. Reached from Mokihinui Station (where there are hotels), on the Westport–Mokihinui Railway. Mokihinui is close to the mouth of the river.

MOKIHINUI River (South Branch).—Shingle bed. Banks low and forest-clad. Wadeable. Landing mostly good. Course, thirteen miles. Contains brown trout. Reached by forest track of fifteen miles up the bank of the " Mokihinui River." For approach and accommodation see " Mokihinui River," already mentioned.

NGAKAWHAU Stream.—Shingle and sand bed for three-quarters of a mile, then rock gorge for five miles. Small branches further up with shingle beds. Banks low for three-quarters of a mile, then rock for five miles. Feeders mostly low banks, and forest-clad. Wadeable partly. Landing deep, also good. Course, eleven miles. Contains brown trout. Reached from Ngakawhau Station (where there is hotel accommodation), on the Westport–Mokihinui Railway. Ngakawhau Station is close to mouth of river.

WAIMANGAROA Burn. — Shingle bed for seven miles, then rock gorges. Banks low mostly, partly clear and partly forest-clad. Wadeable partly. Landing deep, also good. Course, ten miles. Contains brown trout. Reached from Waimangaroa Station (where there are hotels), on the Westport–Mokihinui Railway. Waimangaroa is close to the mouth of the river.

WAREATEA Burn.—Shingle bottom mostly for six miles, then mountain torrent. Banks low, partly clear, partly forest-clad. Wadeable partly. Landing mostly deep. Course, seven miles. Contains brown trout. Reached (to within a mile of the mouth) from Fairdown Station, seven miles from Westport (where there are hotels), on the Westport–Mokihinui Railway.

 OROWAITI Burn.—Shingle and mud bed for four miles, then mountain torrent. Banks low and forest-clad. Wadeable partly. Landing deep, also good. Course, eight miles. Contains brown trout. Reached by a mile and a half of road from Westport (where there ·are hotels), on the Westport–Mokihinui Railway.

BULLER River. — Tidal for a mile or two. Shingle bed and bottom for two miles, then ten miles of shingle bottom and rock gorge, then twelve miles shingle bed and bottom, then shingle bottom and rock gorge for ten miles, then shingle bed and bottom to Hampden, then shingle bed to near where Gowan River joins; from thence a few miles of rocky and boulder gorges, to the junction of the Hope Stream, then shingle bed to Lake Rotoiti. Banks low, partly clear and partly scrub for first two miles, then steep and forest-clad to junction with Hope Stream; then nearly all clear. Wadeable here and there. Landing mostly deep, also good. Course, eighty-five miles. Contains brown trout. Reached (to the mouth) at Westport (where there are hotels), which is reached by frequent coastal steamers. The river is also reached partly by railway and partly by coach-roads from Nelson. One of these roads strikes the Buller River close to Lake Rotoiti and eighty-five miles from the mouth, the other seventy-one miles from the mouth; both follow the bank all the way to the mouth at Westport. The river is also reached from the south: from Greymouth to Reefton by railway, and from Reefton, where there is hotel accommodation, by coach-road to Westport. This road strikes the river twenty-two miles from Reefton, at the mouth of the Inangahua River, where there is hotel accommodation; and here is also the junction with the Westport–Nelson Coach-road, which follows and crosses several important rivers and streams.

OHIKANUI Burn, tributary of Buller River.— Shingle bed and bottom. Banks steep, high, and forest-clad. Wadeable partly. Landing deep, also good. Course, nine miles. Contains brown trout. Reached from Westport by ten miles of the Westport–Nelson Coach-road. For approach and accommodation see " Buller River," already mentioned.

CASCADE Creek, tributary of Buller River.— Shingle bed and bottom. Banks steep, high, and forest-clad. Course, seven miles. Contains brown trout. Reached from Westport by eight miles of the Westport–Nelson Road, to the ferry; then by three miles of track. For approach and accommodation see " Buller River," already mentioned.

OHIKAITI Burn, tributary of Buller River.— Shingle bed and bottom. Banks steep, high, and forest-clad. Wadeable partly. Landing deep, also good. Course, eight miles. Contains brown trout. Reached from Westport by twelve miles of the Westport–Nelson Coach-road. For approach and accommodation see " Buller River," already mentioned.

BLACKWATER Stream, tributary of Buller River.— Shingle bed and bottom. Banks steep, high, and forest-clad. Wadeable partly. Landing deep, also good. Course, thirteen miles. Contains brown trout. Reached from Westport by sixteen miles of the Westport–Nelson Coach-road. For approach and accommodation see " Buller River," already mentioned.

ORIKAKA Stream, tributary of Buller River.— Shingle bed and bottom. Banks steep, high, and forest-clad. Wadeable partly. Landing deep, also good. Course, twelve miles. Contains brown trout. Reached from Westport by twenty-three miles of the Westport–Nelson Coach-road, and then by crossing the Buller River. The nearest hotel accommodation is at Inangahua, three miles off, at the junction of the Reefton–Nelson–West-port Coach-road. For approach and accommodation see "Buller River," already mentioned.

INANGAHUA River, tributary of Buller River.—Shingle bed and bottom. Banks high, low, partly clear, partly forest-clad; upper reaches rock gorge. Wadeable partly. Landing deep, also good. Course, forty-four miles. Contains brown trout. Reached at various points for twenty-two miles from the mouth, to Reefton, by the Westport–Reefton Coach-road, which follows the river for that distance. At the mouth, and along the road, and at Reefton there is hotel accommodation. Above Reefton the river is reached by track, which follows it for twenty miles. For approach and accommodation see " Buller River," already mentioned.

COAL Burn, tributary of Inangahua River.—Shingle bed and bottom. Banks low mostly, partly forest-clad, gorges at head. Wadeable partly. Landing deep, also good. Course, four miles. Contains brown trout. Reached by the Westport–Reefton Coach-road, then by crossing the bridge near the mouth of the Inangahua, and then following up the Inangahua for five miles. For approach and accommodation see " Inangahua River," already mentioned.

LARRY'S Stream, tributary of Inangahua River.—Shingle and boulder bed and bottom. Banks high, low, partly clear, partly forest-clad; upper reaches rock gorge. Wadeable partly. Landing deep, also good. Course, sixteen miles. Contains brown trout. Reached by twelve miles of the Westport–Reefton Coach-road from the mouth of the Inangahua River. For approach and accommodation see " Inangahua River," already mentioned.

Waitahu River, tributary of Inangahua River.—Shingle bed and bottom. Banks high, low, partly clear, partly forest-clad; upper reaches rock gorge. Wadeable partly. Landing deep, also good. Course, twenty-one miles. Contains brown trout. Reached from the mouth of the Inangahua River by eighteen miles of the Westport–Reefton Coach-road, also by four miles of this road from Reefton. For approach and accommodation see " Inangahua River," already mentioned.

Newton Burn, tributary of Buller River.—Shingle and boulder bottom. Banks high and forest-clad. Wadeable partly. Landing deep also good. Course, eight miles. Contains brown trout. Reached from Westport by forty-two miles of the Westport–Nelson Coach-road. For approach and accommodation see " Buller River," already mentioned.

Maruia River, tributary of Buller River.—Shingle bed and bottom for forty miles, then rock gorge and mountain torrent. Banks low mostly, partly clear and partly forest-clad. Wadeable partly. Landing deep, also good. Course, fifty-eight miles. Contains brown trout. Reached from Westport by forty-five miles of the Westport–Nelson Coach-road. Seven miles further on is Hampden, where there are hotels. For approach and accommodation see " Buller River," already mentioned.

Matiri Burn, tributary of Buller River.—Shingle and boulder bottom; after, four miles mountain torrent. Banks low and forest-clad. Wadeable partly. Landing mostly deep. Course, ten miles. Contains brown trout. Reached from Westport by fifty miles of the Westport–Nelson Coach-road. Two miles further on is Hampden, where there are hotels. For approach and accommodation see " Buller River," already mentioned.

Matakitaki River, tributary of Buller River.—Shingle bed and bottom. Banks mostly low, and mostly forest-clad. Wadeable partly. Landing deep, also good. Course, thirty-seven miles. Contains brown trout. Reached from Westport by fifty-two miles of the Westport–Nelson Coach-road to Hampden, where there are hotels within a mile of the mouth. For approach and accommodation see " Buller River," already mentioned.

GLENROY Stream, tributary of Matakitaki River. —Shingle and rock bed and bottom. Banks a good deal forest-clad. Wadeable partly. Landing deep, also good. Course, eighteen miles. Contains brown trout. Reached from the mouth of the Matakitaki River by eighteen miles of track up the river-bank. For approach and accommodation see " Matakitaki River," already mentioned.

MANGLES Stream, tributary of Buller River.— Rock gorge for five miles, then shingle bed and bottom. Banks above gorge low and mostly clear. Wadeable partly. Landing deep, also good. Course, eleven miles. Contains brown trout. Reached from Westport by fifty-two miles of the Westport–Nelson Coach-road to Hampden, where there are hotels within two miles of the mouth. For approach and accommodation see " Buller River," already mentioned.

TUTAKI Stream, tributary of Mangles Stream.— Shingle, rock, and boulder bed and bottom. Banks forest-clad. Wadeable partly. Landing deep, also good. Course, eleven miles. Contains brown trout. Reached by track of eleven miles up the bank of the Mangles Stream. Fer approach and accommodation see " Mangles Stream," already mentioned.

OWEN Stream, tributary of Buller River.— Shingle and rock bed and bottom. Banks low and forest-clad, then mountain torrent. Wadeable. Landing deep, also good. Course, thirteen miles. Contains brown trout. Reached from Westport by sixty-two miles of the Westport–Nelson Coach-road, and is ten miles past Hampden, where there are hotels. For approach and accommodation see "Buller River," already mentioned.

GOWAN River, tributary of Buller River.—Shingle and rock bed and bottom. Banks various and mostly forest-clad. Wadeable partly. Landing deep, also good. Course, seven miles. Contains brown trout. Reached from Westport by sixty-nine miles of the Westport–Nelson Coach-road; two miles further on this road, at the mouth of the Hope Stream, accommodation may be obtained. Also reached from Nelson by twenty miles of this road, from the Motupiko Station (where there is hotel accommodation), on the Nelson–Motupiko Railway. For approach and accommodation see "Buller River," already mentioned.

LAKE ROTOROA, tributary of Gowan River.—Shingle and rock bottom. Banks mostly steep and forest-clad. Wadeable here and there. Landing mostly deep. Length, six miles; breadth, a quarter of a mile. Height above sea-level, 1,623 ft. Contains brown trout. For approach and accommodation see "Gowan River," already mentioned.

D'URVILLE River, tributary of Lake Rotoroa.—Shingle, rock, and boulder bed. Banks mostly forest-clad. Wadeable partly. Landing deep, also good. Course, twenty-one miles. Contains brown trout. For approach and accommodation see "Gowan River" and "Lake Rotoroa," already mentioned.

LAKE CONSTANCE, tributary of D'Urville River.—Shingle and rock bottom. Banks steep and fairly clear. Wadeable here and there. Landing mostly deep. Length, a mile and a half; breadth, a mile and a half. Contains brown trout. For approach and accommodation see "Gowan River," "Lake Rotoroa," and "D'Urville River," already mentioned.

SABINE Stream, tributary of Lake Rotoroa.—Shingle, rock, and boulder bed. Banks mostly forest - clad. Wadeable partly. Landing deep, also good. Course, twelve miles. Contains brown trout. For approach and accommodation see "Gowan River" and "Lake Rotoroa," already mentioned.

HOPE Stream, tributary of Buller River.—Rock and shingle bottom. Banks steep and mostly forest-clad. Wadeable. Landing deep, also good. Course, eleven miles. Contains brown trout. Reached from Westport by seventy-one miles of the Westport–Nelson Coach-road; and from Nelson by twenty-five miles of this road from the Motupiko Station (where there is hotel accommodation) on the Nelson–Motupiko Railway. Accommodation may be obtained at the mouth of the stream. For approach and accommodation see "Buller River," already mentioned.

HOWARD Stream, tributary of Buller River.— Rock and shingle bottom. Banks mostly forest-clad. Wadeable partly. Landing deep, also good. Course, twelve miles. Contains brown trout. Reached from Westport by seventy-six miles of the Westport–Nelson Coach-road, five miles above the mouth of the Hope Stream. For approach and accommodation see "Hope Stream" and "Buller River," already mentioned.

LAKE ROTOITI, tributary of Buller River.— Shingle beaches partly. Banks steep, rock and clay, forest-clad almost to the water's edge. Wadeable here and there. Landing deep, also good. Length, five miles and a quarter; breadth, three-quarters of a mile. Height above sea-level, 1,886 ft. Contains brown trout. Reached from Westport by eighty-five miles of road up the bank of the Buller River, by the last fifteen miles of this road from the mouth of the Hope Stream, where there is accommodation, on the Westport–Nelson Coach-road. The road from Lake Rotoiti continues down the Motupiko River for ten miles from the source, and on to the Nelson–Motupiko

Railway. For approach and accommodation see "Buller River," already mentioned.

ROTOITI Stream, tributary of Lake Rotoiti.— Shingle, rock, and boulder bed. Banks chiefly forest-clad. Wadeable partly. Landing deep, also good. Course, fourteen miles. Contains brown trout. For approach and accommodation see "Lake Rotoiti," already mentioned.

OKARI Burn.—Shingle bed and bottom, with rocky gorges in upper reaches. Mountain torrent. Banks various and mostly forest-clad. Wadeable partly. Landing deep, also good. Course, eight miles. Contains brown trout. Reached from Westport by thirteen miles of road to the mouth, or by eight miles of road to the upper waters at Addison's, where there is hotel accommodation.

TOTARA Burn.—Shingle bed and bottom, with rocky gorges in upper reaches. Mountain torrent. Banks various and mostly forest-clad. Wadeable partly. Landing deep, also good. Course, seven miles. Contains brown trout. Reached from Westport by ten miles of the Westport–Charleston Coach-road. It is four miles past Addison's, where there is hotel accommodation, and three miles from Charleston, on the coast, where there are hotels.

WAITAKERE Stream.—Shingle bed and bottom; boulder and rock gorges in upper reaches. Banks various and mostly forest-clad. Wadeable partly. Landing deep, also good. Course, twelve miles. Contains brown trout. Reached from Westport by seventeen miles of coach-road to Charleston, where there are hotels, at the mouth.

FOUR-MILE Burn.—Shingle bed and bottom, rock in upper gorges. Banks high and forest-clad. Wadeable partly. Landing deep, also good. Course, seven miles. Contains brown trout. Reached from Charleston by five miles of track. For approach and accommodation see "Waitakere Stream," already mentioned.

24—Sport.

Fox's Burn.—Shingle bed for four miles, then mountain torrent. Banks low for four miles, then forest - clad. Wadeable partly. Landing deep, also good. Course, nine miles. Contains brown trout. Reached from Charleston by eleven miles of track to Brighton, where there is accommodation, at the mouth. For approach and accommodation see " Waitakere Stream," already mentioned.

Pororari Burn.—Shingle bottom mostly. Banks low mostly, and forest-clad. Wadeable partly. Landing deep, also good. Course, ten miles. Contains brown trout. Reached from Charleston by twenty miles of track. For approach and accommodation see " Waitakere Stream," already mentioned.

Punakaki Stream.—Shingle and boulder bed. Banks low and forest-clad. Wadeable. Landing mostly good. Course, thirteen miles. Contains brown trout. Reached from Charleston (to the mouth) by twenty-two miles of track. For approach and accommodation see " Waitakere Stream," already mentioned.

Canoe Creek.—Shingle bed and bottom, with rock gorges in upper part. Banks forest-clad. Wadeable partly. Landing deep, also good. Course, six miles. Contains brown trout. Reached from Charleston by thirty miles of track (to the mouth). For approach and accommodation see " Waitakere Stream," already mentioned. Accommodation may be obtained near the mouth. Also reached by twenty-three miles of track from Greymouth, *via* Barrytown, where there is hotel accommodation three miles before reaching Canoe Creek. Greymouth, where there are hotels, is reached by frequent coastal steamers, and by railway from Reefton and Hokitika.

Ten-mile Creek.—Shingle and boulder bottom, rock gorges in upper part. Banks steep and forest-clad. Wadeable partly. Landing mostly deep.

Course, eight miles. Contains brown trout. Reached from Charleston by forty miles of track (see Waitakere Stream," already mentioned), also from Greymouth by ten miles of the same track. For approach and accommodation see " Canoe Creek," already mentioned.

SEVEN-MILE Creek.—Shingle bottom, upper portion rocky gorges. Banks forest-clad. Wadeable partly. Landing deep, also good. Course, seven miles. Contains brown trout. Reached from Greymouth by six miles of road, which continues as a track to Charleston. For approach and accommodation see " Waitakere Stream," already mentioned.

GREY RIVER.—Short estuary, tidal for three miles. Shingle bed, with rock gorges in upper reaches. Banks for forty miles on southern side low and clear ; on northern side forest at intervals, then forest-clad. Wadeable partly. Landing deep, also good. Course to Lake Christabel, sixty-seven miles. Contains brown trout. Reached from Greymouth, at the mouth, where there are hotels. Greymouth is reached by frequent coastal steamers, and by railway from Reefton and Hokitika ; the river is also reached for thirty miles from several stations on the Greymouth – Reefton Railway, which runs near the river. At several of these stations there is hotel accommodation. Also reached for the same distance by the Greymouth–Reefton Road, which keeps near the river, and not far from the railway. At Little Grey, where there is hotel accommodation, a track follows up the river forty miles, to near the source in Lake Christabel.

OMOTUMOTU Creek, tributary of Grey River.— Shingle bottom. Banks high, steep, and scrub-encumbered. Wadeable partly. Landing deep. Course, five miles. Contains brown trout. Reached from Greymouth by two miles of road. For approach and accommodation see " Grey River," already mentioned.

ARNOLD River, tributary of Grey River.—Boulder and shingle bottom. Banks mostly forest-clad and scrub - encumbered. Wadeable partly. Landing mostly deep. Course, sixteen miles. Contains brown trout. Reached from Greymouth to Stillwater Station (where there is hotel accommodation), at the junction of the Greymouth–Reefton and Stillwater–Jackson Railways. Stillwater is near the junction with the Grey River. The railway runs near the river for twelve miles, to its exit from Lake Brunner. For approach and accommodation see "Grey River," already mentioned.

LAKE BRUNNER, tributary of Arnold River.—About three-fourths gravelly beaches with shallow water. Banks mostly low and forest-clad. Wadeable here and there. Length, five miles and a half; breadth, three miles and a half. Height above sea-level, 281 ft. Contains brown trout. Reached from Greymouth by the Greymouth–Reefton Railway to Stillwater, where there is hotel accommodation, and then by the Stillwater–Jackson Railway, which runs along the bank of the lake. For approach and accommodation see "Arnold River," already mentioned.

EAST HOHONU Stream, tributary of Lake Brunner.—Shingle and boulder bottom in lower half, rock and boulder bottom in upper. Banks steep and forest-clad. Wadeable partly. Landing deep. Course, twelve miles. Contains brown trout. Reached by track from the Greymouth–Jackson Railway. For approach and accommodation see "Lake Brunner," already mentioned.

ORANGIPUKU Burn, tributary of Lake Brunner.—Shingle bottom. Banks steep and forest-clad. Wadeable in upper half. Landing mostly deep. Course, nine miles. Contains brown trout. Reached by tracks from Laketown, on the Greymouth–Jackson Railway. For approach and accommodation see "Lake Brunner," already mentioned.

BRUCE'S Burn, tributary of Orangipuku Burn.—
Shingle bottom. Banks steep and forest-clad.
Wadeable mostly. Landing mostly deep. Course,
five miles. Contains brown trout. Reached by
tracks from Laketown, on the Greymouth–Jackson
Railway. For approach and accommodation see
" Lake Brunner," already mentioned.

CROOKED Stream, tributary of Lake Brunner.—
Snow-fed. Shingle bed in lower half; boulder
bottom in upper, with rock gorges. Banks low and
scrub-clad in lower half, steep and forest-covered
in upper. Wadeable mostly. Landing chiefly
good. Course, seventeen miles. Contains brown
trout. Reached by tracks from Lake Brunner.
For approach and accommodation see " Lake
Brunner," already mentioned.

LAKE KANGAROO, tributary of Crooked Stream.—
Shingle bottom. Banks steep and partly forest-
clad. Length, one mile and a half; breadth, half
a mile. Contains brown trout. Reached by tracks
from Lake Brunner. For approach and accommodation see " Crooked Stream," already mentioned.

LAKE LADY, tributary of Crooked Stream.—
Shingle bottom. Banks steep and partly forest-
clad. Length, one mile; breadth, three-eighths
of a mile. Contains brown trout. Reached by
track from Lake Brunner. For approach and
accommodation see " Crooked Stream," already
mentioned.

POERUA Burn, tributary of Crooked Stream.—
Shingle bed. Banks chiefly swampy and forest-
clad. Wadeable partly. Landing mostly deep.
Course, five miles. Contains brown trout. Reached
by track from Lake Brunner. For approach and
accommodation see " Lake Brunner," already mentioned.

LAKE POERUA, tributary of Crooked Stream.—
Muddy bottom. Swampy margin; banks low,
swampy, and flax-encumbered for greater part,
one-fourth steep and forest-clad. Length, one

mile and a quarter; breadth, half a mile. Contains brown trout. Reached by tracks from Lake Brunner, also by road of five miles from Laketown, near Lake Brunner. For approach and accommodation see " Lake Brunner," already mentioned.

Twelve-mile Burn, tributary of Grey River. —Shingle bed. Banks low, partly forest-clad. Wadeable. Landing deep, also good. Course, ten miles. Contains brown trout. Reached from Notown Road Station (which is near the mouth), on the Greymouth–Reefton Railway, thence four miles up the burn is Notown, where there is hotel accommodation. Reached also from Greymouth by sixteen miles of the Greymouth–Reefton Road. For approach and accommodation see " Grey River," already mentioned.

Blackball Burn, tributary of Grey River.— Shingle bed and bottom, rock gorges in upper part. Banks low, mostly forest-clad. Wadeable mostly. Landing deep, also good. Course, six miles. Contains brown trout. Reached from Ngahere Station (where there are hotels), on the Greymouth–Reefton Railway; also from Greymouth by sixteen miles of the Greymouth–Reefton Road. For approach and accommodation see " Grey River," already mentioned.

Nelson Stream, tributary of Grey River. — Shingle bottom. Banks low, mostly clear; the upper portion forest-clad. Wadeable partly. Landing deep, also good. Course, twelve miles. Contains brown trout. Reached from Ngahere Station (where there are hotels), on the Greymouth–Reefton Railway; also from Greymouth by seventeen miles of the Greymouth–Reefton Road. For approach and accommodation see " Grey River," already mentioned.

Lake Hochstetter, tributary of Nelson Stream. —Shingle bottom. Banks forest-clad. Length, two miles; breadth, three-quarters of a mile. Contains brown trout. Reached from Ngahere Station (where there are hotels), on the Greymouth–Reefton Railway, by five miles of road up the bank of the Nelson Stream to Hatter's, then by eight miles of track up the bank of Nelson Stream. For approach and accommodation see "Nelson Stream," already mentioned.

MOONLIGHT BURN, tributary of Grey River.— Shingle bed and bottom, rock gorges in upper part. Banks low, mostly forest-clad. Wadeable mostly. Landing deep, also good. Course, eight miles. Contains brown trout. Reached from Matai Station, on the Greymouth–Reefton Railway. At Ngahere Station, two miles off, there are hotels. Reached also from Greymouth in twelve miles by the Greymouth–Reefton Road. For approach and accommodation see "Grey River," already mentioned.

AHAURA RIVER, tributary of Grey River.—Shingle bed, rock gorges towards the source. Banks both low and high, partly clear, and also forest-clad. Wadeable. Landing deep, also good. Course, including the part called Waiheke, forty-two miles. Contains brown trout. Reached from Greymouth from Ahaura Station (near which there are hotels, near the mouth), on the Greymouth–Reefton Railway; also from Greymouth by twenty-two miles of the Greymouth–Reefton Road. The upper twelve miles, called Waiheke, is reached from the mouth by ten miles of road and twenty miles of track up the bank of the river. For approach and accommodation see "Grey River," already mentioned.

HAUPIRI STREAM, tributary of Ahaura River.— Shingle bed in lower part, upper gorgy. Banks low, partly forest-clad. Wadeable partly. Landing deep, also good. Course, eighteen miles. Contains brown trout. Reached from Ahaura by road following Ahaura River for ten miles, then by track following the river for twenty miles. For approach and accommodation see "Ahaura River," already mentioned.

LAKE AHAURA, tributary of Haupiri River.—
Shingle bottom. Banks chiefly forest - clad.
Length, one mile and a half; breadth, half a
mile. Contains brown trout. Reached from
Ahaura by road following Ahaura River for ten
miles, then by track following the connecting
stream for sixteen miles. For approach and
accommodation see " Haupiri Stream," already
mentioned.

LAKE HAUPIRI, tributary of Haupiri River.—
Shingle bottom. Banks chiefly forest - clad.
Length, one mile and a half; breadth, three-
quarters of a mile. Contains brown trout.
Reached from Ahaura by road following Ahaura
River for ten miles, then by track following the
river and connecting stream for twenty miles.
For approach and accommodation see " Haupiri
Stream," already mentioned.

TUTAEKURI Stream, tributary of Ahaura River.—
Shingle bed, and rock gorges in upper reaches.
Banks mostly forest-clad. Wadeable partly.
Landing deep, also good. Course, eleven miles.
Contains brown trout. Reached from Ahaura by
road following Ahaura River for ten miles, then by
track following the Ahaura and Trent for twenty-
five miles. For approach and accommodation see
" Ahaura River," already mentioned.

TRENT Burn, tributary of Tutaekuri.—Shingle
bed, and rock gorges in upper reaches. Banks
mostly forest-clad. Wadeable partly. Landing
deep, also good. Course, ten miles. Contains
brown trout. Reached from Ahaura by road
following Ahaura River for ten miles, then by
track following the river twelve miles. For
approach and accommodation see " Ahaura River,"
already mentioned. Accommodation may be obtained near the junction with the Ahaura.

SLATEY Burn, tributary of Grey River.—Shingle
bed and bottom, rock gorges in upper part.
Banks low, mostly forest-clad. Wadeable mostly.

Landing deep, also good. Course, ten miles. Contains brown trout. Reached from Greymouth from the Ahaura Station (where there are hotels), on the Greymouth–Reefton Railway; also from Greymouth by twenty-two miles of the Greymouth–Reefton Road. For approach and accommodation see " Grey River," already mentioned.

OTUTUTU Stream, tributary of Grey River.— Shingle bed, and rock gorges in upper reaches. Banks mostly forest-clad. Wadeable partly. Landing deep, also good. Course, eleven miles. Contains brown trout. Reached from the Ikamatua Station, on the Greymouth–Reefton Railway; or by the Greymouth–Reefton Road, thirty-two miles from Greymouth and seventeen from Reefton. At Little Grey, a mile and a half from the mouth, there is hotel accommodation. For approach and accommodation see " Grey River," already mentioned.

MAWHERA-ITI Stream, tributary of Grey River.— Shingle bed. Banks mostly clear, partly forest-clad. Wadeable mostly. Landing mostly good. Course, sixteen miles. Contains brown trout. Reached from the Ikamatua Station, on the Greymouth–Reefton Railway; or by the Greymouth–Reefton Road, thirty-two miles from Greymouth and seventeen from Reefton. At Little Grey, a mile from the mouth, there is hotel accommodation, and from here the road runs up and near the stream for twelve miles. Reached also from the Mawhera-iti Station (where there is hotel accommodation), on the same railway. For approach and accommodation see " Grey River," already mentioned.

SNOWY Stream, tributary of Mawhera-iti Stream. —Shingle bed. Banks mostly clear, partly forest-clad. Wadeable mostly. Landing mostly good. Course, fourteen miles. Contains brown trout. Reached from the Mawhera-iti Station (where there is hotel accommodation), on the Greymouth–

Reefton Railway; also from the Greymouth–Reefton Road, thirty-five miles from Greymouth and fourteen from Reefton. For approach and accommodation see " Mawhera-iti Stream," already mentioned.

BIG Stream, tributary of Mawhera-iti Stream.—Shingle bed. Banks low; mostly clear, partly forest-clad. Wadeable mostly. Landing mostly good. Course, twelve miles. Contains brown trout. Reached from the Mawhera-iti Station (where there is hotel accommodation), on the Greymouth–Reefton Railway; also from the Greymouth–Reefton Road, thirty-five miles from Greymouth and fourteen from Reefton. For approach and accommodation see " Mawhera-iti Stream," already mentioned.

BURTON's Burn, tributary of Mawhera-iti Stream.—Shingle bed. Banks low; mostly clear, partly forest-clad. Wadeable mostly. Landing mostly good. Course, six miles. Contains brown trout. Reached from Hinau Station, on the Greymouth–Reefton Railway; also from the Greymouth–Reefton Road, thirty-seven miles from Greymouth and twelve from Reefton. For approach and accommodation see " Mawhera-iti Stream," already mentioned.

STONY Burn, tributary of Mawhera-iti Stream.—Shingle bed. Banks low; mostly clear, partly forest-clad. Wadeable mostly. Landing mostly good. Course, eight miles. Contains brown trout. Reached from the Maimai Station, on the Greymouth–Reefton Railway; also by the Greymouth–Reefton Road, forty miles from Greymouth and nine from Reefton. For approach and accommodation see " Mawhera-iti Stream," already mentioned.

ANTONIO's Burn, tributary of Mawhera-iti Stream.—Shingle bed. Banks low; mostly clear, partly forest-clad. Wadeable mostly. Landing mostly good. Course, six miles. Contains brown trout. 'Reached from the Maimai Station, on the Greymouth–Reefton Railway; also from the Greymouth–Reefton Road, forty-one miles from Greymouth and eight from Reefton. For approach and accommodation see " Mawhera-iti Stream," already mentioned.

Maimai Burn, tributary of Mawhera-iti Stream.— Shingle bed. Banks low, partly forest-clad, partly clear. Wadeable. Landing mostly good. Course, eight miles. Contains brown trout. Reached from the Maimai Station, on the Greymouth–Reefton Railway; also from the Greymouth–Reefton Road, forty-three miles from Greymouth and six from Reefton. For approach and accommodation see " Mawhera-iti Stream," already mentioned.

Waipuna Burn, tributary of Grey River.—Shingle bed. Banks high and wooded. Wadeable. Landing deep, also good. Course, five miles. Contains brown trout. Reached from Ikamatua Station (where there is hotel accommodation), on the Greymouth–Reefton Railway, thence by track of five miles up the bank of the Grey River. For approach and accommodation see " Grey River," already mentioned.

Brown's Burn, tributary of Grey River.—Shingle bed; rock gorges in upper reaches. Banks forest-clad. Wadeable. Landing deep, also good. Course, five miles. Contains brown trout. Reached from Ikamatua Station (where there is hotel accommodation), on the Greymouth–Reefton Railway; thence by track of nine miles up the bank of the Grey River. For approach and accommodation see " Grey River," already mentioned.

Allen Burn, tributary of Grey River.—Shingle bed; rock gorges in upper portion. Banks forest-clad. Wadeable. Landing deep, also good. Course, seven miles. Contains brown trout. Reached from the Ikamatua Station (where there is hotel accommodation), on the Greymouth–Reefton Railway, thence by track of twelve miles up the bank of the Grey River. For approach and accommodation see " Grey River," already mentioned.

CLARK Stream, tributary of Grey River,—Shingle bed, with rocky gorges in upper part. Banks high and forest-clad. Wadeable partly. Landing deep, also good. Course, thirteen miles. Contains brown trout. Reached from the Ikamatua Station (where there is hotel accommodation), on the Greymouth–Reefton Railway, thence by track of fifteen miles up the bank of the Grey River. For approach and accommodation see " Grey River," already mentioned.

ALEXANDER Burn, tributary of Grey River.— Shingle bed, with rock gorges in upper part. Banks high and forest-clad. Wadeable partly. Landing deep, also good. Course, seven miles. Contains brown trout. Reached from the Ikamatua Station (where there is hotel accommodation), on the Greymouth–Reefton Railway, thence by track of nineteen miles up the bank of the Grey River. For approach and accommodation see " Grey River," already mentioned.

MARCHANT Stream, tributary of Grey River.— Shingle bed. Banks broken, and mostly forest-clad. Wadeable partly. Landing deep, also good. Course, twelve miles. Contains brown trout. Reached from the Ikamatua Station (where there is hotel accommodation), on the Greymouth–Reefton Railway, thence by track of thirty-two miles up the bank of the Grey River. For approach and accommodation see " Grey River," already mentioned.

LAKE CHRISTABEL, tributary and source of Grey River.—Shingle bottom. Banks mostly forest-clad. Length, two miles ; breadth, three-quarters of a mile. Contains brown trout. Reached from the Ikamatua Station (where there is hotel accommodation), on the Greymouth–Reefton Railway, thence by track of forty miles up the bank of the

Grey River. For approach and accommodation see " Grey River," already mentioned.

Paroa Burn.—Shingle bed and bottom. Banks low and forest-clad. Wadeable. Landing mostly good. Course, seven miles. Contains brown trout. Reached from Greymouth from the Paroa Station on the Greymouth–Hokitika Railway, or by five miles of coach-road to Paroa, close to the mouth, where there is hotel accommodation.

New River.—Shingle bed and bottom. Banks low and forest-clad. Wadeable. Landing good. Course, twenty-two miles. Contains brown trout. Reached from Greymouth from the Cameron's Station on the Greymouth–Hokitika Railway, or by eight miles of road. For approach and accommodation see " Paroa Burn," already mentioned. At Marsden, five miles from the mouth of the river, there is hotel accommodation.

Card's Burn, tributary of New River.—Shingle bed and bottom. Banks low and forest-clad about half-way, then high and forest-clad. Wadeable. Landing deep, also good. Course, nine miles. Contains brown trout. For approach and accommodation see " New River," already mentioned.

Caraboo Burn, tributary of New River.—Shingle bed and bottom. Banks low and forest-clad half-way, then high and forest-clad. Wadeable. Landing deep, also good. Course, six miles. Contains brown trout. For approach and accommodation see " New River," already mentioned.

Teremakau River. — Snow-fed. Shingle bed. Banks near mouth high, steep, and forest-clad; higher, low, forest- and scrub-covered, with clear intervals. Wadeable. Lnnding good. Course, fifty miles. Contains brown trout. Reached from Greymouth at the Teremakau Station, near the mouth (where there is hotel accommodation), on the Greymouth–Hokitika Railway, or by road of nine miles *via* Paroa to the mouth.

Big Hohunu Stream, tributary of Teremakau

River.—Shingle bed half-way, boulder bed the remainder. Banks low and clear half-way, then steep and forest-clad. Wadeable. Landing good. Course, eleven miles. Contains brown trout. Reached from Greymouth from the Kumara Station (which is close to the river, and where there is hotel accommodation), on the Greymouth–Hokitika Railway. For approach and accommodation see "Teremakau River," already mentioned.

BLAKE Burn, tributary of Teremakau River.—Shingle bottom. Banks steep and partly forest-clad. Not wadeable. Landing deep. Course, three miles. Contains brown trout. Reached from the Kumara Station (where there is hotel accommodation), on the Greymouth – Hokitika Railway, thence by six miles up the bank of the Teremakau River. For approach and accommodation see "Teremakau River," already mentioned.

WAINIHINIHI Burn, tributary of Teremakau River.—Shingle and boulder bed. Banks low and forest-clad. Wadeable. Landing good. Course, seven miles. Contains brown trout. Reached from the Kumara Station (where there is hotel accommodation), on the Greymouth – Hokitika Railway; thence by thirteen miles up the bank of the Teremakau River. For approach and accommodation see "Teremakau River," already mentioned.

GRIFFIN Burn, tributary of Teremakau River. Shingle bed to half-way, then boulders and mountain torrent. Wadeable. Landing good. Course, eight miles. Contains brown trout. Reached from the Kumara Station (where there is hotel accommodation), on the Greymouth – Hokitika Railway, thence by fourteen miles up the bank of the Teremakau River. For approach and accommodation see "Teremakau River," already mentioned.

TAIPO Stream, tributary of Teremakau River.—Snow-fed. Shingle and boulder bed. Banks partly

TROUT CAUGHT, WESTLAND DISTRICT.

steep and forest-clad. Wadeable. Landing good. Course, eighteen miles. Contains brown trout. Reached from Jackson Station (where there is hotel accommodation), on the Greymouth–Jackson Railway. For approach and accommodation see " Teremakau River," already mentioned.

OTIRA Stream, tributary of Teremakau River.— Snow-fed. Shingle and boulder bed, with five miles of rock gorges. Banks low, high, and forest-clad. Wadeable. Landing good. Course twelve miles. Contains brown trout. Reached from Greymouth by the Greymouth–Jackson Railway to Jackson, where there is hotel accommodation, then by coach-road fourteen miles up the bank of the Teremakau River to Otira, where there is hotel accommodation close to the mouth. For approach and accommodation see " Teremakau River, already mentioned.

DECEPTION Burn, tributary of Otira Stream.— Snow-fed. Shingle bed lower half, boulder and rock gorge upper. Banks, lower half low and forest-clad, upper rocky and forest-clad. Wade-able. Landing deep, also good. Course, eight miles. Contains brown trout. Reached by two miles of the coach-road above the hotel at the mouth of the Otira Stream. For approach and accommodation see " Otira Stream," already mentioned.

KELLY's Burn, tributary of Otira Stream.— Boulder bed, lower half; upper, rocky gorges. Banks steep and forest-clad. Wadeable. Landing mostly deep. Course, four miles. Contains brown trout. Reached by four miles of the coach-road above the hotel at the mouth of the Otira Stream. For approach and accommodation see " Otira Stream," already mentioned.

ROLLESTON Burn, tributary of Otira Stream.— Snow-fed. Shingle bed lower half, boulder and rocky gorges upper. Banks, lower half low and forest-clad ; upper, rocky and forest-clad. Wadeable. Landing deep, also good. Course, eight miles. Contains brown trout. Reached by eight miles of coach-road above the mouth of the Otira Stream. For approach and accommodation see " Otira Stream," already mentioned.

KAPITEA Stream.—Shingle bed. Banks low and mostly forest-clad. Wadeable. Landing mostly good. Course, fourteen miles. Contains brown trout. Reached (to near the mouth) from the Chesterfield Station, on the Greymouth–Hokitika Railway.

FLOWERY Burn.—Shingle bed. Banks low and mostly forest-clad. Wadeable. Landing mostly good. Course, six miles. Contains brown trout. Reached (to near the mouth) from the Awatuna Station, on the Greymouth–Hokitika Railway.

ARAHURA River.—Snow-fed. Shingle bed half, and then boulder and rocky gorge. Banks low and forest-clad. Wadeable. Landing deep, also good. Course, thirty-five miles. Contains brown trout. Reached (to near the mouth) from the Arahura Station, on the Greymouth–Hokitika Railway. A mile from the station is Stafford, where there is hotel accommodation.

KAWHAKA Stream, tributary of Arahura River.— Shingle bed. Banks low and forest-clad. Wadeable. Landing deep, also good. Course, sixteen miles. Contains brown trout. Reached from the Arahura Station, on the Greymouth–Hokitika Railway, thence by ten miles of road to the Arahura River bank. Accommodation may be had within a few miles. For approach and accommodation see " Arahura River," already mentioned.

WAINIHINIHI Burn, tributary of Arahura River.— Shingle bed for lower mile or two, then boulder and rock gorge. Banks steep and forest-clad. Wadeable partly. Landing mostly good. Course, four miles. Contains brown trout. Reached from Hokitika Station (where there are hotels), on the Greymouth–Hokitika Railway, thence by road of seventeen miles to the Arahura River, then two miles up the bank of that river. For approach and accommodation see "Arahura River," already mentioned.

LITTLE HAUHAU Creek.—Mud and shingle bottom about half-way, then shingle bottom. Banks low, partly clear, and partly forest-clad. Wadeable partly. Landing deep, also good. Course, three miles. Contains brown trout. Reached (to near the mouth) from the Ho Ho Station (where there is hotel accommodation), on the Greymouth–Hokitika Railway, or from Hokitika by two miles of road.

HAUHAU Creek.—Mud and shingle bottom for first mile or two, then shingle bottom. Banks low, partly clear, and partly forest-clad. Wadeable partly. Landing deep, also good. Course, six miles. Contains brown trout. For approach and accommodation see "Little Hauhau Creek," already mentioned.

HOKITIKA River.—Snow-fed. Shingle bed for twenty-two miles, then deep rock gorges for a mile, then shingle bed for five miles, then boulder and rock gorges to the source. Banks mostly low, partly clear, partly forest-clad. Wadeable. Landing deep, also good. Course, forty miles. Contains brown trout. Reached (to the mouth) from Hokitika Station (where there are hotels), on the Reefton–Greymouth–Hokitika Railway. Greymouth is reached by frequent coastal steamers.

To the south of the Hokitika River and tributaries the rivers and lakes on the west coast are only reached by uncertain, chiefly forest, tracks. The stranger requires a guide.

MAHINAPUA Creek, tributary of Hokitika River. —Partly tidal. Mud and shingle bottom. Banks low and forest-clad. Not wadeable —must be fished from a boat. Landing deep. Course, five miles. Contains brown trout. Reached from

25—Sport.

Hokitika by crossing the Hokitika River by boat to the mouth, then by boat up the creek. For approach and accommodation see " Hokitika River," already mentioned.

LAKE TARLETON, tributary of Mahinapua Creek. —Mud bottom. Banks low and forest-clad. Not wadeable. Landing deep. Length, quarter of a mile ; breadth, one-sixth of a mile. Contains brown trout. Reached from Hokitika by boat up Mahinapua Creek. For approach and accommodation see " Mahinapua Creek," already mentioned.

SANDSTONE Creek, tributary of Mahinapua Creek. —Mud bottom for half a mile, then shingle bottom. Banks low and forest-clad. Wadeable partly. Landing deep. Course, five miles. Contains brown trout. Reached from Hokitika by boat up Mahinapua Creek. For appoach and accommodation, see " Mahinapua Creek," already mentioned.

LAKE MAHINAPUA, tributary of Mahinapua Creek. Sandy and mud bottom. Banks low and forest-clad. Wadeable only here and there ; can be fished from a boat. Landing deep. Length, two miles ; breadth, one mile. Contains brown trout. Reached from Hokitika by six miles up Mahinapua Creek. For approach and accommodation see " Mahinapua Creek," already mentioned.

FROSTY Burn, tributary of Lake Mahinapua.— Boulder bottom. Banks steep and forest-clad. Wadeable. Landing deep. Course, four miles. Contains brown trout. Reached by boat across Lake Mahinapua. For this approach see " Lake Mahinapua," already mentioned. Reached also by nine miles of the Hokitika–Ross Road. There is hotel accommodation in the neighbourhood on this road.

SOUTH Creek, tributary of Lake Mahinapua.— Mud and sand bottom for a mile and a half, then boulder bottom. Banks low and forest-clad.

Wadeable after first mile and a half. Landing deep, also good. Course, three miles. Contains brown trout. Reached by boat across Lake Mahinapua. For this approach see "Lake Mahinapua," already mentioned. Reached also by eleven miles of the Hokitika–Ross Coach-road. There is hotel accommodation in the neighbourhood.

FISHERMAN'S Burn, tributary of Hokitika River. Shingle bed. Banks low and forest-clad. Wadeable. Landing good. Course, five miles. Contains brown trout. Reached from Hokitika by crossing the Hokitika River by boat to near the mouth. For approach and accommodation see "Hokitika River," already mentioned.

KANIERI Stream, tributary of Hokitika River.— Boulder and shingle bottom. Banks forest-clad. Wadeable. Landing mostly deep. Course, eleven miles. Contains brown trout. Reached from Hokitika to near the mouth by four miles of road to Kanieri, where there is hotel accommodation. For approach and accommodation see "Hokitika River," already mentioned.

KENNEDY'S Burn, tributary of Kanieri Stream.— Shingle and boulder bed. Banks forest-clad. Wadeable. Landing deep, also good. Course, five miles. Contains brown trout. Reached from Hokitika by the road to Lake Kanieri. For approach and accommodation see "Kanieri Stream," already mentioned.

BLUEBOTTLE Burn, tributary of Kanieri Stream. —Shingle bottom. Banks steep and forest-clad. Wadeable partly. Landing good mostly. Course, five miles. Contains brown trout. Reached from Hokitika by the road to Lake Kanieri. For approach and accommodation see "Kanieri Stream," already mentioned.

BUTCHER Burn, tributary of Kanieri Stream.— Shingle and boulder bed. Banks forest-clad. Wadeable Landing good. Course, four miles.

Contains brown trout. Reached from Hokitika by the road to Lake Kanieri. For approach and accommodation see " Kanieri Stream," already mentioned.

LAKE KANIERI, tributary of Kanieri Stream.— Banks forest-clad to the water's edge. Surrounded by high forest-clad hills. A little shingle beach. Landing almost entirely deep—requires to be fished from a boat. Length, five miles ; breadth, one mile. Contains brown trout. There is a trout-hatchery close to where the river leaves the lake. Reached from Hokitika by thirteen miles of road. There is hotel accommodation where the Kanieri River leaves the lake, and where boats can be obtained. For approach and accommodation see " Kanieri Stream," already mentioned.

CAMP Burn, tributary of Lake Kanieri.—Boulder and shingle bed and bottom. Banks forest-clad. Wadeable. Landing mostly good. Course, four miles, with high waterfall half a mile from the mouth. Contains brown trout. Reached in five miles by boat across the lake from outlet of Kanieri River. For approach and accommodation see " Lake Kanieri," already mentioned.

RAFT Burn, tributary of Hokitika River.—Shingle bottom. Banks steep and forest-clad. Wadeable in upper reaches. Landing mostly deep. Course, five miles. Contains brown trout. Reached from Hokitika by three miles of road up the bank of the Hokitika River. For approach and accommodation see " Hokitika River," already mentioned.

WHITE Burn, tributary of Raft Burn.—Shingle bottom. Banks steep, scrub- and forest-clad. Wadeable in upper reaches. Landing mostly deep. Course, six miles. Contains brown trout. For approach and accommodation see " Raft Burn," already mentioned.

DUCK Burn, tributary of Hokitika River. — Shingle bottom and bed. Banks low and mostly clear. Wadeable. Landing deep, also good. Course, eight miles. Reached from Hokitika (to near the mouth) by eleven miles of road up the bank of the Hokitika River. Hotel accommodation at Kokatahi, close by. For approach and accommodation see " Hokitika River," already mentioned.

KOKATAHI Stream, tributary of Hokitika River. —Snow-fed. Shingle bed in lower half, boulder and rock gorges in upper. Banks low in lower half and fairly clear; upper, steep and forest-clad. Wadeable partly. Landing deep, also good. Course, sixteen miles. Contains brown trout. Reached from Hokitika (to near the mouth) by twelve miles of road up the bank of the Hokitika River to Kokatahi, where there is hotel accommodation. For approach and accommodation see " Hokitika River," already mentioned.

MURRAY Stream, tributary of Kokatahi Stream.— Shingle bottom. Banks scrub- and flax-encumbered. Very little wadeable. Landing deep. Course, twelve miles. Contains brown trout. For approach and accommodation see " Kokatahi Stream," already mentioned.

BROWNING Burn, tributary of Kokatahi Stream.— Shingle bed in lower half, boulder and rock gorges in upper. Banks low in lower half and fairly clear; upper, steep and forest-clad. Wadeable partly. Landing deep, also good. Course, ten miles. Contains brown trout. For approach and accommodation see " Kokatahi Stream," already mentioned.

TOAROHA Stream, tributary of Kokatahi Stream. —Snow-fed. Shingle-bed in lower half, boulder and rock gorges in upper. Banks low in lower half and fairly clear; upper, steep and forest-clad. Wadeable partly. Landing deep, also good. Course, twelve miles. Contains brown trout. For approach and accommodation see " Kokatahi Stream," already mentioned.

HARRIS Burn, tributary of Hokitika River.— Shingle bottom. Banks steep and forest-clad. Wadeable partly. Landing deep. Course, six miles. Contains brown trout. Reached from Hokitika by thirteen miles of road up the bank of the Hokitika River, *viâ* Kokatahi, where there is hotel accommodation. For approach and accommodation see " Hokitika River," already mentioned.

Mont's Creek, tributary of Hokitika River.— Mud bottom. Swampy banks, mostly scrub-encumbered. Not wadeable; only fishable from a boat. Landing deep. Course, five miles. Contains brown trout. Reached from Hokitika by fourteen miles of road up the bank of the Hokitika River, *viâ* Kokatahi, where there is hotel accommodation. For approach and accommodation see " Hokitika River," already mentioned.

Falls Burn, tributary of Hokitika River. — Shingle bed half-way, then more or less rock gorges. Banks rather steep and forest - clad. Wadeable. Landing deep, also good. Course, three miles. Contains brown trout. Reached from Hokitika by nineteen miles up the bank of the Hokitika River. For approach and accommodation see " Hokitika River," already mentioned.

Doctor's Burn, tributary of Hokitika River.— Shingle bed lower half, then more or less rock gorges. Banks rather steep and forest - clad. Wadeable. Landing deep, also good. Course, seven miles. Contains brown trout. Reached from Hokitika by twenty-two miles up the bank of the Hokitika River. For approach and accommodation see " Hokitika River," already mentioned.

Granite Burn, tributary of Hokitika River.— Shingle bed in lower reaches, then rock gorge and mountain torrent. Banks low in lower reaches, steep in upper, all forest-clad. Wadeable. Landing deep, also good. Course, five miles. Contains brown trout. Reached from Hokitika by twenty-four miles up the bank of the Hokitika River. For approach and accommodation see " Hokitika River," already mentioned.

WHITCOMBE Stream, tributary of Hokitika River.
—Snow- and ice-fed. Boulder bed chiefly, mostly
mountain torrent. Banks steep, and more or less
rock gorges. Wadeable partly. Landing deep.
Course, sixteen miles. Contains brown trout.
Reached from Hokitika by twenty-eight miles up
the bank of the Hokitika River. For approach
and accommodation see " Hokitika River," already
mentioned.

CROPP Burn, tributary of Whitcombe Stream.—
Snow-fed. Boulder bed chiefly, mostly mountain torrent. Banks steep, and more or less
rock gorges. Wadeable partly. Landing deep.
Course, five miles. Contains brown trout. Four
miles from mouth of Whitcombe Stream. For
approach and accommodation see " Whitcombe
Stream," already mentioned.

PRICE Burn, tributary of Whitcombe Stream.—
Snow-fed. Mostly rock bottom. Banks mostly
rock. Wadeable only in places. Landing deep.
Course, five miles. Contains brown trout. Eight
miles from mouth of Whitcombe Stream. For
approach and accommodation see " Whitcombe
Stream," already mentioned.

MUNGO Burn, tributary of Hokitika River.—
Snow-fed. Boulder bed chiefly, mostly mountain torrent. Banks steep, and more or less
rock gorges. Wadeable partly. Landing deep.
Course, four miles. Contains brown trout.
Reached from Hokitika by forty miles up the
bank of the Hokitika River. For approach and
accommodation see " Hokitika River," already
mentioned.

TOTARA LAGOON and FEEDERS at mouth of Totara
Stream.—Four miles long and forty yards wide.
Lagoon, sand and shingle bottom; banks forest-
clad on one side, sand on the other. Five feeders,
chiefly shingle bottom, with forest-clad banks.
Lagoon not wadeable; feeders wadeable. Landing in lagoon deep, also good; in feeders mostly

good. Course of feeders, three to six miles. Contains brown trout. Reached from Hokitika by twenty miles of the Hokitika–Ross Coach-road. At Ross, which is within a mile of the lagoon, there are hotels.

TOTARA Stream.—Shingle and boulder bottom. Banks steep and forest-clad. Wadeable mostly. Landing mostly deep. Course fourteen miles. Contains brown trout. Reached from Hokitika by twenty miles of the Hokitika–Ross Coach-road, which crosses it two miles from the mouth and a mile from Ross. At Ross, which is within a mile of the mouth, there are hotels.

MIKONUI Stream.—Shingle bed lower half, then boulder bottom. Banks steep and forest-clad. Wadeable. Landing deep, also good. Course, fifteen miles. Contains brown trout. Reached from Hokitika by twenty-three miles of coach-road, which crosses within a mile of the mouth. Three miles before reaching the stream is Ross, where there are hotels.

TUKE Burn, tributary of Mikonui Stream.— Snow-fed. Shingle bottom for half a mile, then rock gorges and mountain torrent. Banks steep and forest - clad. Wadeable in lower portion. Landing deep. Course, seven miles. Contains brown trout. Reached by ten miles from the mouth of Mikonui Stream. For approach and accommodation see " Mikonui Stream," already mentioned.

WAITAHA River.—Snow- and ice-fed. Shingle bed half the length, then narrow rock gorge, then mountain torrent with boulder bottom. Banks low and forest-clad in lower reaches, then steep and forest-clad. Wadeable in lower reaches. Landing deep, also good. Course, twenty-eight miles. Contains brown trout. Reached from Hokitika by thirty-five miles of coach-road, *via* Ross, which road crosses it within three miles of the mouth.

Kakapotahi Stream, tributary of Waitaha River. —Shingle and boulder bed for three miles, then rock impassable gorges for four miles, then shingle bed for two miles, then mountain torrent. Banks steep mostly, and forest-clad. Wadeable mostly where not gorges. Landing deep, also good. Course thirteen miles. Contains brown trout. Reached by a mile and a half from the mouth of the Waitaha River. For approach and accommodation see " Waitaha River," already mentioned.

Barron Burn, tributary of Waitaha River.— Snow-fed. Boulder bed, mountain torrent. Banks steep and forest-clad. Not wadeable. Landing deep. Course six miles. Contains brown trout. Reached by following up the bank of the Waitaha River. For approach and accommodation see " Waitaha River," already mentioned.

Duffer's Creek.—Tidal for a mile, with sand and mud bottom; then boulder bed. Banks steep and forest-clad. Wadeable mostly. Landing deep mostly. Course, nine miles. Contains brown trout. Reached from Hokitika by thirty-eight miles of road, *via* Ross, which road crosses it four miles from the mouth.

Wanganui River.—Snow- and ice-fed. Shingle bed lower half, then boulder and shingle bed, then boulder bottom with rock gorges. Banks on lower half low, partly clear, partly forest-clad; on upper steep and forest-clad. Wadeable mostly. Landing deep, also good. Course, thirty-two miles. Contains brown trout. Reached from Hokitika by fifty miles of the Ross–Okarito Road and track, which crosses it at Hendes' Ferry, fourteen miles from the mouth.

Peterson's Creek, tributary of Wanganui River. —Shingle bottom. Banks steep and scrub-clad. Wadeable only here and there. Landing deep. Course, eleven miles. Contains brown trout. Reached from Hendes' Ferry. For approach and accommodation see " Wanganui River," already mentioned.

Ianthe Creek, tributary of Wanganui River.—Sand and shingle bottom. Banks low and forest-clad. Wadeable partly. Landing deep. Course, two miles. Contains brown trout. Reached (to the mouth) from the Wanganui River, or (to where it leaves Lake Ianthe) in a mile from the Ross–Okarito Road, and forty-four miles from Hokitika. For approach and accommodation see " Wanganui River," already mentioned.

Evans Burn, tributary of Ianthe Creek.—Shingle bed. Banks low and forest - clad. Wadeable. Landing good. Course, seven miles. Contains brown trout. Reached (to the mouth) from the Wanganui River; the upper waters are crossed by the Ross–Okarito Road forty-seven miles from Hokitika. For approach and accommodation see " Ianthe Creek," already mentioned.

Lake Ianthe, tributary of Ianthe Creek.—Mud bottom. Banks steep and forest-clad. Not wadeable—must be fished from a boat. Length, one mile and three-quarters; breadth, one mile and a quarter. Contains brown trout. Reached in a quarter of a mile from the Ross–Okarito Road, and forty-two miles from Hokitika. For approach and accommodation see ' Ianthe Creek," already mentioned.

Lambert Burn, tributary of Wanganui River.—Ice-fed. Boulder bottom and rock gorges, mountain torrent. Banks steep and forest-clad. Not wadeable. Landing deep. Course, five miles. Contains brown trout. Reached from Hendes' Ferry, then by eight miles up the Wanganui River. For approach and accommodation see " Wanganui River," already mentioned.

Poerua River. — Snow- and ice-fed. Shingle bed lower half; upper, rock gorges. Banks, lower half low and forest-clad; upper, steep and forest-clad. Wadeable in lower half. Landing good in lower half. Course, twenty-two miles. Contains brown trout. Reached from Hokitika by fifty-six miles of the Ross–Okarito Road, which crosses it ten miles from the mouth.

McCulloch Burn, tributary of Poerua River.—Shingle bed lower half, then rock-bound mountain torrent. Banks low in lower half, steep in upper; forest-clad throughout. Wadeable. Landing deep, also good. Course, seven miles. Contains brown trout. Reached (to the mouth) at the Ross–Okarito Road. For approach and accommodation see " Poerua River," already mentioned.

Saltwater Lagoon and Feeders.—Tidal. Sand and shingle bottom. Banks mostly low and forest-clad on three sides, clear on seaward side. Landing mostly deep. Two small feeders, with shingle bottom; banks steep and forest-clad; wadeable; landing deep. Length, two miles and three-quarters; breadth, one mile. Contains brown trout. Reached from the Ross-Okarito Road, from a point fifty-eight miles from Hokitika and seven miles from the lagoon.

Wataroa River.—Snow- and ice-fed. Shingle bed lower half, then shingle and boulder bottom. Banks low and forest-clad in lower half, steep and forest-clad in upper. Wadeable partly. Landing deep, also good. Course, thirty-two miles. Contains brown trout. Reached from Hokitika by sixty-seven miles of the Ross–Okarito Road, which crosses it seventeen miles from the mouth. At Okarito, which is seventeen miles further on, there is hotel accommodation. From the point where this road crosses the river a road strikes off towards the coast, touching the river eight miles further down and not far from the mouth of the Rotokino Creek.

Rotokino Creek, tributary of Wataroa River.—Sand and mud bottom. Banks steep and scrub-clad. Not wadeable. Landing deep. Course, two miles. Contains brown trout. Reached (to

the mouth) by eight miles of road from where the
Ross-Okarito Road crosses the Wataroa River.
For approach and accommodation see "Wataroa
River," already mentioned.

LAKE ROTOKINO, tributary of Rotokino Creek.—
Sand and mud bottom. Banks, three-fourths steep
and forest-clad, the remainder low and swampy.
Not wadeable. Landing deep. Length, one mile
and a quarter ; breadth, three-quarters of a mile.
Contains brown trout. Reached by a mile (to the
lower end) from the Ross–Okarito Road, and fifty-
nine miles from Hokitika. For approach and
accommodation see "Rotokino Creek," already
mentioned.

PERTH Burn, tributary of Wataroa River.—
Snow- and ice-fed. Shingle and boulder bed
lower half, then boulder bottom and rock gorges.
Banks steep and forest-clad. Wadeable partly.
Landing deep, also good. Course, eight miles.
Contains brown trout. Reached from where the
Ross–Okarito Road crosses the Wataroa River,
thence by a track for five miles up the bank of
that river to the mouth. For approach and accommodation see "Wataroa River," already mentioned.

WAITANGITAONA River.—Tidal for a mile, with
sand bottom ; then shingle bed. Banks low and
clear on one side, with flax on other side, for
length of tidal water ; then low and forest-clad.
Wadeable above tidal water. Landing mostly
good. Course, twenty-seven miles. Contains
brown trout. Reached from Hokitika by seventy-
three miles of the Ross–Okarito Road, which
crosses it seventeen miles from the mouth and ten
miles from Okarito, where there is hotel accommodation. The mouth can also be reached in eight
miles along the beach from Okarito.

OKARITO LAGOON and FEEDERS.—Tidal. Sand
and mud bottom. Banks on land side low and
swampy ; on sea side low, hard, and clear. Wade-

able partly. Landing deep, also good. Length, six miles and a half; breadth, one mile and a quarter. Three or four small feeders of three miles in length; shingle bottom mostly; banks steep and forest-clad; wadeable; landing deep. Contains brown trout. Reached from Hokitika to Okarito by eighty-three miles of road. At Okarito there is hotel accommodation.

OKARITO Burn.—Boulder bottom. Banks steep and forest-clad. Not wadeable. Landing deep. Course, seven miles. Contains brown trout. Reached from Hokitika by seventy-eight miles of the Ross–Okarito road, which crosses it six miles from the mouth and five miles before reaching Okarito, where there is hotel accommodation, at the mouth.

WAHAPO Burn, tributary of Okarito Burn.— Boulder bottom. Banks steep and forest-clad. Not wadeable. Landing deep. Course, one mile. Contains brown trout. Reached from the Ross–Okarito Road where it crosses the Okarito Burn. For approach and accommodation see " Okarito Burn," already mentioned.

LAKE WAHAPO, tributary of Wahapo Burn.—Mud and shingle bottom. Banks steep on three sides, low and swampy on the fourth, and forest-clad all round. Not wadeable—only fishable from a boat. Landing deep. Length, two miles; breadth, three-quarters of a mile. Contains brown trout. Reached from the Ross–Okarito Road, which skirts it towards where it crosses the Okarito Burn. For approach and accommodation see " Okarito Burn," already mentioned.

LAKE MAPOURIKA, tributary of Okarito Burn.— Mud and shingle bottom. Banks, half steep, the rest low, all forest-clad. Not wadeable—only fishable from a boat. Landing deep. Length, three miles; breadth, one mile and a quarter. Contains brown trout. Reached from where the Ross–Okarito Road crosses the Okarito Burn, thence by following up the burn four miles. For approach and accommodation see " Okarito Burn," already mentioned.

McDonald's Burn, tributary of Lake Mapourika. —Shingle and boulder bed. Banks steep and forest-clad. Wadeable. Landing deep, also good. Course, five miles. Contains brown trout. For approach and accommodation see " Lake Mapourika," already mentioned.

Potter's Burn, tributary of Lake Mapourika.— Shingle bed lower half, boulder upper. Banks low on lower half, steep on upper; all forest-clad. Wadeable mostly. Landing deep, also good. Course, six miles. Contains brown trout. Reached from where the Ross–Okarito Road crosses the Okarito Burn, thence by following up the burn for four miles, and the bank of Lake Mapourika four miles. For approach and accommodation see " Lake Mapourika," already mentioned.

Three-mile Lagoon and Feeders.—Tidal. Mud and sand bottom. Banks mostly low; forest-clad on three sides, clear on sea side. Wadeable partly. Landing deep, also good. Length, one mile; breadth, one mile. Three feeders, mostly shingle bottom, forest-clad; three miles in length. Contains brown trout. Reached (to the mouth) by three miles of beach road from Okarito, where there is hotel accommodation. For approach and accommodation see " Okarito Lagoon," already mentioned.

Totarakaitorea Creek.—Shingle bottom. Banks steep and forest-clad. Wadeable. Landing deep. Course, six miles. Contains brown trout. Reached (to the mouth) from Okarito, where there is hotel accommodation, by three miles of beach road. For approach and accommodation see " Okarito Lagoon," already mentioned.

Alpine Creek.—Mud and shingle bottom. Banks scrub- and forest-clad. Not much wadeable. Landing mostly deep. Course, three miles. Contains brown trout. Reached from Okarito, where there is hotel accommodation, by five miles of track. For approach and accommodation see " Okarito Lagoon," already mentioned.

LAKE ALPINE, tributary of Alpine Creek.—Mud and shingle bottom. Banks, moderate slope, and forest-clad. Not wadeable—only fishable from a boat. Landing deep. Length, three-quarters of a mile; breadth, quarter of a mile. Contains brown trout. Reached from Okarito, where there is hotel accommodation, by five miles of track. For approach and accommodation see " Alpine Creek," already mentioned.

FIVE-MILE LAGOON and FEEDERS.—Tidal. Mud and sand bottom. Banks low and swampy, rock and flax on three sides, sand on seaward side. Not wadeable. Landing mostly deep. Length, two miles; breadth, one mile. Two feeders, with mud bottom for lower half, then shingle bottom. Banks steep, the lower flax, the upper forest. Wadeable. Landing deep. Reached by seven miles of road and track from Okarito, where there is hotel accommodation. For approach and accommodation see " Okarito Lagoon," already mentioned.

WAIHO River.—Ice-fed. Shingle and boulder bed. Banks, lower half low and chiefly forest-clad, upper steep and forest-clad. Wadeable. Landing good. Course, twenty-one miles. Contains brown trout. Reached (to the mouth) from Okarito, where there is hotel accommodation, by seven miles of track. At the mouth there is a ferry and ford. Also reached from the Ross-Okarito Road, from where it crosses the Okarito Burn, and thence by eight miles up that river and the bank of Lake Mapourika, then on Gillespie's Road three miles more to the Waiho River, where the road crosses it nine miles from the mouth.

DRY Burn, tributary of Waiho River.—Snow-fed. Shingle bed. Banks low and scrub-clad. Wadeable. Landing good. Course, ten miles. Contains

brown trout. Reached by following up the Waiho
River five miles from the mouth. For approach
and accommodation see " Waiho River," already
mentioned.

TOTARA River, branch of Waiho River, forming
with Waiho River an island four miles long and
one mile broad.—Shingle and boulder bed. Banks
low and chiefly forest-clad. Wadeable. Landing
good. Course, five miles. Contains brown trout.
For approach and accommodation see " Waiho
River," already mentioned.

KELLERY Burn, tributary of Totara River.—Ice-
fed. Boulder bottom. Banks rocky and forest-
clad. Not wadeable—only fishable here and there.
Landing deep. Course, ten miles. Contains brown
trout. Reached by six miles from the mouth of
the Waiho River, or from Gillespie's Road, which
crosses it three miles from the mouth. For approach and accommodation see " Waiho River,"
already mentioned.

OMOEROA Stream.—Shingle and boulder bed.
Banks, lower half low and chiefly forest-clad, upper
steep and forest-clad. Wadeable. Landing good.
Course, twelve miles. Contains brown trout.
Reached from Hokitika by ninety-three miles of
road, *viâ* Lake Mapourika and Gillespie's Road,
which crosses it eight miles from the mouth. Near
the mouth is a ford.

WAIKUKUPA Stream.—Snow-fed. Shingle bed for
lower two miles, then boulder bed to main road,
then boulder bottom. Banks low, steep, and
forest-clad. Wadeable. Landing deep, also good.
Course, eleven miles. Contains brown trout.
Reached from Hokitika by ninety-six miles of road,
viâ Lake Mapourika and Gillespie's Road, which
crosses it eight miles from the mouth, near which
there is a ford, and accommodation.

HAURAKI Creek.—Shingle bottom. Banks steep
and forest - clad. Wadeable. Landing deep.
Course, seven miles. Contains brown trout.

Reached from Hokitika by ninety-six miles of road, *via* Lake Mapourika and Gillespie's Road, then by a mile or two to the source. For accommodation see " Waikukupa Stream," which is two miles from the mouth.

LAKE GIBBS, tributary of Hauraki Creek.—Mud bottom. Swampy margin and banks. Not wadeable—only fishable from a boat. Landing deep. Length, three-quarters of a mile ; breadth, quarter of a mile. Contains brown trout. Reached by following up Hauraki Creek and Jack's Creek a mile from the mouth. For approach and accommodation see " Hauraki Creek," already mentioned.

LAKE GAULT, tributary of Hauraki Creek.—Mud bottom. Banks, swampy margin. Not wadeable —only fishable from a boat. Landing deep. Length half a mile ; breadth, quarter of a mile. Contains brown trout. Reached by following up Hauraki Creek. For approach and accommodation see " Hauraki Creek," already mentioned.

LAKE MUELLER, tributary of Hauraki Creek.— Sand and shingle bottom. Banks mostly steep and forest-clad, except on the western side, where there is shingle beach. Wadeable partly. Landing deep, also good. Length, three-quarters of a mile ; breadth, half a mile. Contains brown trout. Reached by following up the Hauraki Creek, or from Okarito by twenty-three miles of road, *via* Lake Mapourika and Gillespie's Road. It is three miles from the road. For approach and accommodation see " Hauraki Creek," already mentioned.

WAIKOHAI Creek.—Tidal for about a mile. Sand and mud bottom. Banks steep and swampy, and more or less flax-encumbered. Not wadeable. Landing deep. Course, five miles. Contains brown trout. Reached from Hokitika by 110 miles of road and track, *via* Lake Mapourika and Gillespie's Road, to Gillespie's Beach, near the mouth, where there is hotel accommodation. Reached also by steamer.

26—Sport.

WEHEKA River.—Snow- and ice-fed. Shingle bed for lower half, then boulder bottom in upper. Banks, lower half low and partly clear, upper steep and forest-clad. Wadeable mostly. Landing deep, also good. Course, twenty-one miles. Contains brown trout. Reached from Gillespie's Beach, where there is hotel accommodation, by three miles of track to near the mouth, where there is a ferry and ford: this is 113 miles from Hokitika. Also reached from Gillespie's Beach by six miles of the Gillespie's Beach–Okarito Track, to seven miles from the mouth.

CLEARWATER Stream, tributary of Weheka River. —Shingle bottom. Banks steep, low, scrub- and forest-clad. Wadeable. Landing deep, also good. Course, thirteen miles. Contains brown trout. Reached from Gillespie's Beach by six miles of the Gillespie's Beach–Okarito Track, which crosses it five miles from the mouth. For approach and accommodation see " Weheka River," already mentioned.

Fox Burn, tributary of Weheka River.—Ice-fed. Shingle and boulder bed. Banks steep, low, and forest-clad. Wadeable. Landing deep, also good. Course, ten miles. Contains brown trout. Reached (to the mouth) from Gillespie's Beach by six miles of the Gillespie's Beach–Okarito Track. For approach and accommodation see " Weheka River," already mentioned.

BALFOUR Burn, tributary of Weheka River.— Ice-fed. Boulder bottom. Banks steep, rocky, and forest-clad. Wadeable partly. Landing deep mostly. Course, six miles. Contains brown trout. Reached by thirteen miles from the mouth of the Weheka River. For approach and accommodation see " Weheka River," already mentioned.

OINATAMATEA Stream.—Shingle bottom for the lower three-fourths, then shingle bed. Banks steep and forest-clad. Wadeable only in upper portions. Landing deep mostly. Course, sixteen miles. Contains brown trout. Reached from Gillespie's Beach, where there is hotel accommodation on the Waikohai Creek, by five miles of tracks to near the mouth. This is 115 miles from Hokitika.

KARANGARUA River.—Snow- and ice-fed. Shingle bed lower half, boulder and shingle bed in upper. Banks low, steep, and forest-clad. Wadeable. Landing deep, also good. Course, twenty-three miles. Contains brown trout. Reached from Gillespie's Beach, where there is hotel accommodation on the Waikohai Creek, by seven miles of track to near the mouth. This is 117 miles from Hokitika.

COPLAND Stream, tributary of Karangarua River. —Snow- and ice-fed. Boulder bottom mostly. Banks steep and forest-clad. Wadeable in parts. Landing deep. Course, twelve miles. Contains brown trout. Reached from Gillespie's Beach, on the Waikohai Creek. For approach and accommodation see " Karangarua River," already mentioned.

TWAIN Burn, tributary of Karangarua River.— Snow- and ice-fed. Boulder and shingle bottom, only upper and lower portions accessible. Banks steep and forest-clad. Wadeable where accessible. Landing deep. Course, six miles. Contains brown trout. Reached from Gillespie's Beach, on the Waikohai Creek. For approach and accommodation see " Karangarua River," already mentioned.

HUNT's Creek.—Sandy bottom. Banks steep and forest-clad. Not wadeable. Landing deep. Course, nine miles. Contains brown trout. Reached from Gillespie's Beach, where there is hotel accommodation on the Waikohai Creek, by thirteen miles of track to near the mouth. This is 123 miles from Hokitika.

MANAKAIAUA Burn.—Shingle bottom for a mile, then shingle bed. Banks steep and forest-clad.

Wadeable in upper portion. Landing deep mostly. Course, ten miles. Contains brown trout. Reached from Gillespie's Beach, where there is hotel accommodation on the Waikohai Creek, by fourteen miles of track to near the mouth. This is 124 miles from Hokitika.

MAKAWHIO Stream.—Snow-fed. Tidal for a mile, with shingle bottom; then shingle bed for five miles; then boulder bed. Banks steep and mostly forest-clad. Wadeable above tidal water. Landing deep, also good. Course, fifteen miles. Contains brown trout. Reached from Gillespie's Beach, where there is hotel accommodation on the Waikohai Creek, by sixteen miles of track. This is 126 miles from Hokitika.

MAHITAHI River.—Snow-fed. Shingle bed lower half, then shingle and boulder bed. Banks steep and forest-clad. Wadeable. Landing deep, also good. Course, twenty-one miles. Contains brown trout. Reached from Hokitika by 135 miles of track to the mouth at Bruce, where there is accommodation. A steamer calls occasionally.

OINEMAKA Burn.—Sand and shingle bottom for a mile, then shingle bottom to head of river and branches. Banks steep and forest-clad. Wadeable, except the first mile. Landing deep, also good. Course, eight miles. Contains brown trout. Reached from Bruce, on the Mahitahi River, by five miles of track to near the mouth, where there is a ford. There is also a ford a mile further up. Reached also from Bruce by seven miles of the Mahitahi–Haast Track, which crosses the river four miles from the mouth. This is 139 miles from Hokitika.

PARINGA River. — Snow-fed. Shingle bed for about three-fourths length, then boulder bottom. Banks, lower half moderate slope, upper steep and forest-clad. Wadeable. Landing deep, also good. Course, twenty-one miles. Contains brown trout. Reached from Bruce, on the Mahitahi River, by twelve miles of the Mahitahi–Haast Track, which reaches the river at Paringa, seven miles from the mouth, to which there is a track. About two miles above Paringa there is a ford, and two miles further up another ford. Where the Mahitahi–Paringa Track crosses the Paringa River is 151 miles from Hokitika.

HALL River, tributary of Paringa River.—Sand and mud bottom. Banks steep and forest-clad. Not wadeable — must be fished from a boat. Landing deep. Course, two miles. Contains brown trout. Reached from Paringa, to near where it leaves Lake Paringa, by three miles of the Mahitahi–Haast Track. This is 154 miles from Hokitika. For approach and accommodation see " Paringa River," already mentioned.

LAKE PARINGA, tributary of Hall River.—Has several small feeders. Shingle and mud bottom. Banks steep on three sides, low on fourth; forest-clad. Not wadeable—fishable from a boat. Landing deep. Length, two miles and three-quarters; breadth, half a mile. Contains brown trout. Reached from Paringa by four miles of the Mahitahi Haast Track. This is 155 miles from Hokitika. For approach and accommodation see " Paringa River," already mentioned.

OTOKO Stream, tributary of Paringa River.— Snow-fed. Shingle bed for half length, then boulder bottom. Banks steep and forest-clad. Wadeable mostly. Landing deep, also good. Course, twelve miles. Contains brown trout. Reached from Paringa by following up the Paringa River for five miles. For approach and accommodation see " Paringa River," already mentioned.

MOERAKI River.—Shingle bottom from mouth to outlet of Lake Moeraki, one mile, then to source of river shingle bed and bottom. Banks low, steep, and forest-clad. Wadeable partly. Landing deep, also good. Course, twenty-one miles. Contains brown trout. Reached from Paringa by nine miles of the Mahitahi–Haast Track, which crosses it eight miles from the mouth. A track from here runs near the bank of the river to the mouth. The crossing is 160 miles from Hokitika.

LAKE MOERAKI, tributary of Moeraki River.—Shingle and mud bottom. Banks on north and south steep, high, and forest-clad; on east and west low, scrub - encumbered. Not wadeable—fishable from boat. Landing deep. Length, one mile and three-quarters ; breadth, three-quarters of a mile. Contains brown trout. Reached from the track down the bank of the Moeraki River from the crossing of the Mahitahi–Haast Track; or by ten miles of Matthies's Track from Paringa. Matthies's Track continues along the bank of the lake to the Moeraki River, which it reaches in a further three miles, a mile from the mouth. For approach and accommodation see "Moeraki River," already mentioned.

WAKAPOHAI Stream. — Shingle bed for three-fourths of length, then boulder bottom. Banks low on lower half, then steep and forest-clad. Wadeable. Landing deep, also good. Course, eleven miles. Contains brown trout. Reached from Paringa to within two miles of the mouth, *viâ* Lake Moeraki, by fourteen miles of the Paringa – Matthies Track. Also reached from Paringa by ten miles of the Mahitahi–Haast Track, which crosses it eight miles from the mouth. This is 161 miles from Hokitika.

KOTOKAKORAKOTA Creek.—Shingle bottom. The banks steep and forest-clad. Wadeable partly. Landing deep. Course, four miles. Contains brown trout. Reached from Paringa to near the mouth by nineteen miles of the Paringa–Matthies' Track.

SHIP Creek.—Shingle bottom. Banks steep and forest-clad. Wadeable in upper half. Landing deep. Course, five miles. Contains brown trout.

Reached from Paringa (to the mouth) *viâ* Lake Moeraki, by twenty-one miles of the Paringa–Matthies' Track.

WAITA Burn.—Shingle bed for three-fourths of length, then shingle bottom. Banks low in lower half, steep in upper ; forest-clad. Wadeable. Landing deep, also good. Course, ten miles. Contains brown trout. Reached from Paringa by twenty miles of the Mahitahi–Haast Track, which crosses it five miles from the mouth. A track runs down the river to the mouth from the crossing, which is 171 miles from Hokitika.

LAKES TAUWHERIKITI, tributaries of Waita River. —Mud bottom. Banks steep, swampy, flax- and scrub-encumbered. Not wadeable—must be fished from a boat. Landing mostly deep. A chain of small lakes connected by short deep streams— making altogether, including connecting streams, four miles, as follows : Length one mile, breadth half a mile ; length one mile and a half, breadth half a mile ; length half a mile, breadth quarter of a mile. Contain brown trout. Reached by tracks from the mouth of the Waita River. For approach and accommodation see " Waita River," already mentioned.

HAAST River. — Snow-fed. Shingle bed for three-fourths of length, then boulder bottom. Banks low for half length, then steep and forest-clad. Wadeable. Landing deep, also good. Course, forty miles. Contains brown trout. Reached from Paringa by twenty-seven miles of the Mahitahi–Haast Track, which continues six miles down the river to the mouth at Haast, where there is hotel accommodation. Where the Mahitahi–Haast Track reaches the river is 178 miles from Hokitika. Haast is also reached by occasional steamers from Hokitika. The river is also reached (to the source) from Lake Wanaka by sixteen miles of track up the Makarora River ; this track then continues down the bank of the

Haast River to the mouth. For this approach and accommodation see Chapter XIX., "Middle Island—Rivers and Lakes of the East Coast: Lakes Wanaka and Hawea."

Thomas Stream, tributary of Haast River.—Shingle bed for half length, then shingle bottom. Banks forest-clad. Wadeable partly. Landing deep, also good. Course, fifteen miles. Contains brown trout. Reached (to the mouth) by ten miles of track from the mouth of the Haast River. For approach and accommodation see "Haast River," already mentioned.

Clark Stream, tributary of Haast River.—Snow-fed. Shingle bed for nearly whole length, then boulder bottom. Banks low, steep, and mostly forest-clad. Wadeable. Landing deep, also good. Course, seventeen miles. Contains brown trout. Reached (to the mouth) by twenty-six miles of track from the mouth of the Haast River. For approach and accommodation see " Haast River," already mentioned.

Landsborough River, tributary of Clark Stream. —Snow- and ice-fed. Shingle bed and bottom about half length, then boulder bottom. Banks mostly steep and forest-clad, except last four miles which are clear. Wadeable mostly. Landing deep, also good. Course, thirty miles. Contains brown trout. Reached (to the mouth) by twenty-six miles of track from the mouth of the Haast River, and four miles up the Clark Stream. For approach and accommodation see " Clark Stream," already mentioned.

Burke Burn, tributary of Haast River.—Snow-fed. Shingle bottom for a mile. Banks of lower side fairly clear excepting the first mile ; almost unfishable owing to the precipitous nature of the banks. Not wadeable. Landing deep. Course, ten miles. Contains brown trout. Reached (to the mouth) by thirty-one miles of track from the mouth of the Haast River. For approach and accommodation see "Haast River," already mentioned.

Wills Stream, tributary of Haast River.—Snow-fed. Boulder bottom for three miles, then shingle bed. Banks steep, low, and forest-clad. Wadeable in upper half. Landing deep, also good. Course, twelve miles. Contains brown trout. Reached (to the mouth) by thirty-four miles of track from the mouth of the Haast River. For approach and accommodation see "Haast River," already mentioned.

Okuru River.—Snow-fed. Tidal for two miles, with shingle bottom for five miles, then shingle and boulder bed. Banks low, steep, and forest-clad. Wadeable above tidal water. Landing deep, also good. Course, thirty-one miles. Contains brown trout. Reached (to the mouth) by seven miles of track from Haast and 185 from Hokitika. Also reached by occasional steamers from Hokitika. For approach and accommodation see "Haast River," already mentioned. The tracks about here are uncertain.

Actor Burn, tributary of Okuru River.—Snow-fed. Shingle bed the lower half, then boulder bed. Banks steep and forest-clad. Wadeable mostly. Landing deep, also good. Course, eight miles. Contains brown trout. Reached by following up Okuru River twenty miles from the mouth. For approach and accommodation see "Okuru River," already mentioned.

Turnbull River.—Snow-fed. Tidal for a mile, with shingle bottom for five miles, then shingle and boulder bed. Banks low, steep, and forest-clad. Wadeable above tidal water. Landing deep, also good. Course, twenty-one miles. Contains brown trout. Reached (to the mouth) by eight miles of track from Haast and 186 from Hokitika. For approach and accommodation see "Haast River," already mentioned. Also reached by occasional steamer to Okuru from Hokitika. The tracks about here are uncertain.

Ito Burn, tributary of Turnbull River.—Snow-fed. Boulder bottom. Banks steep and forest-clad. Wadeable partly. Landing deep. Course, six miles. Contains brown trout. Reached by following up Turnbull River for twelve miles from the mouth. For approach and accommodation see "Turnbull River," already mentioned. The tracks about here are uncertain.

Hapuka Creek.—Tidal for about half a mile. Mud bottom. Banks steep and flax-encumbered. Not wadeable—fishable from boat. Landing deep. Course, four miles. Contains brown trout. Reached (to the mouth) by nine miles of track from Haast and 187 from Hokitika. For approach and accommodation see "Haast River," already mentioned. Also reached by occasional steamer to Okuru from Hokitika. The tracks about here are uncertain.

Waiatoto River.—Snow- and ice-fed. Tidal for a mile, with shingle bottom for eight miles, then shingle bed. Banks for a mile low and steep, then high and steep for seven miles, then alternately steep and low. Forest-clad throughout. Wadeable in upper half. Landing deep, also good. Course, thirty-four miles. Contains brown trout. Reached (to the mouth) by eighteen miles of track from Haast and 196 from Hokitika. For approach and accommodation see "Haast River," already mentioned. The tracks about here are uncertain.

Hindley's Creek, tributary of Waiatoto River.—Sand and mud bottom. Banks steep and forest-clad. Fishable from a boat in lower reaches, wadeable in upper. Landing deep. Course, seven miles. Contains brown trout. Reached (to the mouth) at Waiatoto. For approach and accommodation see "Waiatoto River," already mentioned. The tracks about here are uncertain.

Nisson Creek, tributary of Waiatoto River.—
Shingle bottom. Banks low and forest-clad. Not
wadeable. Landing deep. Course, one mile.
Contains brown trout. Reached (to the mouth)
by following up the Waiatoto River four miles
from the mouth. For approach and accommodation see " Waiatoto River," already mentioned.

Lake Nisson, tributary of Nisson Creek.—Mud
bottom and shallow. Banks low, swampy, and
forest-clad. Only fishable from boat. Length,
three-quarters of a mile; breadth, half a mile.
Contains brown trout. Reached from Nisson
Creek. For approach and accommodation see
" Nisson Creek," already mentioned. The tracks
about here are uncertain.

Axius Stream, tributary of Waiatoto River.—
Snow-fed. Shingle bed for half distance, then
boulder bottom. Banks steep and forest-clad.
Wadeable mostly. Landing deep, also good.
Course, eleven miles. Contains brown trout.
Reached (to the mouth) by following up the Waia-
toto River sixteen miles from the mouth. For
approach and accommodation see " Waiatoto
River," already mentioned. The tracks about
here are uncertain.

Arawata River.—Snow-fed. Shingle bed for
three-fourths of length, then boulder bottom.
Banks low, steep, and forest-clad. Wadeable.
Landing deep, also good. Course, forty-five
miles. Contains brown trout. Reached (to the
mouth) by twenty-five miles of track from Haast,
and 203 from Hokitika. For approach and accommodation see " Haast River," already mentioned. The tracks about here are uncertain.
Also reached from Glenorchy, at the head of Lake
Wakatipu. (See Chapter XIX., " Middle Island—
Rivers and Lakes of the East Coast : Lake Wakatipu.") From here a track of 105 miles reaches
the mouth, passing *en route* closely down the
following rivers and lakes : Down the Hollyford

River, along and up Lake Alabaster, Lake Wilmot, and the Pyke River, then crossing the upper waters of the Jerry's and Gorge Stream, then following down Cascade River, which it crosses; then crossing Teer's Creek, Stafford Burn, and Smoothwater Burn.

JACKSON Stream, tributary of Arawata River.— Shingle bed and bottom. Banks low, steep, and forest-clad. Wadeable. Landing deep, also good. Course, thirteen miles. Contains brown trout. Reached (to the mouth) by following up the bank of the Arawata River for five miles from the mouth. For approach and accommodation see "Arawata River," already mentioned.

ELLERY River, tributary of Jackson Stream.— Shingle bottom. Banks steep and forest-clad. Not wadeable—fishable from a boat. Landing deep. Course, three-quarters of a mile. Contains brown trout. Reached by following up the bank of the Arawata River for five miles from the mouth, then two miles up the Jackson Stream. For approach and accommodation see "Jackson Stream," already mentioned.

LAKE ELLERY, tributary of Ellery River.—Shingle bottom, with shallow water and shingle beach on western end; banks on other three sides steep, with occasional beaches and shallow water; forest-clad all round. Wadeable partly. Landing deep, also good. Length, three miles; breadth, half a mile. Contains brown trout. Has one shingle-bottom feeder. Reached by following up the bank of the Arawata River for five miles from the mouth, then Jackson Stream and Ellery River three miles. For approach and accommodation see "Ellery River," already mentioned.

LAKE MARY, tributary of Lake Ellery.—Mud and shingle bottom. Banks low, steep, and forest-clad. Wadeable partly. Landing deep. Length, three-quarters of a mile; breadth, quarter of a mile.

Contains brown trout. For approach and accommodation see "Lake Ellery," already mentioned.

SMOOTHWATER Burn.—Shingle bed and bottom. Banks low and forest-clad. Wadeable. Landing mostly good. Course, five miles. Contains brown trout. Reached (to near the mouth) by 208 miles of track from Hokitika; and from Glenorchy by the Glenorchy–Arawata track, ninety-eight miles.

STAFFORD Burn. — Shingle bed and bottom. Banks low and forest-clad. Wadeable. Landing good mostly. Course, eight miles. Contains brown trout. Reached (to near the mouth) by 213 miles of track from Hokitika; and from Glenorchy by the Glenorchy–Arawata track, ninety-five miles.

TERES' Creek.—Boulder bottom. Banks steep and forest-clad. Wadeable. Landing deep mostly. Course, five miles. Contains brown trout. Reached by 217 miles of track from Hokitika; and from Glenorchy by the Glenorchy–Arawata Track, eighty-nine miles.

CASCADE River.—Snow-fed. Tidal for four miles, with sand and shingle bottom, then shingle bed, then boulder bed. Banks on lower half steep, swampy, flax-encumbered, and partly clear; on upper half steep and forest-clad. Wadeable above tidal water. Landing deep, also good. Course, forty-four miles. Contains brown trout. Reached by 227 miles of track from Hokitika, which track crosses it sixteen miles from the mouth on the Glenorchy–Arawata Track, seventy-eight miles from Glenorchy.

BARN Creek, tributary of Cascade River.—Sand and mud bottom. Banks steep and flax-encumbered. Not wadeable — fishable from a boat. Landing deep. Course, three miles. Contains brown trout. Reached by following down the Cascade River for thirteen miles from where the Glenorchy–Arawata Track crosses it. For approach and accommodation see "Cascade River," already mentioned.

Martyr Burn, tributary of Cascade River.—
Shingle bed and boulder bottom for a mile, upper
portion unfishable. Banks low, steep, and forest-
clad. Wadeable. Landing deep, also good.
Course, ten miles. Contains brown trout.
Reached for six miles from the mouth upwards
from the Glenorchy – Arawata Track. For approach and accommodation see " Cascade River "
already mentioned.

Hope Burn.—Shingle and boulder bed. Banks
steep, low, and forest-clad. Wadeable. Landing deep, also good. Course, eight miles.
Contains brown trout. Reached (to two miles
of the mouth) by a track of twelve miles,
which branches off from the Glenorchy – Arawata Track where that track crosses the Cascade
River, 227 miles from Hokitika and seventy-
eight from Glenorchy.

Gorge Stream. — Shingle and boulder bed.
Banks steep and forest-clad. Wadeable. Landing deep, also good. Course, eleven miles. Contains brown trout. Reached by 237 miles of track
from Hokitika, which crosses the upper waters on
the Glenorchy–Arawata Track, sixty-seven miles
from Glenorchy.

Jerry Burn, tributary of Gorge Stream.—
Shingle and boulder bed. Banks steep, low, and
forest-clad. Wadeable. Landing deep, also good.
Course, ten miles. Contains brown trout. Reached
by 243 miles of track from Hokitika, which track
crosses the upper waters on the Glenorchy-
Arawata Track sixty-one miles from Glenorchy.
For approach and accommodation see " Gorge
Stream," already mentioned.

Awarua Creek.—Sand and shingle bed. Banks
steep, low, and forest-clad. Wadeable. Landing
deep, also good. Course, ten miles. Contains
brown trout. Reached by 248 miles of track from
Hokitika, which track touches the upper waters on

the Glenorchy–Arawata Track, fifty-six miles from Glenorchy, and then by five miles of branch track to the mouth.

HOLLYFORD River.— Snow-fed. Tidal from sea to Lake McKerrow, two miles, with shingle bottom, and banks fairly low and forest-clad. After passing through the lake, shingle and boulder bed. Banks partly low, steep, and forest-clad. Wadeable partly. Landing deep, mostly. Course, including Lake McKerrow, forty-three miles. Contains brown trout. Reached (to within two miles of the mouth) by 251 miles of track from Hokitika, along the Glenorchy–Arawata Track, then by twelve miles of branch track. From here a branch track of sixteen miles up the bank of the river and Lake McKerrow rejoins the Glenorchy–Arawata Track 267 miles from Hokitika and thirty-eight from Glenorchy. The Glenorchy–Arawata Track continues up the bank of the river for fourteen miles, then turns off to Glenorchy. This is 281 miles from Hokitika and twenty-four miles from Glenorchy, making the distance from Hokitika to Glenorchy 305 miles.

LAKE MCKERROW, tributary of Hollyford River. —Shingle bottom. Banks steep mostly, and forest-clad. Wadeable in a few places. Landing deep, also good. Chiefly fishable from a boat. Length, ten miles; breadth, one mile. Height above sea-level, 15 ft. Contains brown trout. For approach and accommodation see " Hollyford River," already mentioned.

PYKE River, tributary of Hollyford River.— Snow-fed. Shingle bed in upper reaches, boulder bottom. Banks steep and forest-clad. Wadeable mostly. Landing deep, also good. Course, including Lakes Alabaster and Wilmot, twenty-six miles. Contains brown trout. Reached (to the mouth) by sixteen miles of track up the bank of Lake McKerrow and the Hollyford River. This is 267 miles from Hokitika and thirty-eight from

Glenorchy. This track skirts it and Lakes Alabaster and Wilmot for twenty-four miles. For approach and accommodation see " Hollyford River," already mentioned.

LAKE ALABASTER, tributary of Pyke River.— Shingle bottom. Banks forest - clad and steep mostly. Wadeable in a few places. Landing deep mostly. Length, four miles and a half; breadth, three-quarters of a mile. Height above sea-level 130 ft. Contains brown trout. Reached (to its outlet) in the same way as Pyke River. For approach and accommodation see " Pyke River," already mentioned.

LAKE WILMOT, tributary of Pyke River.—Shingle bottom. Banks forest - clad and steep mostly. Wadeable in a few places. Landing deep mostly. Length, one mile; breadth, half a mile. Contains brown trout. Reached (to its outlet, ten miles from the mouth of the Pyke River) from the Glenorchy–Arawata Track, which skirts the lake its whole length. For approach and accommodation see " Pyke River," already mentioned.

CLEDDAU Stream (discharges into Milford Sound). —Shingle, then boulder and rock bed. Banks low near mouth; then steep, high, and forest-clad. Wadeable partly. Landing deep, also good. Course, twelve miles. Contains brown trout. For approach and accommodation see " Arthur River," following.

ARTHUR River (discharges into Milford Sound). —Shingle bed. Banks mostly low, and partly forest-clad. Wadeable. Landing good. Course, including Lake Ada, sixteen miles. Contains brown trout. Reached from Milford Sound by coastal steamers that make the trip occasionally to allow tourists to see the Sutherland Falls, the highest known in the world, over 1,904 ft., and also the surrounding scenery, which is of great grandeur. From the landing-place, by track up the bank of the river, and by boat on Lake Ada four miles, is altogether fourteen miles to the falls. A route that is available for the greater part of the year is *viâ* Lake Te Anau. (See Chapter XX., " Middle Island—Rivers and Lakes of the South Coast: Lake Te Anau.") From Lake Te Anau by track to the Sutherland Falls is eighteen miles. To make the trip from Te Anau to the Sutherland Falls and Milford Sound, and *vice versâ*, more easily manageable for tourists the Government have erected a number of huts along the route, and there are regular guides resident on the route. Particulars of these matters will be found in the Government tours and New Zealand excursions books, and also in the " New Zealand Index Annual."

LAKE ADA, tributary of Arthur River.—Shingle and rock bottom. Banks mostly steep and forest-clad. Wadeable here and there. Landing mostly deep. Length, four miles; breadth, half a mile. Height above sea-level 150 ft. Contains brown trout. For approach and accommodation see " Arthur River," already mentioned.

———

South of this on the west coast for 160 miles as far as Chalky Inlet there are a number of sounds of great beauty and grandeur, also streams and lakes; but at present they are difficult of access, and it is almost a *terra incognita.*

ALPHABETICAL LIST

OF

RIVERS, STREAMS, BURNS, CREEKS, AND LAKES.

CHAPTER XVI.—NORTH ISLAND: EAST COAST, FROM DOUBT-LESS BAY TO PORT NICHOLSON.

CHAPTER XVII.—NORTH ISLAND: WEST COAST, FROM AHIPARA BAY TO PORIRUA HARBOUR.

CHAPTER XVIII.—MIDDLE ISLAND : NORTH COAST, FROM CAPE KOAMORU TO CAPE FAREWELL.

CHAPTER XIX.—MIDDLE ISLAND : EAST COAST, FROM CAPE KOAMORU TO LONG POINT (IRIHUKA).

CHAPTER XX.—MIDDLE ISLAND: SOUTH COAST, FROM LONG
POINT (IRIHUKA) TO CHALKY INLET.

CHAPTER XXI.—SOUTH, OR STEWART ISLAND, NORTH AND
EAST COAST.

CHAPTER XXII. — MIDDLE ISLAND: WEST COAST, FROM CAPE FAREWELL TO CHALKY INLET.

By Authority: JOHN MACKAY, Government Printer, Wellington.—1904

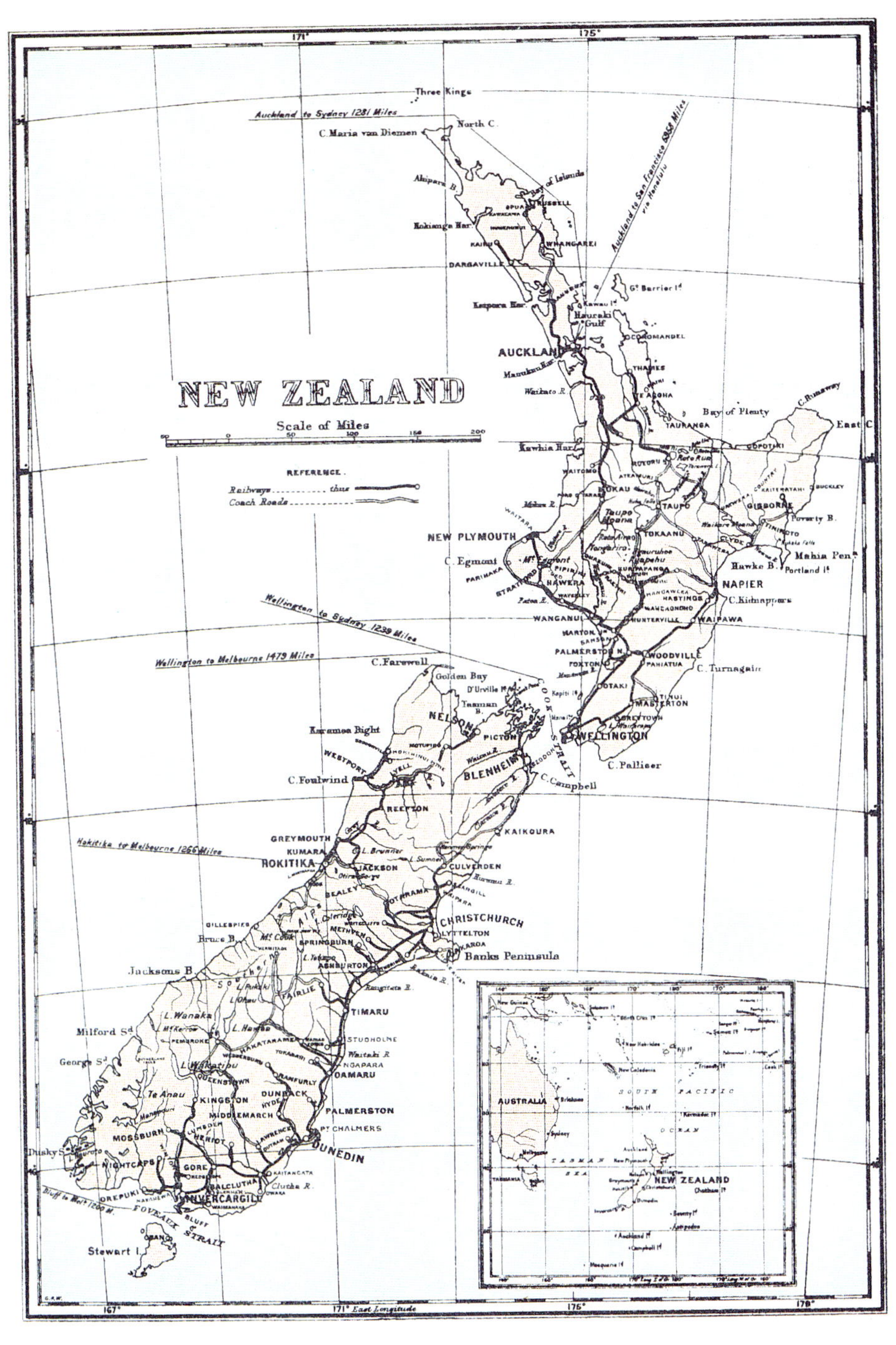

NEW ZEALAND
Scale of Miles
0 50 100 150 200
REFERENCE.
Railways............thus
Coach Roads.............
Three Kings
Auckland to Sydney 1281 Miles
C. Maria van Diemen
North C.
Bay of Islands
Ahipara B.
RUSSELL
Kaipara Har.
WHANGAREI
DARGAVILLE
Gt Barrier Id
Kaipara Har.
Hauraki Gulf
COROMANDEL
AUCKLAND
THAMES
Manukau Har.
Waikato R.
Bay of Plenty
C. Runaway
Kawhia Har.
TAURANGA
East C.
OPOTIKI
OKAU
TAUPO
GISBORNE
NEW PLYMOUTH
Taupo Moana
Poverty B.
C. Egmont
Mt Egmont
HAWERA
Mahia Pen.
STRATFORD
Hawke B.
Portland Id
NAPIER
WANGANUI
HASTINGS
C. Kidnappers
MARTON
HUNTERVILLE
WAIPAWA
PALMERSTON N.
WOODVILLE
FOXTON
PAHIATUA
C. Turnagain
OTAKI
MASTERTON
Wellington to Sydney 1239 Miles
Wellington to Melbourne 1479 Miles
C. Farewell
Golden Bay
D'Urville Id
WELLINGTON
C. Palliser
Karamea Bight
NELSON
PICTON
WESTPORT
BLENHEIM
C. Campbell
C. Foulwind
REEFTON
Hokitika to Melbourne 1266 Miles
KAIKOURA
GREYMOUTH
L. Brunner
KUMARA
CULVERDEN
HOKITIKA
JACKSON
BEALEY
OTIRAMA
Coleridge
CHRISTCHURCH
METHVEN
LYTTELTON
GILLESPIES
Mt Cook
SPRINGBURN
AKAROA
Bruce B.
Banks Peninsula
Jacksons B.
L. Tekapo
ASHBURTON
FAIRLIE
L. Ohau
TIMARU
L. Wanaka
McKerrow
L. Hawea
STUDHOLME
Milford Sd
PEMBROKE
Waitaki R.
George Sd
L. Wakatipu
NGAPARA
QUEENSTOWN
RANFURLY
OAMARU
Te Anau
KINGSTON
DUNBACK
HYDE
PALMERSTON
MIDDLEMARCH
MOSSBURN
LUMSDEN
HERIOT
PT CHALMERS
LAWRENCE
NIGHTCAPS
GORE
DUNEDIN
Dusky Sd
OREPUKI
BALCLUTHA
Clutha R.
Bluff to Hull 1200 M.
INVERCARGILL
BLUFF
FOVEAUX STRAIT
Stewart I.
AUSTRALIA
SOUTH PACIFIC OCEAN
TASMAN SEA
NEW ZEALAND